WHEN MAN
IS THE PREY

Also by Michael Tougias

Ten Hours Until Dawn

WHEN MAN IS THE PREY

*True Stories of Animals
Attacking Humans*

EDITED BY

Michael Tougias

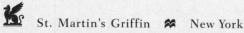
St. Martin's Griffin ❧ New York

www.stmartins.com

ISBN-13: 978-0-312-37300-9
ISBN-10: 0-312-37300-7

10 9 8 7 6 5 4 3

COPYRIGHT ACKNOWLEDGMENTS

CONTENTS

THE WORST OF THE REST: MONKEYS, WOLVES, PIGS, DEER, HIPPOS, AND OTHER ANIMAL ATTACKS

INTRODUCTION

by Michael Tougias

I never saw the black bear until it let out a grunt, which sounded like a deep, guttural "huff." There was only about seven feet between the bear and me.

I was trout fishing in northern Vermont, on one of those achingly beautiful summer mornings that make you wonder why you don't fish more often. The Lamoille River snaked through spruce forest and narrow meadows, sometimes hidden in patches of fog, other times sparkling in the sun. As I worked my way upstream, the section of river before me looked deeper than the top of my hip waders, and I left the water to bushwhack through a thicket of alder saplings and four-foot high ferns. It was in that tangle of vegetation that I first heard the bear and then saw its black bulk directly ahead of me, partly obscured by the green foliage. I froze. A primal fear of something so big seemed to scream in my brain: "run!"

Countering the urge to flee was my mind's inner voice, saying "wait, don't do anything sudden." I retreated a couple paces, never taking my eyes off the bear. The tops of the ferns near the bear shook, and this massive body of jet black fur moved a foot or so off to the side. I felt a rising panic combine with my wildly beating heart, and it took every bit of self-control I could muster not to dash away. I thought the bear would have used this interlude to make its escape but it stayed in place, facing me through the brush. Slowly I started walking backward, hoping I wouldn't trip and fall but not wanting to take my eyes off the spot where the bear held its ground.

Soon I was back by the river, and I went down into the water and crossed to the other bank. I was safe, and I relaxed a bit, wondering what would have happened if the bear had not let out the warning "huff." Would I have stumbled right into the creature? Would it have attacked? Maybe it was sleeping in the ferns, and I was down wind and the bear had no way of knowing of my approach until it awoke from my footsteps. Whatever the reason, the incident was too close for comfort, even if it was just plain bad luck that I unwittingly approached so closely.

A BLACK BEAR ALMOST always avoids contact with humans, using his superior sense of smell and hearing to slip away long before we even know one was nearby. But every once in a great while, a black bear does not flee. This might involve a unique situation such as a mother bear with cubs, or a bear that has grown acclimated to humans, associating us with food (trash, birdfeeders, pet food). Or, as was the likely scenario in my close encounter, a bear is surprised and feels threatened.

I was lucky in my encounter, but many of the people featured in this book were not. Some were simply in the wrong place at the wrong time, while others were in new surroundings they didn't fully understand. They were unfamiliar with the wildlife, and some reacted to their initial encounter by doing exactly the wrong thing, triggering the creature to attack. Others made the right decisions, potentially saving their lives.

I enjoy all books with wildlife stories, from authors as diverse as Thoreau and Jack London. But above all I want to be pulled into the situation and taken out of my suburban home and transported to the forest, the jungle, the sea, or other remote and untamed regions. The stories in this book certainly take us on gripping journeys into the wild, but they also offer lessons so that the reader gleans a few tips on staying safe in similar situations or habitat.

Knowing how and when predators hunt is a key factor in staying safe. For example, the odds of encountering a shark at the beach, even though remote, do increase at dusk, dark, and dawn. Equally important is learning how to react if you surprise an animal, like I did. A slow, measured retreat is almost always preferable to running away. Most prey, once discovered by a predator, flee, and when we do the same we are reinforcing that we too are prey—and man can rarely flee faster than wildlife.

Above all, remember that the wildlife featured in this book is doing exactly what it needs to do to survive. The creatures need to eat, and they are opportunistic, preferring to spend the least amount of energy for the most amount of food. Sometimes we fit that profile perfectly. More often than not a predator's hunt is unsuccessful, so they need to conserve energy, and pick the prey that gives them the best odds of a successful hunt. Slow, sick, or wounded prey falls into this group. (That's why fishing lures usually swim in a jerky motion rather than straight and fluid.)

It is my hope that when you read these incredible stories, many of which are tragic, you don't fall into the trap of viewing the attacking wildlife as villains, but instead marvel at their power, cunning, and stealth. I felt sadness for the victims in these stories, but at the same time I respected the animals, which were simply guarding their turf or following instincts which have evolved over the ages.

When we leave the comforts of civilization, many of us experience a joy and soaring of the spirit because of the very "wildness" of a particular area. The predators that inhabit such regions are an integral part of the food-chain. Without them, the dynamics of the interwoven species inevitably suffers, and the ecosystem is thrown out of balance. Take away the creatures that might do us harm, and we ruin the very places we think are special.

FIVE HUNDRED
POUNDS OF FURY

Bears

one

BEARS

by Peter Hathaway Capstick

ON A GEOGRAPHICAL BASIS, it seems to me a fellow would be hard put to find a more widely distributed form of terrestrial omnivore than bears in general. All sharing remarkably similar characteristics beyond such cosmetic considerations as color and size, bears are found in different flavors just about everywhere but in Antarctica, and if the polar bear ever was able to get past the equator, there's little question that the bottom of the earth would not be bearless.

This not being a zoological reference book, I can't believe that the total readership interest in the South American spectacled bear or the Asian sun or black bears would be worth the calories expended to include them, although Lord knows I have the spare calories. So, it is my dearest hope that you don't feel shortchanged by only being violently dissertated to on matters pertinent to grizzlies, browns, polars, blacks and sloth bears, any one of which, believe me, is better encountered in these pages than in its natural habitat unless you have an emerging death wish.

With the possible exception of the great cats, there probably has been more speculation, both correct and otherwise, written about bears than any other animal group. With good reason, too: they're big, scary looking, and they bite. A recently processed pile of still-steaming blueberries encountered in heavy cover has an astonishingly stimulating effect upon the sense of foreboding of just about any hunter, fisherman, hiker or backpacker you can think of. There is probably a case to be made that this natural apprehension is a residual reaction to the days of yore when we started to solve the housing shortage by some very rude treatment of Pleistocene cave bears, whose rocky homes we undoubtedly usurped. The most recent thinking on the matter, incidentally, indicates that the huge cave bear—whose Latin name I am not about to look up—was most likely a pure vegetarian judging by the cusps of its teeth.

Personally, I doubt this idea of fear of bears stemming from the very old days. It just seems common sense to me to be scared motherless of any animal that has the potential for carnage that any full-grown bear does. As far as I'm concerned, if you're not afraid of bears you're doing something wrong.

With the concept firmly in mind that we have to start somewhere, why not begin this horror-fest with the bear the psychoanalysts would have a ball with: *Ursus horribilis?* Really, now, what sort of behavior would you bloody well expect from an animal named, in formal Latin, no less, the "Horrible Bear"? Perhaps it's one of those chicken-or-the-egg things, but I suppose whether the grizzly is a most terrifying man-eater when so prompted or became such just to live up to his name isn't very important, particularly since he most likely cannot read and understands not a syllable of Latin. Sure, we're kidding around, whistling in the graveyard on our way home through the dark, moonless, bear-filled night. But there have been many times recently when there was nothing funny about spending the night in Montana's Glacier National Park. . . .

The August evening in 1967 was marvelous camping weather although the 60 glaciers and more than 200 lakes in the near 1,600 square miles of Montana wilderness probably had little to do with the coolness. A group of young people were bedded down in an area known as Granite Park, all asleep by midnight. Most probably thought they were having a nightmare when a bloodcurdling scream from 19-year-old Julie Helgerson raped the stillness, the teenager a little way off from the main body of sleepers. In the light of the anemic campfire, she was starkly outlined in the jaws of a tremendous grizzly bear. As she screamed and fought, it appeared for a moment that she might escape as the bear dropped her to severely bite a young man of the group in the legs and back. But, the bear seemed to prefer the more tender Julie and returned to bite her through the body and drag her several hundred feet where, for some unknown reason, he suddenly left the dying girl and ambled off into the night. By the time rangers from the park arrived, she was just a statistic. The young man who was also mauled survived after hospitalization.

It was a very bad night for 19-year-old girls in Glacier National Park. Just a few hours later, at four in the morning and 20 miles away, another group of campers were frightened awake by a grizzly who towered over them, growling like a thunderstorm. Like a flushing covey of quail, girls and boys scampered up trees and scattered into the blackness. All but one. Michele Koons of San Diego experienced the unspeakable terror of the zipper sticking on her sleeping bag! With the bear only feet away, she was bound and trussed by the unyielding nylon skin. The grizzly grabbed her. In numb panic, the rest of the party listened to her describe her own death. "He's tearing my arm off!" was one shriek all agreed upon. "Oh, my God, I'm dead!"

Right she was.

If either of the girls killed that night in 1967 was missing any flesh, the press and my sources did not mention it. I cite the night of terror as a precedent of attack rather than of man-eating, although one must wonder what the bears would have done had they come upon solitary campers and were not disturbed with their kills. The odds against something as rare as fatal grizzly attacks upon two girls the same age, in the same park, 20 miles apart on the same night actually happening have given me a rather eerie feeling when I read the monthly Solunar Tables created and copywrited by my old friend John Alden Knight, which still appear in *Field & Stream*. These tables are purported to forecast periods of peak feeding activity for fish and game. That night they were pretty accurate.

The two grizzlies were shot and killed, proof of their perfidy having been confirmed by blood samples found on claws and muzzles.

Regarding the new class of man-eater, the "park killer," the bear is the classic North American example of this syndrome. Thirty-six people were mauled in less than 20 years in parks by bears and one more killed in

1972 at Yellowstone by a grizzly. Considering that well over two hundred million people (most are repeats) enter national parks each year, this isn't much of a toll. But, don't forget, not many parks have grizzlies.

It was nine years later that the first substantiated case of man-eating, or, if we carefully note the preferences of the Glacier Park bears, woman-eating occurred. If was another college girl, Mary Pat Mahoney of Highwood, Illinois, a student at the University of Montana. Mary Pat was 22 years old. She would get no older.

Camped with four friends, all female, Mary Pat Mahoney's tent was torn open shortly after dawn, and the girl, still in her sleeping bag, dragged away under the ripping, yellow fangs. Her friends, awakened by Mary Pat's screams of terror and agony, attracted the attention of another camper, who ran to get ranger Fred Reese. Reese arrived a few minutes later where he was joined by another ranger, a Californian on a "busman's holiday" named Stuart Macy. Just outside the shredded tent lay the gore-smeared sleeping bag and nearby, a bloody T-shirt. A clear spoor of blood and drag marks led off into a thicket, the partially-eaten body of what used to be Mary Pat Mahoney was found about 300 yards from the site of her probable death.

Fred Reese, half-gagging at the sight, gave his .357 Magnum revolver to Stuart Macy who agreed to stand guard over the remains in case of the bear's return. Reese went for help. No sooner was he out of sight than a grizzly lumbered up and informed Macy that his presence was not appreciated. To top things off, the .357 was either defective or broken, which might be just as well as I, for one, have no interest whatever in putting any close range handgun bullets into any man-eating grizzlies while standing over their kills. Unless he'd gotten lucky with a brain or spine shot, Macy might well have found himself joining Mary Pat. As it was, the bear was sufficiently nasty and Macy had to climb for his life. His shouts and yells brought armed ranger help, two men with 12-gauge shotguns stuffed with rifled slugs. The first shot floored the bear, but, true to grizzly tradition, it got up and took off. Shortly thereafter, one of the rangers was able to pick out the form of a grizzly's head and blew a big hole in it. As it turned out, there were *two* bears, probably siblings, and by the human blood identified on both, they undoubtedly shared breakfast with the body of Mary Pat Mahoney.

A Board of Inquiry was already established after the 1967 debacle, but it could not determine that the girls had done anything to provoke the attack. They had even made a point of not bringing any meat on the trip to avoid bears! They wore no perfume and were in no known way provocative. I do not wish to be in any way indelicate, but I wonder, since so many victims have been female, whether the key factor could be menstruation and the detection of such by a bear?

That the problem is not improving, in fact is eroding into rank man-eating by grizzlies, was proved three times just in 1980 in good old reliable Glacier National Park. On the night of July 24th (and the age factor is starting to get spooky) a grizzly tore into a tent occupied by a young man and a young woman, both 19, (who may have attracted it by the scent and sound of doing what came naturally, although I do not know their relationship). Employees of McDonald Lake Lodge, the two were killed by the bear and the young lady largely eaten.

In October, it happened again. On the 3rd, the mutilated and partly eaten body of a Texas backpacker was also discovered near his camp at Elizabeth Lake (Glacier Park) close to the Canadian border.

The grizzly is such an impressive carnivore that I am tempted to extoll his qualifications in a literary context where this is perhaps not warranted. He may weigh as much as 1,000 pounds, is in big trouble as the world crushes in around him and is the central figure of some of the greatest legends of the American West. He shares a well-earned reputation with the Cape buffalo and sand dunes in general for talent in the field of lead absorption, a characteristic learned by all on the Lewis and Clark Expedition. When he turns rogue, he's a national migraine. One, sporting the title Old Mose, was at last killed in 1904 after having eaten more than 800 head of cattle and killed five men! That must have been a lot of bear!

Another terror, after years of raiding the sheep in the Wasatch Mountains of northern Utah in the 1920's (near the same place where in the winter of 1846–47 the Donner party had been trapped and resorted to cannibalism) was finally killed in 1923 by a sheep rancher and hunter named Frank Clark, who out-foxed the phantom bear with a second or "sucker" trap which sank its teeth into the bear's forearm. After dodging each other through a very nasty night, the bear, christened by the local Mormons as "Old Ephraim," charged Clark, who was armed with only a .25-35 caliber Winchester lever action rifle. (For you gun buffs, this was wrongly called a ".25-.35" in F.M. Young's account of Old Ephraim. It was a "nothing" cartridge in modern terms, firing a light 117-grain factory load bullet which has been called by the expert ballistician Frank C. Barnes, ". . . just about the minimum that should ever be used on deer, and in fact it won't qualify for this purpose in many states.") With the help of his little dog as a distraction, though, Frank Clark, after having twice shot the bear *through the heart*, stopped Old Ephraim with his last and seventh bullet at six feet, a brain shot in the ear. He was an inch short of ten feet long and held in such respect by the ranchers that he was actually granted a grave and buried, a suitable marker erected on the site:

"HERE LIES OLD EPHRAIM.
HE GAVE FRANK CLARK A GOOD SCARE."

You can count on that!

For no particular reason, let's proceed at this point to a perusal of the great bear of the north, the animal sometimes considered the only predator on the North American continent that hunts, kills and eats man as part of his normal prey. A pal of mine who has shot several put it quite well over a few beers the other day when he observed: "Anything on that ice is food for the polar bear. He's at the top of the stack except maybe for the killer whale, and looks at any other animal he can catch as dinner." I suspect he's correct, at least as far as a consideration of the polar bear in an unaltered habitat, shared only with the primitively armed Eskimo is concerned. But, then, with bears, you never know.

My fellow Editor at *Outdoor Life*, Ben East, makes a very good point in his excellent book, *Bears* (Outdoor Life, Crown Publishers, New York, 1977) when he reminds his readers that Fred Bear, president of the archery tackle firm of that name and one of the greatest bowhunters of dangerous game in history, killed both grizzly and Kodiak bears without so much as a severe threat of a charge, but the first two polar bears he punctured with his razorhead trademark arrowheads charged Fred and his guide without a second thought. The men were lucky that both bears were able to be stopped at such close range with the guide's rifle, but neither counted as a bowkill because of the firearm interference. Fred Bear did eventually kill a polar bear according to the rules, but he still is convinced that that chap up north with all the yellowish-white hair is unquestionably the most dangerous. That is not an amateur opinion, either.

So far as I can determine, being a tropical bird by persuasion, and claiming no familiarity with the beastie, the polar bear is the one member of the species that is strictly carnivorous, or at least this is the case for the great majority of the time. Whether or not he eats french-fried tundra at certain times of the year doesn't really interest me, but I think it safe to say he'd probably die of starvation chained to a salad bar.

There is no question whatever that both polar bears and Eskimos spend huge parts of their spare time hunting and eating each other, which seems to be a nice, clear-cut relationship in an otherwise muddy world. As the object of some pretty shabby "sportsmanship" I know several people—I shall not dignify them as either gentlemen or sportsmen-hunters—who obtained their polar bears from the gun rest of an ice-cutter's gunwale off the northern Norwegian Islands. My good friend, David Putnam, son of the well-known publisher and stepson of Amelia Earhart, was part of a polar expedition that roped a female and two cubs under identical circumstances, so shooting a white bear in the water from a ship would be sheer murder. These are the same people who have wolf skins obtained on a trapping license and shot from the air with buckshot. Please, do *not* be tempted to confuse them with legitimate hunters any more than you would lump a jewel thief with a diamond cutter on the basis that they are involved with the same commodity. The use of aircraft in hunting polar bear, although once completely legal, seems outwardly a rather obvious means to an end, yet may not be so. I have not done it and believe it would be unfair to draw any conclusions without tasting the wine. I know too many absolutely ethical people who have hunted in this generally misunderstood mode to believe that it was unsporting. Apparently, the public misconception is that the aircraft is used as a part of the actual hunt itself. From my understanding, it is simply a vehicle to make access to the ice floes possible. A point well considered is the unbesmirched rule of the Boone and Crockett Club, which rules on and records North American game trophies, that the direct use of an aircraft to locate an animal is unethical and any trophy thus obtained will be disqualified as not consistent with the rules of "fair chase."

Well, if you're going to digress, do it properly. . . .

Thalarctos maritimus, whose name I know you were pining to know, is the second biggest of the bears after the Kodiak, which we'll get into in a moment. This position of supreme predator of his world of the Arctic, matched with his physical characteristics as well as the very low population density of people in his range tally up to a most uninhibited and effective general predator. By "general" I mean that man is fair game.

There is, considering how many more seals there are than Eskimos, a pretty reasonable school of thought that bears stalk and eat people because they think they are just another kind of seal. In afterthought, it's a fair notion, in my opinion, because the Arctic aborigines largely dress in sealskin, smear themselves with one form or another of blubber and are about the same size as some of the most populous species of seal. Eskimo hunters commonly, after spotting a polar bear, will lie down in a position a sleeping seal would take to draw the bear into range.

The Barents' Expedition in the 16th century recorded many attacks by polar bears and at least one witnessed case of a member of the company being eaten.

It has been pointed out that perhaps polar bears are, as a group, rather baffled about just what the hell they have ahold of when they catch a man. Some authorities say that a bear normally eats only the blubber (fat) of a seal, discarding the meat, and upon finding none on a man, shows clear confusion. Surely, polar bears in the wild run across precious few humans and fewer live to pass the information along. Plain curiosity may be the reason for such persistent digging-up of Eskimo graves, the bodies exhumed, not eaten. So, precisely why the white bear is a confirmed man-eater may not be so important as just knowing that he is. Personally, I'm not awfully worried about the entire prospect.

Ah, the Alaskan brown. The Kodiak. Now, that's a bear's bear! For quite a few years there has been the same sort of controversy as used to exist around the leopard/panther and who was who and what was what. Is the Alaskan brownie just a super-grizzly or the griz a runt brownie? Does it really matter from a practical standpoint what the relationship is? Only over a couple of sundowners. The Kodiak Island bear is sufficiently bigger in the adult phase to be distinguishable from the grizzly or the Eurasian brown bear that I don't especially care if these are races of the same animal. They all bite.

Beyond this observation, I can find no *specific* instances of man-eating in the Alaska brown bear. For one thing, his range is most likely far too limited to give him much of a chance as well as being greatly underpopulated by man. Of course, many hunters and other outdoorsmen have been killed and injured by the Kodiak, but that's a different story, indicating clear provocation. So much for potentially the most logical candidate for a "disaster" novel. Excuse me, I have been informed that there has already been one, centered around a genetically thrown-back cave bear.

The last American bear that is clearly guilty of chowing down on man is one that most even knowledgeable people would not suspect: the black bear.

Now, sir, it just happens that I have some experience of *Euractos americanus,* acquired about 20 years back, and which to this day still influences my general jaundiced outlook concerning any close association with bears, generally or specifically. I was, in fact, the witness to a savage mauling which, although provoked, gave me a pretty good idea, by interpolation, what it would be like to incur the displeasure of a grizzly, brown or polar bear, let alone a big black.

I was grouse and woodcock hunting with my brother Tom at Loon Bay Lodge in New Brunswick, eastern Canada, probably about 1962. My guide and dog-handler was a young fellow named Sheldon something, with whom I duly wandered off one morning intent upon unspeakable atrocities to the transient flight of woodcock we all hoped had dropped in on the good moon the night before. Before we were even off the lodge's immediate property, I happened to look into a nearby evergreen and spotted a black blob that could be nothing but a bear, and not much of a bear at that.

Well, Sheldon reckoned that was just dandy, as he'd been looking for a cub to raise and tame for, lo, these many years and this was clearly his chance. Handing me a couple of buckshot shells to cover him in case mama, who had apparently gotten a better offer elsewhere, showed up, he started climbing the tree with the serious intention of catching the cub, which couldn't have weighed more than about 40 pounds with a full stomach.

I can capsulize this whole adventure by saying that Sheldon is one lucky guide that he isn't chained up outside some hollow tree to this day! Man! What that little dear didn't do to him you wouldn't find in a "How-To" karate manual. By the time the bear ran off and I regained my strength lost through laughter and was able to stand again, Sheldon looked like he'd been covering the south wall of the Alamo all by himself. He'd been bitten three times, scratched like he'd been hand-sorting wildcats and practically broken his neck (and mine) when the bear dropped smack on his head and knocked him 20 feet out of the tree, bouncing off branches the whole way. I think Sheldon took up the breeding of tropical fish after that morning. Guppies, if I'm not mistaken. . . .

In proper, tradition-steeped bear hunter's terms, there is one whole passel of black bear in these here Yewnited States. Of course, nothing like there used to be, when Seton recorded presumably reliable sources as having killed 11 in one day and as many as 18,000 black bear skins sold by a fur company in a single year. Of the 50 States, Ben East says only a dozen do not have blackies. Alaska, like most everything else, has the most at about 50,000 and there are possibly as many as a quarter million or more conservatively in North America. I can assure you that we have no shortage here in Florida. The guide I used to fish with in the Ten Thousand Islands one morning showed me why we couldn't go out on our usual day. A huge bear had torn his boat apart trying to get the bait out of the livewells just east of Remuda Ranch on U.S. Route 41, the Tamiami Trail, about 25 miles from Naples, Florida.

The few local Seminole Indians with whom I have signed a peace treaty—the United States Government never did—do not opine to be over-fond of the species, either. Actually, the Everglades bears are among the most respected in size, some openly represented as better than 600 pounds, which, when interpolated from the Florida pound to the American pound, would mean something over 350. Don't forget, we're the boys who brought you Ol' Slewfoot!

There are at least seven people recorded who find none of these goings-on in the least humorous, if, indeed, you do yourself. They were all killed and eaten by American black bears. But, before I specify these cases, perhaps a short heart-to-heart would be in order as my approach to the literary side of death has been referred to by some as less than, well, reverent.

I have seen quite a fine assortment of death, some of which I have been responsible for personally. It is my belief that those instances were morally justified either through self-defense, natural adaptation as a qualified predator or indirectly as a taxpayer. My philosophy is identical to that of Woody Allen who once wrote a line that well illustrates my view of life: "I don't want to achieve immortality through my work. I want to achieve immortality through not dying."

Not having any wish to type an inconsistent tumor into a chapter about bears, I shall state my case without benefit of soliloquy by observing that death is the only thing in the world you can absolutely count on. Not even taxes are so reliable. I resent any formalcy, be it a religion or a sanitation law or the perfidy of the rare advantage-seeking funeral director, who mystically, sanitarily, or economically places legal or moral brackets around my final physical rite of passage in which we must all return our salts to the earth. It is my personal view that death deserves no more respect as a human activity than any other; which means, not much. Besides, nobody ever gets very good at it. There's nothing sacred about dying; mystical, maybe. But that's only because we don't understand some of the more involved implications. My personal view is that we *do* have it rather figured out but don't want to face facts. We have an odd tendency to somewhat overestimate ourselves as a species, which insinuates colossal nerve from our kind who have been here an eye-blink compared to the dinosaurs' tenure. I am writing this book, for reasons beside the money, because I find the whole idea of animals that eat people interesting. Not holy, not bizarre, not even horrid (unless I might be personally involved). Yes, I feel sorrow for the youngster maimed or killed by an animal. Yes, I wish there was no cancer. No, I did not send in my Publisher's Clearing House Sweepstakes Entry Form. Not even the *Reader's Digest* sweepstakes form. You see, I'm a pessimist: something will have eaten me before I could possibly have a chance to win. Somehow I just knew you'd want to know my philosophy. Back to bears. And death.

It was May of 1906, not an especially auspicious date for the first recorded case of man-eating by a black bear in North America, and most likely was anything but the original instance. It's just that folks, including Indians, probably had better things to do than write up such matters until this point. Three men were at a lumber camp on the Red Deer River of Alberta in May; two workers by the names of McIntosh and Heffern as well as the cook, a man named Wilson. The woodcutters saw a bear wander out of the woods across the river and shouted for Wilson to come out and have a look.

That bear must have either been starving or gifted with tremendous powers of resolution because, without a hitch, he walked through the river, stopped to shake himself off and without the slightest hesitation charged straight at the astonished group of three men.

The axemen made it safely to the cookhouse about ten yards away, but the cook, Wilson, was leading a losing race with the black bear. The incident was probably funny to everybody but poor Wilson, who, in his enthusiasm to remain uneaten, couldn't slow up sufficiently to get into the cookhouse door. Around and around the shanty went the man and the bear, the black gaining at every yard. With a probably merciful swat, he reared up and broke Wilson's neck with one blow. The man was dead before he hit the ground, at least we hope so.

You'd reckon we were talking about a hardened man-eating lion rather than a lousy black bear, but this animal wasn't about to be driven off his kill. Both McIntosh and Heffern were close enough to hit the animal with, among other items, a square bullseye with a can of lard and the man-eater even ignored a perfect hit with a nasty canthook. He picked up the hopefully dead and certainly unconscious Wilson's body and dragged it a few yards away, giving the other two men in the shanty a chance to run like hell for the bunkhouse where one of them had a revolver. Perhaps they should have thrown it at the bear, based upon their accuracy with canthooks and lard cans, because despite repeated shots, no bear hair flew. Probably tired of the harassment, the man-eater carried Wilson about a hundred yards into the bush, out of range. It is insinuated that he had the chance to eat at least part of Wilson before realizing that discretion was the better part of man-eating when a mediocre rifleman arrived on the scene and demonstrated—unsuccessfully—the error of the bear's ways. Ah, well, style isn't everything: it's results that count.

I wish, at least from my side of the typewriter, that I could give you some good, hairy tales about man-eating black bears that didn't sound like overwritten "What I Did On My Summer Vacation" reports, but the black bear just doesn't have a great deal of thespian presence. In 1961, he ate an Ohioan (which, judging by some of my best friends can be hard to swallow at the best of times) in Ontario—which must violate some sort of international law—and earlier, in 1924, had solved all the problems of a trapper by the name of Waino, also in Ontario. The Waino case, however, reads more like Jim Corbett wrote it as the bear had had a losing brush with a porcupine that had given him both barrels in the face and neck. Although genuine man-eating, the Waino case would have to be considered in the light of a starving, injured bear. I'm sure Mr. Waino would feel much better about that.

A distinguishingly nasty incident that cost the life and much of the body of a tot, three-year old Carol Ann Pomerankey, happened in America's Upper Peninsula of Michigan in 1948 when the little girl, daughter of a forest ranger, was fatally bitten in the neck by a black bear. The bear had come out of the woods where the family was living in the Marquette National Forest, while Carol Ann's dad was at work and her mother involved in the kitchen. The little girl had actually reached the screen door of the cabin under the full view of the mother when the bear executed her. Despite the valiant efforts of the distraught mother to beat the animal off with a broom, it stuck with the body and carried it off.

A posse was formed within a short time, complete with dogs, and the bear was driven away from the body where it had stopped to eat part of the little girl. One of the hunters, a professional fisherman by the name of Weston, volunteered to stay with the remains while the rest of the men went on. Five minutes after the main group had left, Weston practically filled his pants when he turned around and saw the man-eater, standing on its hind legs, not more than 20 feet away. Terrified to chance firing and more terrified not to, he shot the bear square in the chops and then finished it with four more bullets in the body. It wasn't a very big bear, sort of a half-pint, and official examination of the animal's body showed no possible reason for the attack. It might be noted, though, that it was a lousy year for blueberries, a common denominator when black bears take to eating people.

Here's to good blueberry harvests. . . .

Okay, we've clearly established that the American black bear is a people-eater and, when determined, pretty good at it. There has, though, been no case of a bear turning genuine multiple man-eater as the big cats do, so, beyond making the irrefutable point that the black bear does kill and eat man, I think we ought to let the poor chap alone.

There's a weird-looking denizen of India and other less pronounceable places called the sloth bear (*Melursus ursinus*) that everybody who writes about bears seems suspiciously eager to grant the crown for Man-eater of the Year. Were it not for the fact that outdoor writers in general and those specifically who scribble about man-eating animals are conspicuous by their obvious veracity, clear eyes (no smoking permitted in the library) and look of eagles, one might be remotely questioning about the true ferocity of the *Melursus ursinus*. Ah, but having read this far I know you will agree.

Actually, no kidding, I once did an interview with a man who killed a man-eating Indian sloth bear. If you don't know the name Berry Boswell Brooks, you don't own a copy of Rowald Ward's *Records of Big Game,* in which he is prominently featured opposite many of the largest whatevers collected. I just may one day do a book about Berry, who was a character out of a mold that has been somehow misplaced, but since *bwana* Brooks was not himself a man-eater, I feel editorially bound to dispense with further dissertations on his character and hospitality. Berry got a better offer from above a few years back, but I still have the tapes of three days of interviewing him. By God, sir, he was the most willing interviewée I ever ran up against! As I recall, he even bought me some extra tape cassettes in case I ran low! . . .

Whatever the case, the sloth bear is the last one you're going to pry out of me. Rather like a two-headed toad, it's interesting in that it apparently, judging from its constant irritability, suffers from persistent, perhaps terminal constipation. The one Berry shot had killed an even dozen women, the remains of one of which was the bait he sat up over to place a .458 caliber hole through the killer from a .460 Weatherby Magnum. (Don't let Roy Weatherby, ultra-velocity gunmaker, confuse you; he just adds the sales tax to the caliber.)

One of the more interesting aspects of the sloth bear, who is no larger than an average, underprivileged American black bear, is that he tends to kill with his three-inch claws, biting only as a secondary method of attack. This brings to mind a parallel of another very badly confused Asian animal, the Indian rhinoceros. This poor chap generally bites anybody he can catch up with rather than goring, as is more customary among his clan. Well, not to worry. For sure, upon reading these words, one or another of the "preservationist" groups will get up a massive program to teach Indian sloth bears how to bite and Indian rhinos how to gore. If you're interested and they can get the government equally so, you will be proud to know that they may do it with *your* tax dollars, too.

two

"COME QUICK! I'M BEING EATEN BY A BEAR!"

by Larry Kaniut

AS TOLD TO THE AUTHOR BY CYNTHIA DUSEL-BACON

Bears usually will kill humans only when surprised or super hungry.
—Capt. Robert Penman, Alaska Department of Public Safety,
personal interview, Anchorage, February 1977

FIRST HEARD ABOUT Cynthia Dusel-Bacon over a local radio news-cast on August 13, 1977. She had been frightfully mauled by a bear while working for the United States Geological Survey somewhere up north, around Fairbanks. My interest in her experience led me to write her at the University of Stanford Medical Center.

This courageous lady sent me a tape with her story. She was more than eager to offer her experience in hopes of helping others avoid a similar situation, and she wrote in her letter (typed by holding a stylus between her jaws), "I couldn't be more pleased about your efforts to amass all available information about bear maulings in Alaska. I can't think of a greater contribution one could make to educate people about the potential danger of a bear encounter. I believe very strongly in what you are doing."

A short time later I received her tape and her story.

THE SUMMER OF 1977 was my third summer in the Yukon-Tanana Upland of Alaska, doing geologic field mapping for the Alaskan Geology Branch of the U.S. Geological Survey. I began working for the survey in the summer of 1975, making helicopter-assisted traverses in the highest terrain of the six-thousand-square-mile Big Delta quadrangle. The second summer, as our budget did not provide for helicopter expenses, the project chief and I found it necessary to map the geology by backpacking, usually a week at a time. Last summer we were again funded for helicopter transport after an initial month of backpacking. All five geologists in our group, after being transported by air to the field area, usually mapped alone. I personally felt quite comfortable.

Every summer in the upland area we saw bears. The first one I saw was walking slowly along on the far side of a small mountain meadow, and I froze. It didn't see me and disappeared into the forest. Another time I was walking through a spruce forest and saw a black bear moving through the trees some distance away. Again I was apparently not noticed. The second summer while I was backpacking, I encountered a small black bear coming along the trail toward me. I had been busy looking down at the ground for chips of rock when I heard a slight rustling sound. I looked up to see the bear about forty feet in front of me. Startled, it turned around and ran off in the other direction, crashing through the brush as it left the trail. This particular experience reassured me that what I had heard about black bears being afraid of people was, in fact, true.

I SEE MY FIRST GRIZZLY

During my third summer, I saw my first grizzly, but only from the air while traveling in the helicopter. Although other members of our field party had seen them on the ground, I felt myself fortunate to have en-countered only black bears. Grizzlies were generally considered to be more unpredictable and dangerous.

All three summers I had hiked through the bush unarmed, as it was the belief of our project chief that guns added more danger to an en-counter than they might prevent. A wounded, angry bear would probably be more dangerous than a frightened one. She had therefore strongly discouraged us from carrying any kind of firearm. We all carried walkie-talkies and radios to keep in constant touch with one another and with our base camp. And we were warned against surprising bears or getting between a mother and her cubs. Whenever I was doing field mapping, I always attempted to make noise as I walked so that I would alert any bears within hearing and give them time to run away from me. For two summers this system worked perfectly.

Last summer we were scheduled to complete the reconnaissance mapping of the Big Delta quadrangle. Since it covers such a vast area, we needed helicopter transportation to finish traversing all the ridges by mid-September.

At about 8 A.M. on August 13, 1977, Ed Spencer, our helicopter pilot, dropped me off near the top of a rocky, brush-covered ridge approxi-mately sixty miles southeast of Fairbanks. I was dressed in khaki work pants and a cotton shirt, wore sturdy hiking boots, and carried a ruck-sack. In the right-hand outside pocket of my pack I carried a light lunch of baked beans, canned fruit, fruit juice, and a few pilot crackers. My walkie-talkie was stashed in the left-hand outside pocket, complete with covering flap, strap, and buckle. I was to take notes on the geology and collect samples by means of the geologist's hammer I carried on my belt, record my location on the map, and stow the samples in my rucksack.

Standard safety procedure involved my making radio contact with the other geologists and with our base camp several times during the day, at regular intervals. The radio in camp, about eighty miles south of the mapping area, was being monitored by the wife of the helicopter pi-lot. Plans called for me to be picked up by helicopter at the base of the eight-mile-long ridge on a designated gravel bar of the river at the end of the day.

NICE NARROW TRAIL

After noticing, with unexpected pleasure, that I was going to be able to use a narrow trail that had been bulldozed along the crest of the ridge, I started off downhill easily, on the trail through tangles of birch brush and over rough, rocky slides. The ridge was in one of the more populated parts of the quadrangle, as a few small cabins are about fifteen or twenty miles downstream along the Salcha River, and a short landing strip for airplanes is about ten miles from the ridge. Fishermen occasionally come this far up the river, too, so the bears in the area have probably seen human beings occasionally. This particular morning I wasn't expecting to see bears at all; the hillside was so rocky, so dry-looking and tangled with brush, it just didn't seem like bear country. If I were to see a bear that day, it would more likely be at the end of the day, down along the river bar, and adjoining woods.

I descended the ridge slowly for several hundred yards, moving from one outcrop of rock to another, chipping off samples and stowing them in my pack. I stopped at one large outcrop to break off an interesting piece and examined it intently. A sudden loud crash in the undergrowth below startled me and I looked around just in time to see a black bear rise up out of the brush about ten feet away. My first thought was "Oh no! A bear. I'd better do the right thing." My next thought was one of relief: "It's only a black bear, and a rather small one at that." Nevertheless, I decided to get the upper hand immediately and scare it away. I shouted at it, face-to-face, in my most commanding tone of voice. "Shoo! Get out of here, bear! Go on! Get away!" The bear remained motionless and glared back. I clapped my hands and yelled even louder. Even this had no effect on the bear.

Instead of turning and running away into the brush, it began slowly walking, climbing toward my level, watching me stealthily. I waved my arms, clapped, yelled even more wildly. I began banging on the outcrop with my hammer, making all the noise I could to intimidate this bear that was just not acting like a black bear is supposed to. I took a step back, managing to elevate myself another foot or so in an attempt to reach a more dominant position. But as I did this, the bear darted suddenly around behind the outcrop, behind me.

My sensation was of being struck a staggering blow from behind. I felt myself being thrown forward and landed facedown on the ground, with my arms outstretched. I froze, not instinctively but deliberately, remembering that playing dead was supposed to cause an attacking bear to lose interest and go away.

Instead of hearing the bear crashing off through the brush though, I felt the sudden piercing pain of the bear's teeth biting deep into my right shoulder. I felt myself being shaken with tremendous, irresistible power by my shoulder, by teeth deep in my shoulder. Then it stopped and seemed to be waiting to see if I was still alive.

I TRIED FOR MY RADIO

I tried to lie perfectly still, hoping it was satisfied. "I've got to get at my radio in the pack, I've got to get a call out," I thought. My left arm was free so I tried to reach behind me to the left outside pocket of my rucksack to get at the walkie-talkie. The strap was buckled so tightly I realized I couldn't get the pocket open without taking off my pack. My movement caused the bear to start a new flurry of biting and tearing at the flesh of my upper right arm. I was completely conscious of feeling my flesh torn, teeth against bone, but the sensation was more of numb horror at what was happening to me than of specific reaction to each bite. I remember thinking, "Now I'm never going to be able to call for help. I'm dead unless this bear decides to leave me alone."

The bear had no intention of leaving me alone. After chewing on my right shoulder, arm, and side repeatedly, the bear began to bite my head and tear at my scalp. As I heard the horrible crunching sound of the bear's teeth biting into my skull, I realized it was all too hopeless. I remember thinking, "This has got to be the worst way to go." I knew it would be a slow death because my vital signs were all still strong. My fate was to bleed to death. I thought, "Maybe I should just shake my head and get the bear to do me in quickly."

All of a sudden, the bear clamped its jaws into me and began dragging me by the right arm down the slope through the brush. I was dragged about twenty feet or so before the bear stopped as if to rest, panting in my ear. It began licking at the blood that was by now running out of a large wound under my right arm. Again the bear pulled me along the ground, over rocks and through brush, stopping frequently to rest, and chewing at my arm. Finally it stopped, panting heavily. It had been dragging me and my twenty-pound pack—a combined weight of about 150 pounds—for almost a half hour. Now it walked about four feet away and sat down to rest, still watching me intently.

Here, I thought, might be a chance to save myself yet—if only I could get at that radio. Slowly I moved my left arm, which was on the side away from the bear, and which was still undamaged, behind me to get at that pack buckle. But this time the pocket, instead of being latched tight, was wide open—the buckle had probably torn off from the bear's clawing or the dragging over the rocks. I managed to reach down into the pocket and pull out the radio.

"COME QUICK! I'M BEING EATEN BY A BEAR!"

Since my right arm was now completely numb and useless, I used my left hand to stealthily snap on the radio switch, pull up two of the three segments of the antenna, and push in the button activating the transmitter. Holding the radio close to my mouth, I said as loudly as I dared, "Ed, this is Cynthia. Come quick! I'm being eaten by a bear." I said "eaten" because I was convinced that the bear wasn't just mauling me or playing with me, but was planning to consume me. I was its prey and it had no intention of letting the "catch" escape.

I repeated my message and then started to call out some more information, hoping that my first calls had been heard. "Ed, I'm just down the hill from where you left me off this morning . . ." But I got no further. The bear by this time had risen to its feet; it bounded quickly over to me and savagely attacked my left arm, knocking the radio out of my hand. I screamed in pain as I felt my good arm now being torn and mangled by claws and teeth.

I realized I had done all I could to save my life. I had no way of knowing whether anyone had even heard my calls. I really doubted it, since no static or answering sound from someone trying to call back had come over the receiver. I knew I hadn't taken time to extend the antenna completely. I knew I was down in a ravine, with many ridges between me and the receiving set. I knew there was really no chance for me. I was doomed. So I screamed and yelled as the bear tore at my arm, figuring that it was going to eat me anyway and there was no longer any reason to try to control my natural reactions.

I remember that the bear then began sniffing around my body, going down to my calves, up my thighs. I thought, "I wonder if he's going to open up new wounds or continue working on the old ones." I didn't dare to look around at what was happening—my eyes were fixed upon the dirt and leaves on the ground only inches below my face. Then I felt a tearing at the pack on my back and heard the bear begin crunching cans in its teeth—cans I had brought for my lunch. This seemed to occupy its attention for a while; at least it let my arms alone and gave me a few moments to focus my mind on my predicament.

"Is this how I'm going to go?" I remember marveling at how clear my mind was, how keen my senses were. All I could think of as I lay there on my stomach, with my face down in the dry grass and dirt, and that merciless, bloodthirsty thing holding me down, was how much I wanted to live and how much I wanted to return to Charlie, my husband of five months, and how tragic it would be to end it all three days before I turned thirty-one.

It was about ten minutes, I think, before I heard the faint sound of a helicopter in the distance. It came closer and then seemed to circle, as if making a pass, but not directly over me. Then I heard the helicopter going away, leaving me. What had gone wrong? Maybe it was just a routine pass to transfer one of the other geologists to a different ridge, or to go to a gas cache to refuel, and not an answer to my call for help. No one had heard my call.

The bear had not been frightened by the sound of the helicopter, for having now finished with the contents of my pack, it began to tear again at the flesh under my right arm. Then I heard the helicopter coming back, circling, getting closer. Being flat on my face, with the remains of the pack still on my back, and both arms now completely without feeling,

I kicked my legs to show whoever was up above me that I was still alive. This time, however, I was certain that I was to be rescued because the pilot hovered directly over me.

SILENCE

But again I heard the helicopter suddenly start away over the ridge. In a few seconds all was silence, agonizing silence. I couldn't believe it. For some completely senseless, heartless, stupid reason they'd left me for a second time.

Suddenly I felt, or sensed, that the bear was not beside me. The sound of the chopper had undoubtedly frightened it away. Again I waited in silence for some ten minutes. Then I heard the helicopter coming over the ridge again, fast and right over me. I kicked my legs again and heard the helicopter move up toward the crest of the ridge for what I was now sure was a landing. Finally I heard the engine shut down, then voices, and people calling out.

I yelled back and tried to direct them to where I was lying. But the birch brush was thick, and with my khaki work pants and gray pack I was probably difficult to see lying on the ground among the rocks. Ed was the first to spot me, and he called the two women geologists down the slope to help him. Together they managed to carry me up the hill and lift me up into the backseat of the helicopter.

I remember the feeling of relief and thankfulness that swept over me when I found myself in that helicopter, going up and away over the mountain. I knew that my mind was clear and my breathing was good and my insides were all intact. All I had to do was keep cool and let the doctors fix me up. Deep down, though, I knew the extent of my injuries and knew that I had been too badly hurt for my body to ever be the same again.

They flew me to Fort Greely, an army base in Delta Junction, about an hour's trip. There, emergency measures were taken to stabilize my condition. I was given blood and probably some morphine to deaden the pain. An hour or so later I was flown to the army hospital in Fairbanks and taken immediately into surgery. For the first time that day I lost consciousness—under the anesthesia. My left arm had to be amputated above the elbow, about halfway between elbow and shoulder, because most of the flesh had been torn from my forearm and elbow. To try to save my right arm, which had not been so badly chewed, the doctors took a vein out of my left thigh and grafted it from underneath my badly damaged right shoulder, through the torn upper arm, and out to my lower arm. This vein became an artery to keep the blood circulating through my forearm and hand. Four surgeons continued working on me for about five hours, late into the evening. They also did some "debriding"—that is, removing hopelessly damaged tissue and cleaning the lacerated wounds of leaves, sticks, and dirt. I stayed at Fairbanks overnight and then at three o'clock Sunday afternoon was flown to San Francisco.

By this time our branch chief had managed to notify my husband, Charlie (also a geologist for the U.S. Geological Survey), of my accident. They were waiting for me when I arrived at the San Francisco airport at one o'clock Monday morning. I was taken immediately by ambulance to Stanford Hospital and put in the intensive care ward.

ANOTHER AMPUTATION

Then began the vain attempts to save my right arm. For more than a week I held every hope that the vein graft was going to work. But a blood clot developed in the mangled arm and circulation stopped. The pulse that had been felt in the right wrist and the warmth in my fingers disappeared and the whole arm became cold. Although another amputation was clearly going to be necessary, the doctors felt that they should wait until a clearer line of demarcation between good tissue and bad tissue became evident. Then they would amputate up to this point and save the rest.

But before that line appeared, I began to run a high temperature. Fearing that the infected and dying arm was now endangering my life, the doctors took me immediately into the operating room, found the tissue in my arm to be dead almost to the top of my shoulder, and removed the entire arm.

As if this were not trouble enough, my side underneath the right shoulder had been opened up by the bear when he tore out and ate the lymph glands under my right arm. This area was raw and extremely susceptible to infection. It would eventually have to be covered by skin grafts, skin stripped from my own body. But before the skin graft could be done, tissue would have to be regenerated in the wound to cover the exposed muscle and bone. I stayed for weeks in the hospital, absorbing nourishing fluids and antibiotics intravenously and eating high-protein meals of solid foods. Slowly, new flesh grew back to fill the hole, and the plastic surgeon was able to graft strips of skin taken from my upper right thigh to cover the raw flesh under my right shoulder. The thigh skin was laid on in strips like rolls of sod, kept clean and open to the air for many days, until it "took." Those operations hospitalized me for a total of six weeks.

IT HAD BEEN AUGUST 13

During my long days and weeks in bed I had lots of time to review my experience and ponder some of the questions that had puzzled me on that unlucky day of August 13. Why didn't I simply bleed to death after the bear had torn both my arms to shreds and chewed through the main arteries in each? My doctor explained that because I had been in excellent physical condition and my arteries were young and elastic, the blood vessels constricted and cut off the flow of blood quickly after the flesh was mangled. Even the open ends of the arteries closed themselves off and kept me from losing all my blood, and my life.

Had my call for help over the walkie-talkie really been picked up? Or was the helicopter merely making a routine run over the area when Ed spotted me on the ground? I learned later that my first call for help *had* been heard by the helicopter pilot's wife, Bev Spencer. She understood it clearly and immediately radioed her husband that I was in trouble. She gave him what little information I had been able to transmit about my location, and he started right toward my ridge. He had also heard my call, but not clearly enough to be sure of the message. But why did he leave my ridge after he flew over me the first time? And where did he go?

Actually, Ed hadn't been able to spot me from the air the first time, and realizing that he couldn't fly the helicopter and look for me at the same time, he decided to pick up another geologist first.

The second time over he did spot the bear, and hence, me, from the air, but he also saw that the terrain was too rough for only two to get me up the ridge to a landing spot, so he flew back to pick up a third geologist from another area. Finally, with two assistants, he made his landing and led the successful search and rescue. I only wish I'd known why that helicopter kept leaving me again and again, though. I didn't need that additional mental torture.

WHY WAS I ATTACKED?

But why did the bear attack me in the first place? I see three possible reasons: (1) the bear may have been asleep in the brush and I startled it; (2) the bear may have seen me as a threat, not only to itself but also to any offspring that might have been nearby; or (3) the bear was very hungry. I do not even consider a fourth possibility, one that has often been suggested as a reason for discriminating against women in similar situations—namely, the possibility that wild animals, particularly bears, are often attracted by the scent of menstrual blood of women at times of their periods. For the three summers I worked out in the bush, I was never approached by any wild animals, and my periods came and went regularly. On the day of the attack I was not menstruating.

Regarding the first possibility, which I believe is the most likely one, the bear may have been asleep in the brush and woke up startled when it heard me chipping on rocks. It should have had plenty of time to collect its wits, however, as it stared at me and circled me before charging. Although the terrain seemed rather unsuited for a comfortable lair—large, rectangular blocks of broken-off rubble covered the ground and were almost covered by birch brush—this hidden spot may have seemed ideal to the bear.

It is also possible that the bear was instinctively fearful for the safety of a cub in the area. I never saw any other bear that day, but the helicopter

pilot, after he left me off at the Fort Greely hospital for emergency treatment, asked Fish and Game officials to find the bear that had attacked me
so that it could be checked for rabies. They did and shot what they believed
to be the guilty one—a 175-pound female. They reported the presence of
a year-old cub in the area, but left it to take care of itself. If the mother encountered a strange creature in its territory and simultaneously noticed
the absence of its cub, it could have reacted violently out of rage or fear for
its cub. Given that I saw no cub, it may have felt, in sudden panic, that I
had something to do with its disappearance.

As to the third possibility, extreme hunger of the bear, the post-
mortem analysis of the bear's stomach revealed only a few berries and
some "unidentifiable substance" that may have been parts of me. I hadn't
noticed any blueberry patches on the ridge, so the bear could have been
tired of hunting for berries and decided to try for larger game, since it
came upon me, either unexpectedly or deliberately, at a distance of only
ten feet.

One fact is certain: that bear wanted me for dinner—my flesh and
blood—and once having tasted it, did not intend to let me get away. But I
did get away. Furthermore, I'm up and around again. The bites on my
head have healed and my hair has grown back to completely cover the
scars. My right side is covered with new skin, my left stump is strong and
has good range of motion. I'm fitted with artificial arms and am ready to
resume my interrupted careers as wife and geologist.

It will be difficult for me to operate a workable arm on my right side,
where I have no stump, and to manage the use of the arm and hook on
the other side, where I have no elbow. But with practice I know that I
will eventually be able to make my prosthetic devices and my feet and
mouth do many of the things my hands did for me before.

I plan to continue in my job with the U.S. Geological Survey. Both
Charlie and I have loved our work there, and our colleagues have been
tremendously supportive of me throughout the ordeal. I'd like to stay
with the Alaskan Geology Branch, perhaps specializing in petrography—
the examination of sections of three-hundredths-of-a-millimeter-thick
wafers of rock under the microscope to determine their mineral compo-
sition and texture. With only minor adaptations to the microscope, I

should be able to do this work as effectively as I was able to do it before my accident.

I am determined to lead as normal a life as possible. I know that there are certain limitations I can't get around, having to rely on artificial arms. But I'm certainly going to do the best I can with all that I have left. And that's a lot!

three

THREE BEARS RIGHT THERE!

by Ralph Borders and Bill Gonce

ALTHOUGH WE DEPARTED ON our hunting trip Saturday, 5 September 1992, our hunt began years before. Ours is a hunting heritage. We've shared many hunting adventures, but we'd never hunted sheep. The thrill of the outdoors and sharing a campfire fueled our enthusiasm. The opportunity to pursue Dall sheep produced an added dimension.

My brother-in-law, Bill Gonce, came from Juneau to my home in Haines, Alaska, where we completed our plans and preparation. We enjoyed discussing old times and anticipated the next two weeks, hunting sheep for the first week, followed by a moose hunt. We were eager to see Alaska's interior, knowing that it offered country far different from southeast Alaska's heavily timbered and lush rain forest.

We had taken great effort to select the lightest foodstuffs for the sheep hunt to reduce the weight of our packs. Our meals would consist of things that could be eaten dry (pilot bread, cheese, smoked salmon, hard sausage, candy) or mixed with hot water (instant oatmeal, Top Ramen soup, MRE-meals ready to eat, hot cider mix, tea bags, and Kool-Aid).

We are both experienced hunters, in good shape for hiking but not used to packing. We didn't anticipate much packing on the sheep trip because we would be dropped off in the mountains by a bush pilot. We were filling a fly-in trip that other hunters had been unable to complete.

Bill is a carpenter-contractor who came to Alaska in 1971. He is 41 years old with graying red hair, 6-feet-1-inch tall, and weighs 180 pounds. He has hunted an abundance of deer.

Bill got me a meat-cutting job in the Haines grocery store in 1973. For the past five years I've helped maintain roads, water and sewer lines, and vehicles for the Haines Department of Public Works. I'm 43 years old and have graying brown hair. I'm 5-feet-10-inches tall, weigh 160 pounds, and am blind without my glasses. I enjoy photography and have shot a lot of bears with my camera.

On Saturday we left Haines at 6:30 A.M. It was a beautiful, clear forty-degree day. We talked sheep hunting as we enjoyed the journey north. Stopping at the beautiful turquoise Kluane Lake in the Yukon and watching one hundred Dall lambs and ewes heightened our excitement. When we reached Tok, I purchased a bear tag, in the event we ran into a bear worth collecting. Our trip went without a hitch, and we arrived in Fairbanks at 6:30 P.M., where we spent the night in a motel.

Sunday and a beautiful, clear day beckoned. That afternoon we began the last leg of our journey. As we drove toward the airstrip at Salcha forty miles to the south, we encountered local hunters with three- and four-wheelers, as well as tracked off-road vehicles. The annual excitement of moose fever prevailed.

We finally reached the dirt airstrip between the river and the highway. A half-dozen variously colored, single-engine airplanes dotted the strip near the bush pilot's home. We noticed two Super Cubs fitted with special tundra tires. This Piper aircraft is the bush pilot's plane of choice for getting into and out of tight strips, such as high-mountain gravel stream bars. The twenty-nine-inch-tall balloon tires add to the plane's performance and its look of strength and superiority. The pilot, Bill Sewell, stowed our gear in his plane, and before we knew it, we were airborne, flying into an area where neither Bill nor I had previously been. On our way in we saw a few caribou and one black bear.

Forty minutes later we landed on a gravel strip in the middle of the river. For the uninitiated, an Alaskan bush "strip" is not an asphalt runway a mile in length. A bush strip is a level stretch of ground one hundred yards long or longer, which could be rocky or mushy firmament. We noticed an old wrecked plane off to one side, the result of an inexperienced pilot, a sudden wind shift, or too much weight aboard to maintain flying status. This did not dampen our hunting desire.

This strip was not the object of our hunt but would have to do until the weather permitted our pilot to move us. We were fifteen miles from our planned drop-off point at a miner's cabin at 4,000 feet. If the wind died down in two days, Bill would return to ferry us away from this 1,500-foot elevation, deeper into the mountains and closer to ram country. Before the pilot left, he flew Bill around the area for twenty-five minutes, looking for rams and pointing out various drainages.

Along the river was a packer's hunting camp with four moose hunters. The packer had mules and horses for hire, should a hunter want a moose packed to camp. He had a spare wall tent, eight-by-ten-feet, that he let us use. It was much nicer than our two-man tent. We went to bed anticipating hunting in the vicinity until Bill returned.

On Monday (Labor Day) we loaded our packs and hiked from the packer's camp carrying our spike camp: tent, single-burner Coleman stove, sleeping bags, and a two-day food supply. We crossed the river, skirted some muskeg, climbed a hill, and set out for the mountains three to four miles away.

We set up camp around 5:00 P.M. at the base of a mountain. Packing our gear had taken its toll, but a plus was my Danner boots: they kept my feet dry and comfortable. There was no water in the area, and were we glad the packer had told us to take along canteens!

While resting we saw a ewe and a lamb above camp. Later we watched a wolf cross a ridge in front of us. I decided to shoot it but overestimated the range and missed with the only shot I fired. The wolf was still running two miles away.

On Tuesday we climbed the mountain behind camp and noticed two more ewes. We spotted one hundred caribou, but the season was closed that year. We also saw a wolf and three Dall ewes by afternoon, when we heard wolves howling. We ran into another sheep hunter who said he'd seen no legal rams.

Deciding to return to base camp, we trudged down the mountain to camp, packed our gear, and headed for base camp by 5:00 P.M. We retired for the night hoping the pilot would show up in the morning.

Wednesday surprised us with a snowstorm and wind. There would be no hunting or flying. We spent the time with the other hunters around the stove in the packer's tent waiting for the weather to change. Thursday the tenth dawned clear and cold with a low of twenty degrees during the night.

The packer told us about the hunting possibilities and two cabins where we could spend the night, nine miles away and deeper into ram country. Two miles beyond the cabins at timberline was another spot to set up camp. He said if we'd flag a spot at timberline to drop our gear, he'd bring it up the next day.

With that in mind we took sleeping bags and a little food to last until supper Friday. Upon reaching the cabins and discovering other hunters, we were surprised. The packer had not known they were there. They had come in by three-wheeler part of the way, having left the machine two miles away because they couldn't descend the steep sidehill.

They occupied the newer cabin, so we took the old cabin, which was a twelve-by-fourteen-foot log structure. It was built over a spring and had a rotten wood floor, two stories, and no windows on the first floor. The rusty woodstove had no damper, making it nearly impossible to boil water, much less heat the room. Nevertheless, we prepared hot water, mixed instant oatmeal chased down with hot chocolate, and hit the sack. The temperature dropped to ten degrees that night.

On Friday we prepared for rams. My wool pants and Pendleton shirt were comfortable. Before leaving the cabin we split our gear, which included a spotting scope and tripod, knife-steel, ammo, extra sweater, gloves, lunch, and survival gear (space blanket, candles, matches, nylon cord, emergency flares).

Two miles up the valley from the cabin we reached timberline, where we flagged the drop-off spot for our gear. We dropped our sleeping bags off amidst six-inch-wide trees fifteen to twenty feet high along the riverbank. We headed up the mile-and-a-half-wide valley. Mountains rose from the valley floor. High tundra and rocks led the way toward the head of the valley ten miles beyond. We saw caribou again. After three miles we spotted twenty lambs and ewes across the valley. Realizing our best chance for rams was ahead, we pushed on.

Our objective was a 6,500-foot peak. Stopping for lunch, we glassed for rams. I observed what appeared to be old bear tracks in the snow—that of a sow and two cubs. We crossed a 5,500-foot pass around 3:00 P.M., stopped, and glassed for an hour. With darkness only four hours away, we decided to make a hurried search of a bench about one hundred feet above us. We thought the hike would eliminate another place to look later and warm us up before returning to set up spike camp.

It had just begun snowing and we had a mile-and-a-half visibility. With an eye peeled for rams we climbed the ten to twenty-degree slope. As we neared the bench, we noticed wolf tracks. Then we saw a single set of bear tracks going downhill that was fresher than the wolf's. The vegetation consisted of berry bushes. We scanned the valley through the falling snow but saw nothing. While I looked downhill, Bill looked uphill. Suddenly, Bill said, "There they are . . . RIGHT THERE!"

I followed his gaze and saw three bears. The sow, which had been lying down and looking over her shoulder, exploded into action. The cubs followed suit and all three bears came for us. Bill and I stood side by side. There was no growl, no noise. The bears came quickly and silently through the fresh snow. We were eyeball to eyeball with three bears.

I watched the sow looking from Bill to me, sizing up the situation and deciding which one to go for. She came for me. One cub was just behind her off her right flank, and the other was the same distance off its twin's flank.

My brother-in-law said later, "It was like three large dogs and they were rushing up to play. It was like, 'Well, fancy meeting you here.' It seemed so innocent."

Bill carried a bullet in the chamber of his .06 and he was shooting, handloaded 180-grain Nosler seconds. I was trying to get my gloves off so I could chamber a round. (My .338 Ruger has always had a problem getting a shell from the clip to the chamber.)

Within four seconds of sighting us, the bears were on us. The sow ran past Bill and grabbed me above my left bicep, pulling me off my feet and carrying me thirty to sixty feet downhill. She slipped or rolled onto her back, dropping me. Just as the sow grabbed me, Bill fired from his hip at the closer cub. His shot spun the cub around, rolled him onto the other cub, and spooked them. Both cubs turned and took off.

The bear and I rolled over and over down the slope. I kept thinking that I should play dead; I made no attempt to fight back. The sow bit my face rapidly. It wasn't a tearing, just bite, bite, bite. I yelled to Bill, "Get her off of me!" Suddenly, she bounced up and grabbed me by the left foot and chewed on it. I didn't hear it, but Bill had shot her. I hadn't heard his first shot when he hit the cub, either.

While she was chewing my left foot, Bill fired again, hitting her and knocking her off me. Bill timed his shots to shoot the bear when she rose above me. I had told him enough over the years that he knew to break the bear down in order to disable it (shoot it in the shoulder, spine, or hip). She came down the next time and grabbed my right foot and chewed on it. I wasn't concerned as long as she chewed on my leg and Bill kept shooting. I didn't think her bites were life-threatening. She bit into my foot at the same time I heard Bill's final shot. The pain was so intense that I knew he had shot my foot. The bear went limp, and I realized he had hit her in the spine, killing her instantly.

Thinking I wouldn't be able to walk on a shot foot, I stood up. I could walk. I hadn't been shot after all. Bill reloaded immediately, fearing the return of the cubs. I yelled, "Find my glasses! We gotta go!" Then I crawled around on all fours feeling through the snow for my glasses. Halfway between where the bear grabbed me and where she died, I found my glasses.

Bill thought I was done for. He didn't tell me that he could look beyond my lipless mouth and see raw flesh and teeth and the back of my throat. He also saw holes in my temples and head. He was concerned that I might have other injuries hidden by my clothes, but I figured as long as I could walk I was okay. I didn't bleed much. I pulled my cap over my head to slow the bleeding. I knew I was okay and refused to let him look for other injuries.

The only major injury was to my lips. I lost about two-thirds of my upper lip and a third of my lower lip. We found part of my upper lip frozen to my coat (they tried to sew it on, but it didn't take). There were a number of puncture wounds to my face and feet. It was hard to believe that the entire attack took thirty seconds.

Bill saw blood on the snow from the cub. The bears were the least of our concerns, and we started out. Bill followed me down the mountain. Convinced I was going to bleed to death, he kept looking for spurting blood.

Although hiking out was difficult, I was buoyed by adrenaline and an eagerness to receive medical help. I stopped periodically and cleaned the blood off my glasses. Within an hour we'd covered four miles to the drop-off site we had marked for the packer and where the packer happened to be. It was 5:05 P.M. We'd covered four miles in fifty-five minutes.

The packer boosted me aboard a horse and led me out, while Bill jogged behind with the day pack. We reached the hunters' cabin, and the packer yelled, "Bear attack!". We could never have known when we met these men that they would play a huge part in my rescue.

The pilot's brother, Leroy Sewell, volunteered to make the trip out for help. His plan was to retrieve his three-wheeler and drive to a mining camp to radio for help. Concerned that I could bleed to death, he grabbed his Mauser rifle and took off. Leroy crossed and recrossed the creek many times, climbing uphill for two miles from 3,000 to 4,000 feet before he reached his machine. (Ralph and Bill never got to speak to Leroy again.)

At the mine camp, Pat Peedle called 911 on a cellular phone. Although low on fuel, a helicopter was dispatched from Fort Greely. Some confusion followed, as the pilot could not locate the cabins and mules nearby. Peedle finally made it clear via radio contact that the helicopter was going in the wrong direction, and the bird landed for specific directions from Sewell. Once he got his bearings, the pilot flew to pick me up. During our wait Bill attended me, mostly dabbing at the blood on my face to keep it from going down my throat.

The mauling took place at 4:10; the helicopter came in at 8:30. The medic cut my clothes off and they loaded me into the chopper. Thinking I would die before he saw me again, Bill talked them into letting him ride in the upper rack. The crew wore night-vision goggles. They flew me to

Fairbanks. Just before arriving at Fort Greely, the chopper encountered a snow squall, reducing visibility to zero. The pilot was redirected. However, since he was on bingo fuel (nearly depleted), he blasted through the squall and landed safely.

My medical treatment and care in Fairbanks was superb. I was there a week, then went to southern California where my folks live. Both my wife and I were enrolled with Blue Cross, and they covered $40,000 in medical expenses. The psychological effect of the bear attack is negligible to both Bill and me.

The week following the attack it snowed three feet, covering the sow, and we never went back to retrieve her. We don't know what happened to the cubs. The fish and game officer wanted us to retrieve and give up the bear, but Bill refused, since he had a bear tag. I wanted the beautiful hide but the snow depth negated the retrieval. The officer finally relented since the bears were all the same size, it was self-defense, and the snow was so deep.

Most people knowledgeable of bears think the attack was the result of the bears' staking out a game trail in hopes of ambushing a caribou or sheep.

Bill Sewell volunteered to take us back in the spring to look for the bear and Ralph's lost rifle. We're not eager to run into another bear family, but we would like to get back into sheep country to bag a ram.

four

A THOUSAND STITCHES

by Stephen A. Routh

I WAS A FAIRLY new float pilot in 1980. July 29 was such a pretty, sunny day that I invited my wife to flight-see with me. I planned to practice landing and taxiing with my Citabria. We were out cruising, landing on a few lakes, and enjoying the weather.

As the day wore on, the weather kicked up with high gusty winds. Since my piloting skills were limited, I thought the proper move was to overnight. It was late in the day, and I had a tent and camping gear on board. We sought a lake with a nice spot to pitch the tent, where we could have some food and return to Anchorage the next morning.

After flying over two lakes, we found one that looked like a good camping area. The lake had nice high banks and level ground surrounding the beach. It appeared to be an adequate place to tie a float plane down, pitch the tent under the trees out of the weather, and spend a nice evening.

I set up for my approach: pulled the carb heat, trimmed the plane, reduced power, and settled safely onto the lake. We taxied to one area where I got out and looked. It was swampy and inappropriate to camp. We taxied to another place and looked that over. It wasn't appropriate either. We taxied to a third place. The bank's height contained the crescendoing noise of the plane's engine as we taxied on step. There was no doubt that any animal within miles would have known that there was an airplane on the lake.

I nosed the airplane in, then heeled it around. With power off, I turned around so the float heels were up on the shore, I had a twenty-foot rope tied to the rear cleat on one float. I grasped the rope in one hand and walked up the little bank, looking for a spot to camp as well as something to anchor the plane to.

I wasn't particularly concerned about animals. Over the years I've followed all the rules to avoid animal problems. My outdoor experience is extensive. I've spent a great deal of time fishing. I have good survival skills. I've been in a lot of bear areas and have avoided bears by making noise and keeping food away.

I looked to the left and didn't see much. I looked to the right. I looked back to the left. Something caught my eye, and I looked back to the right. In my face was a bear. I don't know where he came from, but he was right there. His jaw was a little lower than my chin. It was so startling and so close that I involuntarily screamed. It wasn't the approach I'm used to with bears. Normally man and bear run in opposite directions. But he was within a foot of me standing up on his hind legs, mouth open, nose to nose.

I remember thinking, *This is great. I'll run down my side of the hill, and he'll run down his side of the hill. We're both scared to death. I'll laugh and joke telling my wife. I'll sit in the airplane and probably shake for a while. Then we'll figure out something to do . . . maybe sleep in this airplane in the middle of the lake.*

I turned to run back to the airplane, thinking he was going in the other direction. I also figured the lake would be my salvation should the bear pursue. As I turned to get out of there, he grabbed me. The bear's big, hairy armlike forelegs shot around me literally in a bear hug, *chunk.* Then I felt him snapping at the back of my head. He was all over me. His jaws kept snapping, and I kept moving my head so he couldn't gain purchase on my neck. We were both in a hunting-survival mode. He was snarling and pummeling me. He bit me, grabbing my skull and hair. I felt the back of my head crunch and tear. He grabbed my lower ear in his teeth. I felt my left ear go *huunk.*

At 6-feet-2-inches tall and 195 pounds I was in great shape, but I was no match for this animal. He stood with his forelegs around my torso, and his back legs were hanging on me or clawing me. He was a little shorter than me. Gauging from the fact that my legs buckled with him on my back, and from the length of it's legs, the bear probably weighed 350 pounds. The power of the animal was phenomenal. I kept thinking, *This is a black bear; it can't be that strong.*

I couldn't support his weight, and I fell. Since we were heading downhill, we tumbled together to the lake. All the while he snarled and bit and snapped. I thought, *This is a strange way to die.* I was convinced that I wasn't going to make it.

We fought near the shore in ankle-deep water, and I was on my knees most of the time. He was all over me, and I didn't have time to get up. Somehow I got turned toward him and I was staring him right in the eye. I tried to reason with him. Thinking it might calm him, I said, "You don't want to do this."

There was incredible fury in that animal's face. It was in every sense a WILD animal. There was no appealing to him; he had his mission, and that was to eat me. That was all he knew. It seemed that he was just incredibly angry.

I had to get something to try to kill him. I felt that one of us wasn't going to leave there, and I began to fight back. I couldn't stop his forelegs from coming around me. He reached around and raked my back with those claws. I was amazed by the length of the bear's forelegs. I have long arms and wide shoulders (I wear over a size thirty-seven shirt). The bear's outstretched paws went beyond mine. With my arms outstretched I could actually grab him by his wrists, but he still had claws behind them. Even with that leverage and me holding his wrists, I could not stop the arms from coming around, and I'm strong. I could have done that with most people; not many could bring their arms around me if I was holding their wrists from an interior point because I would have the leverage.

Over and over I felt the claws rip into my sides and back as those powerful paws raked me. I reached into my back pocket hoping I could get my Buck knife. I reasoned that I'd kill that bear. He was so busy attacking he wasn't concerned about being counterattacked. I figured I could jam my knife in his throat, or jam it in his mouth. Since I didn't have my knife, I probed for my comb. My theory was that I was going to jam it into his throat and maybe choke him.

But I couldn't stop those arms from coming around, and I couldn't stop that mouth from working on me. And the mouth kept going for my throat. He bit the back of my neck, my hamstrings, and down my spine, where he tried to break the spine to disable me. He was a very efficient killing machine.

I decided that the best way to survive would be to give him something to chew on. Finally I decided to sacrifice my left arm. I jammed it inside his mouth at the forearm. He kept busy gnawing on that. He tried to move his head to get around my arm so he could come back at my throat, but I kept my arm jammed into his mouth.

While I was being torn apart, my wife was watching from the floats a mere fifteen to twenty feet away. She had no idea what to do and stood screaming at the top of her lungs.

I had no knife, no comb. I thought I could get a rock from the beach to crush his skull, but the shoreline was silty and muddy. It was covered with organic stuff, with no rocks visible. There was an old log where we wrestled in the shallows. The log had old, moldy, dead leaves on it. At one point I saw a branch on the log. I ripped it off and slashed the bear in the face with it.

He didn't like me messing with his face. He protected himself more than he was attacking me. I hit him in the eyes with the branch. He dodged and backed off. That's when the bear noticed my wife and went after her. Joanie climbed into the airplane and managed to close the door. In two jumps the bear was at the heels of the float. The water was shallow, about six inches deep. There was a bench there before it got deeper. The bear jumped onto a float and ran to the cabin, where he stood up and clawed at the Plexiglas windows, trying to get at Joanie.

I thought about my chances of survival on shore, knowing I might well bleed to death in the water. On the other hand the cold might stop the bleeding. I decided that my best chance for survival was to get into the water so I headed out into the lake. I think it's a deep lake. I was in water twenty to thirty feet deep.

I managed to get one hip wader off, but I couldn't remove the other one. I must have been in shock because I've never had a problem in the water. I've been a champion swimmer, but I couldn't get the wader off. I kicked out in the water to get away.

The bear clawed on the plane for a while. Then he ran to the end of the float and looked up and down the beach hunting me. Suddenly he focused on me and entered the water and headed for me. As much as I had a glimmer of hope before, I figured he was far more equipped than I for this battle. I thought of myself, *This is where you're going to die.* He swam toward me, mouth open and snarling.

I did something instinctual: I splashed water. I would give him the slip—lie back in the water and then push water, which would propel me away from him while sending a wave into his mouth. I'd push, and he would cough—*aarrffff*—and spit the water out, then snarl around, come up, look, and see me. Then I'd do it again. I don't know how long we did that, but I must have poured a ton of water down the bear's throat before he finally gave up and headed back to shore.

I found that I could keep myself up, but I couldn't maneuver well. I realized that I had serious injuries. I determined, *There's no way I'm going back to shore. If I'm gonna die, I might as well die in the water and not be eaten by a bear.*

I was shouting at my wife to start the airplane. If she could get the airplane going and step on a rudder to get to me, I could climb on a float. That would be one positive step. She repeatedly pushed the start button . . . *rrraaahhhrrruuuhhhrruuuhhh*; it wouldn't catch. I kept shouting, "PUSH IN THE RED BUTTON! PUSH IN THE RED BUTTON!" That's all I could think about, the mixture control. (You pull the mixture control out to stop your airplane and cut the engine down. No gas gets to the engine if you don't have the red mixture button in.)

Finally she said, "Oh!" Though she'd never flown alone, she'd flown with me enough to know where the mixture button was. She pushed that in and *vroom*, the engine came to life. Then Joanie came taxiing out. What a wonderful sight!

I had a tough time getting onto the float. Joanie had to drape me over the float, and finally I was able to crawl up. It was difficult getting inside the airplane. Joanie pushed me and I tumbled in, one leg after the other. My left arm was in bad shape. I saw the bone inside and thought, *This is not a good deal here at all.* Then I reached to the back of my head and felt my ear dangling. I touched the back of my neck and it was covered with blood. Joanie tried to figure out how badly injured I was. She lifted up my shirt. Then she put it down and didn't say anything. After seeing the look of horror in her eyes, I thought, *I still might die.*

I was afraid to go to shore because I thought the bear might come back—even though I didn't see the bear after reaching the safety of the plane. I got into the pilot's seat, and she helped get the radio on. I wasn't functioning well. I was messed up, but I got on the radio and started talking, pleading, saying, "Somebody help."

There was a DC-6 flying five miles overhead, and it began circling. We couldn't see him, but I was talking to him. Rescue Coordination Center sent an Otter out. Everybody was looking, but nobody could figure out where I was. I didn't even know the name of the lake, or if I knew it, I had forgotten it because of my condition.

I was a mass of injuries. There wasn't much anybody could do. Where would you start? I was bleeding all over the place. The bear had shredded my new Levi's, causing me to ponder his power (I knew a man couldn't rip Levi's in his hands).

We sat in the middle of the lake, and it got darker and darker. I knew that after a period of time nobody could land: It was too high sided, and you can't see the water, the beach, or the land. People kept assuring, "Yeah, we're on the way. We'll be there any minute." But they had no idea where I was. The ELT (Emergency Locator Transmitter) was going, but it was frustrating observing how the systems didn't come together quite right.

My wife had the foresight to pull out the emergency gear, which included flares. She shot off a flare, followed by another. A pilot flew over, circled, and landed. Since it was close to the Fourth of July, he initially thought this was part of the celebration. But then he thought, *Wait a minute. This can't be right.*

I was in the back of the airplane and too messed up to even transfer airplanes. He took one look at me and knew that there was trouble. He

said, "Can you get into my airplane?" Then seeing blood and my condition, he said, "Don't even try."

He decided to taxi my wife and his passenger across the lake to a
cabin, then return for me. They knocked on the door. An occupant
opened the door, looking half-asleep, and said, "We're on our honeymoon,
leave us alone," and slammed the door. They sat outside for a while, and
finally my wife couldn't stand it anymore and said, "I'm not going to stay
out here anymore." They knocked on the door again, and when the folks
realized there was an emergency, they let them in to spend the night.

Meanwhile, the pilot returned, got into my airplane, and took off for
Anchorage. We landed at Elmendorf. Because it was so late with no
lighted landing areas on water, they had cars shining their headlights
across the water so he could see to land. From Elmendorf I was taken to
Providence Hospital, about seven miles away in east Anchorage.

AFTERWARD

Our flight-seeing trip was an intended campout. I was in good physical
and mental shape. I had planned to fly for a few hours and then spend
the night somewhere. We had our food and a tent, and everything would
be comfortable.

The mauling seemed to last a lifetime but I think the actual attack
took less than ten minutes. Things happened so fast but seemed like they
were happening so slow. The first phase was probably over in two to
three minutes, and the second in the water took a minute or two. If it
was ten minutes from the time I first saw the bear until I got on the float,
I'd be surprised. It seemed like half-an-hour, but it must have been much
less than that.

I survived the shock; I think going into the cold water was the best
thing I could have done. The cold water probably saved me, slowing the
bleeding substantially. If I had been on that lake another hour or two,
however, the loss of blood or hypothermia would have done me in.

My injuries included a severely mangled arm; lacerations to my head,
neck, and legs; and a nearly severed ear. My worst wound was to my arm,

where I had jammed it into the bear's mouth. I got a deep wound infection. They treated it with a machine that circulated water, slowly cooking my arm in an effort to beat the infection. I was on different types of IV antibiotics. Finally one, Keflex, killed the infection. I was told that the next stage of antibiotic would probably have cost me my hearing.

My dangling ear was sewn back in place. There are a bunch of stitches where three areas come together. They did such a fine job in the ER that people can't even tell my ear was chopped off. I ended up with about one thousand stitches, but if you looked me over you wouldn't know it. I was in the hospital ten days. I was fully insured. To be honest I don't recollect how much treatment was. Five thousand dollars for the hospital bill comes to mind. I signed the forms and the hospital took care of the rest.

I had a .44 Magnum pistol at that time. I guess I'd grown careless and I didn't have it with me on the beach. A month ago I shot a good-sized black bear on my porch at my cabin at Lake Creek. I dropped him at six feet in the shoulder with my .44 Magnum. He ran up a tree and fell out. I tracked him by his blood spoor for three miles and never did find him. My confidence in the .44 Magnum is down to zero now, and I wouldn't use it again, except to shoot myself to avoid the agony.

I'm an advocate of fighting back. I hear people talk about rolling over and playing dead. With this black bear I wouldn't have had to play dead, I would have been dead. I have no doubt that he would have munched on me while I was hiding my head and trying to survive.

I don't think the bear was surprised. Anybody would have known that there was a man out there because there's no missing the sound of a float plane taxiing, especially when you have a high-sided lake.

I received numerous phone calls and input in the hospital and thereafter. One caller said that two weeks earlier on that lake some kids had been taking shots at a bear with a .22 just for fun, not to kill it but just to hit it. And the bear had run off.

I think black bears are more dangerous than grizzlies. Grizzlies will maim you, but there's a chance you'll survive. But the black bear is the killer. He's going to eat your liver. The bite pattern on me is consistent with injuries to animals by bears: sever the spine or cut the hamstring. Bears are far stronger and more resilient than people give them credit for.

I'm impressed with the black bear's strength and survivability. I think they're much underrated.

In the future I'll always be armed. If I'd had my pistol strapped to my side, I could have done more than I did with a twig. I would also carry a knife. Your adrenaline is going so high that you become super human, and I think I could have killed that bear with a knife. I might be the world's biggest fool, but I think I could have sliced the bear's throat or even jammed a knife into his throat and pushed on the end of it so it went into his mouth and he swallowed it. It's good practice to carry a knife.

I have no idea what became of that bear. The fish and game people laughed when I asked them what they were going to do with the bear. They said they never go after a bear unless it kills someone.

Incidentally, today that airplane still has the claw marks on the back window where the bear was trying to get to my wife. But we haven't flown out to Cow Lake for any overnight tenting.

five

IN WITHOUT KNOCKING

by Helmuth A. Port

IN THE FALL OF 1990 I was on the upper Eli River enjoying the out-doors. The Eli is 65 miles north of Kotzebue, Alaska, about 475 miles northwest of Fairbanks. I always fly with my friend and guide Johnny Walker when I'm in the Kotzebue area.

Johnny had out-of-state sheep hunters at his base camp. My plans included sheep hunting, hiking, fishing for big char, and searching for fossils and minerals. Since I had a sheep permit and Alaskans are not required to employ the services of a guide for sheep, I hunted alone. I'd been out ten days. Desiring to shower and clean up, I asked Johnny to fly me to his Squirrel River cabin. The cabin provided most of the comforts of home and was only a thirty-five-minute flight in Johnny's Super Cub. After a brief and comfortable stay at the cabin, I went out again to the mountains.

On the way from the Squirrel River to the Eli River we encountered some light turbulence. For the most part the skies were clear, but we saw little spots of clouds to the west.

Johnny's camp was in the Maiyumerak Mountains and part of the Baird Mountains. It was the 26th of August and the fall colors were at their peak. Creeks and rivers provided willow and some spruce tree cover, but other than that the country is wide open. Our camp was located in typical sheep country: rocky ridges covered by caribou lichen and interspersed with valleys.

As we landed, we saw clouds in the distance. Johnny said, "Don't set up your tent. You can use the kitchen tent. I'll get the other hunter and come right back; he's a doctor from San Diego."

It never happened. The beautiful day ended abruptly when clouds moved in. The wind picked up and rain fell. The weather changed so fast that within two hours the temperature plummeted from sunny and sixty-five degrees to the thirties.

Warned by the weather I put my tent up before the snow started. I took a bucket five hundred yards to the river, filled it with water, and returned to the kitchen tent. I wasn't concerned about the weather because I was dressed properly. I wore Timberland hiking boots (Sorrel boots around the tent and for short tundra hikes), insulated hunting clothes, and rain gear from Helly Hansen. Feeling I'd done all I could in preparation for the next day, I crawled into my tent for the night, wrapped in my longjohns.

It was a rough night. The storm blew in and the tent stakes came out of the ground. I spent most of the night outside the tent replacing stakes and putting big rocks on the bottom to hold the stakes down.

When I awoke the next day, the wind was still blowing, and it was still snowing. I went out hiking and saw caribou everywhere. They were moving in from the Kugururok area, across the Noatak River south of the Sekuiak Bluff and into the Maiyumerak Mountains. In that classic caribou mile-eating migration pace, the animals fanned out and never slowed their stride toward the south and the Kobuk River.

Around 5:00 P.M. I returned to camp. Sleep was difficult because high winds hammered the tent, causing the tent fly to pop and snap. The noise was endless and the tent shuddered with each blast. Finally about 1:00 A.M. I got to sleep. Tucked into the cozy comfort of my sleeping bag I slept on my right side, cushioned by three inches of down and Hollofill in my waterproofed cocoon. My right arm stretched out over my head, which rested on my bicep. The top of the sleeping bag covered my head.

About 3:00 A.M. I awakened from a sound sleep. I felt something damp on my face and weight on my chest. I wondered what was happening. It's not easy waking up, knowing that something is happening and not knowing what. You're wide awake feeling something deadly but you don't know what to expect.

I thought, *It's a bear!*

I felt the bear's mouth at the back of my head and I moved my right arm. That's when I felt his wet face hair brush my cheek. The animal instantly went for my right arm. Evidently he saw a danger or considered my moving arm a threat. He sank his teeth into my elbow and tried to rip it apart. With his jaws locked on my arm, his ear was right in front of my mouth. I feared for my life. Knowing that bears have sensitive ears, that I could not move with his weight on me, and that I was locked in my sleeping bag, I screamed into his ear in a loud, shrill, piercing voice.

The noise must have startled him because he pushed me away and jumped from the tent. He had come in the back side and jumped out the same way. It was dusky but light enough to see. He stood ten feet away on all fours with his head down, swaying it from side to side. I thought, *Any second he could attack.*

I tried to grab my .300 magnum. I felt it, but I couldn't lift it. I screamed again. Next to the tent was a bluff maybe three yards high. As he heard my second scream, he jumped up on this ridge, which had been the edge of the riverbed several thousand years before. He stood there and looked at me, continuing the side-to-side swaying of his head.

I would have shot the bear, but I realized that I couldn't use my right arm anymore. I couldn't lift the rifle, aim, and pull the trigger with one arm. I grabbed my rifle with my left hand and opened and closed the bolt with my mouth. Holding the rifle between my left upper arm and my body, I placed the stock on the ground, pointed the barrel straight up, and pulled the trigger. He turned and slowly moved away, disappearing from my view.

I went to work salvaging my gear and preparing for the bear's return. My tent was destroyed. I took my sleeping bag and rifle and walked the twenty-five yards to the kitchen tent. Our food was stored in fifty-five-gallon barrels in the kitchen tent. I rolled one behind me and one to the door, making a fortress. I put my rifle on the barrel for support, pointing it toward the door. I took two other sleeping bags and made a warm area to keep my body temperature up and prevent hypothermia.

Although the bear was not in sight, I was waiting for him. He knew he had me and that nobody could take me away from him. I thought, *He's coming back.* I was protected for his return, sitting and waiting for the bear. I took a ballpoint pen, and on my raincoat I wrote a note for my wife Gisela, letting her know what had happened in case I didn't make it. I told her that I loved her.

After I wrote the note, I took my Swiss army knife and cut my right shirt sleeve open from the wrist to the shoulder. I tied my arm with a tourniquet made of tent rope. I left it on until my fingers got numb. Usually every twenty minutes, I loosened the tourniquet and the arm started bleeding again. I wiggled my fingers until they had feeling, then I tightened the tourniquet with my left hand and teeth for another twenty minutes.

I opened my shirt and discovered serious wounds on my left side. I had enough antiseptic solution made of twenty Swedish herbs soaked in vodka to last for fourteen days. I washed my wounds with this antiseptic solution. Finally I wadded up toilet paper and placed it into the gaping wounds to absorb blood (there were several rolls of toilet paper in the kitchen tent). I cut my shirt into strips to hold the toilet paper in place. Every two hours I changed the dressing, tossing the bloody stuff in front of the door; I wanted the bear to come through the front door, to my face rather than behind me.

I was waiting and thinking, *What now?* As long as I was busy doing something it wasn't so bad, but when I wasn't busy, I thought about the bear. The first bright light of morning came into the tent, bringing hope and emotional feelings. Tears ran down my face. Then I thought about something to drink. I was glad I had the water from the river. I drank honey and water and that was good.

I was not concerned about bleeding to death, but I thought if I didn't get help within three days, infection would set in. Then I would get a fever and die. I made other provisions because I didn't want to die this way. I determined once the fever came I would shoot myself. I had two bullets left in the rifle. I would use one for the bear, and if I couldn't kill him with a single shot, the second would be for me. It was easy to make this decision out there under those conditions. I couldn't make this decision now. I wouldn't have the courage to think it to the end.

I reconstructed the mauling in my mind and tried to determine the cause of the attack. The weather had been so nice the last fourteen days that we had not been using the kitchen tent; we'd been cooking under a fly. Two sheep, over forty inches each, had been shot, and we cooked and ate sheep meat. In another wall tent Johnny had fleshed the capes, and perhaps there were some fat strips on the ground. I think the bear smelled sheep from the campfire place. Maybe I smelled like a sheep to him, and he just opened my tent. He ripped the tent open with one paw and came in. This was also a poor berry year in the area, and few salmon spawned in the rivers.

As nearly as I could tell, the bear jumped in and was on me instantly. He first hit my side and held me down by standing on me. He went for my neck (you can see the tooth marks at the head area on my sleeping bag). When I moved my right arm, he bit it. Then I screamed in his ear and he cleared out. It was an old, skinny bear looking for food. Although I never saw the bear after the attack, I kept thinking, *Sooner or later, he's coming back.*

Forcing thoughts of the bear from my mind, I kept up my routine of loosening the tourniquet, wiggling my fingers, and changing the dressing. Thoughts about my life filled some of the time.

After my first trip to Alaska in the 1970s, I decided to quit architecture in Germany and move here. It was neither the fishing nor the hunting that brought me, but rather the closeness with heaven. I was not a religious person. I was raised as a Catholic—Christmas time and Easter we went to church. But Alaska touched me like nothing I'd ever experienced, and I simply had to come to Alaska.

Although I had to participate in World War II and although I came home unhurt, I decided, "No more rifles. I don't touch any gun anymore." I came to Alaska with the attitude "no more shooting, no more killing." When I catch a fish, I can take the hook out and say, "Bye, bye." I cannot take the bullet out of a hunted animal and say, "Hey, go again."

Alaskan friends wanted me to take my camera afield. Of course, you have to take your rifle with you for protection. Then your friends want you to get a bear tag, a moose tag. Before you know it, you're hunting. I've hunted fifteen years in Alaska.

I kept wondering how long it would be before Johnny could come back for me . . . wondering if the bear would return . . . wondering if I'd have to use the last bullet on myself. I knew that nobody would come to me in this weather. Who would? Not Johnny. He was a good caretaker. We were so often together that we know how each would react.

I waited at the tent, where I felt protected. I couldn't move. I kept watching, looking through the tent door to see what was going on. I'd used about six rolls of toilet paper when I heard the first sound of a motor out of the skies. My reaction was, *Calm down. It's only the commuter going to Point Barrow with the mail.*

Then the sound got a little bit louder, and a little bit louder. It took me a while, but I finally got out of the tent. I saw only the tail of Johnny's Super Cub close above me. Now maybe I could forget about the bear's return. I was happy. He was a mighty pleasant sight. The attack took place at 3:00 A.M., and Johnny got back to me at 6:00 P.M.

Johnny dropped in low over the ridge. His flaps were down. He pulled power and glided silently in. His over-sized tundra tires skimmed over the tundra and actually rolled through some low bushes on his touchdown. As he flew over camp, he noticed the wall tent up the ridge where he'd skinned the sheep. It was flattened. The bear had been there on its way to me. Realizing that a bear had visited his camp, Johnny had turned around and made a big loop to look for the bear. Thinking that I might be dead and that the bear might return, Johnny said to the hunter, "Throw a bullet in your gun." But they never saw the beast.

He helped the doctor hunter from the plane and said, "You will have to stay here. I will pick you up later. You can stay at the kitchen tent. If you want, you can look around for the bear. I have to fly Helmuth to the hospital in Kotzebue right away."

The doctor didn't want to stay. "Noooo, I won't stay here! I won't stay here."

Johnny's Super Cub was not designed for more than one passenger, and he said, "You have to."

The doctor said, "If you try to leave, I'll jump on the tail." (Only a few days before this the doctor had read halfway through *More Alaska Bear Tales,* and he told John that he would never read it again.) You could see that he was serious. Reluctantly Johnny changed his mind and said, "Okay then, throw all the other stuff out and crawl in the tail section. You can sit behind Helmuth." He flew us both out, with the hunter holding me upright.

We had no problems getting to Kotzebue. En route, Johnny radioed the flight station and made arrangements with the hospital. After landing safely Johnny drove me in his pickup a mile to the hospital, arriving at 8:00 P.M.

They X-rayed me and contacted the emergency doctor at Providence Hospital in Anchorage, who directed them on proper medical treatment. Although the elbow joint was dislocated, no bones were badly broken. The Anchorage doctor instructed them to relocate the elbow. They put it in, then X-rayed it. Ten minutes later, it was out. They relocated it three times. Out, in, out again; they couldn't keep it in. I was bleeding but hadn't experienced any pain the previous seventeen hours due to heavy doses of morphine. I felt pain when they tried to bring the elbow back.

X-rays did not reveal the total damage—all the ligaments and tendons were torn from the bone. There was no connection between the lower and upper part of the arm. The pulse in the arm faded away, alarming the medical staff. A pilot and copilot flew a doctor and two nurses from Anchorage to Kotzebue to return me to Anchorage. The Life Guard unit plus the Lear jet cost me $10,200—the most expensive flight I've ever taken.

During my ten days in the hospital, I was in surgery three times for the elbow and my deep belly wounds. One claw opened the upper cavity on the edge of the lung. The other went in the belly and was close to the colon. Two claws ripped through the ribs, which the bear broke. I had a cast on for five weeks, then I started physical therapy that continued for eight months. At the end I gained half of the normal elbow movement back. I'm back to normal now and no worse for the wear.

I still love the outdoors and spend as much time in Alaska's wilderness as I can. I don't have bad feelings about bears. Bears don't kill for fun. I was not a bad human being. I was in his territory, and he was going for food—me. Although I've had about fifty encounters with bears, I've never been afraid of brown-grizzly bears. But I don't like going close to black bears because I can't determine what they have in their minds.

Going into the bush after such an experience is not easy. When night falls and I crawl into my sleeping bag, memories of the attack come back. My heart beats faster and my ears tune in to the night sounds. When the slightest noise alerts me, I sit straight up in the tent, a gun in my hand, awaiting developments.

Hunting alone in Alaska is dangerous and foolish. Since my bear encounter, I make sure I don't go out alone. And I'm always on the alert for uninvited visitors . . . especially those who enter without knocking.

six

ONE MAULING WAS PLENTY

by Tom Jesiolowski

CHIP AND I WERE awake again before the first of light on the third day of our hunt. We fixed and ate some hot grub. We thought it might be another long, cold, wet, windy day. I prepared my hunting pack while Chip got his things in order. His motor was running early as we had spent quite a few hours in our tent the day before, the wind howling and the rain blowing through even the most microscopic holes in our new North Face tent. He was anxious to see if we could find the bear that we had watched leave our valley for a high mountain sanctuary two days before.

We had waited for the big bear six hours that day. I told Chip that as long as he didn't wind us, the chances were good he would come back. It was a well-worn bear trail he'd followed in and out of our valley. There were still some late salmon in the river that drained our hunting area, and it would be awhile before he would take to his den in the high country. The pouring rain never let up, and dark shut us out. He didn't come back.

On day four we left camp before the sky showed much light. I felt the best bear area was several miles back in our valley where we could watch the trail the bear had taken on two days before. I wanted to be back there at the first of light.

I spotted a bear almost as soon as I started to glass that morning. It was a large bear. After we moved closer, we discovered it was a sow with two large cubs. I told Chip they were probably the bears that had made all the tracks around my tent four days earlier.

We watched and admired them for a while. I answered lots of questions for Chip: How big? How old? What would we do if? Before too long I decided we'd better move. They might wind us and spook another bear that we might really want.

The wind was blowing into our faces and quartering up the mountain, following to our right side. It did not spread any scent out into the valley; the wind was good for us that morning. We walked along the river and passed the bears, noting many partly eaten and rotting salmon scattered along the bank amidst lots of bear tracks.

I was headed for a lookout I had known from a previous hunt. It was a small hill, part of the mountain. From there we would be directly across from the place we saw the bear two days before, which would give us a commanding view of the valley.

As we progressed up the hill, I turned several times to check the view. Before we reached the top, there was the big bear again, coming down the same trail it went up two days before! I needed only a moment to study it in my spotting scope. It was a large, lone bear. He was headed for a long narrow alder patch in the valley floor that grew on each side of a stream that tumbled down from his mountain retreat.

We had to move fast. It was a considerable distance across the main valley. There were lots of small alder patches, little sloughs, and ditches to negotiate. I thought the bear would follow the alder patch along the stream till it ended, then head for the larger river and the fish. I figured we could get into a good position if we arrived at the end of his alder patch before he came out. I should have known better. We waited what seemed like hours, but no bear. He either lay down in the alder patch or sneaked out some unknown way. It was going on 10:00 A.M. when I decided to move.

We climbed up on the hill on the downwind side of the alders, hoping to see into his hideout. After watching for just a few minutes, we spied another bear over a mile away up the big valley. If it turned out to be a good bear, I wanted to be on his side of the alder patch we were now watching. We had to drop down and cross a small ravine that the stream had gouged out of the mountain. We lost sight of the bear for only a few moments, but it was gone when we topped out on the other side. There were small alder patches close to the bear, so I figured it walked into one for a nap. That was not unusual at this time of day, as it was 11:00 A.M. now.

Chip and I talked things over and I suggested dropping down on the upwind side of the alders in front of us where we'd last seen the first bear. I left him in position and went down one hundred yards or so. If my scent blew through the alders and the bear was in there napping, it would get him out.

I started back to Chip. When I was halfway, I saw Chip jump up. I turned to see a bear busting out of the alders in front of us. I ran the rest of the way to Chip and quickly calculated the situation. So many things went through my mind that my thought process had to speed up.

The bear didn't appear as large to me as I had thought when I studied it in my spotting scope. Maybe because it was moving so fast now, I felt it was a good bear. Chip was yelling for instructions and asking how large the bear was, was it nine feet? (That was the minimum requirement he placed on the size bear he wanted.) I told him it was close. I also remember saying the bear had winded us and wouldn't be back. If he wanted it, he needed to take it now.

Chip fired, and within moments the bear was down. We moved in on it cautiously to make sure it was dead. When that was confirmed, there was a lot of backslapping, yelling, and handshaking done.

We had one problem, though. Chip's camera was not working and I had left mine at camp because of the drenching we had got two days before. Chip wanted pictures badly. I said okay. I figured we had just enough time. We could make it to camp, get my camera, and be back to the bear in time to take pictures and do the skinning before dark. Taking the hide back after dark wouldn't be much of a problem.

We would have to move fast. We had quite a few miles to cover. We marked the location of Chip's bear with a plastic bag high on an alder bush. I then checked with Chip on his rifle. I always create an awareness with anyone I hunt with on firearm safety. He had already removed the round from his chamber. It's a rule I maintain when someone is following directly behind me. That way I didn't have to worry about them falling or tripping and shooting me in the back.

I decided to take a shortcut straight through the alders, the same path from where the bear had previously emerged. I knew of a bear trail on the other side that would lead for several miles toward the beach and camp. We hiked toward the alders several hundred yards distant, elated with the good luck we just had and making plans for the rest of our hunt. We needed only to tip over a caribou, and we could enjoy some real good fishing and goose hunting for the remainder of the hunt.

We were soon in the alders, still talking, daydreaming, and trying to soak in the morning's events. A few minutes later we reached a stream running through the center of the alders. The banks were fairly steep, and it appeared to be slippery.

I turned to Chip as a courtesy and showed him I was removing the round from my chamber for safety's sake. I crossed the stream and climbed the bank on the other side, continuing on a few yards after reaching the top of the bank. I then stopped and turned to wait for Chip. Chip was just coming into sight when I heard a bear. He was huffing and popping his teeth.

I turned to see a large brown bear coming down on me with a full head of steam only about twenty yards distant. I realized this was a serious charge, not a bluff. A lot of things were going through my mind. Oddly enough, one thing that stood out was the light coloration of the bear's ears as it bore down on me. The closer it came, the more I noticed the huffing-puffing, guttural noise it made.

I didn't think I had time to swing my rifle from its hanging place on my pack frame, let alone bolt a round into the chamber. I knew it wasn't loaded, but things were happening so fast that I shoved the barrel at the bear's chest and jerked the trigger on the empty chamber just as he hit me.

What a sick feeling.

He hit me with his mouth open and wrapped both front paws around me before I could get my back turned fully toward him. The impact of the bear was incredible, like being hit by a runaway truck. I felt immense pressures, as if my guts were coming out my mouth.

I was hoping he'd bite into my pack. No luck again! He carried me about a half-dozen yards, where we piled up into the base of some alders. For a few split seconds he tried to get a mouth hold on me. His jaws popped together continuously.

I yelled to Chip to get the bear but not to shoot me. The bear picked me up by the side in its jaws and gave me a few quick shakes, then dropped me just as I heard Chip's rifle crack.

I managed to hold onto my .338 Winchester rifle. The bolt was open as I hit the ground, and I instantly slammed a fresh round into the chamber. I thrust the barrel behind me expecting the bear to get on me again, but Chip hollered that he was circling back into the alders.

When the bear let go of me, I dropped with one leg in an awkward position and I couldn't spring right up. When I got turned around, the bear was moving off just out of sight. Chip said his shot hit the bear for sure. I thought the bear would make a second charge, but he kept his distance. I said to Chip, "Let's get the heck out of here."

We retreated the same way we had entered. A lot was going through my mind now. I had one bear down, another one wounded, and I hadn't yet calculated my own condition. I knew I was going to need medical attention and was upset that this bear had wrecked the rest of my hunt with Chip.

As soon as we reached the open, I wondered whether to check my back first or look for the bear that had just jumped us. I asked Chip again if he was sure he had hit the bear. He said he was. Just then the bear broke out of the alders, turned, and looked at us. I thought for a moment he was coming after us again. He turned, though, and made a break for it, running with a limp.

I ran after him. In a few seconds I had a clear shot and dropped the bear, then gave it one more shot to be sure. I walked over and kicked the bear in the butt. I felt sick. It wasn't a good feeling having to kill that bear, and at the same time I was still upset because I knew the rest of my hunt with Chip was ruined.

Now I had to decide how to handle the situation we were in. We were quite a ways from the beach and our camp. I had two bears that needed skinning, and I still hadn't checked my wound. Already my side hurt quite a bit. When I asked Chip to check my bites, he wasn't even aware that the bear had bitten me.

He helped me get my shirt off. I had a few puncture wounds below the armpit and in my back under the shoulder blade, but they weren't bleeding badly. A hole had been scooped out of my back. My back didn't bother me as much as my side.

The most memorable part of the whole incident was taking the first hit of being run over by the bear. It felt as though all my insides were going to burst. (I found out later the bear broke my ribs when it slammed into me.) It remained a mystery as to why the bear hadn't cleared out, with all the racket and the man scent in the immediate area.

I thought I would skin Chip's bear and leave it to pack out after I got patched up, but before we went back to it, I started getting muscle spasms under my ribs. I didn't know if I might be bleeding inside, so I figured we had better head for the beach. I wasn't in shock and could walk, so we left. Chip would have a lot more problems if I passed out or went into shock where we were.

As we headed for the beach, I couldn't help wondering how long it might be before Rich would come by. The weather could get bad, and we might not see him for three or four days. I soon passed it off. It was a good flying day and Rich is good about checking on us regularly. I was hoping the tide would be out so he could land on the beach. We had a signal worked out in the event that we needed him.

As soon as we got to the beach, I piled the washed-up fishing float high on the bank according to our plans. We scuffed out a "HELP" in the sand. I undressed and Chip tended my wounds. I hadn't felt bad while I was walking, but now I started to stiffen up and hurt. Chip got a charge out of putting the nozzle of the First Aid cream into the tooth holes in my body and squeezing the tube.

We wondered how long we would have to wait for help. It was unlucky that the bear jumped me, but everything else fell into place that day. Rich came by in about fifteen minutes, even before I could get my belongings together. We flew back to where the bears lay so Rich would be able to find them easier from the ground when he returned. Then we headed toward Cold Bay.

In a short time Rich had Cold Bay on the radio and they in turn were diverting a flight from Dutch Harbor, as I had already missed the scheduled flight from Cold Bay to Anchorage. Paramedics met me at the Reeves' Airline hangar and fifteen minutes later I was headed for Anchorage, where by 7:00 P.M. of the same day I was in the hospital getting patched up. My injuries included four broken ribs, and the ribs on the right side of my rib cage were torn from the breastbone.

The next day Richard and Chip returned to retrieve the two bear hides. Chip's bear was in good shape, but the one that mauled me had been torn to pieces by other bears during the night. Both animals were enormous females.

The following spring when brown-bear season opened, I was back at my camp on the Alaska Peninsula. My hunter was Willard Ryan of Jackson, Mississippi. Willard was an old friend, having already hunted with me in the Brooks Range.

We hunted the same valley where my bear incident had occurred the fall before. After hunting this valley hard for ten days unsuccessfully, we decided to move. We would have only two days left in the season, but a fresh area might help to change our luck.

Rich flew us to another spot not far away. Things started picking up even before I got my new camp set up. I was preoccupied with getting the tent up in a light drizzle, when Rich spotted a bear sleeping in some alders only two hundred yards from us. Law prohibits us from hunting the same day we've been airborne, so all we could do was keep an eye on him till dark. This was the boost we needed to rejuvenate our optimism.

We were up before light the next morning. The sleeping bear was gone! I glassed the slopes of the mountains surrounding our camp at first light. The scenery here is spectacular: the mountains form a natural amphitheater and steep alder-grown slopes are rimmed by high, rugged, snowy peaks. Almost immediately I spotted a bear. It was moving from behind the highest peaks directly above our camp. It ran downhill till it reached the first high alders on the mountainside, where it took refuge.

There was nothing tricky we could do here. Geography prevented all but a direct climb up a line that would take us to the bear's elevation, just left of his hideout in the alders. I anticipated the climb would take almost two hours. I knew as the air warmed that it would carry our scent uphill and most likely alert the bear to our presence. I thought we would lose this bear, but we had no other options.

Willard was slightly below and a little to the right of me. I was crossing up to the left, as I figured we were getting very near to the bear's position. Just as I reached the top of the alders, Willard ran up from behind hollering, "The bear is coming!" Willard moved uphill slightly.

I gave Willard some instructions, then remembered thinking to myself, well, the bear winded us like I thought and is probably making his escape. I remember checking my rifle chamber to make sure it was loaded, and turning my scope down from 5X to 1½X. All the while Willard was hollering, "The bear is coming!"

Because the slope of the mountain curved, a small ridge prevented me from having the same view as Willard had. To my astonishment, my first sight of the bear came less than forty yards distant! As he crossed the mountainside, he appeared to run more over the alders rather than through them. I could hear the same guttural chugging of his breathing as the bear from the previous fall. I couldn't believe this was happening again.

The bear disappeared into some thicker alders. As it emerged, my mind was racing faster than normal function allows. I remember thinking, *I hope Willard doesn't need for me to tell him to shoot.* The bear was so close that I didn't know if I'd have time for more than one shot.

We must have fired simultaneously. The bear slumped onto his front elbows and came right back up, hardly slowing down. I was trying to calculate my next shot from the hip so I could turn myself in a defensive posture, when Willard's second shot rocked the bear a full foot to the side. The bear wasn't more than a dozen feet from me. I actually saw the round pass through the bear as it carried dust and debris, exiting the backside of the animal. I'll never forget the relief I experienced the instant I realized that the shot had finished him. Several more shots were fired.

Then several minutes were spent sitting and collecting our thoughts.

As I sat there soaking things in, trying to analyze the event, I still couldn't believe it. This bear had winded us. Instead of running away, he circled downhill till he struck our ground scent, then came on it like a hound dog.

Rich told me later that there was a carcass on the beach on the opposite side of the mountain where the bear came from. Maybe our bear had a confrontation with another bear. Maybe it had lost its meal and was taking its frustrations out on us. Whatever the reason, I still believe most bears will avoid human contact. These instances of bears deviating from what we consider normal behavior keep us aware that we need to always be alert in bear country.

seven

HELL HATH NO FURY . . .

by Jan Thacker

YOU NEVER FORGET THE really bad things that happen to you—it's like they're branded in your mind. Two years after his friend was almost ripped apart by a crazed sow grizzly, Alaskan hunter Gary Corle can still shut his eyes and hear Johnny McCoy's agonized screams and the crunch of breaking bones.

Time has healed the horrendous wounds in McCoy's head and arms. The casts that immobilized his broken and crushed bones are long gone, too. But that terrible morning is still just a flash of memory away. The hunting buddies thank God and good friends that McCoy, a Baptist preacher, survived the attack at all. And McCoy's survival also bears witness to the power of friendship and the determination of a community to keep him alive.

Until the huge sow grizzly and her two cubs showed up that day in September 2002, the moose hunt that McCoy and Corle had embarked on promised to be just another adventure in the Alaskan outback. Mc-Coy, 53, is a former mayor of North Pole, Alaska—a small community 15 miles south of Fairbanks—and for 22 years was pastor of First Baptist Church of North Pole. Corle, 59, is one of the church deacons and works at nearby Eielson Air Force Base. Hunting buddies for almost

20 years, they had been flown to their base camp by pilot Art Ward for a moose hunt they expected to resemble many others that came before.

A HUNT LIKE NO OTHER

After landing on the Little Delta River about 40 miles west of Delta Junction, they spent the first day setting up camp and preparing for their hunting adventure. The next morning after breakfast, they packed their backpacks with food and equipment, headed upriver and began scouting for moose and marking trails. They followed the stream for a couple of miles, then turned inland. The pair saw bear scat and tracks but paid little attention. Such sign was as common to the landscape as the distant mountains. The men hiked along quietly until McCoy told Corle he had to stop to relieve himself. Corle continued flagging and minutes later McCoy was back on the trail, hurrying to catch up.

Almost at the same instant that he saw Corle again, McCoy spotted a sow grizzly with two cubs in tow suddenly rush out of the bushes that fringed the river and charge at his friend. McCoy raised his rifle to shoot but the bear was on Corle so quickly that he feared hitting his friend.

"I saw that bear and didn't even have time to alert Gary," McCoy remembers. "I thought she was going to kill him." Corle, taken completely by surprise, was sideswiped by the massive bear and sent tumbling face first into a thick clump of brush.

"I heard something behind me and the first thing that came to my mind was that it was Johnny," Corle recalls. "I turned my head toward the sound and looked and it was the darnedest thing I ever saw—a huge grizzly bear and that sucker was coming full bore toward me."

The backpack Corle was wearing became tangled in the vegetation and it helped save his life. The frenzied bear pummeled him repeatedly but couldn't roll him because the pack was caught in the bushes.

Corle managed to get partly turned and jammed the rifle into the sow's thick brown fur. He pulled the trigger and, at the report, the bear suddenly let him go and wheeled away. When he looked back Corle half-expected to see her lying dead nearby, but the sow had only shifted the focus of her fury.

"As I was trying to get up I heard the most agonizing scream I have ever heard," says Corle. "Then I saw Johnny was literally being torn to pieces by the grizzly. They were ten yards away and the bear was slashing away at him. I could hear the sound of her tearing the flesh off his bones."

Grabbing his rifle and chambering a round, Corle followed the blurred frenzy with his .30/06. Moments before, McCoy had been the one afraid of shooting at the bear and hitting Corle. Now it was Corle's turn to feel powerless to help. The entire attack lasted less than a minute, but the bear's savagery resulted in horrible wounds to McCoy. The bear bit through his arms and shoulder and the preacher could feel and hear his bones crushing. Hanging onto McCoy's damaged arm, the sow swung him around like a rag doll.

Even in his terror, McCoy tried to fend off the sow with his .300 Winchester Magnum. He shoved the rifle barrel into her mouth and the bear ground her teeth into the metal. He pulled the trigger repeatedly but the rifle wouldn't fire. Then the bear quit worrying about the rifle barrel and directed her attention to McCoy's head.

"I could feel her trying to grab hold of my whole skull. I kept thinking, 'This isn't happening to me. This isn't happening to me,'" he says.

Inexplicably, the bear's fury ebbed and she released her grip. McCoy remained still, playing dead, thinking that "if I moved one foot she'd finish me off." The sow bounded away a few feet and then glanced back at him. Then the bear tossed a quick glance at Corle and fled into the underbrush.

For a moment, Corle thought about shooting the grizzly as she left but he had a more important task at hand. One look at his friend convinced him that he needed to focus on saving the preacher's life.

"Johnny was in bad shape," recalls Corle. "His ear was attached to a flap of skin under his chin and his eyeball had been swatted from its socket and was dangling on his cheek. Blood was everywhere. One arm looked like it had gone through a meat grinder."

Realizing his friend was losing blood at an alarming rate, Corle quickly attempted to stanch the flow. He pulled off his and McCoy's backpacks and started reassuring his injured companion, who was in agonizing pain. Then he checked both rifles to make sure that they were ready in case the grizzly returned for a second attack.

A PRAYER FOR STRENGTH

Undaunted by McCoy's terrible wounds, Corle immediately went to work. First he pushed the preacher's ripped ear and scalp back in place and wound game bags from his backpack under McCoy's chin and around his head. He replaced the eyeball as best he could, wound the makeshift bandage over the socket a few turns and then tied it off.

Because of the excruciating pain, McCoy wouldn't let Corle check his bleeding arms, both of which had multiple compound fractures. The man's muscles and skin were lacerated by the bear's claws and teeth. "Johnny had a hole in his hand as big as a nickel and the blood was spurting out," says Corle. "I bandaged it, too, but I thought he might still bleed to death because there were so many other wounds."

Realizing they needed to move toward help quickly, Corle put on his backpack and slung the rifles. The lean, 5-foot, 11-inch hunter struggled to get his heftier companion to his feet.

"He was so weak," says Corle. "I told him, 'You have got to get up. I can't do it alone. We have to get you out of here. Ask God to give you the strength to make those legs work.'"

Nauseated and in horrific pain, McCoy managed to gain his feet and stood there tottering as Corle tried to figure out how to help him move. Since McCoy's arms and hand were in such pain, he couldn't bear being touched. He was blinded from injuries, blood and layers of bandaging.

In the end McCoy solved the problem himself by feebly grabbing onto Corle's backpack with two severely injured arms and saying he'd stumble along behind.

"I told him he was going to have to do more than just hang on," Corle recalls. "I told him, 'You need to pray for strength. You need to do your share and be brave.' And everything I asked him to do, he did."

The journey back to the river camp was an arduous three-mile hike over rough terrain. The trip took a couple of hours. As the two trudged along, Corle warned McCoy of every patch of mud, every hill and every creek they had to cross—all the time praying his friend wouldn't fall.

"I knew if he went down he'd go unconscious and I'd never get him up again," Corle says. "He was bleeding bad and making funny noises in his throat. When we came to a place where I thought we'd probably never get across, we'd stop and pray. When we'd get across, we'd stop and offer thanks. We prayed the whole way."

In between prayers, Corle wondered what he needed to do to keep McCoy alive if they made it back to camp. The men weren't due to be picked up for another eleven days and there was no way McCoy would survive without immediate medical attention.

The pair eventually reached the river. It was there, while they took a break to catch their breath, that McCoy revealed to Corle that he had a cell phone with his gear at their base camp—another mile or so away.

The men finally struggled into their camp several hours after the bear attack. Corle got McCoy into a camp chair and checked the bandages. He added more game bags over those now soaked and dripping with blood but was pleased to see the back of the severely injured hand had stopped bleeding and a huge blood clot covered most of it. He warned McCoy to keep the hand still, knowing it would start gushing again if the clot was jarred loose.

CALLING 911

Then he retrieved McCoy's cell phone. He tried to call Art Ward, the pilot who had flown them out the morning before. The line was busy. Corle tried the church, but that line was busy, too.

"So I called 911," says Corle. "I thought they might not be so busy."

The phone was answered by a dispatcher at the North Pole Police Department, which handles calls for Delta Junction, the nearest town. Within 45 minutes of Corle's 911 call, a team of rescuers from Fort Wainwright's 68th Medical Company Air Ambulance was airborne on a UH-60 Blackhawk helicopter and headed south.

Corle saw the helicopter in the distance but realized it was hugging a ridgeline more than five miles away, instead of following the river. There was little time to make course corrections. McCoy had grown quiet. He was suffering. If he didn't have help soon, the copter might be carrying him home in a body bag. Then despair was replaced with hope as Corle spotted Art Ward's Super Cub flying down the river. News about McCoy had spread.

Corle already had cleared a small patch of ground he thought would be big enough for the rescue helicopter and was astounded when Ward set the Super Cub down on the tiny bit of land. Once he stopped the plane, the pilot leapt from the cockpit, took McCoy's phone, punched in the numbers and explained to the 911 dispatcher exactly where the helicopter was in relation to the injured hunter.

When another Super Cub, whose pilot was also searching for the pair, flew overhead, the two pilots used radios to vector in the Blackhawk.

Twenty minutes later, medics on the chopper had McCoy's wounds redressed, except for the ear, which they realized would fall off if they removed Corle's field bandage. A trail of blood trickled from the gurney as medics loaded McCoy into the chopper and whisked him to Fairbanks Memorial Hospital's emergency room.

After he watched the helicopter disappear in the distance, Corle gathered up the pair's rifles and other equipment and climbed into Ward's Cub. Within minutes he was on his way back home, worried about his friend.

Doctors spent six hours putting back together what took the grizzly a moment to rip apart. Dr. William Wennen, a renowned plastic surgeon who has pieced together several bear attack victims in his career, was in the hospital and took over repairing McCoy's head wounds. Another doctor, Jim Tamai, pinned and repaired the fractured arms and tended the preacher's badly damaged hand.

McCoy's left eye, miraculously undamaged, was properly refitted into its socket. His left ear, which had been left dangling around his chin, was sewn back into place.

A MAJOR PATCH JOB

The doctors made more than 1,000 stitches—some 35 inches of them—in treating McCoy's injuries. For weeks both of his arms and hands were swathed in casts and bandages, and his head and body were covered with massive bruises.

Recovery took months, but McCoy healed well. Today, his face and head are crisscrossed with fading scars. His injured arms and hand took many weeks to heal and he still suffers from a weakened grip.

Corle escaped the incident relatively unscathed except for a few bruises and a bite wound on his arm. His clawed and chewed backpack revealed that he, too, could have been critically injured. Both men realize what the eventual outcome would have been had Corle been more seriously hurt.

Good friends before the hunt, McCoy and Corle are even closer now and still hunt together. They agree that the ordeal with the grizzly was the result of an accident. It was just an unlucky coincidence that their paths crossed that of a grizzly sow who assumed her cubs were in danger.

The bear paid a price, too, as Corle discovered when he returned to the scene weeks later to retrieve McCoy's backpack. When the sow plowed into Corle and knocked him to the ground, he shoved the muzzle of his .30/06 into her thick hide and fired. At that point the bear turned on McCoy. Until he returned to the site, Corle was unsure whether the bullet had hit its mark. It had. Corle found the rotting carcass of the grizzly in the dense bushes, several yards away from where she had almost taken McCoy's life.

eight

LAST STAND

by Larry Mueller and Marguerite Reiss

.

GENE MOE SNAPPED HIS head around at the ferociously loud and deep bawling roar of a close and angry bear. At first glimpse, he knew he was in for the fight of his life. This was no trotting charge of a bluffing bear. Both front paws reached forward together in each leap of a galloping bear going in for the kill. Gene made one instinctive step toward his rifle, just five feet away, and then recognized the futility of dropping an inferior weapon to grab a superior one he'd never have time to shoot. The knife he had been using to skin a Sitka blacktail deer was still in his hand, so he thrust it forward to meet the raging bear's wide-open mouth, hoping to shove it down her throat. He was keenly aware that he could lose a hand, or more, but no better defense presented itself.

Gene might not have been in this life-threatening predicament had his partner of the day been able to follow their plan. Two years earlier, the same partner and Gene had just skinned out the hindquarters of a deer when a Kodiak bear appeared and plopped down 100 yards away, probably called by the dinner-bell shot. "Hey, we've got company," Gene said. "Get the two quarters onto my backboard, and let's get out of here." They were a meager 50 yards away when the bear arrived to carry off the rest of the deer.

This year, they were camped on Afognak Island northwest of the village of Kodiak, but Gene, 69, and his son, Karl, 44, and their two partners, Tom Frohlick, 44, and Steve Fitzpatrick, 48, both employees of Gene's concrete contracting business, motored their skiff across the straits and down about ten miles to the lower end of Raspberry Island to hunt Sitka blacktails. Gene's plan was to position Steve on a ridge, move out about 200 yards, and circle to move a deer toward him. If by late in the day Steve hadn't gotten a deer, and Gene got a chance for a buck, he would take it. The rules called for the partner to be alert for the shot and then listen for the owl hoot. It would then be the partner's job to join Gene and watch his back during the field-dressing. About that time Steve dropped his cap's earflaps.

"Can you hear with those flaps down?" Gene asked.

"Oh yeah," Steve answered, but later he heard neither shot nor hoot. And the bear bearing down on Gene wanted and needed more than a gut pile. This was November 1, 1999. The berry crop had been poor, a severe previous winter had killed an estimated third of the deer, and Asian ships with 20-mile nets were making clear-cuts in the ocean's fishery. Few Pacific salmon came upstream at Raspberry Island to spawn, die and provide the fat-building nutrition essential for bears to hibernate.

THE BATTLE BEGINS

Raspberry has an open grassy top, but at lower elevations moss hangs from big timber in the world's northernmost rain forest. That year, snows had driven the deer down to the forest. Gene did watch a beautiful buck for 20 minutes, but it spooked before his partner could get a shot. About 2 o'clock, he saw another buck and decided to take it while there was still enough daylight to get it back to Afognak. Steve didn't show up, so he began skinning it out alone. All the meat was off the carcass and laid out on plastic, and the heart and liver were in his hands when he heard the bloodcurdling roar. His only chance of survival depended on what he could do quickly with the three and three quarter-inch blade on his Model 110 Buck folding knife. And that chance was rapidly diminishing.

Foam does bubble forth profusely from the mouths of excited bears, and this hungry sow was so excited that Gene now saw more foam than head. He could only aim his blade at the center and hope.

The knife slid alongside her head, and the bear bit Gene's right arm above the elbow, taking out a big chunk of flesh. He could feel her trying to tear off the arm completely. He quickly reached over her head with his left hand to jab a finger in her eye, but came to an ear first and rammed his finger in as hard and far as it would go, then twisted. This experience proved to be so new and so intolerable that she relaxed her grip on his arm and tried to pull away, but Gene's left arm was over her neck. Thinking he might put her on the ground in a more helpless position, he attempted to bulldog her as he had young bulls during his youth on the farm in Minnesota. Big mistake. She flipped her neck and threw him eight feet.

Having watched bears doing lots of berry picking and digging, Gene knew she'd swing at him with her right paw. Like humans, the majority of bears are right-handed. This one stood up on her hind legs, arms outstretched in scarecrow fashion, and began circling, picking her moment to end this confrontation. A grizzly can decapitate a cow with one swipe; a Kodiak brown is even bigger, and Gene knew his head would come off a lot easier than a cow's. He was also certain that she was standing on her hind legs to place that right paw at the best level to accomplish this. He tried to move closer to his rifle while focusing his eyes on nothing but that right paw. He saw it coming the instant it started. And at that same instant, he jerked his head back the way a boxer dodges a right hook. She missed, but came close enough that one claw split his ear and almost tore off the earlobe.

Since that failed, she dropped to all fours, hit his legs and knocked him on his back. She'd be on top of him next, bouncing or biting to crush his ribs or skull, so he jerked both heavily booted feet together and kicked upward with all his strength as she came flying in. The collision knocked her off to the side, and Gene leaped to his feet.

She began circling him again, and like a prizefighter up against a taller man with a longer reach, Gene knew that he had to get inside that right paw to survive. She was beating him to death. She came at him fast on all fours, and this time Gene was stepping off with his left foot, right foot still on the ground, as the paw started to swing. The paw missed and swung around his back, so she bit a large chunk out of his right leg above the knee instead. The pain was severe, but now Gene was inside the right front paw and against the bear's shoulder with his left arm over her neck. His right arm had no feeling, and flesh from above the elbow hung down to his fingers. He reached over the neck and stabbed four times as hard as he could. Then, changing tactics, he moved closer to the jaw to slice the neck so he could push his knife and fist into the cut to stab deeper.

STANDING TALL

The sow tried to stop Gene by raising him off the ground with her right paw. He hung on and kept cutting the hole deeper, but he couldn't hold her when she dropped him to push away with both front feet. Nevertheless, before her head pulled out from under his left arm, he managed one more hard stab into the deep slash near her jaw. Blood squirted all over them both. Immediately, this Kodiak brown wanted a breather between rounds and circled out beyond the little arena of beaten-down snow.

Noticing that some of the fight was going out of her, Gene yelled, "Bear, the Lord's on my side, so come on!"

She did. And as she ran, Gene could see blood still gushing from the cut nearest the jaw. He also noticed that her head was cocked oddly sideways, suggesting that the last stab had probably gone deep enough to injure a vertebra. Terribly battered with loose skin and flesh hanging from his arm, claw gashes in his shoulders, and painfully dragging his right leg, 6-foot 3-inch Gene tried to stand tall and move toward her looking as menacing as possible. He would not allow her the added confidence of thinking the fight had gone out of him.

Whatever she thought, it did not stop her from charging—though not with the speed demonstrated earlier. All Gene had left now was a little prayer and the advice of a dog-musher friend who said a blow to the nose from a light club he carried would stop nearly any animal. Gene drew back his left fist, and as the bear leaped at him, he threw the hardest punch of his life. He missed the nose, but struck her cocked head just under the eye. The impact of the punch combined with the momentum of the 750-pound brown was so powerful that his arm and hand went white and he had no feeling left in the knuckles. The sow's head twitched, and she bared two front teeth that were still covered with Gene's "meat," as he tells it, before suddenly dropping with her paws under her body. Her cocked head straightened with the blow, and her nose pulled downward during her fall, ramming it into the moss. She lay motionless.

CRAWLING FOR HELP

Gene had seen so many animals go down that he knew it's a brain or spine shot when one drops with its feet under it. Hit other organs, it will go down with its feet or legs out from under its body. He believed this one was dead from damage he had inflicted to the spine with his knife and fist. But he wasn't taking any chances; he stepped back to get his rifle. Before he could shoot, however, he had to first free his hand of the knife—but found he couldn't relax his grip. Eventually, he was able to pull his fingers from the knife with his teeth, but then the loose skin and flesh from his arm fell over the scope of his rifle. Finally, he managed to raise the rifle high enough to get the flesh off to the side, and then lower it to shoot the bear twice in the chest.

A little fur flew both times, but the bear never twitched. Clearly, Gene's lethal punch had finished breaking the vertebra of his 750-pound opponent. Gene's ordeal, however, was far from over. He was two miles from the boat, feeling dizzy from loss of blood and still bleeding badly. He pulled the hanging flesh back up on his right arm and wrapped a plastic bag around it as best he could. His hunting pants—purchased in 1948, made of quarter-inch thick wool and worn only for the annual hunts—had probably reduced the potential damage when the bear bit a chunk out of his right leg. At least for now, he could still move on his feet. He had not seen the cubs, which later evidence showed the sow had, but as a precaution, he picked up his rifle as he left. He could easily meet other bears on Raspberry Island.

He doesn't know how far he got before exhaustion forced him to lie down in the snow. When he felt it was time to move on, however, he couldn't sit up. Finally, he struggled onto his stomach and pushed himself off the ground with his left arm and leg. At this point, he recognized what carrying extra weight was doing to the limits of his strength. Meeting another bear now seemed less of a gamble than whether he'd reach the beach at all. He abandoned his rifle.

At least twice he had to again lie down in the snow to rest. During one of those rests he remembers trying to die. "Lord, take me home," he begged, but it wasn't his time. So Gene struggled on, sometimes walking, sometimes crawling.

At one point, it appeared as if he was about to lose in the gamble of discarding his rifle—and his death wish would soon be fulfilled. He was hearing sounds from an animal too big to be anything but another bear. Yet being eaten alive did not exactly seem like a reasonable answer to prayer, so Gene remained motionless long after the noises ceased. If it had been a bear, wind direction had played in his favor.

REACHING SAFETY

Struggling through alder thickets was the most difficult challenge of the entire two-mile trek. The tree limbs would snag the plastic bag and yank it off his right arm. He'd stop, pull the hanging flesh back up and rewrap it, only to have it happen over and over again.

Finally, Gene spotted an opening in the woods and knew he was right on target. Within 200 yards of the beach, he could go no farther. He wearily halted, yelling for help, hoping somebody was near the boat. He was fortunate. Tom and Steve were already there and responded immediately, warming him with another coat and a full-length flotation vest. Steve had not heard the last two shots, either.

It was the custom among these hunters that the first to get back to the boat around 4 P.M. would fire his rifle as a signal that it was time to come in. The others would return answering shots, and everybody would be out of the woods before dark. They fired the routine shot and Karl answered, but then Tom and Steve began calling excitedly, trying to hurry him in so they could get Gene to medical help more quickly. Karl could not understand their words and concluded that a shot followed by loud, excited voices meant that a bear was somewhere between him and them. Instead of hurrying him in, the calls slowed Karl into greater caution, but he speeded up when he got close enough to understand. He was thoroughly shocked by his father's appearance. The three quickly got Gene into the skiff and headed for the nearest habitation: the Silver Salmon Lodge owned by Peter and Barabel Guttchen.

TOO OLD TO HEAL?

Peter saw the skiff motoring into the bay with men waving wildly. As he walked down to ask what was wrong, he was astonished to see a man chewed and torn beyond belief step out of the boat and walk up the beach toward the lodge. A new front room was being built on the beach side of the lodge, so Gene also walked around to a door in the rear, refusing to be carried. He lay on the living room floor while Tom carefully rearranged the flesh on his right arm and bound it with an Ace bandage provided by Barabel. Karl wrapped his dad's right leg with strips torn from her apron.

The Guttchens had the only radiotelephone in the vicinity, and immediately called the Coast Guard at Kodiak. By luck, they were going on maneuvers and had a helicopter already ten feet off the ground. They quickly arrived at the lodge. By that time, the bandaging was finished and Gene was in a sleeping bag. Gene was flown to the then three-year-old, 23-bed hospital at the little fishing village of Kodiak, where, without a break, Dr. Barry Goldsmith spent twelve hours caring for him, seven of them stitching the wounds. Four years later, the feeling had not returned in two of the knuckles in the left hand.

The day after the attack, Gene's hunting partners returned to Raspberry Island to find the rifle and knife and skin the bear. Alaska law requires that any bear taken in self-defense without a tag must be turned over to Fish and Game. Gene later bought back the hide at the annual auction. The partners found the blood trail very easy to follow—sometimes drops, sometimes a spray, some smears on branches, some on trees he had leaned against, and three pools where he lay down. Behind a log with a large smear of blood, they found the rifle. Finally, as they followed the trail back to the attack site, two young bears were standing over the few remains of Gene's deer. They were probably the dead bear's 2½-year-old cubs, which she was trying to drive off so she could have more offspring that winter during hibernation.

Back in the hospital, Gene overheard two nurses discussing how he was too old to heal properly. The next day, however, the doctor was asking what medic put his arm back together so expertly. "Tom Frohlick," Gene answered, "a cement finisher who works with us." (Annually, to make his employees more aware, careful and competent in an emergency, Gene has them take an 8-hour class in first aid. Gene himself certainly benefited from his employees' training.) Two other reasons he could outfight a bear? He never smoked and he worked hard all his life. The doctor would later say that Gene has the muscle tone of a 33-year-old man.

Gene offers one more tip to those who hunt in bear country. Something he has noticed many times, but never told anyone until now, is how raven behavior ties in with deer hunting in bear territory. "When a raven flies over and sees you," Gene says, "he'll give a squawk or two. If you keep watching him, you'll probably hear him squawk again and notice that he's flying over another ravine. I figure if he squawks when he sees me, he's squawking when he sees something else. When the wind has been in my face, I've sneaked over to see what's there, and sure enough, I'd find a deer in that ravine. But you have to be careful. It could be a bear with a kill or cubs to defend. About half of the time, when I'd start to get close, I'd see a bear coming from the other direction. I don't know for sure if bears are smart enough to catch on to raven behavior, but I take the possibility seriously. I've certainly had enough experience with rifle shots calling bears to dinner."

nine

MOMENT OF TRUTH

by Bob Humphrey

WE TAKE SO MUCH for granted as we go about our daily lives, seldom considering that in the blink of an eye fate could place us in a situation that will test our mettle—a situation where failure means death and even success will leave us indelibly changed. Such was the case for Pete Karels. One moment he was settling against the bole of a spruce tree, enjoying a peaceful sunset in the splendor of a remote Canadian wilderness. The next, he was face to face with the most dangerous animal in North America and almost certain death. His fate rested solely on how he would react in the ensuing seconds.

It all began a year earlier, when Karels' friend and fellow Minnesotan, Ron Bice, invited him along on a bowhunting trip for moose in Alberta. Bice had hunted this region for black bear several times with guide Everett Martin, and over the years the two had become friends. Following one of these bear hunts, Bice and Martin decided to go after moose the coming season; upon returning to his home, Bice asked Karels to join in. They planned their adventure in the intervening months, and when September finally arrived the duo gathered their gear, loaded up their truck and made the long trek from Minnesota to Alberta.

Along the way, Karels read an article about pepper spray for bears. He told Ron about it one morning over breakfast. Bice said, "I'm gonna get some of that. How about you?"

Karels replied, "No, it's sixty dollars." Then he drolly added, "Besides, more than likely I'll be hunting with you, and I know I can outrun you."

Upon arriving at camp, Karels and Bice met their outfitter and discussed their plans. They would be hunting from tree stands, overlooking natural mineral licks. These minerals are an important dietary supplement for moose; the animals are drawn to low muddy swales where the licks are concentrated. Bice and Karels spent the first day scouting licks, hanging stands and cutting shooting lanes. With their mission accomplished, they headed back to camp for dinner.

As is often the case in that part of the world, the subject of grizzlies came up while the hunters ate. Martin and some of the other guides related various tales of grizzly encounters to a captivated audience. Having grown up in the area, Martin was familiar with the big bears, and though he respected them, he did not fear them.

By the light of the glowing lantern, Martin offered some advice to his wide-eyed clients on how to react should they encounter a bear. "Forget what the books tell you," he said. "Your best chance is to stand your ground and try to act bigger and meaner than the bear." Even after hearing the guides' stories, Bice thought the odds of a grizzly encounter were extremely remote. Karels summarily dismissed the idea. Still, both kept Martin's advice in mind during the hunt.

"To be honest, I was looking for grizzly tracks from the very start," said Bice. Seeing no evidence of the big bears the first day put him more at ease. "I felt an encounter was unlikely, which boosted my confidence to walk through the brush with only my bow and arrows." While Karels maintained his nonchalant attitude about the bears, he sensed Bice's trepidation. It became a running joke between the two. "That night old Pete was teasing me about my fear of and respect for these bears. He laughed and joked about it pretty much throughout the hunt," said Bice.

The days passed with no moose sightings, but each night there was more grizzly talk among the hunters and their guide. Their discussions took on a more serious tone when a problem bear was reported within four miles of camp. Hikers had encountered the bear over a moose kill.

Because it was on a hiking trail and roughly a mile outside the town of Hinton, the bear was classified as extremely dangerous; people were advised to steer clear of the area. The bear was eventually tranquilized and relocated 200 miles to the north.

With that potential danger removed, fear of the bears once again subsided, until Bice noticed some fresh sign near one of his moose stands. It was a rubbing tree, the kind bears sometimes use to scratch their backs and perhaps deposit scent. The tree was covered with coarse grizzly hair. It was also right on the half-mile trail that Bice had to travel each day walking to and from his stand. Bice admitted that his bow and arrows offered little comfort on those daily walks, particularly at night in the dark. "For the first time in my life I knew what it felt like to be potential prey for something," he said. Meanwhile, Karels continued to make light of his partner's growing concern.

Whether it was his respect for the bears or the lack of moose sightings, Bice decided to shift his attention to a different stand, some 30 miles from where he'd been hunting. The choice ultimately turned out to be a good one. That evening Bice had his first chance at a big bull. "Shortly after getting settled in, I heard a loud crash to my left," he said. "It was a cow and calf coming my way, passing by about 20 yards out." A few minutes later he heard the grunting of a bull approaching on the same path. The 40-plus-inch rack of the bull materialized out of the dense spruce, as the moose headed straight for Bice.

"I couldn't draw the bow because he seemed to be staring straight at me the whole time as he came closer, approaching straight-on." The bull eventually stopped at the base of Bice's tree, a mere six feet away. "I couldn't believe he hadn't heard me hyperventilating," said Bice. Astonishingly, the bull never offered Bice a clean shot. Now the Minnesotans were down to their last day of hunting.

With the final day of his clients' hunt looming and nothing to show for it, Martin offered to let the pair stay on another couple of days. Bice decided to take advantage of the extra time by catching up on some much-needed sleep. He suggested that Karels head back to the site of his most recent moose encounter, hoping the big bull would return and perhaps offer him a better shot.

The afternoon passed without event, however. Karels planned on hunting again the next morning, and because Alberta law doesn't allow hunters to carry a bow on a four-wheeler until noon, he decided to leave his bow in the stand. He also considered leaving his fanny pack, but almost as an afterthought, he remembered Martin's advice. If he should encounter a bear, the air horn he carried in his pack might deter it.

After a three-quarter-mile hike to the road, Karels arrived at the pick-up spot. Another of the camp's guides, Dan Abei, was scheduled to pick him up at 8 o'clock. Karels was early so he decided to lie down in a little hut the outfitter had made out of evergreen boughs. His repose was short-lived, however. Barely five minutes had passed when, lying on his side and looking up the four-wheeler trail, Karels suddenly perceived a horrifying sight: a full-grown sow grizzly, with two cubs in tow, headed straight for him. Their eyes met, both becoming aware of the other's presence at the same instant.

Karels was overwhelmed with a feeling of helplessness, but he knew he didn't want to be lying down. He scrambled to his feet. Whether because of his sudden movement, their proximity or perhaps both, when Karels stood, the bear charged.

There was no time for fear. Karels acted on instinct and adrenaline. With 600-plus pounds of pure fury bearing down on him, and his life hanging in the balance, he had to make a split-second decision. His initial, gut instinct was to go behind the hut, but as he turned and took half a step the outfitter's advice raced through his mind: "Don't ever run from a grizzly bear."

Most people wonder how they would react in a life-or-death situation. Animal behaviorists call it a fight-or-flight response. Soldiers call it trial under fire—the test of battle. Karels now faced that test. He turned back toward the bear, then waved his arms and yelled with all the force he could muster.

The bear, perhaps taken aback at Karels' audacity, checked her bluff charge. Standing mere feet from Karels, she rose up on her hind legs, towering over him, and let out a roar that shook Pete to his very marrow. Meanwhile the little 150-pound cubs had also stood up and were now bouncing on their hind legs, as if to say, "Go get him, Mom, go get him!" Somehow, Karels stood his ground.

To an onlooker, the scene might have seemed almost comical, had it not been so frightening. Here was a man, 6 feet 3 inches tall, weighing 220 pounds, trying to face down a bear that towered three feet over him and was nearly three times his weight. Both were standing, staring at each other, screaming and roaring and flailing their arms. Saliva, snot and the foul odor of bear breath filled the tiny space between them. But the bear came no closer.

Karels turned slightly and reached down for his fanny pack and the air horn inside it. As soon as he did, the bear dropped to all fours and got ready to charge again. Karels frantically pulled the air horn from his pack, then came to the horrific realization that the horn was still in its plastic container. Screaming at the bear, Karels desperately tried to free the horn. That screaming gave him the few extra seconds he needed. Just when it seemed the bear would lunge forward, Karels freed the horn and blasted her.

It startled the bear momentarily and, still standing, she backed off. Then, to Karels' dismay, the horn quit, and the bear came at him again. Karels challenged her once more. Roaring and advancing on her, he managed to tighten the top and get the horn working again. The bear backed down, turned and headed away. By now adrenaline was surging through Karels' body and he chased after the bear, yelling and blowing the horn. He had seemingly escaped with his life, but the bear was not done with her terrorizing.

No sooner had she disappeared from Karels' sight than Abei came riding up on his four-wheeler. Both bear and four-wheeler rounded the same corner at the same time. "I saw a flash of gray go through the bushes and thought it was too small to be a moose," Abei later related. "First I saw a cub, then the sow. She reared up and roared. Spit was coming from her mouth. I reached for my rifle, but I didn't know if Pete might be somewhere behind her in the bush." The bear hesitated, turning from Dan back toward Pete. Then she dropped to all fours and, choosing flight over fight, hurried her cubs uphill and out of view.

When Dan finally got to Pete he was so stunned he appeared almost calm, except for his ghostly white complexion. "Did you see the bear?" Dan excitedly asked, breaking Karels' trance. "She charged me; she charged me!" Karels shouted.

That night by the glowing lantern, Karels, still shaky from his ordeal, told and retold his story. He humbly averred, "I don't know what most people would do in that situation. I just did what I had to do." He also acknowledged that Martin's advice had probably saved his life. "He prepared us well by telling us not to run." Karels' nonchalant attitude about bears had also changed. "I've been a hunter for years," he said. "It's a little different when something's after you."

BLINDSIDED!

by Sharon Rushton

JEFF DYCHE HAD BEEN dreaming about this Alaskan hunt for a long time. Alaska native Mark Rutledge saw it as a chance to repay his old friend Jeff, who had taken him hunting and fishing when he had visited Colorado. The trip was set for early September and the two rendezvoused at the Anchorage airport. "I was like a kid at Christmas," says Jeff. "Thank heaven Mark had almost everything packed, so it wasn't long before we were heading down the Denali Highway."

At the trailhead the two men loaded a ten-day supply of food and gear into a trailer, which they hitched behind an Argo, a six-wheeled ATV. It was late afternoon when their journey into the marsh and bog of the Monahan Flats began. A well-marked trail provided easy going for two miles—the farthest point most hunters make. Mark's hunting site was twelve miles farther on. Drizzling rain and low-hanging clouds gave the area an ominous feel. Lightning closed in around them and delayed their progress.

About six miles in, the two men finally called it a night. "This wasn't like camping in Colorado," says Jeff. "I felt alive. I knew there were bears and wolves around. All my senses were working."

Jeff awoke before Mark the next morning and was amazed by the surrounding beauty. A mist hung over the ponds scattered throughout the area. A loon broke the early-morning silence. Mark finally stirred, and it wasn't long before the two pulled on their hip boots and headed toward the West Fork Glacier.

The terrain became increasingly challenging for the Argo, with swamp, mud bogs and water everywhere. They bogged down often and had to use alder bushes and trees to wrench the Argo and trailer out of the muck. One bog held them hostage for an hour and a half. Finally, they unhitched the trailer, got the Argo out and winched the trailer across. "It was like no country I've ever been in," says Jeff. "Colorado was a desert compared to this."

About four that afternoon, as they were heading out of the bogs up a hillside, Mark turned off the ignition and announced that this would be home for the next eight or nine days. The two quickly set up their tent and unloaded the backpacks, sleeping bags, propane heater and rifles. The rest of the gear could wait until after supper. Hamburger Helper prepared on the cookstove never tasted better. With an hour of daylight left, they decided to grab their guns and take a short walk to scout for moose.

About 600 yards from camp, they overlooked the Big Susitina River headwaters and spotted five cow moose . . . a good sign. With a dollar bet on who would see the first bull moose, they were both intent on scanning the area. A nearby knoll would provide a better view. The terrain was changing into thick brush, and Jeff, a seasoned hunter, turned his riflescope from 9X to 3X. As they reached the hilltop, a grizzly suddenly came charging over the top of the knoll.

"The bear made three strides and was on top of us. There was no time to get off a shot," says Jeff. "We were standing only a few feet apart so I didn't know if it was heading for me or Mark.

"It's amazing how your adrenaline rush slows things down. In my mind I saw things as snapshots. The first frame I can remember is how big and round the bear's head was. It was huge. The second snapshot I recall is his large right paw raised in the air."

The grizzly never stood up but bore straight down on them like a semi-truck on a superhighway. Jeff dove backward into the brush. He fell to the ground, covering his neck with his hands, expecting to feel the hot breath of the grizzly at any moment. "Chills went up and down my spine and the hair on my neck stood up," he says. "At first I thought he had overrun me and was coming back. But the grizzly had zeroed in on Mark."

The bear tried grabbing Mark's leg with its paw but missed. It then grabbed hold of his leg with its teeth, knocking him to the ground. The bear shredded Mark's backpack with its claws while going for his head. Mark looked and saw the nose of the grizzly against the side of his face. To avoid having his face ripped off, he turned his head quickly away as the bear grabbed hold of the back of his head. Mark could hear bone crunching and feel the bear's breath. He also heard gurgling as blood ran into his ear. When Jeff heard Mark scream, he immediately jumped up. The first thing he saw was Mark's head totally engulfed in the bear's mouth. "It was like watching a snake trying to swallow its prey," Jeff says. "The grizzly was growling 'grrrr' and shaking Mark . . . flopping him around like a rag doll. The strength of a bear to be able to lift a grown man with just its head didn't seem real."

Jeff instantly shouldered his .30/06 rifle, steadily zeroed the crosshairs of the scope on the bear's heart, and squeezed the trigger. "I could clearly see the bear's shoulder in my scope," says Jeff. "But had the scope still been on 9X, I wouldn't have been able to get a clean shot and the bear probably would have killed us both."

At the shot, the bear released Mark, who was on his feet before the bear hit the ground. "My first thought was, thank God he's alive," Jeff says.

The bear was off its feet but still growling.

"Shoot him again, shoot him again," Mark yelled. Stepping around the back of the bear, Jeff shot the grizzly at the base of its skull. The bear's eyes rolled back and it finally lay silent and still.

"Though everything appeared to be moving in slow motion, it happened fast. From the time we first saw the bear to when I pulled the trigger was less than fifteen seconds," says Jeff.

Now the gravity of the situation sank in. Blood was oozing out of Mark's head. Jeff knew that Mark needed immediate attention. He picked up Mark's rifle along with shells and other items scattered from his torn backpack. As they began walking back to camp, Jeff could see a tear where Mark's hair was tucked up underneath his skull, exposing a large section of his skull. Jeff also realized Mark's left ear was hanging by a small piece of skin near his neck.

Mark was bleeding badly and so they ran the 600 yards back to camp. Halfway back they heard a loud noise. Again, an adrenaline rush sent everything into slow motion. Jeff says his heart just dropped. "Now what? Here I am with all this stuff in my arms," Jeff thought, "and I can't even shoot whatever this is." Suddenly, a dozen ptarmigan erupted at their feet. After the initial shock, both were relieved, and they regained their quick pace back to camp.

Jeff told Mark to sit down and hold still as soon as they reached camp. Mark wasn't saying anything. "I think he was in denial, like it was a dream," says Jeff. Thankfully for Mark, Jeff was a trained emergency medical technician. He didn't panic. Jeff knew he had to stop the bleeding and work to keep Mark from going into shock, but he couldn't find the first-aid kit. "I tore the camp apart looking for that kit," Jeff says. Finally, he couldn't look any longer. He had to use what he could access quickly or he was going to lose Mark.

"I grabbed a roll of electrical tape from my backpack and a roll of paper towels. I fixed his ear first, pulling it to where it should be, covering it with paper towels and asking Mark to hold the towels against his ear with pressure. Next, I stuck my finger between his skull and his scalp and pulled the scalp out so it would sit as it should. Then I covered it with paper towels and electrical tape." Mark had another gash about eight inches long on the top of his head. It ran almost ear to-ear and was cut clear to his skull. Jeff wrapped paper towels tightly over the gash.

It was starting to get dark. Jeff knew that Mark needed immediate medical attention and feared he wouldn't make it for 24 hours. Yet they were 12 to 14 hours from the nearest hospital, with no means to call or radio for help. Fourteen miles of rough, marshy terrain separated them from their truck. The trail was hard enough to decipher in the daylight. Now they would have to try to get out in the dark.

They unhitched the trailer and gathered up warm clothes, two sleeping bags, a can of gas, food, a flashlight with extra batteries and the spotlight that plugged into the Argo.

To keep Mark from going into shock, Jeff kept up a barrage of questions. "What's your name? What happened? Where are you from?" he asked. Mark usually responded with one word—Mark, bear, Anchorage—but as long as it was the right word, Jeff knew he was okay. A wrong answer would have meant Mark was becoming disoriented and going into shock.

With Mark stabilized, a more serious threat now loomed. Jeff had never learned to drive the Argo, which has a difficult lever steering mechanism. He knew it would take valuable time to learn so he put Mark in charge of driving, hoping the task would keep him focused on something besides his injuries. Mark grabbed the controls and put the Argo in high gear.

"Mark was driving really fast," says Jeff. "I kept saying 'slow down.' At one point we hit a tree straight on and it almost tipped us over. I said, 'If this thing breaks, we're definitely going to have to walk out of here.'" But Mark never slowed down.

As they did on the way in, the two continually got stuck. "The first couple of times my adrenaline was so high I just picked up the back of the Argo and got us going again," Jeff says, but adrenaline didn't always help. It took them 20 minutes to get out of one hole. In the darkness, the two lost the trail a couple of times and had to backtrack.

About halfway back to the truck Mark's leg started to become more painful. In their rush to return they had never taken a look at it in camp. When they removed Mark's waders and shined a light on his leg, they saw a puncture wound down to the bone on one side of the leg and tears on the other side. Mark wasn't bleeding badly, Jeff noted, so they pulled the tight-fitting waders back on to give his leg support.

The temperature was falling and both men were soaking wet. Mark was getting cold. Jeff dug out a jacket from their supplies and gave it to Mark. If Mark went into shock, Jeff would be unable to get the Argo unstuck by himself. If the Argo got stuck, Jeff would have to carry Mark out and probably wouldn't be able to get him out in time.

Mark never let up on the throttle and Jeff never stopped asking questions. "What's your name? Where are you from?" The temperature continued to drop to just above freezing. Mark now had five jackets wrapped around him and he was still cold. Jeff gave Mark the jacket he had on. Now he was down to just his soaking-wet shirt and he was getting very cold himself.

Half an hour later, Mark said, "I know where we are." They had reached the main trail and were only two miles from the parking lot.

Twenty minutes later they reached the truck. It was 2 A.M. Jeff started the engine to get the heater going and covered Mark in sleeping bags.

Flooring the gas pedal, Jeff worked to keep the truck on the dirt highway. It was 38 miles to the nearest phone. Mark kept saying he was cold, but all Jeff could do was keep heading toward Cantwell.

When they finally reached the State Trooper's Office in Cantwell, it was quiet and dark. Jeff locked up the brakes on the gravel driveway and honked the horn, but no one came out. Jeff left the heater running in the truck to keep Mark warm as he went to find help. He ran to the sleeping quarters and pounded on the first door; no answer. He tried a second and third door, but no one answered.

As Jeff finished pounding on the last door, he saw a call box and picked up the phone.

"Cantwell emergency. Do you have an emergency?" the voice asked. "My friend's been mauled by a bear and needs help," responded Jeff. The operator said an ambulance could be there in ten minutes. A moment later Trooper Curt Bedingfield came out of the first door and helped Jeff look after Mark until the ambulance arrived a few minutes later. The emergency medical technicians found Mark shaking, close to shock and hypothermic. They gave him an intravenous drip and wrapped him in blankets but left the paper-towel bandages and electrical tape in place. Mark was still not out of the woods; it would be another three-hour ride to the Fairbanks Memorial Hospital. The sun was beginning to peek over the horizon as the ambulance pulled up to the emergency room door. The doctors took Mark directly into surgery. Working intensely for more than four hours, the surgeons were able to reattach Mark's ear, and with more than 300 stitches, they sewed up the severe gashes in his head. The wound on his leg was left open to drain.

Jeff never got a moment of sleep. Not only was he concerned for

Mark, but every time he closed his eyes, he relived the grizzly attack. When Jeff was allowed to see Mark, they grabbed each other's hands. "Thanks for saving my life!" Mark said, knowing that if Jeff had waited two more seconds to shoot the bear, he would have been dead.

Jeff and Mark are now planning the trip they never finished . . . same time of year, same place. Mark says he's a little "bearanoid," but they are both ready for a new adventure.

eleven

BUSHWHACKED!

by Colin Moore

STEVE LEVI SWUNG HIS right leg over the saddle and dropped his foot to the ground. It landed with a flattened thud that raised a miniature cloud of dust. After four days of hard riding, creeping along ridgelines and climbing on and off horses, there wasn't much bounce left to Levi.

Hunting wasn't so physically demanding back in Georgia, but then home didn't have elk like Wyoming did and Levi was determined to endure whatever it took to get a good bull. This could be the place, or at least Levi's guide, Mike Potas, thought there was a chance.

After making sure the horses were secure, Levi removed his rifle from its scabbard and followed Potas through the trees. The two hunters left the cover of the lodgepole pines and slinked along a barren promontory that jutted out from the rim of a basin on the Keller Fork of Bruin Creek in the Bridger-Teton National Forest. The point was about 100 yards long and covered with football-size rocks and a few small spruce trees. A boulder the size of a coffee table at the ridge's end was where the two hunters set up a spotting scope to sweep the valley below.

"Potas must not have too much faith that we'll see a shooter here," Levi thought as the guide squinted through the scope's eyepiece. "He

didn't even bother to take off his chaps when he dismounted." Just then
Levi heard something behind him.

"Whooof!"

At first he thought the sound might have come from an elk that had
winded the hunters and was in the process of bounding away. One glance
at Potas told a different story, however, as Levi saw him staring over his
shoulder in wide-eyed horror. Levi followed Potas's eyes to the source of
the noise. Less than a dozen yards away, on the crest of the point, a sow
grizzly was charging toward them at full speed as her two cubs stood and
watched.

"Unreal," Levi thought. "Maybe she's just bluffing."

Potas was convinced the bear meant business, however. He cursed
once, then yelled "Run!"

And they ran.

HUNT OF A LIFETIME

Anticipation is one of the sweetest parts of hunting, and Steve Levi of
Athens, Georgia, had a good taste of it months before he headed west for
his Wyoming elk hunt. He had signed up to hunt elk with Gary Fales
Outfitting just outside Cody, presuming he drew a tag. No sweat. Although Levi had never hunted elk before (much less applied for an elk
tag) he got one. Even more fortunate, he drew a mule deer tag as well.

Friends who had hunted western Wyoming had recommended Fales's
outfit to him. "If you want an authentic high-country elk hunt without
any fancy trimmings but with the chance to bag a trophy-size bull, line
up Fales," they said. So Levi booked a seven-day hunt and, on September 7,
flew from Atlanta to Cody with his father, James, who went along as an
observer.

Their base camp on the Thorofare River was 26 miles from the trailhead at the end of a butt-numbing seven-hour horseback ride. The trail
threaded up, down and around the rugged Absaroka Mountains, through
forested passes and across meadows lush with the sweet grass that fed
elk until the first snows of winter.

"We were taking horses through places I never knew horses could go," Levi recalled. "We would leave before daylight and ride to a vantage point where we could glass for elk, then return to camp around ten o'clock, eat lunch and loaf until three o'clock or so. Then we would go back out and hunt until dark. You got so tired that the soreness you felt didn't bother you so much after a while."

One reason Levi never seemed to get enough rest was his guide. Fales had paired Levi with Mike Potas, an energetic 32-year-old from Meteestse, Wyoming. Potas had been guiding since his teens and specialized in bighorn sheep and mountain lions. A lanky six-footer, he was as durable as whet leather and had previously won the local Tough Man Contest in Cody. Potas drove himself and his customers hard to succeed, and he was popular with younger hunters. Fales figured the 31-year-old Levi could handle Potas's daily regimen, which included long rides through some of the most rough-hewn country this side of Alaska.

"The first morning we weren't far from camp when we heard a bull bugling," said Levi. "After we dismounted, we spotted two decent five by fives. Because it was the first day, we decided to pass on them. Later we saw a nice six by six, but he was about seven hundred and fifty yards off and there was no way to get closer."

Levi was hunting with a custom rifle chambered for a .300 wildcat based on a necked-down 8mm Remington cartridge that utilized 180-grain bullets. The rifle was sighted in to be dead on at 300 yards, and Levi had practiced even longer shots at a local range. He was confident he was as prepared as most Western hunters for any reasonable opportunity and, on Friday, September 13, he got a chance to prove it. While riding along a ridge between two bowls, Potas spotted a 160-class mule deer watching the hunters pass. He told Levi the muley was a good buck, and the Georgia hunter elected to have a go at it.

Levi quickly dismounted, chambered a round and, while standing within yards of his horse, took an offhand shot at the buck 175 yards away. As the sound of the shot reverberated through the mountain canyons, the buck dropped in its tracks and slid about 20 yards down the mountain toward the hunters. Potas told Levi that, as a shooter, he would do.

ONE LAST TRY

On the final morning of the hunt, Levi was still determined to go home with a trophy rack or none at all. It was a cold morning, with temperatures in the 30s, and the hunters had layered on clothing. Potas was wearing thick long underwear under his blue jeans and chaps and he had a thick jacket on over his shirt. The coat kept him warm, but it also concealed the .44 Magnum revolver he wore in a shoulder holster for backup. Bears— blacks and grizzlies—were a fact of life in the mountains of the Bridger-Teton and six rounds of lead was standard insurance against attack.

As they reached the basin where Potas figured they might see elk, Potas cautioned Levi to stay close to him and be ready to shoot if he saw a bull that passed muster.

"We eased out to the end of the point when Mike motioned me to get down because he had spotted elk," said Levi. "We got next to the only big rock out there. It was off to one side and I was planning to kneel behind it and use it as a rest if I got a shot. The valley was about six hundred and twenty yards across, according to my range finder, and we saw a few small bulls browsing around in an opening. We waited, hoping a good bull would eventually move out of the timber."

When the grizzly sow winded the hunters, she answered the supposed threat in typical fashion of her kind: straight ahead, with no benefit of the doubt extended to the intruders.

"Mike went one way and I started to go the other, but I was kind of dumbfounded at first," said Levi. "The grizzly came on so fast I knew I wouldn't have time to raise my gun. Mike took off down the hill and probably that's why the bear veered off toward him. She just went right after him. I shuffled a step to my right and before I knew what was happening, the bear had caught up with Mike."

Potas leaped into one of the scraggly spruce saplings but the bear was on him instantly. "Shoot it, shoot it," screamed Potas, who didn't have time to retrieve his handgun from under his jacket before the grizzly clamped his leg in her jaws. He was holding onto the tree's upper branches and kicking at the sow with one leg while she attempted to pull him out of the tree.

"I chambered a round, but even then I was wondering, 'Am I going to shoot the bear, or shoot Mike?'" Levi said. "In a split second I made the decision not to shoot and lowered my rifle. The next thing I know, Mike is flying out of the tree and rolling and stumbling down the hill for about thirty yards. The bear didn't follow him; instead, she turned and came for me."

The grizzly apparently had spent much of her fury on the guide but still perceived Levi to be a menace to her cubs. Suddenly, she rushed him. With nowhere to run, Levi stood his ground, but the grizzly moved so quickly that he didn't have time to raise the rifle to his shoulder. When the bear was within ten feet, Levi fired from the hip and instantly chambered another round. The shot froze the sow in her tracks for a second or two. That was Levi's cue to leave and he bounded down the slope to Potas's side. Both men looked back up the incline but the bears had disappeared over the skyline.

The guide was spoiling for a rematch with the grizzly. He had drawn the handgun from its holster and fired a couple of rounds in the air while shouting a string of challenging curses.

"When he settled down some we looked at his wounds. The bear had bit him in the upper thigh of his left leg and it was bleeding pretty good," Levi said. "But thanks to the thick leather chaps, the bear couldn't tear his leg with her teeth or get her claws in him."

RIDING FOR HELP

Potas asked Levi to fetch the horses, and by the time he returned, the guide's lower leg was drenched in blood. Levi cut his long underwear and bound Potas's wounds as best he could to stop the bleeding. He then helped Potas mount his horse, but the smell of blood made the mare jumpy.

The guide told Levi he would have to ride for help and instructed him on how to follow the stream to its confluence with the Thorofare. Once Levi reached the river, camp would be a few miles downstream. Minutes after Levi left Potas in the basin, he spooked a big bull from the aspens flanking the opposite ridge. The hunter didn't give the elk a moment's notice, however, and continued his descent toward camp. Not long after he reached the river, Levi encountered two hunters with packhorses. When he caught up with them, Levi discovered they were both doctors making their way out of the high country after a successful hunt. Levi told them what had happened. It was agreed that one of the men would take Levi's fresh horse and seek help at the camp while the other would accompany Levi back to where he had left Potas.

As they were making their way back to the site of the grizzly's attack, Levi spotted Potas coming toward them on his horse. Having decided that it was safer to take his chances on the trail than to wait for more bears, Potas was making a beeline for the Thorofare.

"By the time we reached Mike he was pretty wobbly and lying over in his saddle," Levi said. "The doctor made sure the bandages would hold and then we rode to camp. Another doctor there had medical supplies and gave Mike some painkillers while he examined the wounds. Potas had three deep punctures in his leg between the groin and the knee and was bleeding pretty bad. The doctors determined that no major veins were touched, but they were concerned that the femoral artery might have been nicked."

A Life Flight helicopter called to the scene with a satellite phone airlifted Potas to a Cody hospital for treatment. The guide spent the night in the hospital and was released the next day.

An investigation by the Wyoming Game and Fish Department concluded that Levi shot at the bear in self-defense and missed it. No charges were filed. Levi returned to Georgia without an elk but with something rarer still: an adventure story any mountain man would envy.

By the time elk season was over the grizzly episode had created quite a stir in hunting camps up and down the Thorofare. Potas's celebrity status increased a few notches and Fales's other guides elected to name the scene of the attack "Potas Point."

It is safe to assume that the hunting guides also started paying almost as much attention to what was behind them as they did to what was in front of their spotting scopes.

twelve

ROGUE BEAR ON THE RAMPAGE

by Lyn Hancock

HAVING DELIVERED THE LAST of his explosives to seismic crews working on the Alaska Highway, Ray Kitchen, a 56-year-old trucker from Fort Nelson, B.C., decided to stop off at the Liard River Hotsprings Provincial Park. There, his 11-year-old daughter, Joline, and her friend Sarah, who were along for the ride, could enjoy a swim.

A tropiclike oasis in the boreal forest, the hot springs were a popular tourist haven complete with campsites and a playground. It was August 14, 1997.

As Kitchen relaxed beside the springs, watching the girls play, terrifying screams suddenly erupted from the park's famous Hanging Gardens. The sound jolted Kitchen to his feet.

He rushed along a rain-slicked boardwalk and up some wooden stairs to reach the gardens' viewing platform—and stopped, horrified. On the wooden structure, a huge bear straddled a young boy beside the motionless form of a woman. Both were covered with blood from deep gashes in their swimsuit-clad bodies.

* * *

PATTI MCCONNELL HAD BEEN driving north from Paris, Texas, for over a week, heading for Alaska to start a new life. The vivacious 37-year-old mother hoped to get a job there and raise her two kids, Kelly, 13, and Kristin, seven.

It had been a tiring trip, and the children were delighted when McConnell turned off the Alaska Highway and into the Liard River park.

The family wasted no time slipping into their swimsuits, and in bare feet they hurried along the boardwalk and into the crystal-clear 53°C water of the lower pool. After a long, hot soak, they headed for the more secluded upper pool some 340 metres farther into the bush.

Kristin soon got bored and raced back along the boardwalk to the lower pool, where she'd made some friends.

"Slow down or you're gonna slip!" McConnell yelled as her daughter tore off around a bend. She and Kelly got up to follow. As they reached the turnoff leading to the Hanging Gardens, Kelly said, "Let's go see them, Mom."

Climbing a flight of steps through the bush, they came to a viewing platform. So intent were mother and son on identifying the exotic plants, they paid no attention to a rustling in the bushes beside the boardwalk. McConnell glanced at her watch. "Kelly, I'm worried about Kristin. I'm going to find her."

McConnell started down the wet steps. As she reached for the railing to steady herself, something drew her attention. She looked up into the eyes of a black bear—a big adult male sitting in the shrubbery chewing on a dogwood branch.

McConnell froze. "Kelly . . . bear!" she hissed.

"Sure, Mom!" With his back to her, Kelly thought she was kidding.

"Kelly!"

This time he turned round to find an animal taller than him staring intently at his mother. Remembering what he had heard about bears, he said, "Mom, don't make any sudden movements."

Cautiously, Kelly edged towards his mother. The bear snorted, then lunged through the railing and onto the boardwalk. "Mom! Run!"

Galvanized by her son's screams, McConnell moved as fast as she could, the bear charging after her. She ran up the steps to the viewing platform—and was trapped.

Kelly saw in horror the bear engulf his mother's almost naked body with its own. Despite his slight stature, the 13-year-old ran at the creature and kicked it in the face. "Get off my mom!"

The bear looked up, grunted and went back to its prey.

Searching for a weapon, Kelly snatched up a sawed-off tree limb. With a strength born of anger, he smashed at the bear's head, all the while screaming for help.

The sight of his mother's blood on the bear's canines spurred Kelly on. Lunging furiously with his stick, he hit the animal squarely on the nose, drawing blood. The bear growled and swung a paw at Kelly, ripping deep claw marks into his neck and shoulders.

Then he came after the terrified boy. Kelly crumpled under the animal's massive weight. He felt its teeth crunch around his waist as it lifted him into the air and swung him around like a dog playing with a rag doll. Just as he was about to pass out, the animal flung him to the deck. Kelly rolled into a ball.

His mother lay beside him, her skin ashen, her eyes open and unblinking. He tried to crawl towards her, but the bear pounced again, tearing chunks out of his flesh. The animal's foul, rancid breath made Kelly want to vomit. He closed his eyes. He knew he was about to die.

RAY KITCHEN QUICKLY TOOK in the horrifying scene. Grabbing a fallen tree branch, he hammered it against the railing.

"Hey! Get off!" he yelled. The bear paid no attention. Kitchen tore off a bigger branch and rammed it into the bear's stomach, hoping to push the animal away from the child.

The bear rose from his victim and charged towards Kitchen. The impact knocked him right through the railing, bear and man tumbling into the bush. Clad only in his swim trunks, Kitchen tried to protect his body from the bear's slashing claws by scrambling on his knees to a tree and covering his head with his hands. He began yelling for help.

* * *

FRANK HEDINGHAM, 71, WAS lounging on a deck overlooking the lower pool when he heard the screams. *Just a bunch of kids,* he thought. Then he heard shouts: "Help!" "Bear!" "Get a gun!" He immediately took off in their direction.

Just ahead of him on the boardwalk were Ingrid Bailey, a wilderness firefighter and paramedic from Felton, California, and her friend, Brad Westervelt. News that a rogue bear was about had spread quickly, and frantic people were fleeing towards the parking lot.

But Bailey, who regularly parachuted into fires in remote areas, was used to bears. She, Westervelt and Hedingham pressed on, gathering sticks and chunks of wood as they ran.

At the viewing platform, they saw two bloodstained bodies on the deck. But it was the terrifying scene below the deck that riveted them. Kitchen, still alive, was struggling weakly. The bear's jaws were clamped tight around his upper arm and shoulder, its claws slashing at his already torn and bloody body.

Bailey began hurling her chunks of wood at the bear. "Get off him!" she screamed, stamping her feet and pounding the railing with a stick. She felt no fear, just anger, then helplessness as her efforts did nothing to distract the animal.

Hedingham and Westervelt, meanwhile, had spotted a long, thick tree trunk. It was heavy and cumbersome, but they levered it over the railing. Using it as a battering ram, all three heaved together, but that, too, failed to drive the animal off.

We need a gun, Bailey thought desperately. *Where's the park ranger?*

As if reading her thoughts, Westervelt dropped his end of the tree. "I'm going to find a ranger," he yelled and raced off. Hedingham, with a history of heart attacks, was exhausted but vainly continued to pound away at the bear.

Suddenly the bear shifted its position, clamped its jaws around its victim's neck and threw him into the air. "No!" Bailey screamed frantically.

The bear hesitated and dropped Kitchen to the ground. His face gouged, his windpipe ripped out, his neck almost severed, Kitchen was dead.

Bailey turned to the other victims. She knelt beside McConnell and felt for a pulse. She knew the woman was dead, but her training dictated that she try to resuscitate her. She set to work.

Just then Kelly moaned, and Hedingham rushed to his side.

Suddenly the bear's left paw curled over the edge of the deck centimetres from Kelly's feet.

Furious, Hedingham stood up and delivered a vicious kick with his hiking boots. The animal staggered back, but instead of retreating, it moved down the slope towards the boardwalk, where people were still passing.

Hedingham turned back to the boy, who was trying to crawl to his mother. "Help my mom," he pleaded in a whisper.

"Don't worry," Hedingham said. "We're doing all we can. You mustn't move. Breathe slowly."

Hedingham, who had first-aid training, took a handkerchief from his jacket to mop blood from the worst of the gashes. "What we really need," Bailey said, "are towels to act as compresses and two more pairs of hands for CPR."

As if in answer, several men bounded up the stairs. One had a towel and knew CPR (cardiopulmonary resuscitation). He helped Hedingham bind the boy's wounds. Another man assisted Bailey, compressing McConnell's chest while Bailey breathed into her mouth.

The bear had gone. *But where was the ranger?* Bailey wondered.

"We must get them to hospital," Hedingham said desperately. "I'm going for help."

Suddenly, new screams rang through the trees. *Oh, God,* Hedingham thought, *the bear's at it again!*

ARIE VAN DER VELDEN, 28, a research assistant from the University of Calgary, had been soaking in the upper pool when he became aware of a commotion coming from the bush. Along with other bathers, he left the pool and hurried down the boardwalk. He had almost reached the turnoff to the Hanging Gardens when someone yelled: "A bear's coming! Run for your lives!"

Everyone turned and ran, but Van der Velden slipped and fell into the bush. In seconds the bear was there and launched itself on top of him, slashing at his body. Van der Velden kicked the animal's nose, he even tried pulling the bear's ears, but nothing could deter the beast. Van der Velden felt a searing pain as the bear's claws hooked into his flesh, and then the bear bit deep into his left thigh.

DAVE WEBB, A 49-YEAR-OLD businessman from Fairbanks, Alaska, had just arrived at the park when an exhausted man dripping blood from his temple ran up. "You've got to do something. There's a bear up there!" Hedingham panted, explaining what had happened. Webb nodded, raced back to his motor home and brought out two rifles—a Winchester 30.30 and a Remington 223.

To a young man standing nearby, he shouted, "Do you know how to use a gun?"

"That 30.30 I do," said Duane Eggebroten, 27. They loaded up and set off at a run down the boardwalk.

Eggebroten arrived at the scene first. He heard low groans coming from below the boardwalk. The bear now had Van der Velden propped against a log and was feeding on him. Eggebroten aimed carefully for the back of the bear's neck, then fired. The bear slumped down. Eggebroten knew it was dead, but he fired twice more to be sure.

Up on the viewing platform, Bailey, still tending to McConnell and her son, heard the shots. All the pent-up tension and anger poured out of her. "Shoot it again!" she cried. "Shoot it again!"

The horror at Liard River Hotsprings was finally over.

Patti McConnell died that afternoon. But thanks to the courage of Ray Kitchen, Ingrid Bailey, Frank Hedingham and the others, Kelly McConnell and Arie Van der Velden survived. Flown out to a hospital, they both eventually recovered from their terrible wounds.

In Fort Nelson on August 22, more than 500 mourners turned out to honour the bravery of Ray Kitchen. In a letter to Kitchen's wife, U.S. President Bill Clinton wrote, "The heroism and selflessness that your husband displayed coming to the aid of Patti and Kelly McConnell is an example of all that is noble and good in human nature."

From Canada, Kitchen received the Star of Courage posthumously in September 1998. Frank Hedingham, Kelly McConnell, Ingrid Bailey and Brad Westervelt were also awarded decorations for bravery.

thirteen

TOUGHER THAN A SPEEDING BULLET

by Mike Lapinski

TODAY'S HIGH-POWERED RIFLE IS capable of delivering a heavy lead bullet encased in a copper jacket at velocities approaching three thousand feet per second. But this dubious miracle of modern technology saves the best for last. Packing hundreds of foot-pounds of pent-up energy, the heavy slug arrives with the subtlety of a cruise missile, reducing living flesh in its path to a pulverized, atomized, homogenized mass of sliced, diced, tenderized bloody gel, and hard bone to a jumble of tiny white shards.

The big cats—leopard, tiger, lion—terrible and lethal in their own right, are easily felled by a well-placed bullet. Even the great pachyderms plow a deep furrow in the African savanna when hit with a .375 H&H magnum.

But against a charging grizzly, it's not enough. No doubt harking back to its behavior during the Pleistocene epoch, a grizzly's rage increases when injured. It's a disturbing fact for a gun owner to accept: a salvo of hot lead smashing into a charging grizzly just tends to spur it on toward the source of its pain.

More often than not, the grizzly has gained its fierce reputation when it was dead on its feet, having already been shot through and through. Yet to the shock, the horror, and occasionally the demise of the shooter, the great bear kept coming—its heart shot to pieces, its lungs blown out—until bear or man, or both, found their final peace.

Bear number 34 was such a grizzly. He was a bad bear, and he needed to be killed before he killed someone. At 670 pounds of taut muscle, the big grizzly was a berserk, rage-filled beast that had been killing cattle on a ranch near Dubois, Wyoming, in the summer of 1994.

Like Charles Manson, his psychotic human counterpart, bear 34 didn't become a killer overnight. It took years of pain and suffering to produce something so horrible.

The story of bear 34 actually began twenty-two years earlier when a beautiful young male grizzly bear with a lustrous charcoal-colored coat was live-trapped near Dubois. Biologists fastened an ear tag—number 34. They also fitted the bear with a radio collar.

To avoid damaging a bear's neck, these radio collars are connected with a canvas band that rots away after a few years, allowing the collar to drop off. But something went terribly wrong. Long after the radio had stopped transmitting, the collar stayed snapped around bear 34's neck.

Like all male grizzlies, the young bear's neck grew thick with muscles, but the collar stayed fastened around his neck like a garrote. First it cut through the bear's hide, then into his neck muscles, where it grated against festering flesh and squeezed his upper neck so severely that the nerves near the ears were permanently damaged, rendering him deaf and near-mad with pain. And when a grizzly feels pain, rage is a by-product.

Bear 34 was live-trapped again near the Diamond G Ranch in 1992, and it was then that state biologists discovered the old radio collar embedded in his neck. One can only guess at the fury that bear 34 must have felt, tranquilized and conscious but unable to move while he again endured excruciating pain at the hands of men while the radio collar was finally removed.

The next year, bear 34 became a cattle killer on the Diamond G Ranch, as did two other grizzlies. One of the grizzlies disappeared, and the other one was euthanized, but bear 34 was caught and released several miles from the ranch because he was a study bear.

With teeth worn down, his neck wound still festering, and his food source of cattle removed, bear 34 roamed the remote black timber forests of the Bridger–Teton National Forest near Jackson, Wyoming, in a rage—a 700-pound time bomb waiting to explode.

Clayton Peterson is a no-nonsense Westerner, tough and straightforward as a Wyoming winter. He loves to hunt elk, but in recent years he and other hunters found their pursuit of elk near the game-rich Davis Hill country disrupted by the growing presence of grizzly bears. There had already been a few incidents involving bears and humans, and many hunters had quit coming to the area, but Clay loved the high alpine summits and black timber pockets.

Clay knew that the longer he hunted there, the greater his chances were of encountering a grizzly. He purchased a .375 H&H magnum rifle. It was much bigger than he needed for elk hunting, but Clay wanted the security of the big gun just in case he ran into a cranky bear.

On a frosty, late September morning in 1994, Clay moved stealthily along a low ridge in a dense stand of black timber near Davis Hill. As he crossed a small draw littered with fallen trees, Clay eased over a log and caught movement out of the corner of his eye. A large, dark-colored bear about sixty yards away was moving toward him. He raised his rifle but hesitated, thinking it was just a big black bear. The bear disappeared behind a screen of trees, and he guessed it caught his human scent and scampered off. Suddenly the bear's head popped up above a log just ten feet away. One look at the bear's face and he realized it was a grizzly. Although Clay didn't know it at the time, this was not just any grizzly. It was bear 34.

The next instant the bear lunged at Clay, and Clay blasted him, sending a bullet into the grizzly's hump. The 200-grain slug disintegrated upon impact with the bear's spine, sending hot lead fragments ripping through both lungs. The remainder of the bullet traveled along the underside of the bear's spine, tearing away the main aorta. For all practical purposes, bear 34 was dead on his feet. He was also pissed off.

The grizzly lunged as Clay frantically worked the gun's bolt. The bear's teeth clamped down on Clay's arm, snapping the bone at the elbow. The bear picked him up and shook him violently, then threw him over a blown-down tree.

Bear 34 then staggered backward, but he came looking for Clay Peterson once again. Though stunned and in pain, Clay was able to chamber another shell but inadvertently flipped on the safety. He squeezed the trigger hard enough to bend it, but nothing happened.

The massive grizzly swung a vicious paw one last time at Clay Peterson. The four-inch claws ripped Clay's face away, sending him flying backward. Blinded by his own blood, Clay pulled out his .44 magnum pistol but could not find the bear.

Clay lay in shock for several seconds. He didn't know if the bear was nearby and bent on finishing the job. He gingerly touched his face. It was gone. Hanging by a large flap of skin was his dislodged nose and an eyeball. And blood was pouring everywhere. He gingerly took the face flap and laid it back into place, allowing him to see somewhat out of one eye.

He knew the country well and stumbled down a ridge to find his brother-in-law, the man with whom he had gone hunting. When the brother-in-law saw Clay, he almost fainted. When they arrived at their tethered horses, Clay's faithful horse, seeing the bloody, disfigured person approaching, went berserk and refused to allow him to mount. A helicopter was called in, and Clay was flown to the hospital in Jackson.

Authorities found bear 34 dead a few hundred yards from the attack scene. For the big grizzly, the pain was finally gone. A necropsy confirmed the damage from the radio collar, including the bear's deafness.

But the assault on Clay Peterson was not over. While lying in a hospital bed, an agent for the U.S. Fish and Wildlife Service interviewed Clay, refusing to accept his story about the attack and attempting to cajole him into admitting he had somehow gotten between a sow and her cubs. Clay, still fuming during our interview as he recalled the conversation, said, "The guy was trying to talk me into admitting that it was all my fault, that no grizzly would purposely attack a human. If I could have somehow got out of that hospital bed, I'd have decked him."

Later, Clay was visited by a more tactful officer from the Wyoming Fish and Game Department. When Clay described the bear, he noticed the officer's eyes register recognition. Clay became suspicious and began investigating. It was then that he discovered the dreadful history behind bear 34.

Clay has mended well, considering the tremendous damage inflicted by a virtually dead bear. Surgeons were able to reattach his face, using part of his hip to rebuild his nose. They were also able to save his eye, though the nerves in the eyelid were damaged beyond repair and he now has to sleep with one eye open. Medical costs exceeded $158,000.

Though Clay harbors no animosity toward grizzly bears, and especially the unfortunate animal that attacked him, he remains bitter toward the Fish and Wildlife Service and the state of Wyoming for allowing such a bear to be injured and then protected.

Clay Peterson is also adamant that it won't happen again. Next time a grizzly comes after him, he'll be ready. He's adopted a bigger, more sturdy bullet that he believes will surely get the job done.

FRED WOODS RAISES HIS eyebrows at this philosophy of increased firepower to stop a bear. He went after a bear with a bigger bullet, even a bigger gun. It didn't help. Fred is the host of the Portland, Oregon, sportsman's television program *Northwest Hunter*. Fred's choice of caliber for a brown-bear (grizzly) hunting trip to Alaska was the .416 Remington magnum. It's an elephant gun whose 400-grain bullet and case resemble a small mortar. And yet it wasn't enough.

One morning, Fred spotted a big brown bear and moved to within two hundred yards before carefully placing the crosshairs of his scope on the bear's shoulder. The big gun roared, and the bear dropped. Fred jumped up, exulting in his quick kill. But the bear struggled to its feet, spotted him, and charged. Fred rammed another bullet into the chamber and took careful aim at the chest of the oncoming bear. The bullet literally knocked the bear backward, and it landed in a heap, where it lay heaving its last breaths.

Fred thought, *Whew, that was close!* As a precaution, he chambered the last bullet. When he looked up, he was startled to see the bear back on its feet, coming at him again.

Fred's third shot knocked the big bear sideways but didn't put it down. The bear, now less than a hundred yards away, hobbled toward him on three legs. Fred frantically grabbed for extra shells from his pockets and shoved them into the rifle's magazine. He threw up his gun and fired again when the bear was sixty yards away. This time he heard the loud *splat!* as the heavy slug pulverized the bear's chest.

But the bear didn't go down. As Fred hastily rammed the next bullet into the chamber, he thought, *Two more shots, and then this bear's gonna be on me.*

The bear was thirty yards away when the next slug smashed into its chest, sending forth a crimson plume of blood and gore. The bear went down, but as Fred rammed his last bullet into the rifle's chamber, he had no more illusions that it was over. He brought the rifle to his shoulder as 800 pounds of pulverized brown bear struggled to its feet and lurched forward to fulfill its death wish.

Fred looked through his scope at the bear's eyes, filled with rage and pain. He had one last bullet. When the concussion of the blast echoed through the barren hills, the bear nose-dived into the earth less than ten feet from Fred Woods.

Realizing he'd been fortunate that the bear's charge had begun far enough away that he could get off six shots, Fred began investigating bear pepper spray as an alternative, just in case a grizzly should jump out of the brush at close range. Fred told me, "I knew from personal experience that if you don't kill a bear immediately, shooting it some more only increases its rage. I chose pepper spray because I became convinced that it canceled that rage factor."

Fred drew a few chuckles and smirks when he strapped on a can of bear pepper spray on the first day of an Alaska guided hunt for caribou in the fall of 1999. That afternoon, Fred and another hunter, plus the guide, went on a scouting trip. Four hours later, Fred was in the lead as the men returned to their camp. As they came around the front of the first tent, a brown bear cub ran away squealing. A huge brown bear sow exploded out of a tent thirty feet away and charged them. While the other men frantically struggled to get their rifles off their shoulders, Fred pulled out his bear pepper spray and gave the sow a full blast at twenty feet. The bear skidded to a halt, pawing at the air, then swapped ends and galloped away with her cub close behind.

"A guy with a big game rifle is actually handicapped if he's suddenly charged," Fred said. "These guns have to be free of dirt and snow, so most hunters keep them on a sling over a shoulder. No way can you get that gun off your shoulder, chamber a shell, and then make a killing shot at a bear barreling at you through the brush."

A cadre of outdoors people who recognize the logistical nightmare of unslinging a rifle and then trying to find a charging grizzly in the crosshairs of a scope have opted for a sidearm, namely the .44 magnum pistol. Fred Woods snorts at such logic. "The old-timers in Alaska tell those people that if they're gonna use a .44 mag for self-defense against a brown bear, they should file down the front sight. When the nimrod asks why, the old-timer tells him, 'That way when the bear takes it from you and shoves it up your ass, it won't hurt so much.'"

Besides the obvious ballistic inadequacy of a pistol, the fact remains that very few people can shoot one accurately. At a gathering of outfitters and guides in Wyoming, a state official hooked up a black-bear decoy to his all-terrain vehicle, using a hundred feet of rope. Six guides, experienced in pistol shooting, emptied their sidearms as the decoy was pulled by at thirty yards. Out of thirty-six shots, one bullet struck the black bear—in the rear paw! The nervous driver was overheard swearing, "And I thought that was the wind whistling past my ears!" No doubt another section of rope was added on subsequent exercises.

WYOMING RESIDENT PAT VAN Vleet realized he needed something for self-defense when he started seeing grizzly sign in his favorite hunting area in the Bridger–Teton National Forest in 1993. At first it was just sign, such as huge bear tracks in the mud and massive claw marks on trees. In 1994 he saw his first grizzly, a sow with cub that spotted him at seventy-five yards and ran away.

The increasing amount of bear sign changed the way Pat and his dad, Ken, hunted the vast series of drainages. They no longer felt free to hike for miles in the dark to get to a secluded meadow where the elk were rutting. And they became very careful about leaving food in camp. They hoped these precautions would reduce their chances of encountering a grizzly. They didn't.

An incident on an elk-scouting trip into Grizzly Creek in the fall of 1997 brought the situation to a head. As Pat and his dad entered a dark draw choked with blown-down spruce and Douglas fir trees, they heard shuffling and pawing ahead. They weren't sure if it was an elk, so they eased forward until they stood in the heart of the blowdown, yet no elk was visible.

Suddenly a huge brown grizzly boar stood up and stared at them from less than fifty yards away. Pat's dad had the rifle up, crosshairs on the tiny white star on the bear's chest. For five minutes, the grizzly and the two men stared each other down in silence. The bear slowly dropped down and walked away, occasionally throwing a glance back at them. The bear had not charged, nor had he acted aggressively, but neither was he afraid of them.

Pat's dad was adamant. From now on, one of them would carry a shotgun loaded with rifled slugs. They tried that tack a few times, but it meant one of them could not hunt with bow or rifle, so Pat investigated bear pepper spray as a defense against bears. He visited a sporting goods store, unsure of what he needed and totally ignorant of the importance of knowing. A salesman shoved a can of cheap pepper spray into his hands and told him all pepper sprays were the same.

The next fall, Pat and his dad bowhunted in the area, but the presence of so much grizzly sign, plus a few unnerving nights in camp when they smelled the powerful stench of a bear nearby, convinced Pat's dad that they should leave the area rather than chance a bear encounter.

On September 27, Pat, his dad, his uncle, and another man, E. J. Steigelweir, traveled into Grizzly Creek to set up camp the day before elk rifle season. Pat's dad was edgy. Bear sign was everywhere. Huge logs were turned over, and bear scat littered every trail. Either there was a very busy grizzly nearby, or there were a lot of bears in the area: Only later did they learn that biologists estimated that up to seventeen grizzlies had descended upon Grizzly Creek and other side drainages.

That evening Pat and his dad rode an all-terrain vehicle (ATV) in as far as they could go, then hiked for almost an hour to the top of Black Rock Creek to scout for elk. There was a lot of fresh elk sign, so they decided to hunt there next morning. On the way back to camp a blizzard set in, dumping six inches of wet snow before the sky cleared and the temperature dropped below freezing.

The next morning the four men drove their ATVs to the end of the trail in the dark. The two older men planned to hunt the elk herd from the bottom of the Black Rock drainage while Pat and E. J. hiked to the top to watch the large meadows below in case the elk came up.

Pat recalled, "Dad was really freaking out. He had this bad feeling about us sneaking through the dark. He wanted us to wait until daylight, but we wanted to be up on top at first shooting light."

Pat and E. J. made it to the top of Black Rock Creek in plenty of time to set up before dawn. The meadow below was empty, so Pat bugled, making a sound like the mating call of a bull elk. Four bugles erupted from a half mile below, but a narrow finger of timber blocked their view of one corner of the meadow. Pat decided to move down to it. That way, E. J. could watch the main meadow and Pat could keep an eye on the other opening.

Pat eased down the slope about a hundred yards, then sneaked along the finger of timber to a small rise, where he sat on a large log that afforded him a view for three hundred yards below. After five minutes, he took off his fanny pack and began munching on a candy bar.

Some animals trotted into the open area below, and Pat cranked up his scope to nine power. He was trying to find the animals in the scope when he heard a shuffling sound behind him. His first thought was, *Wow! The elk are right behind me.*

When he turned around he saw fur—brown, grizzled fur. A sow and two cubs were nosing along the log just twenty-five yards away. His heart felt like a giant fist was squeezing it. *Maybe they won't notice me,* he thought. As he lowered the rifle, a cub spotted him and began squealing. The sow instantly charged.

Pat recalled, "I grabbed the pepper spray and sprayed the sow when she was fifteen feet away, but the stuff just sputtered out of the can in a thin stream, maybe ten feet. The sow hesitated, and I sprayed at her again, then she just barreled through the cloud. I was out of spray by then, so I turned and ran. It was an impulsive thing."

The sow bit Pat's left ankle, sending him sprawling, then bit into his right arm. Pat curled into a fetal position. The sow swatted him and lunged for his head, but he tucked it down.

The sow then bit into his right side and shook him hard before flinging him to the ground and biting into his stomach. Fortunately, Pat's heavy hunting coat took the brunt of the bear's powerful jaws. The bear literally pulled him to his feet before furiously shaking him again and throwing him down. Pat hit the ground hard, with the bear right on top of him again, slashing and tearing.

"I was getting knocked around pretty good," Pat said. "Then the bear suddenly leaps straight into the air, bellowing and biting and pawing at the air. Then I heard a loud *whop!* and the bear pitched over backwards."

Pat didn't know what was going on, but at least the bear wasn't on him anymore. As he scrambled away, he thought, *All that, and I only got a sprained ankle.*

"Then I brought up my right hand," Pat said, "and saw a big hole through the palm, and I looked at my ankle and saw the bone sticking out. I was finding bite marks and tears on every part of my body. But when I looked down at my belly and saw the blood, that was too much. I didn't know whether the bear had torn my guts out. It was horrible working my fingers under my coat, feeling my belly. The muscle was torn, but my intestines were still inside."

As shock set in, Pat's knees buckled and he crumpled to the ground. Crimson fingers of blood slowly spread out from his ravaged body. And then a worried voice called out, "Are you all right?" It was E. J.

E. J. had heard and seen a far different version of the attack than Pat, who thought the attack had lasted only a few seconds. E. J. had come running when he heard the commotion below, then heard Pat yell, "She's gonna get me! She's gonna get me! Get her off me!" As E. J. ran downhill, he saw Pat and the sow in a desperate struggle, with Pat punching and kicking at the bear.

E. J. was frantic. He had to stop the bear, but he didn't want to shoot his friend. When he first found the bear in his scope, the animal had just pulled Pat upright, and he dared not shoot, but after the bear threw Pat down and started in on him again, E. J. squeezed the trigger, then shot the sow again as she whirled above his fallen friend, madly pawing the air.

There was no reason for Pat's dad to be suspicious about the two shots that came from above, but some inner voice told him his son was in trouble. Five minutes later when Pat's dad and his uncle arrived, they found Pat in a desperate condition, lying in an ever-widening pool of blood. It appeared that every part of his body was bitten, torn, bloody.

Pat's dad sank to the ground, wringing his hands in anguish. He's a tough man not prone to tears, but as he watched his son moaning in agony, he began to weep. Their situation was desperate. They faced a long, difficult hike down to the four-wheelers, then a one-hour ride along a rough trail back to the pickups, which were parked an hour's drive from a paved road.

Pat's dad had accidentally brought along a cell phone, but he doubted it would get any response in the middle of nowhere. He threw the phone to E. J. and ordered him to race to the top of the divide and call for help. The younger man ran for forty yards, then stopped and yelled back, "What should I tell them?"

"Tell them there's a man up here bleeding to death!"

For an hour Pat lay in the snow, and hypothermia began to set in. His skin turned blue and his teeth chattered uncontrollably as his dad and uncle worked in vain to start a fire in the wet snow.

And then they heard the *whop-whop-whop* of a helicopter echoing off the mountains above.

E. J. had been able to contact a 911 operator in Idaho, who transferred his call to a 911 operator in Wyoming. When the helicopter pilot spotted the red snow, he banked the craft and executed a tight landing just one hundred yards away and Pat was evacuated to a hospital.

Doctors worked feverishly on Pat in the emergency room. In addition to his obvious wounds, they also discovered that his left shoulder and right hip were dislocated. He was in the hospital for eight days. On the second day, Pat received a phone call from someone who wanted to talk to him about pepper spray. Unable to hold the phone in his bandaged hands, and seething over the inadequacy of the spray he had used, he had his wife bring the receiver to his ear, intending to give the guy a good piece of his mind.

The man on the other end of the line was Mark Matheny, owner of

Universal Defense Alternative Products, maker of UDAP Pepper Power. Mark told Pat that he also had been attacked by a grizzly and assured Pat that his wounds would heal. Despite his resolve to the contrary, Pat found himself responding to the sensitive approach of a stranger who had endured a similar nightmare. Before Mark hung up, he promised to send some of his UDAP Pepper Power to Pat's house.

When Pat arrived home, the box containing several cans of pepper spray was sitting on his front porch in a FedEx overnight delivery box. A week later, while Pat waited for a friend to take him to the hospital for physical therapy, he picked up a can of the UDAP spray and limped out to his back deck, still dubious at that point about all pepper sprays.

He flipped off the safety and pressed the trigger. He was startled by the loud, intense blast of red pepper. "That stuff must have shot out fifty feet," Pat said. "This was the stuff I should have had against that bear."

Then a slight breeze brought the orange cloud drifting back to Pat's face. He howled in pain and was instantly blinded. When his friend arrived ten minutes later, he thought Pat had gone mad. He found Pat thrashing around in the bathtub, bandages soaked and drooping, working desperately to get the hot pepper off his burning skin.

Pat and Mark Matheny became friends over the phone, and it was then Pat learned that all pepper sprays aren't the same. Rather than lament his ordeal, Pat stepped forward to become a vocal proponent of EPA-listed pepper spray, often speaking at sportsman's meetings and Boy Scout camps.

To those who wonder if he would have been better off shooting the grizzly, Pat adamantly replies, "No way could I have shot that bear. She came so fast, I wouldn't have had time to find her in the scope. I would've just wounded her and made her even madder than she was."

Pat recovered and is back on the job driving a truck for UPS. His left shoulder is still sore and probably won't get any better. But Pat has turned even that into a positive. He says it reminds him how fortunate he was, and how much worse it could have been.

THERE HAVE BEEN INSTANCES in which a gun has stopped a charging grizzly. But even those success stories can be tainted by the guilt some shooters feel after wasting the life of such a magnificent beast. And when it involves a sow, the tragedy is increased because the cubs are usually too young to survive alone. EPA-registered bear pepper spray could have accomplished the same results for the person being attacked but would have allowed the bears to live.

Several conservation groups, concerned with the needless killing of grizzly bears by hunters who are defending themselves, have petitioned those states surrounding Yellowstone National Park to require hunters to carry bear pepper spray. In 2000, thirty-two grizzly bears died in the Yellowstone ecosystem. Twenty-three of those deaths were caused by humans, and at least eleven were due to conflicts with hunters.

"The hunter issue is popping up as the primary cause of grizzly bear mortality in the greater Yellowstone ecosystem for the past several years now," said Sierra Club spokeswoman Louisa Wilcox in an interview with the *Missoulian* newspaper. "I think this is certainly cause for alarm."

Many people who respect the bear believe it's time for sportsmen who hunt near Glacier and Yellowstone National Parks in the states of Idaho, Montana, and Wyoming to step forward and make a conservation statement by publicly advocating pepper spray as an alternative defense against bears. There's even a catchy slogan ready-made by bear spray enthusiasts: "Spray 'em, don't slay 'em!"

fourteen

PHOTOGRAPHERS AND BEARS

by Mike Lapinski

WILDLIFE PHOTOGRAPHY IS almost as dangerous as bowhunting in bear country. Some say it's even more dangerous. That's because stealth and an unobtrusive presence are as much a part of an outdoor shutterbug's outfit as a camera and telephoto lens. These laudable attributes allow a photographer to move unnoticed among wild animals. If that wild animal happens to be a furtive little deer, no problem. If it's a grizzly, big problem.

Wildlife photographer Tim Christie, whose photos appear in outdoor and nature books and magazines, found that out when he took a short walk to snap a few photos of deer and ended up almost dead. Tim was driving along Camas Road in Glacier National Park in October 1987, looking for any photo subject. A hundred yards ahead, two whitetail bucks trotted across the road and headed for a secluded meadow a short distance from the pavement.

Tim pulled his pickup off the road and wavered for a few seconds, trying to decide whether he should take the time to replace his light tennis shoes with sturdy hiking boots before going after the deer. Tim has weak ankles, and he almost never goes afield without boots. But these were big bucks, perfect magazine cover material, and they'd be gone soon. So he grabbed his camera gear and slipped into the dense forest in his tennis shoes with the thought, *It won't be too bad. I'll be close to the road.*

Tim shadowed the bucks as they fed along the edge of the meadow, staying back about a hundred yards to avoid pressuring the animals. Using his 600-millimeter lens, Tim shot several rolls of film as passing vehicles roared by just out of sight behind him.

Suddenly the bucks stiffened and stared nervously at a thicket of trees to his right. Tim wondered if another photographer was coming, or maybe a ranger was checking on him. The deer had been aware of his distant presence and had not shown alarm, so he was a bit perplexed when they bounded into the forest. But Tim was also a student of wildlife behavior, and he was well aware of the furtive nature of the white-tailed deer, so he merely shrugged and turned back, content with the photos he had taken.

He'd walked only a short distance with the camera and tripod slung over his shoulder when he caught sight of a small brown animal moving out of the thicket. A tiny cub stepped into the open, spotted him, and began squealing.

It's a grizzly, Tim thought. He immediately discarded his camera gear and looked for a tree to climb. A limby red fir stood just ten yards away, and he scrambled onto it. As he worked his way up through the limbs, Tim heard crashing through the brush, followed by growling. Then the tree shook so hard he almost fell out. He looked down into the eyes of a snarling sow grizzly just a few feet below. That gave him incentive to quickly climb higher.

Tim breathed a sigh of relief to be sitting fifteen feet above the bear, secure in the knowledge that grizzlies can't climb trees. The sow was not aware of that fact, because she started up the tree after him.

"She came up as fast as I had," Tim said. "She just hooked her paws over the branches and pulled herself up. I was frantic. I was almost to the top of the tree, and she was right behind me."

Tim climbed until the tree trunk became too thin. He glanced down, and the sow was right there, jaws snapping mere inches from his feet.

The tree limbs were spindly, but Tim frantically tried to climb a foot higher. He glanced down just as the sow launched upward and clamped her jaws onto the heel of his right tennis shoe. "It felt like my foot was in a vice," Tim said. "I really thought she'd snap my heel off."

The sow released her grip around the tree trunk and all 300 pounds of bear just hung there, pulling on Tim. His hands were slowly losing their grip around the tree as the bear continued to jerk and pull; the bear was about to pull him out of the tree and have her way with him on the ground.

Then Tim felt his tennis shoe slip off his foot and glanced down to see the bear, shoe still in its mouth, crashing down through the limbs. Not only was he fortunate that the shoe came off his foot, but the falling grizzly also wiped out most of the limbs, making another assault near impossible.

The sow, still agitated, loped over to a large blown-down spruce tree and climbed to the top of the root wad. "It was really unsettling," Tim said, "because when she stood on her hind legs, she was almost at my level."

Even during this traumatic moment in his life, the photographer in Tim Christie surfaced as he thought, *Gee, she has the most beautiful eyes. I wish I had a camera.* The sow punctuated that thought with a surly *woof!* and scampered away with her cub.

"I was less than a hundred yards from my car," Tim said, "but I didn't want to chance coming down, not knowing where the bear was. A couple times other vehicles stopped next to mine, and I yelled my lungs out to get their attention, but they drove off. After an hour I slowly shimmied down the tree and hurried to my car."

Tim's experience with the sow grizzly prompted him to do some hard thinking about his wildlife photography profession. He now takes fewer chances and has started carrying bear pepper spray. "I think it's insane," he says, "for anyone in bear habitat to take to the woods without it."

CONRAD ROWE AND MICHAEL Francis, also professional wildlife photographers, agree wholeheartedly with Tim Christie. Fortunately it didn't take a near-death experience for both men to carry bear spray as a vital part of their camera gear. A wise choice, considering the predicament they found themselves in while photographing a bull elk near Jasper in Canada's Banff–Jasper National Park.

The two men had become good friends after meeting while photographing elk in Yellowstone. In 1996 they made plans to rendezvous at the Whistler Campground just outside Jasper and team up to photograph rutting bull elk. Both men carried Counter Assault bear spray.

On the frosty morning they got together, they were photographing a big bull elk that was rutting near an old road. Impatient to find some cows, the bull set out at a fast pace toward a meadow two hundred yards away. Michael and Conrad followed at a safe distance.

The bull entered the meadow and turned left. Conrad followed, staying back in the trees. As he edged forward, he spotted movement out of the corner of his eye and turned to find a large brown grizzly forty yards away, coming toward him.

"The first thing that entered my mind," Conrad said, "was to warn Michael. I yelled, 'Michael, a grizzly!' I left my camera and tripod and started backing away, looking for a tree to climb while Michael edged my way."

The bear, now twenty yards away, was coming fast. Michael waved his arms and yelled, and that caused the bear to veer to the right, thereby exposing two tiny cubs. "As soon as I saw the cubs," Conrad said, "I glanced over at Michael, and we both yelled, 'Get out your spray!'"

"The sow ignored Michael and came at me low and fast. It was obvious she wasn't going to stop. We both sprayed her at about six feet. She got hit good with a heavy blast of spray, and it stopped her like she'd run into a wall. She spun around, bellowing, and ran back into the heavy timber with her cubs."

TIM CHRISTIE, MICHAEL FRANCIS, and Conrad Rowe are ethical photographers who care for the welfare of the animals they photograph. Sadly, there is another breed of photographer roaming the wilds whose blind ambition to secure coveted bear photographs has led to wanton disregard for the welfare of the bears.

Montana bear management specialist Tim Manley, during our interview, shook his head and complained, "In my opinion, wildlife photographers are some of the worst habituators of bears. It's a well-known fact that a habituated bear, having lost its fear of humans, is going to end up dead sooner or later unless it's rehabilitated. Yet I've seen photographers do the dumbest, most dangerous things in their headlong zeal to get the close-up shot."

Standing out in Manley's memory is a case that unfolded near Polebridge, Montana, a village on the banks of the North Fork Flathead River along Glacier National Park's western boundary. As reported in the *Missoulian* newspaper, residents began noticing an increase in bear activity in 1997. Grizzly sightings had averaged one or two per year. Now they were seeing more than a dozen a year, and the bears had begun to act strangely. In the past the bears ran away when confronted by a human, but now they walked brazenly through front yards and ignored barking dogs and yelling humans. Tim Manley was at a loss to explain the sudden increase in bear activity.

Later that year, Forest Service surveyors working in the area reported an unusually large number of grizzlies, and when Manley investigated, he quickly discovered the reason. Fifty-pound bags of corn, oats, and barley were strewn on the ground around the property of a wildlife photographer.

"There was bear scat all over the place, filled with corn, oats, and barley," Manley said. "The feed was so thick on the ground that it would require machinery to remove all of it."

The photographer claimed it was leftover grain from winter feeding of deer and elk to keep them from starving. After strongly advising the man that placing out any kind of feed would bring in bears, Manley used aversive conditioning methods such as shooting rubber bullets against their rumps to put the fear of humans back into the bears and drive them into the deep woods. Concerned that the scattered corn would bring in more bears, the state even strung an electric fence around the man's property.

The next winter, the photographer announced that he intended to feed the deer and elk again. Tim Manley visited him and strongly discouraged the practice. The man, known as a bear lover, compromised and said he would place the grain on his frozen pond. That way, he explained, by the time the bears came out of hibernation in spring the corn would have sunk to the bottom of the pond. Manley just shook his head at that odd reasoning.

The next spring, Manley was tracking a radio-collared female grizzly. The bear led him to the photographer's property—and to a pile of bird-seed hidden behind a log. Manley discovered other piles of birdseed and grain behind logs and stumps.

When confronted, the man claimed the grain and seeds were for ducks. This time Manley didn't buy it. "He told me he wasn't going to feed the bears anymore," Manley said, "but I firmly believe he was put-ting the grain out in strategic places, hidden from sight, so he could pho-tograph grizzlies." Unfortunately the state's hands were tied. It is illegal to feed bears in national parks, such as nearby Glacier, and on national forest land, but not on private property.

And then fate intervened. Manley was waiting in a Salt Lake City air-port for a flight when he noticed a copy of *National Wildlife* magazine with an article about grizzly bears promoted on its cover. When he saw the photographer's name, his pulse rate shot up, and when he opened the magazine to the article, his blood ran hot. Real hot.

"The photograph showed a sow grizzly and cub climbing on a sup-posed abandoned bird feeder in the Flathead National Forest," Manley said. "I knew exactly where that bird feeder was located—about twenty feet behind the guy's house. I recognized other bears, too. They were problem bears I'd been dealing with."

Even when confronted with evidence that he'd been baiting grizzlies onto his property to photograph them for financial gain, the man contin-ued to deny any wrongdoing. The state considered charging him with baiting and endangering bears, but the laws were so vague that officials reluctantly dropped the case.

Not Tim Manley. He wrote to the magazine and told the editor that the manner in which the photo was taken had created exactly the condi-tions the author complained other people were causing. Local newspa-pers ran stories detailing the incident, and the state of Montana began looking into the possibility of prohibiting bear-baiting practices even on private land.

"It's ironic that the cub in that magazine article about saving the grizzly is no longer alive," Manley said. "It was illegally killed, largely due to its habituation to people. It died with a belly full of birdseed."

The photographer later sold the property and moved on, leaving Manley with the herculean task of rehabilitating the bears. "There were about a dozen bears feeding on that property when the guy left," Manley said, "and they picked up bad habits that will cause problems with local residents for years. We've had to use Karelian bear dogs, rubber bullets, and other adverse conditioning methods to put the fear of man back in them."

Two years later Manley was still dealing with fallout from the situation. "Late last fall," Manley said, "we had a young sow grizzly walk right into the town of Whitefish and start eating apples under trees. We trapped and relocated her up north in the Whitefish Mountain Range. She hibernated there over the winter, but when she came out of her den in the spring, she headed north for thirty miles in a straight line and ended up on the property where the bait had been placed out, looking for corn and birdseed."

YOU'D THINK IT COULDN'T get any worse than that, but it does. A report in June 1998 in the *Hungry Horse News*, of Columbia Falls, Montana, told of a group of hikers that had banded together on the trip from Red Rocks Lake to the trailhead in the Swiftcurrent Area on Glacier National Park's east side. Among the hikers was an amateur photographer hoping to get some bear photos.

When the group rounded a corner, they spotted a yearling grizzly bear above the trail. The curious young bear began following the hikers at a distance. Anxious to get some close grizzly pictures, the photographer advanced toward the bear—ignoring warnings from the group that what he was doing was illegal and dangerous.

The man wasn't overly concerned, since it was a smallish bear. And besides, he carried a pistol illegally brought into the park, concealed under his jacket. At first the bear retreated, but with the photographer pressuring it, the bear began walking stiff-legged and then turned to face its antagonist.

The photographer continued taking pictures of the agitated bear, holding the camera in one hand and the pistol in the other. Finally the bear had enough. It began popping its teeth and making bluff charges. Now frightened, the man fired warning shots above the bear's head and into the dirt. Then he backed away and hurried past the hikers.

If not for the quick thinking of a teenager in the group who had videotaped the incident, the man might have escaped punishment. The group alerted a ranger, and the man was cited for illegally carrying a weapon inside a national park.

I also witnessed the disregard some photographers show toward the welfare of bears. It was the spring of 1996, and I was taking pictures of black bears feeding along Camas Road in Glacier. Hoping to escape the crowds of people who cruised the road to view the bears, I turned onto a little-used side road. I came around a corner and spotted a medium-size black bear standing in the open, with a man photographing the bruin from about thirty yards away.

I grabbed my camera and tripod and eased out of my car to join the man. He looked back and frowned when he saw me. I assumed his look of dismay grew from his reluctance to share the photo opportunity. As I moved closer, he grabbed his gear and hurried away without a word. A minute later his car roared off.

The man's abrupt departure left me frowning, but the bear's actions had me even more perplexed. Rather than grazing on the new grass shoots, the bear seemed intent on pawing and chewing at something. And then I saw it—the flash of metal. *Could that guy have been feeding this bear?* I wondered.

After the bear wandered off, I walked over and found a well-chewed tuna fish can that reeked of bacon grease. The next day I found another chewed tuna can lying near a meadow where bears often appeared. My guess is that the guy had filled cans with the smelly bacon grease and was enticing wary bears to leave the safety of the dark forest and move into optimum camera position by throwing the grease-filled cans into sunny places with the best background. (Unfortunately I had failed to notice the license number on his car, which carried Washington state plates.)

PHOTOGRAPHERS WHO FEED A bear for the purpose of luring the animal into close camera range usually escape prosecution and injury. But the habituated bear they leave behind is a danger to the next unsuspecting photographer who encounters it. Such was the case, as reported in the *Anchorage Daily News,* in what happened to Michio Hoshino, a wildlife photographer who lived in Anchorage, Alaska. In his native Japan, Michio often hosted wildlife programs on the nature channel.

In July 1997, Michio arrived on Kamchatka Island in Russia's remote chain of Far East islands. The place was famous for its large population of brown bears that showed up at the Khakeetsin River rapids to feed on spawning salmon. Michio was guiding a Japanese film crew that was gathering material for a TV program. He also planned to photograph bears on his own.

There was an immediate problem. The summer salmon run was late, resulting in only a few brown bears roaming the area near the rapids, waiting impatiently for the fish to arrive. Some of these bears went hungry; others took matters into their own hands. The week before, a big boar had broken out a window in the single lodging cabin on the island and climbed through it and ransacked the place. Newly arrived photographers quickly boarded up the window and moved into the cabin. But with several photographers and the Japanese crew inside with all their gear, there was not enough room for everyone, so Michio Hoshino chose to sleep outside in a tent beside the crowded cabin.

Several nights while he slept in the tent, the big boar roamed through the camp, working feverishly but unsuccessfully to break into the underground food cache. A Russian photographer tried a number of times to use bear pepper spray on the bear, but the animal had learned to stay just far enough away to avoid the spray.

In the meantime, the photographers were growing as impatient as the bears. A cameraman from a Russian TV station arrived by helicopter and, finding the bears in short supply, did the wrong thing. Several times the man was observed feeding the big boar to get close shots. Not content with the paltry offerings of the Russian cameraman, the surly boar broke out the windows of the man's helicopter in its drive to get at the food stored inside.

Before this information could be spread to everyone in the camp, the salmon run began, putting aside any concern about the problem bear. With the salmon crowding through the rapids, even the big boar was seen fishing. Everyone thought the worst was over with this animal. They did not know that a habituated bear, hooked on human food rewards, is an incorrigible animal who has lost much of its natural fear of people and who maintains an insatiable desire for people's food even when natural food is abundant.

That night, the photographers in the cabin were startled awake by a man screaming outside. They heard Michio Hoshino yell over and over again, "Tent! Bear! Tent! Bear!" The men dashed outside, armed with a single can of bear spray, and saw Michio's tent being destroyed by the big boar.

They yelled and threw things at the bear, but the beast didn't even raise its head. One photographer grabbed a pail and shovel and banged loudly from just five yards away. The bear finally raised its head, eyed the man, then took Michio's limp body in its massive jaws and carried it into the darkness. The next day, a professional Russian hunter arrived and shot the boar from a helicopter. What was left of Michio Hoshino's body was then recovered. By that time, the Russian cameraman who had fed the boar was long gone—and no doubt receiving accolades for his ability to get so close to a bear.

AL JOHNSON PAID A high price for his close-up photos of bears. Johnson, an Alaska state game biologist, had been sent to Denali National Park to photograph moose and other wildlife. Al was an experienced photographer, and on this trip he carried a 1,000-millimeter lens (which has about twenty-power magnification), along with 300- and 105-millimeter lenses for closer work.

While driving through the park, Al spotted a sow grizzly with three cubs about a half mile away. He brought along all three lenses as he hurried toward the bears. He didn't pressure the bears, staying back more than a hundred yards on the downwind side to avoid alarming the animals—and he always kept a good-size spruce tree close at hand, just in case.

As the story is told in Larry Kaniut's *Alaska Bear Tales*, Al followed the bears for more than two hours, using the 1,000-millimeter lens to capture crisp images as the bears fed on huckleberries in the brilliant autumn sun. But by late afternoon, the light was beginning to fade, making it difficult to use the light-hogging longer lens. The bears were also ambling closer to the road and away from the larger trees that Al sought for safety.

At this point, Al Johnson's desire for the perfect bear photo caused him to abandon the caution he'd so prudently employed throughout the afternoon, and he joined the cadre of wildlife photographers who have pushed their luck too far.

Al decided to lure the bears back toward his position with a predator call, a device that, when you blow into it, simulates the distress cry of a small animal. The call has been known to bring in a predator such as a bear, looking for an easy meal.

Al sought the largest spruce in the area, about eight inches in diameter at the base, and climbed to about fifteen feet. He began using the predator call, hoping the bears would come close to investigate and that he would then be able to use the shorter lenses.

At first there was no visible response from the bears. Then the cubs stood on their hind legs, but the sow still ignored the call. After five minutes of wailing on the call, Al was about to stick it back in his pocket and return to his vehicle when the sow began to show interest.

She looked in Al's direction for a few minutes, then headed toward the tree in a circular path. When the sow was forty yards away, Al yelled to stop her so he could begin taking photos, but his voice had no visible effect on the sow, though the cubs stopped and milled around about thirty yards from the tree. Al began taking pictures of the cubs as the sow continued toward the base of the tree.

Al heard the sow below, but the lower limbs obscured his vision. However, he heard her grunt and slap at his pack, which he had left at the base of the tree. The sow then continued past the tree and stood, waiting for the cubs.

Al was adjusting the focus on his camera when one of the cubs spotted him and began squealing. The sow instantly charged the tree, and a short time later Al felt a tremendous impact as the bear hit the trunk.

Because of the dense foliage, Al didn't know what was happening below, though he could hear branches snapping and claws scraping on the tree. As he squinted down through the limbs, he was horrified to see the sow's head and shoulders burst through the foliage. The bear's jaws clamped onto the heel of his hiking boot. An instant later, he was being dragged down through the branches.

As soon as he hit the ground, Al covered his face with his arms. The sow pounced, biting his arms. Then she gnawed at his skull, removing pieces of his scalp. Several times the sow was distracted by her cubs and stopped the attack long enough to look over and make sure they were safe. She returned each time to biting and pawing at Al.

Throughout the entire ordeal, Al played dead. After what seemed like an eternity to the ravaged man, the sow ran off in the direction of her cubs. As soon as the bear was out of sight, Al struggled to his feet and stumbled three hundred yards to his vehicle. A short time later a park employee who had been a registered nurse stopped and administered first aid. Another vehicle stopped, and Al was taken to park headquarters. He was rushed to a hospital, where he spent two weeks. He has since recovered.

WILDLIFE PHOTOGRAPHY IS ONE of the most coveted occupations among shutterbugs. And why not? You get paid to roam the great outdoors among a variety of wildlife. But there is a downside. The quality telephoto lenses required to get crisp close-up photos of reclusive wild animals from long distance can cost ten thousand dollars or more. An enthusiastic amateur, anxious to move up to professional status, can sometimes avoid this cost by using smaller lenses and getting closer to the animals. With benign animals such as deer and elk, it's doable. With a grizzly bear, it's a death wish.

Montana resident Bill Tesinsky was an amateur photographer who had found some success selling his wildlife photos. He had done admirably well with just an inexpensive camera and a 200-millimeter lens, which is considered too small to get the coveted close-ups that galleries and magazines seek and will pay well for. Bill had relied on his abilities as a woodsman to stalk in close, undetected by the animals.

Tesinsky had one big hole in his photography portfolio. He lacked grizzly bear photos. He knew the market was ripe for good grizzly shots, especially the close-ups that showed the beauty and power of the great bear.

In October 1987, Tesinsky drove to Yellowstone National Park to find a grizzly. He got lucky, in a manner of speaking, when he spotted a smallish female grizzly near the road a few miles south of the Canyon Village area. The bear was well-known to park raugers, having a remarkable ability to feed close to roads while accommodating the crowds of people who quickly jammed the pavement for a look at her. But she had also become a pest and had been trapped and relocated several times, each time quickly returning to her favorite haunts near Canyon Village.

No one saw or heard anything of Tesinsky for three days. Rangers finally investigated on foot. They quickly found the female grizzly, jealously guarding the remains of Bill Tesinsky. Because the bear had not only killed a human, but had also fed on the flesh, the rangers were ordered to kill the bear.

From evidence pieced together afterward, authorities speculate that Tesinsky followed the bear up a draw, no doubt easily coming close while the bear dug for roots and rodents. But Tesinsky encountered a problem that threatened to ruin this most fortunate encounter. The bear had a bright orange radio collar around her neck, which would render the photographs useless.

Unless, that is, he could somehow make the collar disappear. Most wildlife photographers know from experience that the large head of a grizzly, when looking directly at the camera, effectively hides the collar. Tesinsky probably knew this, so he apparently proceeded to use his stalking ability to get within the thirty-yard range needed to get effective photos with the little 200-millimeter lens.

Then something went very wrong. When she was feeding along the road, this grizzly had ignored up to a hundred humans clamoring around close by. But away from the road, the bear probably became alarmed and agitated by the sudden intrusion upon her safety zone. Exactly how the attack went down remains a mystery. What is known is that the bear had been feeding on the body for three days and had cached parts of it in holes.

The incident was given widespread exposure in the newspapers, and Tesinsky's fatal mistake of advancing toward the bear became the subject of many conversations among wildlife photographers. It was hoped that some good would come from Tesinsky's death, by serving to illustrate to others the danger of approaching a grizzly. Not everyone got the message.

Six months later, Montana resident Chuck Gibbs was hiking along the southern edge of Glacier National Park with his wife when he spotted a sow grizzly and three cubs. He sent his wife ahead to the trailhead. Gibbs, known as a great admirer of bears, felt that if he showed respect toward the animal, it would not hurt him. He was wrong.

When he didn't return, authorities were notified, and they soon discovered Gibbs's ravaged body lying among his photography equipment. Investigating rangers were surprised to find a .45-caliber pistol in Gibbs's backpack, unfired. When the film was developed, early frames showed a sow with two cubs at long range and appearing unconcerned, with succeeding frames showing the bears closer and closer, with the sow appearing more and more agitated. The last images show the sow looking his way from a distance of about fifty yards, then advancing toward the camera. The sow had not fed on the body, and the decision was made not to kill her because she had acted in defense of her cubs.

ONE SOLUTION TO THE problem of fledgling wildlife photographers putting themselves, and the bears, at risk would be for recognized professionals to step forward and speak out against taking chances. But sometimes these very professionals are the source of unwise behavior around bears.

A good example is provided in a story that appeared in the *Bozeman*

Daily Chronicle, featuring the work of an internationally known wildlife photographer. In the article, the man said, "Most people think wildlife photographers are using 1,000-millimeter lenses. The closer the better, I say. You get better images. About 80 percent of my work is shot with an 80–200-millimeter lens."

The photographer proudly recounted a recent black-bear photo trip. "I was able to follow the bears on their daily routines. Three of the five of them were confident enough to let me tag along through the brush. I was charged many times. When a sow charged, I just stood my ground. They would hit the brush and try to intimidate me."

The man went on to say that he's more afraid of ticks and Lyme disease than of bears. But he just hasn't met the wrong bear yet. Bill Tesinsky did; so did Chuck Gibbs.

Wildlife photographers should follow the first commandment of proper behavior in bear country: never advance toward a bear. In our national parks, it is not only illegal but also dangerous to approach a black bear, and it is suicidal to approach a grizzly.

STALKED BY SILENT DEATH

Lions, Tigers,

and Other Big Cats

fifteen

THE REIGN OF TERROR

by Lt. Colonel J.H. Patterson, D.S.O

T**HE LIONS SEEMED TO** have got a bad fright the night Brock and I sat up in wait for them in the goods-wagon, for they kept away from Tsavo and did not molest us in any way for some considerable time—not, in fact, until long after Brock had left me and gone on *safari* (a caravan journey) to Uganda. In this breathing space which they vouchsafed us, it occurred to me that should they renew their attacks, a trap would perhaps offer the best chance of getting at them, and that if I could construct one in which a couple of coolies might be used as bait without being subjected to any danger, the lions would be quite daring enough to enter it in search of them and thus be caught. I accordingly set to work at once, and in a short time managed to make a sufficiently strong trap out of wooden sleepers, tram-rails, pieces of telegraph wire, and a length of heavy chain. It was divided into two compartments—one for the men and one for the lion. A sliding door at one end admitted the former, and once inside this compartment they were perfectly safe, as between them and the lion, if he entered the other, ran a cross wall of iron rails only three inches apart, and embedded both top and bottom in heavy wooden sleepers. The door which was to admit the lion was, of course, at the opposite end of the structure, but otherwise the whole thing was very much on the principle of the ordinary rat-trap, except that it was not necessary for the lion to seize the bait in order to send the door clattering down. This part of the contrivance was arranged in the following manner. A heavy chain was secured along the top part of the lion's doorway, the ends hanging down to the ground on either side of the opening; and to these were fastened, strongly secured by stout wire, short lengths of rails placed about six inches apart. This made a sort of flexible door which could be packed into a small space when not in use, and which abutted against the top of the doorway when lifted up. The door was held in this position by a lever made of a piece of rail, which in turn was kept in its place by a wire fastened to one end and passing down to a spring concealed in the ground inside the cage. As soon as the lion entered sufficiently far into the trap, he would be bound to tread on the spring; his weight on this would release the wire, and in an instant down would come the door behind him; and he could not push it out in any way, as it fell into a groove between two rails firmly embedded in the ground.

In making this trap, which cost us a lot of work, we were rather at a loss for want of tools to bore holes in the rails for the doorway, so as to enable them to be fastened by the wire to the chain. It occurred to me, however, that a hard-nosed bullet from my .303 would penetrate the iron, and on making the experiment I was glad to find that a hole was made as cleanly as if it had been punched out.

When the trap was ready I pitched a tent over it in order further to deceive the lions, and built an exceedingly strong *boma* round it. One small entrance was made at the back of the enclosure for the men, which they were to close on going in by pulling a bush after them; and another entrance just in front of the door of the cage was left open for the lions. The wiseacres to whom I showed my invention were generally of the opinion that the man-eaters would be too cunning to walk into my parlour; but, as will be seen later, their predictions proved false. For the first few nights I baited the trap myself, but nothing happened except that I had a very sleepless and uncomfortable time, and was badly bitten by mosquitoes.

As a matter of fact, it was some months before the lions attacked us again, though from time to time we heard of their depredations in other quarters. Not long after our night in the goods-wagon, two men were carried off from railhead, while another was taken from a place called Engomani, about ten miles away. Within a very short time, this latter place was again visited by the brutes, two more men being seized, one of whom was killed and eaten, and the other so badly mauled that he died within a few days. As I have said, however, we at Tsavo enjoyed complete immunity from attack, and the coolies, believing that their dreaded foes had permanently deserted the district, resumed all their usual habits and occupations, and life in the camps returned to its normal routine.

At last we were suddenly startled out of this feeling of security. One dark night the familiar terror-sticken cries and screams awoke the camps, and we knew that the "demons" had returned and had commenced a new list of victims. On this occasion a number of men had been sleeping outside their tents for the sake of coolness, thinking, of course, that the lions had gone for good, when suddenly in the middle of the night one of the brutes was discovered forcing its way through the *boma*. The alarm was at once given, and sticks, stones and firebrands were hurled in the direction of the intruder. All was of no avail, however, for the lion burst into the midst of the terrified group, seized an unfortunate wretch amid the cries and shrieks of his companions, and dragged him off through the thick thorn fence. He was joined outside by the second lion, and so daring had the two brutes become that they did not trouble to carry their victim any further away, but devoured him within thirty yards of the tent where he had been seized. Although several shots were fired in their direction by the *jemadar* of the gang to which the coolie belonged, they took no notice of these and did not attempt to move until their horrible meal was finished. The few scattered fragments that remained of the body I would not allow to be buried at once, hoping that the lions would return to the spot the following night; and on the chance of this I took up my station at nightfall in a convenient tree. Nothing occurred to break the monotony of my watch, however, except that I had a visit from a hyæna, and the next morning I learned that the lions had attacked another camp about two miles from Tsavo—for by this time the camps were again scattered, as I had works in progress all up and down the line. There the man-eaters had been successful in obtaining a victim, whom, as in the previous instance, they devoured quite close to the camp. How they forced their way through the *bomas* without making a noise was, and still is, a mystery to me; I should have thought that it was next to impossible for an animal to get through at all. Yet they continually did so, and without a sound being heard.

After this occurrence, I sat up every night for over a week near likely camps, but all in vain. Either the lions saw me and then went elsewhere, or else I was unlucky, for they took man after man from different places without ever once giving me a chance of a shot at them. This constant night watching was most dreary and fatiguing work, but I felt that it was a duty that had to be undertaken, as the men naturally looked to me for protection. In the whole of my life I have never experienced anything more nerve-shaking than to hear the deep roars of these dreadful monsters growing gradually nearer and nearer, and to know that some one or other of us was doomed to be their victim before morning dawned. Once they reached the vicinity of the camps, the roars completely ceased, and we knew that they were stalking for their prey. Shouts would then pass from camp to camp, *"Khabar dar, bhaieon, shaitan ata"* ("Beware, brothers, the devil is coming"), but the warning cries would prove of no avail, and sooner or later agonising shrieks would break the silence and another man would be missing from roll-call next morning.

I was naturally very disheartened at being foiled in this way night after night, and was soon at my wits' end to know what to do; it seemed as if the lions were really "devils" after all and bore a charmed life. As I have said before, tracking them through the jungle was a hopeless task; but as something had to be done to keep up the men's spirits, I spent many a weary day crawling on my hands and knees through the dense undergrowth of the exasperating wilderness around us. As a matter of fact, if I had come up with the lions on any of these expeditions, it was much more likely that they would have added me to their list of victims than that I should have succeeded in killing either of them, as everything would have been in their favour. About this time, too, I had many helpers, and several officers—civil, naval and military—came to Tsavo from the coast and sat up night after night in order to get a shot at our daring foes. All of us, however, met with the same lack of success, and the lions always seemed capable of avoiding the watchers, while succeeding at the same time in obtaining a victim.

I have a very vivid recollection of one particular night when the brutes seized a man from the railway station and brought him close to my camp to devour. I could plainly hear them crunching the bones, and the sound of their dreadful purring filled the air and rang in my ears for days afterwards. The terrible thing was to feel so helpless; it was useless to attempt to go out, as of course the poor fellow was dead, and in addition it was so pitch dark as to make it impossible to see anything. Some half a dozen workmen, who lived in a small enclosure close to mine, became so terrified on hearing the lions at their meal that they shouted and implored me to allow them to come inside my *boma*. This I willingly did, but soon afterwards I remembered that one man had been lying ill in their camp, and on making enquiry I found that they had callously left him behind alone. I immediately took some men with me to bring him to my *boma*, but on entering his tent I saw by the light of the lantern that the poor fellow was beyond need of safety. He had died of shock at being deserted by his companions.

From this time matters gradually became worse and worse. Hitherto, as a rule, only one of the man-eaters had made the attack and had done the foraging, while the other waited outside in the bush; but now they began to change their tactics, entering the *bomas* together and each seizing a victim. In this way two Swahili porters were killed during the last week of November, one being immediately carried off and devoured. The other was heard moaning for a long time, and when his terrified companions at last summoned up sufficient courage to go to his assistance, they found him stuck fast in the bushes of the *boma*, through which for once the lion had apparently been unable to drag him. He was still alive when I saw him next morning, but so terribly mauled that he died before he could be got to the hospital.

Within a few days of this the two brutes made a most ferocious attack on the largest camp in the section, which for safety's sake was situated within a stone's throw of Tsavo Station and close to a Permanent Way Inspector's iron hut. Suddenly in the dead of night the two man-eaters burst in among the terrified workmen, and even from my *boma,* some distance away, I could plainly hear the panic-stricken shrieking of the coolies. Then followed cries of "They've taken him; they've taken him," as the brutes carried off their unfortunate victim and began their horrible feast close beside the camp. The Inspector, Mr. Dalgairns, fired over fifty shots in the direction in which he heard the lions, but they were not to be frightened and calmly lay there until their meal was finished. After examining the spot in the morning, we at once set out to follow the brutes, Mr. Dalgairns feeling confident that he had wounded one of them, as there was a trail on the sand like that of the toes of a broken limb. After some careful stalking, we suddenly found ourselves in the vicinity of the lions, and were greeted with ominous growlings. Cautiously advancing and pushing the bushes aside, we saw in the gloom what we at first took to be a lion cub; closer inspection, however, showed it to be the remains of the unfortunate coolie, which the man-eaters had evidently abandoned at our approach. The legs, one arm and half the body had been eaten, and it was the stiff fingers of the other arm trailing along the sand which had left the marks we had taken to be the trail of a wounded lion. By this time the beasts had retired far into the thick jungle where it was impossible to follow them, so we had the remains of the coolie buried and once more returned home disappointed.

Now the bravest men in the world, much less the ordinary Indian coolie, will not stand constant terrors of this sort indefinitely. The whole district was by this time thoroughly panic-stricken, and I was not at all surprised, therefore, to find on my return to camp that same afternoon (December 1) that the men had all struck work and were waiting to speak to me. When I sent for them, they flocked to my *boma* in a body and stated that they would not remain at Tsavo any longer for anything or anybody; they had come from India on an agreement to work for the Government, not to supply food for either lions or "devils." No sooner had they delivered this ultimatum than a regular stampede took place. Some hundreds of them stopped the first passing train by throwing themselves on the rails in front of the engine, and then, swarming on to the trucks and throwing in their possessions anyhow, they fled from the accursed spot.

After this the railway works were completely stopped; and for the next three weeks practically nothing was done but build "lion-proof" huts for those workmen who had had sufficient courage to remain. It was a strange and amusing sight to see these shelters perched on the top of water-tanks, roofs and girders—anywhere for safety—while some even went so far as to dig pits inside their tents, into which they descended at night, covering the top over with heavy logs of wood. Every good-sized tree in the camp had as many beds lashed on to it as its branches would bear—and sometimes more. I remember that one night when the camp was attacked, so many men swarmed on to one particular tree that down it came with a crash, hurling its terror-stricken load of shrieking coolies close to the very lions they were trying to avoid. Fortunately for them, a victim had already been secured, and the brutes were too busy devouring him to pay attention to anything else.

SOME LITTLE TIME BEFORE the flight of the workmen, I had written to Mr. Whitehead, the District Officer, asking him to come up and assist me in my campaign against the lions, and to bring with him any of his *askaris* (native soldiers) that he could spare. He replied accepting the invitation, and told me to expect him about dinner-time on December 2, which turned out to be the day after the exodus. His train was due at Tsavo about six o'clock in the evening, so I sent my "boy" up to the station to meet him and to help in carrying his baggage to the camp. In a very short time, however, the "boy" rushed back trembling with terror, and informed me that there was no sign of the train or of the railway staff, but that an enormous lion was standing on the station platform. This extraordinary story I did not believe in the least, as by this time the coolies—never remarkable for bravery—were in such a state of fright that if they caught sight of a hyæna, or a baboon, or even a dog, in the bush, they were sure to imagine it was a lion; but I found out next day that it was an actual fact, and that both station-master and signalman had been obliged to take refuge from one of the man-eaters by locking themselves in the station building.

I waited some little time for Mr. Whitehead, but eventually, as he did not put in an appearance, I concluded that he must have postponed his journey until the next day, and so had my dinner in my customary solitary state. During the meal I heard a couple of shots, but paid no attention to them, as rifles were constantly being fired off in the neighbourhood of the camp. Later in the evening, I went out as usual to watch for our elusive foes, and took up my position in a crib made of sleepers which I had built on a big girder close to a camp which I thought was likely to be attacked. Soon after settling down at my post, I was surprised to hear the man-eaters growling and purring and crunching up bones about seventy yards from the crib. I could not understand what they had found to eat, as I had heard no commotion in the camps, and I knew by bitter experience that every meal the brutes obtained from us was announced by shrieks and uproar. The only conclusion I could come to was that they had pounced upon some poor unsuspecting native traveller. After a time I was able to make out their eyes glowing in the darkness, and I took as careful aim as was possible in the circumstances and fired; but the only notice they paid to the shot was to carry off whatever they were devouring and to retire quietly over a slight rise, which prevented me from seeing them. There they finished their meal at their ease.

As soon as it was daylight, I got out of my crib and went towards the place where I had last heard them. On the way, whom should I meet but my missing guest, Mr. Whitehead, looking very pale and ill, and generally dishevelled.

"Where on earth have you come from?" I exclaimed. "Why didn't you turn up to dinner last night?"

"A nice reception you give a fellow when you invite him to dinner," was his only reply.

"Why, what's up?" I asked.

"That infernal lion of yours nearly did for me last night," said Whitehead.

"Nonsense, you must have dreamed it!" I cried in astonishment.

For answer he turned round and showed me his back. "That's not much of a dream, is it?" he asked.

His clothing was rent by one huge tear from the nape of the neck downwards, and on the flesh there were four great claw marks, showing red and angry through the torn cloth. Without further parley, I hurried him off to my tent, and bathed and dressed his wounds; and when I had made him considerably more comfortable, I got from him the whole story of the events of the night.

It appeared that his train was very late, so that it was quite dark when he arrived at Tsavo Station, from which the track to my camp lay through a small cutting. He was accompanied by Abdullah, his sergeant of *askaris*, who walked close behind him carrying a lighted lamp. All went well until they were about half-way through the gloomy cutting, when one of the lions suddenly jumped down upon them from the high bank, knocking Whitehead over like a ninepin, and tearing his back in the manner I had seen. Fortunately, however, he had his carbine with him, and instantly fired. The flash and the loud report must have dazed the lion for a second or two, enabling Whitehead to disengage himself; but the next instant the brute pounced like lightning on the unfortunate Abdullah, with whom he at once made off. All that the poor fellow could say was: *"Eh, Bwana, simba"* ("Oh, Master, a lion"). As the lion was dragging him over the bank, Whitehead fired again, but without effect, and the brute quickly disappeared into the darkness with his prey. It was of course, this unfortunate man whom I had heard the lions devouring during the night. Whitehead himself had a marvellous escape; his wounds were happily not very deep, and caused him little or no inconvenience afterwards.

On the same day, December 3, the forces arrayed against the lions were further strengthened. Mr. Farquhar, the Superintendent of Police, arrived from the coast with a score of sepoys to assist in hunting down the man-eaters, whose fame had by this time spread far and wide, and the most elaborate precautions were taken, his men being posted on the most convenient trees near every camp. Several other officials had also come up on leave to join in the chase, and each of these guarded a likely spot in the same way, Mr. Whitehead sharing my post inside the crib on the girder. Further, in spite of some chaff, my lion trap was put in thorough working order, and two of the sepoys were installed as bait.

Our preparations were quite complete by nightfall, and we all took up our appointed positions. Nothing happened until about nine o'clock, when to my great satisfaction the intense stillness was suddenly broken by the noise of the door of the trap clattering down. "At last," I thought, "one at least of the brutes is done for." But the sequel was an ignominious one.

The bait-sepoys had a lamp burning inside their part of the cage, and were each armed with a Martini rifle, with plenty of ammunition. They had also been given strict orders to shoot at once if a lion should enter the trap. Instead of doing so, however, they were so terrified when he rushed in and began to lash himself madly against the bars of the cage, that they completely lost their heads and were actually too unnerved to fire. Not for some minutes—not, indeed, until Mr. Farquhar, whose post was close by, shouted at them and cheered them on—did they at all recover themselves. Then when at last they did begin to fire, they fired with a vengeance—anywhere, anyhow. Whitehead and I were at right angles to the direction in which they should have shot, and yet their bullets came whizzing all round us. Altogether they fired over a score of shots, and in the end succeeded only in blowing away one of the bars of the door, thus allowing our prize to make good his escape. How they failed to kill him several times over is, and always will be, a complete mystery to me, as they could have put the muzzles of their rifles absolutely touching his body. There was, indeed, some blood scattered about the trap, but it was small consolation to know that the brute, whose capture and death seemed so certain, had only been slightly wounded.

Still we were not unduly dejected, and when morning came, a hunt was at once arranged. Accordingly we spent the greater part of the day on our hands and knees following the lions through the dense thickets of thorny jungle, but though we heard their growls from time to time, we never succeeded in actually coming up with them. Of the whole party, only Farquhar managed to catch a momentary glimpse of one as it bounded over a bush. Two days more were spent in the same manner, and with equal unsuccess; and then Farquhar and his sepoys were obliged to return to the coast. Mr. Whitehead also departed for his district, and once again I was left alone with the man-eaters.

sixteen

TIGERS

by Peter Capstick Hathaway

ON THE BASIS THAT the great cats are pretty unquestionably the leaders of those terrestrial mammal forms that tend to snack on *Homo sapiens,* it follows that there's a pretty good body of opinion that the largest of these cats is probably the most successful as a man-eater. As far as the records indicate, this is true; or, it's true if the records themselves are true. The individual cat with the highest number of recorded human kills is the Champawat tigress who, after being chased out of Nepal in the first few years of the 20th century continued its career in the Himalayan foothills of India, finished with the round, simple, easy-to-remember official tally of 200 Nepalese souls. Arriving in the Naini Tal area of Jim Corbett, the Champawat tigress fell at last to the borrowed bullet of that great corrective dietician of man-eating leopards and tigers with the rather untidy and sloppy final bag number of 436 kills, which must have irked the hell out of the neater, officious types all over the *Raj.* Point is, we'll never know whether or not this tigress actually killed more people than her closest competition, the Panar leopard, with whom officialdom had its way, sentenced to moulder away in the history books with a nice, concise credit of precisely 400 Indian hill people.

Whatever the logistics, a grand total of 836 people shared between just two wild animals is still one hell of a lot of death!

Conjecture momentarily aside, there's no argument that a tiger turned to people-eating is one major flash of bad news. Personally, if forced to make a choice of having to try to sort out and kill A) a man-eating tiger; B) a man-eating leopard; C) a man-eating lion; or D) none of the above, beyond the obvious choice of the last category, I would far rather tackle the tiger. There is, in glaring contrast to most of my decision-making processes, some very solid logic behind this: what I know first-hand about wild tigers from personal experience would fit with great gaps of leftover space on a note of apology from Ivan the Terrible. I have never seen a wild tiger and probably never will. On the other hand, I have practically had lunch with far too many man-eating lions and leopards and they continue to scare the Holy Deuteronomy out of me. I would, on that basis, opt for the devil I don't know.

Practically every researcher involved with tigers discovers that the primary source of information on the subject of man-eating behavior in this species is Colonel Edward James Corbett, who wrote well and with the advantage of experience and perspective. Many books on the subject bear his authorship, including the immortal *Man-Eaters of Kumaon*. Well, except for acknowledging Corbett as the man who killed the two greatest man-eaters of all time, you may now go and pour a fresh brandy, snug in the knowledge that you have probably heard the last of *sahib* Corbett, at least as far as this chapter is concerned.

The tiger, that striped, sleek, sinuous symbol of the quiet, jungled Asian places, is the largest, strongest and unfortunately the most ecologically vulnerable of the race he tops, *Felidae*. Even more than a hundred years ago, before the internal combustion engine, he was so numerous that some experts, in retrospect, wonder today if there wasn't a point at which it was questionable whether man or the tiger would ultimately be the master of that sprawling continent. One authority quasi-documents that there may have been between a minimum of 300 and a maximum of 800 man-killing tigers operating at the same time just in India alone in the 1800s. Yet, as has been the cry of the anti-hunter far more interested in the sentiment his position represents than the facts of the matter, the question of the tiger is at least closer to the truth than that of any other species beyond the American bison, who was, unlike the tiger, not slaughtered by sportsmen but by official interests to break the economy of the Indian tribes. The truth about the decline of the tiger lies in three areas, two of them common contributors to wildlife downfall. First, habitat and the destruction thereof. Today, to create the perfect tiger sanctuary, an area of about 3,000 square miles would be needed—appropriately stocked with wild food—to accommodate about 300 breeding tigers. This would be roughly three times the size of Haiti. Of course, no people could be permitted to disrupt the arrangement with human habitation and climatic conditions would have to be right, offering fertile soil to provide vegetable food for prey. So, unless you know of a real estate agent who can put you on to a place with these requirements at a reasonable price in a starving world, you will see the hopelessness of trying to save the tiger in his natural surroundings in direct competition with man and his population explosion.

The second factor, although not in my opinion nearly as important as loss of habitat which seems to be primary to every species, is that of poaching and market hunting. As we have successfully proved and have had corroborated by the International Union for the Conservation of Nature and Natural Resources, the leopard has easily evaded poaching pressure throughout its range and has demonstrated an ability to adapt to constantly changing conditions for the worse in its environment. But, perhaps leopards are smarter than tigers, or maybe just smaller and less obvious. Tigers can weigh better than a quarter-ton and are considerably more highly profiled on the list of predators than the secretive, nocturnal leopard. In any case, the tiger has suffered terribly from *illegal* commercial pressure and fur collection which has led to drastic local population reductions.

Third, it is true—and important that the real sportsman realize that there were times, even recently, when such a thing could happen—that the tiger was over-shot for sport, albeit under governmental and social prestige conditions unlikely to exist elsewhere.

India is a strange and fascinating land, to a stranger a rather maggot-ridden enigma contrasting the very wealthy with the very needy in a degree rarely seen. The hard economic facts of life point up only too clearly that some people are smarter, luckier, stronger, more fortunately born or generally more successful than others, and *not* necessarily because they worked harder; keeping one's nose to the grindstone may produce either a bloody grindstone or a calloused nose, it rarely produces a princehood and a palace in India along with one's own stable of hunting elephants. Whatever the case, there were enough Indian nobles controlling enough land, local people and tiger hunting equipment, as well as having the spare time in which to indulge in the sport of tiger hunting to equate into bad news for poor old *Felis tigris*. Additionally, there were British troops in the country for generations and, along with pig-sticking and other forms of *shikar* (the sport of hunting, roughly translated) the most popular way for an officer to take his leave was to go tiger shooting. Between the Brits and the Maharajas, there's pretty good reason to believe that at least 100,000 tigers got the deep six over the past hundred years. (Personally, since this is only 1,000 per year, I can't see the harm.) Some researchers will tell you that this number was killed since the beginning of the 20th century alone, and, when we look at the number of survivors through the haze of now-settling dust of the great *Terai*, they might be right. Through the incredibly expensive machine that was the Indian tiger hunting establishment, official guesstimates (now a couple of years old) are that, in India, of the some 40,000 left about 1930, less than 2,000 may yet exist. Sumatra has less than 1,000 left, and Java, once a real stronghold, probably has less tigers than one of us has fingers and toes.

Some of these hunts, especially those organized by the Indians themselves for British or other foreign dignitaries, were for sure not the equivalent of a fast-food operation. Take, for example, the comments of one Captain Thomas Williamson in his *Oriental Field Sports* (Orme, presumably London, possibly Bombay, 1807). After 20 years in Bengal, which would bring his service back to at least the 1780s, Williamson describes a tiger "beat" or "drive" as using as many of 3,000 trained elephants, 30,000 to 40,000 (!) horses and unnumbered human beaters. The Indian nobility, who were the primary patrons of the emerging double-barreled British rifle trade, those most expensive of all heavy express rifles, encrusted with gold and engraving, (sometimes as many as six perfectly matched rifles being made to order for a particular potentate) had not yet the advantages of modern firearms. Still, bags of 30 or more tigers were not particularly rare in a single hunt.

Actually, consulting various journals and antique books, it becomes clearer where many of those tigers went: the Maharaja of Surguja in the late 1960s had personally killed 1,150 tigers by that date. One mere British Army major, hunting in his "spare time" in the State of Rajasthan, shot and killed or wounded over 150 tigers! Even King George V of Britain in a single *shikar* in 1911, personally put blue-edged .470 caliber dots between the stripes of an incredible 39 tigers.

Perhaps the last really big hooplah involving a member of the British Royal Family "coming out" for a state visit/tiger shoot was that of Queen Elizabeth II in 1961, who was a guest of the Government of Nepal. As might be expected, the Nepalese really pulled the plug!

The campsite for the exercise was reported as two miles square from which all insects and snakes were removed by hand and exterminated. Electric generators and even sprinkling systems were installed and the Queen, in the shade of a royal purple umbrella held over her head, led the hunting procession while riding behind the mahout of the lead elephant. In her not inconsiderable wake followed another entourage of 18 elephants and an undisclosed number of cars full of VIPs. The Queen, alas, was not a knock 'em, sock 'em tiger shot, but after several tries did manage to kill a smallish female, which monumentally irritated quite a few of the loyal bird watchers back home. Over the years, there has been, at least in my observation, in Britain a growing, and not very pleasant, feeling of shooting being more than simply a presumably horrid blood sport but a rite of the privileged; an occupation of the rich which has somehow clung to their socialist culture rather like some leftover conservative pterodactyl roosting bat-like in the national hall closet.

Of course, the equivalent of a full-dress rehearsal of the Battle of Waterloo was hardly necessary for the killing of a tiger or two. Among ordinary officers, a *Shikari* or Indian professional hunter was often employed under whose directions live baits, usually bullocks or buffalo calves, were tied out within shooting range of a tree platform called a *machan*. Theoretically, the tiger or tigress would collect an impressive series of perforations when it came to kill the bait or when it returned to feed on the carcass of the bait later.

In the context of *machan* hunting possibly appearing unsporting to the uninitiated tiger hunter, it should be pointed out that contrary to most beliefs, tigers can and do climb well, although not frequently. In fact, they've been reported as far as 60 feet above the ground in a tree. One man-eater, somehow captured, was released years ago into an enclosed arena by some Maharaja who apparently could think of nothing of greater interest that particular afternoon. The blood of a lot of tiger hunting onlookers must have been chilled about proper for serving champagne as the tiger scampered without the slightest hesitation 30 feet up a smooth limbless tree trunk.

Tigers are also pretty fair at climbing elephants to get at the hunter, and many's the chaperoo for whom the regimental band turned out next day to solemnize his funeral. This nasty habit of tigers charging the hunting elephants and reaching the shooting party atop, led in earlier days to the custom of carrying those peculiar pairs of heavy caliber handguns called Howdah pistols, so named for the *howdah* or platform fixed atop the elephant in which the hunters rode.

The third method of basic tiger hunting was to combine the first two, driving the tiger with beaters and, perhaps, elephants past an ambush point, commonly a *machan*. The main difference in this bit was that it always took place in daylight, whereas, waiting up over a bait, dead or alive, was normally a nocturnal affair. Concerning this last method and the potential hairiness thereof, I cannot resist recounting the incredible adventure during a beat shared by a Mr. and Mrs. E. A. Smythies, around Christmas, 1925, in India's Haldwani Division. It so nicely reflects the flavor of the time that I believe it best quoted directly from the Bombay Natural History Society's *Pioneer* of January 30, 1926.

"We were staying for Christmas in a good shooting block, and one night we had a kill by a tiger in one of the best small beats in the area. So my wife and I went off to the beat, and I fixed up two machans, my own in front, and hers about 40 yards to the right and behind, thus avoiding the risk of ricochets. Her machan was in the first fork of a tall cylindrical tree, 14 feet from the ground, the tree being 4 or 5 feet in girth. Just in front of my machan was a patch of heavy *narkal* grass about 25 yards in diameter, and there was a good deal of grass and undergrowth all round. Soon after, the beat started, and I heard a 'stop' clapping, and the tiger roared twice. About three minutes later, I heard it coming through the *narkal* grass, and presently it broke cover at a fast slouch. My weapon was a H. V. .404 Jeffrey magazine rifle, with which I have killed several tigers. I had 4 cartridges in the magazine and chamber and several more loose on the machan. As the tiger broke cover, I fired and missed, whereupon he rushed back into the *narkal*. Presently the beat came up to the *narkal*, and almost simultaneously the tiger again broke cover, this time at a full gallop with a terrific roar. I fired at it going away on my left and again missed. The beast went by my wife's machan at a gallop about 30 yards from her, and as soon as it had passed her, she fired and hit about 6 inches or so above the heart and just below the spine. This stopped it, and it rolled over roaring.

"Here the incredible part of the story begins. The tiger, mad with rage, turned round, saw her in the machan, and made for her, climbing the tree for all the world like a huge domestic cat, with its forearms almost encircling it. Up it went vertically under her machan, and as I turned round hurriedly, I knocked the loose cartridges out of my machan to the ground. As things were, I had no option but to take the risk of hitting my wife. I fired at the brute when it was half-way up the tree, but only grazed it. As I looked to work the bolt and reload, I realized I had only one cartridge left, and, looking up again, saw my wife standing up in the machan with the muzzle of her rifle in the tiger's mouth—his teeth marks are 8 inches up the barrel—and he was holding on to the edge of the machan with his forepaws and chin. In this position she pulled the trigger—and had a misfire! You must realize that at least two-thirds of the tiger's weight was now on the machan, for, except for his back claws, he was hanging out from the tree by the width of the machan, which was rocking violently from his efforts to get on to it. The next thing I saw was my wife lose her balance and topple over backwards, on the side away from the tiger.

"The beast did not seem to notice her disappearance, and, as I again aimed at him, I saw him still clawing and biting the machan—the timber was almost bitten through, and the strings torn to shreds. I fired my last available cartridge, and, by the mercy of Heaven, the bullet went true. It took the tiger in the heart and he crashed over backwards on to the ground immediately below the machan, where he lay hidden from view in the grass. I did not know at the time that he was dead; nor of course did my wife. All I knew was that my wife had disappeared from the machan on one side of the tree and the tiger on the other, and that I had no cartridges left; and that I was helpless for the moment to give any further assistance.

"Whether my predicament was as bad as my wife's can be judged from her view of the incident. I quote her words:—'When I fired again, he turned round and saw me, and immediately dashed, roaring, towards my tree. I thought he was galloping past, but suddenly realized that he was climbing up, and only just had time to stand up in the machan before his great striped face and paws appeared over the edge, and his blood and hot breath came up to me with his roaring. I pushed the barrel of my rifle into his mouth and pulled the trigger, but the rifle would not go off. Then I really did feel helpless and did not know what to do. We had a regular tussle with the rifle and then I saw his paw come up through the bottom of the machan, and, stepping back to avoid it, I must have stepped over the edge of the machan, for I felt myself falling. I thought I was falling into the jaws of the tiger and it flashed through my mind "Surely I am not going to be killed like this." I never felt hitting the ground at all and the next thing I knew was that I was running through grass and over fallen trees, wondering when the tiger would jump on me.'

"She arrived at my tree almost simultaneously with the mahawat, Bisharat Ali, who had rushed up his elephant, regardless of wounded tigers or anything else, and she hastily mounted and cleared off into safety, unhurt except for a sprained wrist and various scratches and bruises from the fall. One of the 'stops' was calling that he could see the tiger and that it was lying dead under the machan. So, when a supply of cartridges arrived, I went up cautiously and verified his statement, recovered my wife's hat and rifle, and went off with her to the forest bungalow, leaving the 'stops' to bring in the tiger.

"It was a nice male 9 ft. 3 ins. in length with three bullets in it, one between the heart and spine, one cutting the bottom of the chest, and one in the heart. It will be a long time before we try and get another! This is a plain unvarnished account of an incident which must, I think, be unique in the annals of tiger shooting. At least, I have never heard of a lady being hurled out of a high machan by a climbing tiger and her husband killing it up in the air with his last cartridge."

The tiger as a man-eater varies clearly in several areas of technique and habit compared with both the lion, his largest rival in size, and the leopard, the differences concerning the latter cat and the tiger covered, at least from the basis of Jim Corbett's viewpoint, in the leopard chapter of this book. I know I promised not to bring Corbett back into this, so hope I may be forgiven for a couple of purely peripheral observations simply because that individual did his man-eater hunting under conditions that no longer exist and are thus interesting as a point of comparison. Yet, before we gits over our 'ips, it's best we have a look at the tiger on his own before comparing him with any relatives.

I suspect, without running tallies on my pocket calculator, that with the exception of the leopard, the tiger was, until very recent times (as close as 50 years) the most widely distributed of the great cats. Old African hands, I can assure you, have never had to do battle with the widely envisioned "lions and tigers" as perceived by the general public. True, the lion was within the past 200 years widely distributed in Asia and even India, but now exists in that subcontinent only in the Gir Forest where it is distinguished by little more than a slightly broader muzzle than the standard East African issue or is perhaps identical, dependent upon whose taxomony one chooses as gospel. If you think the tiger has problems, the Asian lion must have originated the principle of diminishing prospects. Things don't look good for the few left, heavily protected or not.

I was, however, reasonably surprised upon reading in the late paleoanthropologist Louis S. B. Leakey's 1969 book, *Animals of East Africa*, a part of the National Geographic Society "Wild Realm" series, that there probably *were* tigers in East Africa based upon a fossil jaw recovered from Bed II in 1957, from the now famous Olduvai Gorge.

This largely contradicts—or appears to—the idea that since tigers do very nicely in freezing weather and obviously suffer from the heat of much of their current range, often lying in the water or very deep shade during the heat of the day, that they were originally predators of the far north, gradually filtering south.

Putting the tiger and the lion in the same ball-park points up some interesting comparisons. Perhaps it's not the most logical first consideration, but lions are still doing a pretty good business because there didn't happen to be any Maharajas in Africa, although the British equivalent of U.S. $150 worth of Denis D. Lyell's improbably titled *African Adventure*. (John Murray, London, First Edition, 1935) points out that few men since, for an arbitrary date, 1890, and the date of publication (when lions were considered vermin over much of their territory) ever shot many more than 50 or so, despite their fame as hunters. A couple are guessed by presumably unbiased contemporaries at around 200, but I strongly suspect this a bit high for a guesstimate. One very highly respected lion hunter opined that it would be impossible to hunt and kill on foot 100 lions and stand a chance of surviving. I'm inclined to agree. They sho' does bite!

Further, the history of Africa is not built around the sociality of abundant labor such as India, steeped in the pigeon-holing that the caste system could provide. There were no real beats, hunting elephants, drivers and the rest of the *pukka* rot that brought down the tiger. Had there been, the lion would be nothing but a remote memory. He's a social animal, living lazily and generally ineffectively in groups still called "prides."

I remember very well an incident told me by the late Peter Hankin who was himself a victim of a man-eating lioness. With one client and a couple of his staff, he was tracking what looked to be a very big male lion. It showed up at close range on a rocky, heavily vegetated hill, apparently on cue for the client's bullet. Peter, however, gifted with what I always think of as prudent peripheral vision, urgently suggested that the client not shoot. When asked to desist at the rates Peter was charging, *bwana* Hankin pointed out, I believe, 22 *other* lions who were taking a rather intense interest in the proceedings. That, ladies and gentlemen and members of the press, is a lot of lions. Mr. Hankin and his paying guest did an excellent job of respooring to the Land Rover and returned to camp where I presume they had the sense to drink something suitably fortifying.

I once walked good-morning-madam neat into six most irritated lions, none of which showed any indication of a need for dentures, and I will not forget it quickly. Another night, in Ethiopia, I had a running, score-less skirmish with at least eleven visible lions. The odd thing about large collections of well-maned lions is the uncanny way they have of turning up immediately after your client has shot one that looks as if it just left a Hari Krishna barber shop. While your lion looks like the before picture in an ad for mange cure, the assembled pride all sport manes that would cause them to be instantly hired by MGM or the Where-To-Go section of a sporting magazine. Tigers, on the other hand, are notably unsocial and rarely embarrass Indian *shikaris*.

It appears high time that we got into the tiger as a processor of people meat rather than trying to pass his chapter off as *The Child's Guide To Garden Carnivora*. To be perfectly honest, I don't know what I'd do with-out "Table Two" of Peter Turnbull-Kemp's "Age and Condition Data on 241 Known Man-eaters at Death" to be found in *The Leopard* (Howard Timmins, Cape Town, 1967) which I have no knowledge of having been reproduced elsewhere than South Africa. Turnbull-Kemp is a great writer who, handily enough, writes about my favorite animal, the leopard, in terms that only a professional game ranger or hunter could. I repeat that I know not if the volume has been reproduced for sale in other countries, but if you want my copy, acquired under duress in Botswana, you had better come armed. . . .

The point of this exercise is that the tiger is definitely of a different man-eating temperament (nonetheless deadly, though) and of apparently different collective motive than the lion or the leopard.

On a practical basis, let me demonstrate, courtesy of *Nkosi* Peter and his superb table, what I mean.

The data is based upon what Turnbull-Kemp considers reliable infor-mation, which is good enough for me. In his short introduction in this portion of the book (Chapter Ten) before the Table, he points out the ob-vious differences between lions, leopards and tigers as man-eaters on many bases, although both tigers and leopards are correctly considered "solitary" insomuch as they do not display group behavior as do lions.

Based upon a breakdown of confirmed man-eaters, a sampling of which was composed of 89 lions, 74 tigers, and 78 leopards, it's difficult to find a statistical variation in validity of what I seem to remember as "reliable sampling." Perhaps it would be literary piracy, but considering the completely statistical nature of the table, by Turnbull-Kemp's own commentary assembled from other sources, I would like to extract the obvious differences in categorical behavior from lions, leopards and tigers.

The first screaming difference in percentages expressed as statistics is in the initial category, concerning "age." Of the tigers, age, as subdivided by Uninjured / Injured by Man / Other Factors (presumably porcupine quills, etc.) / and Teeth Affected by Age; the tiger glows as if radioactive as being the most reticent of the man-eaters. The totals for the previous groupings for lions was a mere 18 percent. For leopard, the great hunter, it was even down to 11.5 percent. But, for the tiger, it was a dizzy 55.1 percent! Conclusion? Sick, injured, old tigers eat people on a percentage basis far more frequently than do the nice, healthy sleek tigers.

Interestingly, it was the leopards that clearly took the lead among "Mature" man-eaters, most especially those who were "Uninjured." Under the heading "Mature, Uninjured," the leopard swept the contest with an 84.7 percent correlation, whereas the tiger rated only 47.3 percent and the lion but 32.6 percent. This is a critical statistic because it tends to bear out the concept which I, at least, champion, that the leopard is a natural, matter-of-fact, everyday man-eater of primates, be they baboons, gorilla young, monkeys, chimps or people.

The "Immature" category (three years or under) goes to the lion over the tiger by nearly triple; 49.4 percent against 17.6 percent. The leopard hardly counts, with only two immature, uninjured cats involved out of 78, only 2.5 percent. One of the obvious reasons for this is the same as why we don't tend to have waves of maneating from Siamese cats: they're too small. A leopard at less than three years would not be inclined to take on game as big as a man.

After having waded barefoot through all those fang-studded statistics, I suppose it's time to draw some conclusions. The first, and most pertinent to this tiger chapter, is that the tiger, once he's had some practice, is pretty fair at his man-eating trade, but he's not as inclined to become involved as is the lion or leopard. It would appear, contrary to the reports of African hunters on man-eaters contemporary with Corbett's Asian experience, that the tiger is statistically different from the lion and leopard, at least on the basis of Turnbull-Kemp's *Table Two*. To justify the conclusion reached by Corbett that only tigers incapacitated through injury (infected porcupine quills, gunshot wounds, etc.) ever turn to man-eating were his own experiences. Every man-eating cat he killed was or had been partially crippled. As we've seen, this is by no means the case with the lion or leopard, and seems to be less the case with the modern tiger. But, at least at the turn of the previous century, man-eating tigers appear to have been generally injured.

One point covered by *Table Two* does point up a similarity to some degree between lions and tigers. Although the lion had a slightly larger sampling, and the animals studied were killed much more recently than Corbett's dozen or so tigers, both species were within about 5 percent of each other in terms of condition at death. Of 74 tigers, 59 or about 75 percent were in "good" condition. In the case of the lions, 67 out of 89 were ranked the same, which is about 80 percent. It's interesting to note, however, that almost 94 percent of the 78 leopards were in fine fettle. But, then, why not? People are notoriously nutritious.

If your interest runs to the man-eaters of old, there are reams of books from which to choose, although they might these days be considered almost capital investments! Corbett is the primer and most libraries carry at least some of his work, and much more is available through secondhand booksellers. On the reasoning that if I advise the purchase of, for example, the Corbett omnibus, *Man-Eaters of India* (Oxford Press, New York, 1957), I should also vent my extremely low-profiled opinion that one is better without Kenneth Anderson, who, in my personal consideration, is a bad imitation of Corbett. He closely followed Colonel Jim, literarily, and wrote to formula such blood-curdling chapters as entitled by the stirring sobriquets of "The Striped Terror of Chamala Valley" or "The Spotted Devil of Gummlapur," "The Mauler of Rajnagara" and even the "Marauder of Kempekari." There is a name for much of this material which, according to a friend of mine, certainly not me, is synonymous with that matter which issues from the south end of a bull heading north. Unfortunately, I tend to see Mr. Anderson quoted in truly erudite works of large *carnivora* being as gospel as Baby Jesus and Sunday morning. If you should doubt my observations, note that of Mr. Anderson's three books of which I am aware, *The Black Panther of Sivanipalli, Man-Eaters and Jungle Killers* and his first, *Nine Man-Eaters and One Rogue* (the rogue presumably thrown in in case the reader tired of man-eaters) all are by different publishers, chronologically E. P. Dutton, New York, 1955; Thomas Nelson and Sons, New York, 1957; and finally George Allen & Unwin, Ltd., 1959; the American edition by Rand McNally in 1961.

To be completely frank, for every hour I spend at what Ruark called the "Iron Maiden" pounding out material, I spend at least five in research, digging out reliable tales such as the one you just read concerning Mr. and Mrs. E. A. Smythies. Do you have any idea what is involved in getting hold of a copy of the January 30, 1926 issue of the Bombay Natural History Society's *Pioneer*? Ha! And you think hardback books are getting expensive? That's why I am not about to give away any more source material on early people eaten by tigers. Anyway, you might not buy my next book if I did!

Today is another matter. I know, whaddya mean today! You thought I said that the tiger has been closed down as a species, eliminated as a menace, terminated as a threat to man. Nope. They still bite.

If your sentiments toward endangered species *really* run deep, I mean past the button-wearing stage, may I gently suggest that you visit that gem of tropic charm, the emerald necklace of the Bay of Bengal where the Ganga Mai, the Gangese, and the Brahmaputra Rivers enter the sea, that charming little corner of torrid hell known as the Sundarbans. Who knows, even today you might give your all—literally—to an endangered species.

Okay, let's not lose our perspective: you are not likely to be eaten by one or more tigers even if you happen to be an Indian woodcutter, although if such is the case the odds have vastly improved. Still, the really "in" place for getting eaten by *Panthera tigris* is the Sundarbans, which is sort of odd because they're not particularly attractive to man nor beasts, being mostly mangrove swamp islands or, as it is pronounced where I live at the edge of the Florida Everglades, *"Swowmp."*

I have a suspicion that any place the Gangese and Brahmaputra get together could not be much more unsanitary than ebb tide at Coney Island. Well, whatever the reason, the region appeals to tigers to beat hell. Largely mangrove, which proves that tigers are not guilty of either forethought or judgment, the Sundarbans still have the reputation of being the most likely place to get tigered that comes immediately to mind beyond having a pass key at the Bronx Zoo. In fact, the whole area has been famous since the first European exposure as being notorious for maneaters, reports going back to the mid-1600s of tigers actually swimming out to sea, climbing aboard boats and eating folks. In fact, these reports are so strung-out and consistent that their veracity can't really be reasonably doubted. According to Ricciuti, presumably quoting another source, 275 people were taken by tigers between 1961 and 1971 in the Sundarbans and at least five lives were taken during the month of April, 1973, when the local people were hunting honey.

During the Vietnamese conflict, there were several cases of genuine tiger attack on U.N. Troops, including Americans. In fact, one of the most realistic portrayals of the stealth and surprise factor of a big cat like a tiger was in the hit movie, *Apocalypse Now*, which you probably saw, and which had an excellent tiger scene. Unquestionably, soldiers from both sides were killed and eaten by tigers—as well as by leopards—and much of this may have been generated by the abandonment of bodies in the jungle when fire-fights or other conditions made body retrieval impractical. The tiger is no less a scavenger than the lion.

It has been postulated that, over the last 400 years, at least a half-million Indians alone have been eaten by tigers and, considering the vastness of Asia, the totals of humans must run several times that number. Today, it is common to think of the "Bengal" tiger as being the predominant species or subspecies, however, there are other branches of the family well worth noting. The Siberian snow tiger is the largest of the clan and, although it's stock is sinking like the rest, is certainly an impressive creature by any standard.

There is a reliable tradition that, in Russia, in the *taiga*, that marvelously mysterious veil of evergreens that so fascinated the late zoologist, Ivan Sanderson, to the extent that he believed all sorts of presumed extinct animals might live there, the tiger yet holds a traditional sway if not physical. It would seem that it was a custom of the Cossacks to lash criminals to certain trees as punishment of a one-way variety: tigers were familiar with the trees and ate the offenders, probably developing regrettable manners in the meanwhile.

The tiger, as a man-eater, although astonishingly effective, is probably the least *innately* offensive of the great cats that are established as eaters of men, the truth lying more on the side of the historical traditionalist inasmuch as the majority do seem to prefer nonhuman fare. Unfortunately, the tiger turned man-eater is very possibly the most dangerous animal on earth. If you have any doubt, see how many survivors there were of the Champawat tigress.

I think you get my point.

seventeen

THE LAST SHOT COUNTS

by John H. Brandt in collaboration with Pat Byrne

DURING THE WANING YEARS of World War II the focus of the world was on far more lofty events than to be concerned about a terrorized group of villagers in a remote corner of India. Villagers too frightened to gather wood, too terrified to till their fields or drive cattle to pasture. Too paralyzed with fear to even venture out to market unless every such activity could be undertaken in large groups to assure protection at least to a minimal degree. The inattention to such matters continued on during the years of euphoria related to Indian Independence. During this traumatic period some 2½ million Muslims and Hindus died in search of their political destinies. The government could not really be blamed for neglecting the deaths of a few dozen illiterate natives. But for those unfortunates who lived in the depths of the Orrissa forests in eastern India the word *"Sher,"* "tiger," struck fear such as no city dwellers could ever comprehend. Especially when the tiger, for whatever reasons, took on the grisly custom of killing people and eating human flesh. Such was the case for an unusually long period of horror in the general vicinity of a small place called Phulbani.

Lest someone think such events are only happenings of the past, as I write this (1993) a man-eating tiger is again stalking the area of Koraput in Orrissa, and man-eaters and man-killers, both tiger and leopard, will take an annual toll in rural India of dozens of victims. Villagers now may have access to TV and more motor vehicles stir dust on the rural roads than before, but the silent death awaiting those who must, of necessity, venture into the forests and other remote rural areas, is no different. Although death by any definition may be unpleasant, a more horrible death than to be pulled down by a man-eater is hard for anyone to envision.

The tally of lives lost to the tiger, which became known as the Sudrukumpa Man-eater, came close to 400 and equalled some of the most notorious man-eaters killed by the famous Jim Corbett some twenty years earlier. Why this claim to notoriety was not recorded deserves telling.

Had the beast been slain by a prominent sportsman, international hunter, or a politically and socially well ensconced individual, there is no doubt that the killer of the Sudrukumpa Man-eater would have been acclaimed and stories documented, told and retold, with all appropriate recognition to the person who removed this terror from the area and allowed life to return to a more tranquil state. Neither my colleague and mentor, the famous tiger hunter, Pat Byrne, of Calcutta, nor I, was the slayer of this beast although we both would have been delighted in this accomplishment. All too often the best efforts of important professional hunters are unsuccessful and the old hunting adage of "being in the right place at the right time" comes into being when some novice, through no concerted effort on his part, stumbles into the tiger, through dumb luck, and kills it. I guess we must remember that no one ever said life was fair.

This particular man-eater met another fate and, because of the circumstances of its death, dropped away into literary obscurity. A small, turbaned, village *Shikari*, named Dhondopani, with a homemade muzzle loader that most of us would fear to pull the trigger on, possessed that irreplaceable courage to face instant death and come away the victor. Also, he was the person in the right place at the right time. He will be remembered, but probably only in the village where the deaths occurred and the name, Dhondopani, will soon only be recalled in tales around the evening fires in the small village of Sudrukumpa, from where he came. His name was never known to the outside world and his stature as a respected

Shikari will only stay in the memories of those who knew the sequence of events which led to his brief moment of recognition.

It all began one evening on a more normal tiger hunt in the deep Sal forests surrounding the Dak Bungalow at Sonawani in central India. Pat and I chewed on our pipe stems belching out clouds of foul tobacco smoke as we sat close to the fire on a cold night in January. The local help, staying discreetly on the outer perimeter of the firelight, wrapped in their white dhotis, listened carefully as the story of the Sudrukumpa Man-eater was told.

On a late morning in December 1944, a contractor named Marattah, had gone to survey some road construction work at the Vetkhal Ghat. Completing his routine survey, he mounted his bicycle to ride back a short distance to his home in Phulbani. He had barely reached his house when some of his workers, yelling loudly, ran down the road to join him. Breathlessly they informed him that not ten minutes after his departure and only a few yards from where he had completed his paper work, a tiger had attacked, killed and carried off his crew chief.

Quickly grabbing a single barreled shotgun he returned with the workers to the construction site and began casting around for tracks or blood. These soon led him to the bottom of a small hill where it was evident that the tiger had started his meal with bits of bone, flesh and blood stained clothing scattered about. The group, with Marattah in the fore, followed carefully along the trail the disturbed tiger had taken. Soon however, the adrenalin wore off, and logic prevailed over misguided courage, as the trail led into a densely wooded ravine. Prudently they decided to call off the search and report the death to the Phulbani police station. No further evidence or recovery of the crew chief's body was ever made.

When news of the tiger attack, within three miles of the town, reached the village, instant terrified paralysis set in. Shops closed early, and few people ventured out after dark unless it was in a large crowd whose numbers conferred comfort to overcome fear. The Phulbani police made a few unsuccessful efforts to locate the tiger but not being hunters they soon came to recognize their limitations and the year ended with no further killings. The beginning of the New Year soon changed that complacency.

During January, several people were killed along a twenty-two mile stretch of roads from the Vetkhal Ghat to the beginning of the nearby Ranspathan Ghat. The area is hilly and densely wooded and although normal prey animals such as Sambar, Chital and Boar were common, the tiger apparently was directing his gourmet interests to more gruesome fare.

During that time a man from Mulkipore Village, named Madhu, left his home early one morning to collect palm sap, locally called *"Rosso."* Two of his brothers in the village remained behind but not wanting to miss out on the labors of their brother, they went to his hut in mid-day to see if he would share with them. When they found he had not come back they inquired as to his whereabouts from other family members. When everyone realized that Madhu should have returned long ago, the whole group became suddenly silent and began looking about apprehensively.

Someone, perhaps with more confidence than the others, suggested they form a search party to at least get some of the *"rosso"* before Madhu consumed it all. The others were more realistic and no one laughed at the poorly timed joke. All harbored a cold chill in their innards already anticipating what they might find.

The group of some ten men walked toward the place in the forest where the palms grew and soon found two of Madhu's pots, one full and the other empty. They puzzled over why Madhu had left a full pot and had not replaced the empty one on the palm to collect the sap drippings. With no apparent answer they called loudly and spread out looking for signs. Although the man-eater had until then not killed anyone from their village, all the men knew of the tiger and soon everyone assumed some tragedy had befallen Madhu. They were quickly to find what it was.

They located another collecting pot along with some leaves folded in the manner that the villagers used as a drinking cup. One of the leaves was still wet, as if recently used.

Near the end of a small hill one of the searchers found horrifying evidence that something terrible had happened to Madhu when he saw entangled on a bush, a blood-stained *dhoti* such as Madhu had been wearing. Not far below in a rocky gully, another searcher found what they had feared most. Only portions of Madhu's body remained. The tiger had consumed over half of him.

As they gazed in petrified horror at the body, the tiger suddenly roared in the bush nearby and in one mass movement the entire group charged, as one, back up the trail to the village where they soon arrived bruised and shaken. Others in the village began beating drums and gathering axes and farm implements to serve as weapons in case the tiger had followed the men. No one had looked back in their flight to see if the tiger was behind them. Perhaps no one really wanted to know. The important lesson was not to be the last person in the rapid retreat.

When calm had again returned, the villagers decided that a delegation should go to the village of Sudrukumpa to enlist the help of two local *Shikaris* that possessed muzzle-loading weapons. Bolstered by this new fire power, inadequate though it may seem by modern standards, the group returned to the hill site but found that the tiger had removed the remains of his victim. After several hours they gave up the search and dejectedly returned home to mourn Madhu's death.

A week later, three brothers, Bhimo, Basso and Khusso, from the nearby village of Sudraja, undertook a journey to another small community named Tikripara, to buy a new plow buffalo. They passed through Sudrukumpa on the way and the villagers there cautioned them about the man-eater although by then virtually everyone in the area was already aware of the dreaded presence of the tiger.

Several more men, seeking the security of a larger group, joined them and although the party decided to take a short cut to Tikripara, which went through a densely jungled area, they arrived safely with no sign of the tiger.

Completing the purchase of their new buffalo the following morning, the three brothers set out for the return walk to Sudraja. Prodding the reluctant buffalo before them they soon reached the shortcut junction which lead through the forested area they had crossed the preceding day. Here the buffalo made it known that he had no desire to proceed beyond this point and all efforts to push him on failed. Unaware that there was any danger, Khusso stepped to the side of the road to pick up a stout branch to get the buffalo to change his mind. A huge tiger suddenly jumped on Khusso and with one swipe of his paw slammed him to the ground.

Bhimo, with great courage, jumped forward at extreme risk to himself and dealt the tiger a blow on its head with the blunt side of his axe. The startled tiger dropped Khusso and bounded away but in that brief instant a fatal bite had already been made and Khusso bled to death before the brothers could get him to a village for help. The killer did not return and the blow to the head was obviously also a new experience for the beast. All the previous human victims had proven to be such easy prey.

The police at Phulbani made a record of the new kill but everyone knew that unless some action was soon taken the situation would only get worse.

Two weeks after Khusso's death, a party of villagers enroute to the Phulbani Market was attacked by a tiger in mid-morning. The tiger ran off with the screaming victim in his teeth until the momentarily mesmerized group collected themselves and gave chase. Not to be deprived of his now limp kill, the tiger turned with the man still hanging from his jaws and loudly growled. This was more than the unarmed group could take and they turned and ran for their lives lest the tiger considered a second morsel more appetizing than the first!

At weekly or bi-monthly intervals the killings continued into a dreadfully monotonous routine. Villagers remained behind barricaded doors after dark and few dared venture out into their gardens or pastures to do the farming chores so necessary for life. With horrible resignation and numb apprehension the villagers would pass the days hoping that something or someone could bring an end to the man-eater. By this time the Phulbani police had recorded nearly 200 deaths attributed to the Sudrukumpa Man-eater.

At that time I was hunting near the Tarasingha Forest Bungalow and since my hunting permit was about to expire I proceeded to Russelkhonda, (which became known as Bhanjanagar after Independence) where I intended to spend a few more days. I was soon approached by local officials requesting my help in tracking down the man-eater. A letter of confirmation went to the Phulbani Special Agent and a prompt reply saying "Please come at once" was returned to me that same evening. Two days later I set up my headquarters for the hunt at the Sudrukumpa Reserve Bungalow in the center of the area where most of the killings had occurred. I spent the first several days interviewing relatives of the dead and generally familiarizing myself with the area. I drove many of the forest roads at night but saw no signs of the man-eater. Although no new kills had occurred for some time a villager showed me tracks on a road nearby of a large male tiger, well past his prime, which we assumed were the tracks of the killer.

Two village *Shikaris*, Dhondopani and Krishna, who were fully familiar with the area, accompanied me on the patrols. We pulled into the village of Sudraja, where two people had already been killed, and found the place in a high state of agitation. Dhondopani got a man aside and in questioning him we found that just prior to our arrival some villagers who had ventured out to gather firewood had seen the tiger on a hillside above them. Thoroughly frightened they had all run back before the tiger could attempt to make a kill. The timing of our arrival could not have been better. Dhondopani carried a shotgun and the other *Shikari*, Krishna, a disreputable-looking muzzle loader. I was armed with a 10.75 Mauser. Proceeding cautiously we soon reached the hillside where the tiger was nowhere to be found. Since the sun was going down quickly and none of us wanted to be out after dark with the man-eater in the vicinity, we struck a quick pace to cover the six miles back to Sudrukumpa which we reached without further incidence.

The following morning accompanied by Dhondopani, we returned to Sudruja where the headman informed us that the villagers had decided to abandon the place if any more killings occurred. I tried to assure them that every effort would be made to protect them and trying to bolster their confidence, a sensation I didn't personally feel very strongly, I proceeded on to Vetkhal.

A few miles from Sudruja we met a party of men on the road who had stopped and were staring into a clearing in the forest. They informed us that they were coming to tell us that a kill had occurred some seven miles west of Vetkhal, at a small hamlet known as Bundi. They were stopped at the moment because one of the group thought he had seen a tiger across the clearing and they feared they were now being stalked. Everyone seemed sincerely happy that we had arrived when we did!

Since every tiger, no matter how normal its behavior, was now suspect,

I went to check out the tracks and felt fairly comfortable in judging that the paw marks appeared similar to the splayed out tracks of the man-eater that had been pointed out to me earlier. Since no useful purpose could be served in trying to track a tiger in dense bush we returned to the group of men still waiting for us on the road. Too frightened to continue on, the group asked if I might drive them to Vetkhal. Loading twelve villagers, plus myself and the *Shikaris* into the vehicle, we presented a site so ludicrous that even the man-eater might have been tempted to smirk!

Arriving home well after sunset we were serenaded periodically throughout the night by loud roars on the adjoining hills which I felt sure were being made by the man-eater.

The tiger made no reported kills for several days and although I frequently ran across his tracks or other signs of his presence he apparently managed to successfully kill some other normal prey animal.

For well over a week no further news of the man-eater was heard and I felt that I had to leave and get on with other neglected facets of my life. I told the villagers I would return as soon as possible and although they were terribly upset on being left again to the mercies of the man-eater I knew that they realized I had done the best I could and I felt as bad as they that the man-eater was still patrolling in the area. I turned the remaining bait buffalo, that I had periodically unsuccessfully staked out, over to Dhondopani, and left the area for home stopping to advise the officials in Phulbani that I intended to return for another try at the man-eater but that I couldn't set a time. Unable to do much on their own, they assured me that they would welcome my early return.

Several weeks after my departure, a young woman named Mala, about to be married, went to gather flowers in preparation for the wedding ceremony. Accompanied by family members she approached a flowering tree when suddenly a tiger pounced on her from its hiding place behind a boulder and carried her off. Quickly raising the alarm, the two local *Shikaris*, Dhondopani and Krishna, gave chase accompanied by a number of village men. Throwing stones and shouting loudly brought a roar of response from the tiger which left its kill and bounded away up a slope. Both hunters fired their weapons and were confident that some of the slugs had hit the beast since it had reacted with a fierce growl. The party retrieved the remains of the ill-fated girl and carried her back to the village. The wedding was not to be and the village households went into mourning instead. The report filed the next day with the Phulbani police added one more victim to the ever growing file of "Unnatural Deaths" attributed to the Sudrukumpa Man-eater.

Again, for many weeks nothing was heard of the man-eater and the *Shikaris* hoped that perhaps their slugs had hit something vital and that the man-eater had died someplace from its wounds.

The hot season had now started and in the village of Duarpalli, the resident priest, Tuli, suggested to his son that they should go up the hillside together to gather leaves as fodder for their three buffalos. The son declined the offer and as evening approached it was soon apparent that Tuli had not come back. An old village woman volunteered the fact that she had seen him go up the hill alone with a basket and an axe. The two armed *Shikaris* were summoned, and with a retinue of villagers following them, proceeded up the hill calling out loudly. Only silence and echoes answered their calls. At dark still no sign of Tuli had been found and the villagers decided to call off the search till morning.

Dhondopani and Krishna split the searchers into two groups and soon Krishna's party found a fragment of bloody garment hooked in a thorn bush. A short distance away they found Tuli's basket, filled with leaves, and his axe but no trace of the priest was found then or later. Tiger tracks were evident and everyone felt convinced that the man-eater had taken another victim.

Other killings followed, as the seasonal monsoons began, including a village teacher in Tikripara who was killed in full view of his students in the small village school.

On August 15th of that year the colonial rule of the British Raj came to an end. Major changes in rural administration took place all over India. Phulbani became designated as the headquarters for a new district with a Deputy Commissioner. The man-eater however conveniently ignored such political berthing processes as the local death toll approached the 250 mark.

Late that year, as winter was well underway, I returned to Bhanjanagar and was, through mutual acquaintances, introduced to the Patio of

Nuagam who invited me to spend Christmas with him. After a few weeks as the guest of the Patio, I received a summons to again go to Sudrukumpa and was informed that the tiger's death toll had now reached 278. I left Nuagam and arrived on the twice weekly bus in Phulbani where I received a briefing update on events involving the man-eater. From Phulbani it was a short half hour drive to Sudrukumpa and I was soon back at the village bungalow only to find it locked and unused.

I walked into the main village and located the *chowkidar* (watchman) who opened up the building while I went off in search of someone willing to gather firewood for me. Two young men volunteered to gather, provided I went with them to guard against any attack by the tiger of which they continued to live in daily dread.

A short distance up the road we came to a large tree that had fallen across the now largely unused path. Few villagers had wandered here for fear of the tiger and the dry branches I felt, would make good kindling. Suddenly, my two companions stopped, and wide-eyed with terror they said they had seen movement beyond the tree and were sure it was the tiger preparing to attack us. I looked long and carefully, checking the safety on my rifle several times in the process, but could see nothing. Telling the men to climb a nearby tree, I proceeded alone very slowly and carefully towards the tree. I too soon saw movement but it was dark brown rather than the expected orange-red of a tiger. Close inspection revealed it to be a blood soaked shred of a woman's sari. I retrieved this and beckoned my men to climb down and explain to me what I had found.

I was told that a woman had been attacked at this very place some three months earlier but the group with her had driven the tiger off from the badly mauled victim. They had carried her back to the village where she died shortly of excessive hemorrhage from her wounds.

With heavy loads of firewood we returned safely to Sudrukumpa late that afternoon. At the bungalow I was relieved to receive word that Dhondopani and Krishna would arrive in a day or two to join me in the hunt.

That night huddled near the fire, Ghasi, the *chowkidar* and Mahades, my servant, regaled each other with bone chilling stories of tigers and ghosts until the *chowkidar* decided it was in his best interest to spend the night with us rather than venture out alone to make his way home. It started to rain and soon, other than the patter of droplets on the grass thatch, we were all quickly asleep probably jointly wondering if the man-eater was prowling around outside.

At 2:00 A.M. I awoke to soft shuffling sounds accompanied by deep breathing. Quite certain that it must be the tiger sizing up his next meal, I quietly attached the flashlight to my shotgun. I pressed the light to assure myself that there was nothing in the house. The sounds continued as I made my way to the door waking Ghasi and Mahades on the way. I soon regretted having done so because they immediately began to quake with fear and began moaning, certain they were about to become a late night snack for the man-eater.

Before opening the door I managed to pinpoint the sound as coming from the veranda near the window. I very cautiously opened the shutter, which in spite of my best efforts, made a loud creaking sound. Simultaneously the veranda sounds stopped and I heard a loud "whuff" as I snapped on the light. The beam caught the rapidly retreating rear end of a sloth bear disappearing into the darkness! My night's sleep was shortened and Ghasi and Mahades looked bleary eyed although grateful that they were both still alive!

In mid-morning, with dark rain clouds threatening, I walked to the main road junction and before long spotted in the distance a group of men approaching, led by my two expected *Shikaris*.

The group had brought many supplies with them from the market and I started the servants in getting busy to prepare a meal. While waiting, we discussed our plans to kill the tiger, which we all realized was becoming much easier to discuss than to do! We planned on staking out some more buffalo calves with one site on the Mulkipore road, and another at the place near where Tuli had been killed. I would place the third calf a short distance beyond Sudraja.

In the process of staking out the bait neither Dhondopani nor I saw any evidence of the tiger but shortly Krishna came in and said that he had heard a barking deer call an alarm in the general vicinity of where the village priest had been pulled down. He felt this may well have been prompted by the presence of the tiger. It may have been a very normal alarm call, perhaps even precipitated by Krishna himself. Now all forest activities were viewed with suspicion.

A heavy downpour came that night causing us to make numerous adjustments of our gear, our supplies, and ourselves, from becoming drenched from the badly leaking roof. Everyone was happy to see day dawn with a clear sun beaming down on a sodden misty morning. All three of us went out in separate directions to see how the staked out buffalo had survived the night.

My buffalo was serenely feeding when I approached and taking him for water I made my way back to the village. I was met by some people who informed me that the tiger had been seen shortly before walking on the main road near the hamlet of Pachiamba, not far away.

I left with a villager to show me the place and soon met Dhondopani who joined us. On the rain-soaked trail we easily spotted the tracks of a tiger which we followed up the road till it branched off into some rock-strewn hills. We followed the pug marks for some distance but soon lost them in the gravelly sand. Dhondopani was sure that the tiger was laid up in one of the many caves in the honey-combed rocks. We decided that to try to search for him in such a locale was futile and we returned to camp where we found Krishna waiting. His buffalo bait had also been untouched.

The three of us debated the next move and jointly decided we would walk to Panisal Village, looking for the tiger or signs of his presence, and then return by way of Mulkipore and Tikripara. All three sites had suffered enormous losses of human life to the tiger. The day proved fruitless and added to our frustrations was the fact that no one, including ourselves, had seen any presence of the tiger for several days.

Knowing how large a hunting range a male tiger can have, it was useless to try to speculate where he would strike next or if a message that a kill had occurred would reach us in time to do any good. Usually, remains of tiger kills reported to the police, were promptly collected by bereaved relatives for proper disposal. If a kill was found early enough it was often difficult to get relatives to agree to leave the corpse lay while a sit-up over the kill was attempted in hopes the man-eater might return. To get any of these scenarios to fall into place properly was difficult at best. Yet official recognition for killing the "right man-eater" was often only given if the killer was destroyed in the act of attacking someone or if shot on a human corpse left as bait. It is easy to envision the impossibility of achieving the former and the difficulty of arranging the latter. Hunting man-eaters bears no resemblance to sports hunting!

Checking our staked-out buffalo again in late afternoon we returned to the bungalow only to hear the tiger roaring after sundown at a distance that I figured couldn't be more than half a mile away. He continued to call intermittently all night as if daring us to come after him. The tiger had again chosen to ignore our buffalo baits and after watering the animals we decided to walk towards Vetkhal where the roaring sounds had seemed to originate the night before.

Some men approached us on the way to tell us that a forest guard, who had spent the night in Tikripara, had been killed by the tiger that morning as he was preparing a fire to cook his breakfast on the veranda of his home. The tiger had seized the man and, jumping over a boundary wall, had disappeared into the forest. They volunteered to take us to where the killing had taken place. Only a small pool of blood remained on the veranda to mark the place where the guard had been overwhelmed. I questioned the other rangers who had been in the house when the tiger attacked and they confirmed that all they had heard was a sharp thump followed by an anguished scream. Running to the door they had seen the tiger jumping the wall with the guard in his mouth. The irony was that the guards had a rifle in their possession which was leaning against the wall. In the brief moment of the attack no one had thought to use it to shoot the tiger!

We promptly organized a group to attempt to recover the guard's body. The ranger judiciously informed us that he was "very busy" and decided not to go along. One night of the man-eater had apparently been enough for him! A local villager led the way and we made rapid progress trailing the tiger with occasional blood spots, broken branches and pug marks to guide us. The trail unfortunately led into thick grass and boulders. In order to better cover the area we split into three groups with Dhondopani and Krishna covering the flanks and me and the village guards in the middle. We made a wide circle which brought us back almost to where we started. The guide climbed upon a large boulder and excitedly whispered down to me that he could see the tiger! I motioned to him to stay put as I began to climb up to join him. I had barely reached the top when a loud shattering boom from Krishna's muzzle loader blasted off just below me. I looked up just in time to see the tiger bounding away!

I momentarily felt like throttling Krishna who should have waited a bit longer but decided that since the villagers had already suffered so much from the man-eater that his responsive enthusiasm couldn't be criticized. Walking to where the tiger had been we found the remains of the forest guard and several large splashes of congealing blood.

Daring to speak now for the first time, Krishna said that as I was climbing the rock, the tiger had stared intently in my direction and he feared that a good opportunity would be lost if he had not fired a spontaneous shot.

The Sudrukumpa Man-eater had indeed been hit. We followed the trail for a long way till it entered some low hills near Mulkipore. Sure that we would soon again find the tiger, we enlisted a large group of Mulkipore villagers who eagerly agreed to help us search. The search unfortunately proved to be in vain. It began to rain and whatever spoor we had earlier seen now quickly washed away and soon vanished.

We tied out our baits again but checking each day, no sign of a tiger anywhere near them would be found. The villagers, ever observant of the jungle life around them, also saw nothing. Soon everyone was hopefully thinking that perhaps Krishna's slug had indeed killed the man-eater. We all fervently hoped this was right but we also remembered we had shared similar hopes many months before only to have the man-eater return.

I left the area later that month with the gnawing feeling that the tiger was still alive somewhere nursing his wounds and that the last hadn't been heard of the Sudrukumpa man-eater.

Three months passed with no more reported human kills from the known range of the killer. Slowly village life was starting to resume a normal pace.

At that time Dhondopani and his younger brother Gopal had made plans to visit a contractor's camp located near Panisal. A short-cut trail there led through a heavily wooded area which made the walk to Panisal nearly two miles shorter than going there by road. Dhondopani had his muzzle loader, which he carried by force of habit, even though now few thoughts were still being given to the man-eater, and the two brothers felt perfectly safe. Reaching the top of the hill, Gopal excused himself for a moment to go into the bushes on the side of the path. Dhondopani kept up the conversation from a discreet distance when he suddenly heard a choking sob which made him whirl around. The sight he beheld momentarily froze him in horror. Gopal, hanging limply, was in the jaws of a large tiger which was already turning to leave with its prey. Courage born of anger at the sight of his younger brother being killed by the tiger which he had so long hunted, made him spring into action. He bounded through the bushes after the tiger who, in its astonishment, dropped Gopal to face its new attacker. Sliding to a stop, only a short distance in front of the tiger, which had taken a glowering stance, over the dead body of Gopal, Dhondopani shouldered his relic of a rifle and pulled the trigger at point blank range. The loud roar shattered the stillness of the forest and when after what seemed like an eternity till the smoke cleared away, he could see the tiger rolling on the ground before him, mortally wounded. Dropping his rifle, he grabbed his brother's axe and in maniacal fury began chopping the broad head of the still twitching tiger. Only when the skull had been virtually pulverized did Dhondopani stop. Slowly the painful realization came that his brother had forfeited his life so he could bring the Sudrukumpa Man-eater to the final end of its long reign of terror.

Word soon reached the outside world, which was any place more than twenty miles from Sudrukumpa, that the man-eater was dead. The Phulbani Superintendent of Police passed the message on to me. Everyone rejoiced and soon carts had been sent to retrieve the man-eater so all could view it. Another cart also went to bring down the body of Gopal so he could be properly mourned.

Fifteen years later, Sudrukumpa had changed markedly as we revisited the old village. The bungalow had long been torn down. Shops had been built along the main street and people were no longer afraid to walk alone after dark. Only the old remembered what had been and the young had no point of reference to understand their fear when old stories were told and retold.

India is no longer as it was then, as few places are. Man-eaters still take an annual toll of life throughout the huge subcontinent but man-eaters are now rarely allowed to carry on such outrages for any length of time. Police, game guards or military personnel with modern automatic weapons now usually put a quick end to such an aberrant practice as eating human beings.

In death the Sudrukumpa Man-eater has now joined a long infamous roster of notorious killers; the Champawat, Panar, Muktesar, Gubari, Kanda and Pipal Pani tigers, among others, who all left bloodstained chapters in the recent history of India. Its story would have been properly documented long ago had it been killed by a personage other than an obscure *Shikari* named Dhondopani. His name may be forgotten, perhaps even in the village from which he came, as years go by. It is said that as long as one's name is still thought of in stories that a person is not truly forgotten. Whenever the essence of a story revolves around courage and bravery, the name of Dhondopani deserves to be remembered.

eighteen

LEOPARD REVENGE!

by John B. Snow

IN THE FADING LIGHT of the last day of a two-week safari, Doug Hidden figured that he and his client were finally about to catch a break. They had spent the better part of the hunt trying to tempt a leopard into gun range without success. The haunches of waterbuck and kudu that had been hung in various trees to ripen in the strong African sun had attracted plenty of attention, but from the wrong kind of cat. Lions had been worrying the baits, and with the big cats around, the leopards, reclusive by nature, had become extremely skittish.

For three evenings Doug and his hunter had sat in this particular blind overlooking the flat brushy landscape of western Zimbabwe's Gwayi Valley. Doug knew that a leopard had been feeding on the bait late at night, but they had yet to spot it during hunting hours. This evening, however, their luck seemed about to change.

Doug and his client were about 80 yards from the tree that held the pungent, rotting meat when they heard a rustling sound that meant a leopard was shaking the leaves off the bait. The leaves were there to keep vultures off during the day. More important, they served to signal that a leopard, otherwise silent and all but invisible, had arrived.

For several minutes the cat refused to settle down. Perhaps the lingering odor of the lions made it fidgety; whatever the reason, it didn't present a good shot.

Finally, it started to feed and the crack and crunch of breaking bones coming from the leopard's powerful jaws easily carried over the distance to the hunters. Even now, however, the leopard was uncooperative. The bait had been hung to position the cat broadside to the hunter, but the leopard had twisted itself into an awkward posture straddling the branch, facing toward them.

Despite this, Doug's client felt he had a good target and was certain that his .375 H&H would flatten the leopard without difficulty. With Doug's blessing he shot. The cat snarled and twisted as the bullet bit into it, and then it tumbled from the tree. As soon as it hit the ground it disappeared into the bush. The client's smile gave way to a look of surprise when Doug told him the cat was only wounded. The hunter thought he had made a clean killing shot, but Doug had seen many leopards wounded before and knew it wasn't yet dead.

Doug slowly approached the baited tree with his tracker, Muzungese, their eyes carefully scanning the bush for any movement, their ears straining for any sound. Doug held his .416 Remington at the ready while the tracker swept the bush with a powerful handheld spotlight to pierce the now complete African night.

They found just a little blood and some shards of bone at the base of the tree. The bone was particularly bad news. It meant the leopard had been hit in the leg—very unlikely a fatal wound. Doug and Muzungese followed the leopard's spoor about 150 yards through the tangle of vegetation, but as the batteries drained in the spotlight and their illumination faded, they gathered their client and turned back to camp.

In the pre-dawn darkness the next morning Doug and Muzungese put on thick overalls, not only to ward against the chilly winter air but also to provide an extra layer of protection against the leopard's claws in case it attacked. They drove back to the blind with the hunter and an apprentice guide. Once there, Doug told the hunter and the apprentice to stay with the truck. Having the extra gun along would likely do more harm than good. Doug had witnessed this firsthand when he was an apprentice professional hunter about twelve years earlier. A wounded leopard managed to maul four men, one right after the other, and by the time the gunfire died down a fifth man had been hit with buckshot. Doug's boss, the third man the leopard mauled during its lightning blitz, had also been wounded by a shotgun blast.

During his nine years as a professional hunter, Doug had tracked more than a dozen wounded leopards, and he thought about that mauling every time. He had been charged twice before. One leopard he shot four times with a semi-automatic shotgun as it came in before stopping it; the other leopard he shot "off the barrel" of the .416 he carried this day.

Doug and Muzungese quickly picked up the spoor of the leopard from the night before. Steady rains in recent weeks had spurred the growth of the underbrush, and the dense mix of shrubs, grasses and trees provided poor visibility. Doug and Muzungese had worked together for about five years and each was confident in the other's abilities. The two worked as a team: Muzungese sought out telltale signs of the leopard's movements—a drop of dried blood or an impression of a paw print that would be invisible to someone not raised in the African bush—while Doug remained vigilant for the cat.

About 15 minutes after they started they heard the leopard moving. Doug could tell it was coming fast but he couldn't see it. Suddenly, the leopard exploded out of the bush only ten feet in front of them, leaping for Doug. Doug tried to raise his rifle but the speed of the cat was too great. He shot underneath the leopard as it hit him and knocked him backward.

In its fury, the leopard bit down repeatedly on Doug's right hand and wrist, ripping through tendons and crippling his arm. At the same time its back legs pumped up and down in a blur, raking Doug's belly in an attempt to disembowel him with its bladelike claws.

Muzungese quickly discarded the ten-inch knife he had at the ready in his hand. The writhing mass of leopard and professional hunter made it impossible to stab the cat without risk to Doug. Instead, he ran up to the leopard and started beating it on the head with a wooden cudgel he carried in his other hand.

The attack had proceeded so quickly that Doug had been unable to differentiate one instant from the next. But now, with the adrenaline coursing through his body, he experienced the sensation of time slowing down. After savaging his hand, the leopard started to bite at his face. With his good hand, Doug gripped the leopard's neck to keep the cat's jaws at bay. With only one good paw—the .375 had all but ruined one foreleg—the leopard was unable to pull Doug's head into its mouth, but with only one good arm Doug couldn't get the cat off him either.

Their eyes were separated by fewer than twelve inches. In a moment of near absurdity, Doug recalls the leopard wincing, cartoonlike, each time Muzungese's club cracked on its skull. With the suddenness of a room going dark after a light has been turned off, Doug realized the leopard was no longer on top of him. He looked up and saw that the cat was now on Muzungese, biting and tearing through the tracker's clothes and cutting him badly.

In shock, Doug rolled over and groped for his rifle, which had been knocked from his hands at the leopard's first rush. Pinning the rifle in the crux of his otherwise useless right arm, Doug awkwardly worked the bolt with his left hand, chambering a fresh cartridge and yelling at Muzungese to free himself from the leopard.

Of course, the tracker was as helpless in the leopard's clasp as Doug had been, and with each second that ticked by, new slashes and punctures appeared on Muzungese's body, spouting crimson.

Doug knew that a rushed shot could easily kill the tracker. He kneeled and waited for what felt like an eternity for an opening. Rolling and twisting in the sandy dirt, Muzungese and the leopard were so close to Doug that he could have reached out and touched them. Finally, Doug had a clear shot. He pulled the trigger and blew the leopard off his partner.

As soon as the sounds of the melee died down, the client and apprentice hunter rushed to the clearing, where the leopard's body lay sprawled. They saw Doug doubled over, clutching his midsection. With all the blood they thought he had been gutted. As they peeled away the bloody tatters of clothing, they realized that the claws hadn't cut through to his abdomen, although Doug's arm and hand were an awful mess. The same went for Muzungese. The thick clothing had served its purpose; neither man was mortally wounded.

But they weren't out of danger yet. The filth from the leopard's mouth and claws quickly infected the men's wounds. Within an hour it became clear that both were at risk of dying. The nearest adequate hospital was in Harare, Zimbabwe's capital, 800 kilometers away by road. To get there they chartered an airplane; even so the journey took several hours to complete. The doctors in Harare carefully scraped away the infected tissue—in some spots right down to the bone. Both men spent the next few days in the hospital recovering.

A couple of weeks after the attack, the Zimbabwe Professional Hunters and Guides Association honored Muzungese with its bravery award for saving Doug's life.

But neither Muzungese nor Doug needs a plaque to remind them of what happened that winter morning. A glance at the latticework of scars the leopard carved into their flesh is all they require.

nineteen

THE CASE OF THE BLACK DOG

by John H. Brandt

I WAS AT BANGKOK'S Don Muong airport when the big C-130's began landing, discharging cargo and American infantrymen. It was a comforting sight because the Pathet Lao Communists and their Vietnamese colleagues had just pushed the Loyalist troops to the Mekong River and there were fears in northern Thailand that the impetus of this advance could splash across the river on into Thailand. This didn't happen but the sight of the American combat troops made me think that soon now the turmoil in southeast Asia could be brought to an end and stability returned. Little did I, or anyone else, realize that the turmoil would become known as the Vietnam War and how many years or how many lives would be lost before it came to its tragic conclusion.

My plane left shortly for the flight down the Malay Peninsula to the airport of Songkhla, on the east coast, a few miles north of the Thai-Malay frontier at Sadao. At that time most all of the Malay Peninsula from the Isthmus of Khra down to Singapore was still covered with beautiful montane rain forest. There were no east-west roads across the Peninsula and the best roads anywhere were dusty red laterite and others still dirt track that were reasonable when dry and bottomless morasses when wet. With almost continuous monsoons they were rarely dry! No one foresaw in those years that the hardwood forests would soon be contracted away to greedy lumber barons and that chain saws would soon shatter the stillness. Within two decades only a few reserve forests and National Parks would survive the onslaught. By the early 1990s most of the pristine forests were gone and catastrophic mud slides, from denuded hillsides, killed numerous villagers. Then the government belatedly banned further timbering and export of logs. Unfortunately by this time the damage had been done!

As my plane skimmed in for the descent into Songkhla you could occasionally see clear cut holes in the forest with smoke haze surrounding it where the government was establishing communes called *"nikkoms."* Land hungry peasants and city folk ignorant of slash and burn agriculture were being encouraged to settle with promises that they would soon turn the jungle into a productive garden paradise. That this would not, and could not happen, from lessons learned in other destroyed rain forest areas, was ignored and disregarded.

In Songkhla I was met by a government messenger in a *Khaki* uniform who saluted and handed me some papers tacked together with a straight pin. One was a telegram in Thai which I could not read and the other was a short note in English from the *Balat Changwat* (Deputy Governor) who was a friend of mine. It said in short choppy sentences, "need to talk—my office—leopard problem—hope you have time." The *Balat Changwat* was an avid outdoorsman and competent hunter who had killed his share of tiger and leopard. I was intrigued and interested and told my driver to proceed to the Governor's office in hopes I could catch him before the day slipped away.

At the government building I was quickly ushered into the office where the *Balat*, a short muscular man, was seated at a small carved gilded table. He clapped his hands as I entered to have tea brought in for us. Then with an apology, he began to tell me how busy he was and that he never had time any more to do things he really liked. I began to wonder why I was being given this prelude and wondered when he would tell me about the telegram and why he had called me in.

After proper protocol, with the second cup of tea, he picked up the

telegram and began to translate. "Two boys badly hurt by leopard—
stop—livestock killed—stop—villagers afraid—stop—need your help—
stop—can you come?" The message was from a *Gamnan* from the
remote area near Ban Khao Yuan who was the nominal head of several
rural villages in a remote district south of the Na Thawi to Pattani road
and east of the main peninsula road leading to the Malay border. The
Balat felt it was his responsibility to help but most of his armed personnel, such as the Border Police, were involved in chasing Communist Ter-
rorists (CTs) back and forth across the frontier. Many of the jungle areas
were not particularly safe to be in and hot pursuit arrangements between
the Thai and Commonwealth Forces were in effect. I knew what was
coming, but I waited for him to ask, since I knew if the request was a formal one that he would extend whatever official support he could to assure that the leopard problem would be taken care of.

After a few more laments of overwork and no time, the *Balat* asked if
I might be able to go down to help and kill the leopard that had caused
the problem.

He assured me that he would arrange payment for bait animals and
also supply me with a guide to the village and a letter indicating that local *Gamnans* and *Phuyaibans* (Village Headmen) would give me whatever
help I might require for camp help, to build machans, or whatever else
might come up. He and I had a good rapport and he already knew I
would say "yes." I sent a cable to establish my leave time and then went
home to get my gear, rifle, lights, tinned food, water bags and a good
pocket book in anticipation of long uncomfortable sit-ups in cramped
machans. The *Balat* assured me that he would have an officer who knew
the area available to accompany me as soon as I returned.

I picked up a map at my home and looked at the ground area but it
showed a large blank void. There were a few villages marked along a few
water courses but I knew that most of these could only be reached by
foot path and what appeared as "cities" on the map were in reality only a
cluster of a dozen or so thatched roofed stilted houses. There were some
newly established *nikkoms* to the east and I knew forest damage was already underway in many places. I wondered what the access was to the
area and how far we would have to walk.

We stopped at the District Officer's home on our way and when I asked about roads he smiled that all-knowing Thai smile of *"Mai Pen Rai,"* which literally translates as "not to worry." If the road was dry then all was well and good. If not, there was no need to make worries since it couldn't be changed anyway. A fine philosophy for a developing country.

We drove east on the main Pattani road towards the Thephaa settlement where I had earlier killed a troublesome tiger. The government officer soon tapped the driver's shoulder and directed him to turn south on a track that without some vivid imagination would not pass for a road.

We had proceeded several kilometers with the driver confidently proclaiming that his four-wheel-drive vehicle could do anything but climb trees. I had some misgivings and before long, on a level piece of track, a huge hole covered with water, hiding its presence, engulfed the right front fender and we sank away in the ooze. A drover with a two-wheeled oxcart coming along at that moment didn't realize how quickly I would have swapped him a nice new Jeep 4×4 for his primitive conveyance. At least he didn't get stuck!

Fortunately, we were only a short way from our destination and we decided to leave the mired vehicle to the driver and a few other officials that we had given a lift, to extricate it as best they could. With most of our gear on our backs, my guide and I headed towards a grove of sugar palms visible across some new rice paddies where he assured me the *Phuyaiban's* house was located.

News of strangers travels quickly and we were soon surrounded by children and staring adults long before we reached the houses. The Thais have an irritating custom called *"tai mong"* which means unrestrained gawking at anything unusual or strange. I fit that description well since the coming of eco-tourists to the area was still many years in the future.

We stopped to see the *Phuyai* and asked if he could summon the two herd boys that had been mauled so I could find out what had happened. The *Phuyai* did as he was told but I found his conversational drift was far less concerned about the wounded boys than about his constant reference to livestock killing. The village had goats and I was sure if a leopard was taking these in any numbers that a report would have trickled in much earlier. I felt the behavior of the leopard was far from normal since maulings are not every day occurrences and a leopard so bold as to attack two humans was a time bomb waiting to explode. Then I found the primary reason for the *Phuyai's* concern.

These villages were Buddhist, in an area predominately Malay Muslim, and ordinarily feel that everyday events are pre-ordained and there is little control on their part of what happens. A leopard taking an occasional goat was an accepted event since everyone knew that Buddha had already determined when the day of the goat's demise would occur. The goats were penned at night and although they knew the leopard came around the compound by hearing the milling of the livestock and seeing his tracks, he had, so far, made no effort to break into the pens. One major devastation had occurred however that had prompted the *Phuyai* to action. The leopard had made the terrible mistake of killing the *Phuyai's* dog!

The dog was not just any pariah mutt, that thrived in Thai villages, but a large black dog that was fed special fattening foods. The *Phuyai* had been cultivating him for sale to a gourmet Chinese trader in Haadyai, the nearest large town, who would render him into a delicacy called *"mah dam"* (Black Dog). Now why a black dog should taste differently than a brown one or a white one escaped my judgement and I decided to leave such delicate matters to those with a more discriminating taste than I.

The dog had begun barking at night and the *Phuyai* had opened the door to let him out. Silence had again reigned and in the morning it was obvious what had happened. The dog had blundered into the leopard and the leopard also quickly figured *"mah dam"* to be a delicacy worth trying and had made off with the *Phuyai's* prize.

The two boys, wrapped up in gauze like Egyptian mummies, came and sat by the door step. Each appeared to be some eight to ten years old. Judging by the amount of bandages it appeared the leopard had not missed many places on their bodies. Fortunately they had managed to cover their faces and had escaped disfigurement.

The boys had not been attacked at the same time, they told me. The first herd boy to be mauled had been out with his dozen or so goats, grazing them in an old paddy field not far from the village. He had been day-dreaming in the heat when suddenly his goats bleated and made a unified scramble to get away from the paddy embankment. Then he saw, as the dust settled, that one of his goats was on its side, spasmodically kicking, while a huge leopard held it firmly by the throat.

The herd boy, knowing what his father would do to him if he lost a goat, picked up a stick and a stone, and with more courage than brains, charged the leopard. Shouting and throwing rocks, he closed the distance between them!

Ordinarily a leopard is a stealthy hunter endowed to be as effective a killing machine, pound for pound, as any devised by nature. Often leopards are cautious to the point that trying to lure one by enticing it to a bait or getting it to return to a kill is made doubly difficult by the shy, retiring and ultra cautious demeanor of the animal. Jumping a leopard however, that has just made a kill, who's adrenaline is pumping, and who's killer instincts are at that moment aroused to their fullest, is a foolish transgression. This the herd boy quickly found out!

Whether the stone actually hit the leopard is irrelevant because with a snarling growl he flashed his teeth and launched a lightning spring on the startled boy. By body weight they were about equal but by sheer strength there was no contest as the boy crumbled under the attack.

He was lucky in that he pulled up his knees as he fell backwards and covering his face tried to roll into a ball as best he could. The leopard bit deeply into his shoulders and raked his forepaws across the boys back and chest. The greatest potential damage would have occurred if the leopard could have gotten him into an embrace with his forepaws and then brought his hind feet into play which would have raked him in a way that would have easily disemboweled the boy.

One blessing, if it could be interpreted as such, is that leopard attacks are often very fast, "Biff-Bop-Bam-Thank-You-Mam!" type of attacks. They are quick, lightning fast and deadly in intent, but if the onslaught is survived and there is no bite through the head or neck, the victim often recovers. Because of the imminent danger of septic infection from the leopard claws, each slash often becomes infected and even though the victim survives the attack he frequently dies later from bacterial complications. The advent of antibiotics and techniques for draining the deep lacerations made survival rates better, but it was hardly an experience to be recommended for anyone.

The leopard after his attack had returned to his goat, leaving the boy bleeding in the field, too overcome to yell for help, and in a profound state of shock. Women coming back from gathering firewood had heard the commotion and soon men and dogs came running from the village. This was more than the leopard had counted on and apparently had decided discretion was the better part of valor and had retreated. He had lost his intended meal but he had made his point—don't mess with me!

The boy had been taken, quickly as possible, to a rural Health Center where a medic sewed up the lacerations and pumped the boy full of antibiotics. Two days later, the leopard, apparently still hungry and in a foul frame of mind, attacked another small herd of goats. The description of what happened to the second boy was almost identical to the first except this time the leopard managed to drag his goat kill off. The villagers decided it was not prudent to go into the thick brush to attempt to retrieve their goat and the village mongrels also decided that barking from the safety of the paddy field was sufficient demonstration of their courage. None dared go near the vegetation at the end of the field.

The taking of an occasional goat by a tiger or leopard or the killing of chickens by any of a multitude of lesser predators is an accepted way of rural life. Normally, there were sufficient wild pigs and barking deer in the area to take care of the needs of leopards. Tigers were in actual fact more common than leopards in most of the forested Peninsula Provinces since it is known that tiger actively kill leopard whenever the opportunity allows. Tigers rarely killed cattle or water buffalo in my area and apparently had sufficient natural prey in sambar, pigs, gaur and barking deer to stay away from villages. In northern Thailand, tigers had developed the technique of hamstringing large prey such as water buffalo which allowed them to attack and kill the largest of such animals. In the south this was rarely, if ever practiced, and because of the constant fear of hurting itself in an attack that every carnivore fears, only small cattle and occasional young water buffalo were taken. Interaction between tigers and man was still so unusual that many villagers in the new settlements were ignorant of their very existence.

Leopards, being much more adaptable than tigers to the presence of people, also rarely presented a problem and although they were occasionally seen and heard coughing around villages at night they were not an animal of concern. Neither tigers nor leopards carried the fear in villages that a honey bear or black bear could invoke. These animals often attack unprovoked and cause horrifying mutilation with their large claws. Also, it seemed a strange paradox that although leopards often became notorious man-eaters in India, this was a very poorly documented happening in the rest of Asia, or even Africa, for that matter. Leopards were maulers, and often man-killers, but had rarely developed the epicurean taste for human flesh that so often happened with tigers, or for whatever reason, with leopards in India.

The leopard that had mauled the two boys and who it was assumed had carried off the *Phuyai's* dog, was a dark spotted male that had been seen for some time on and off, in the area. No one had given him much concern. Spotted leopards were actually far less common on the Peninsula than the melanistic variety of jet black leopard often referred to as the "Black Panther." They are the same animal but the black variety seemed more successful and adaptable to the dark rain forest than the spotted one. An estimated 85% of leopard in the south were black.

Apparently the change in the biological balance of the area came about with chopping down of the forests and the poaching and snaring of many of the local animals as food for the subsistence farmers. Thai police, with spotlights on their vehicles, were notorious for jack-lighting barking deer which could often be seen for sale in local markets. Encroachment on its normal hunting area and the ever decreasing number of normal prey animals had apparently driven the leopard into taking prey that unintentionally sealed its fate. Interaction between man and the great carnivores was ever increasing in the area and I often felt empathy for the cats because we were forcing them into abnormal behavior patterns. Such niceties were not a consideration of the villagers, however, who had to live with this potential threat on a daily basis.

The *Phuyai* sent the boys off at dark and had his wife prepare some rice and fish curry for me. He offered me the use of his home and politely followed the normal Thai tradition of hospitality known as *"liang du, puh siia."* This meant the host would offer his guest food to eat, a mat to sleep on and a girl to sleep with. I profoundly thanked the *Phuyai* and tried to diplomatically assure him that I would be the last person in the world to disrupt his solicitous concern for my comfort and well-being that night but that I had to reluctantly decline because of the task at hand. I'm not sure, but I think he understood.

Next morning with the help of several village men, my Jeep was freed and pulled into the village. The government guide had been given funds to purchase some goats that I planned to tie out as bait animals. Within a short time we had three goats tethered to the Jeep bumper. The sales had been quickly negotiated because the village entrepreneurs knew that if the leopard didn't kill the goats on a live stake out that they would get them back anyway which seemed like a quick profit for them.

The villagers told me that often when the paddy fields were full that the leopard walked along the divider berm. This was often overgrown with weeds and occasional bushes allowing him plenty of cover. It had now been over a week since the last attack and I could only assume that during that time the leopard had managed to catch some normal prey since no other attacks on the village goats had occurred.

I selected a small tree, with thick foliage, at a place some two miles from the village where two paddy dikes intersected and where a trail led into the secondary forest which woodcutters often used. Village women gathering fruit in the forest had often seen leopard tracks on the trail. I assumed this was part of the leopard's normal hunting range and that he used it at frequent intervals. I securely pegged the goat out and had the village men tie a rattan chair into the branches for me. The tree didn't lend itself to building a machan, with only spindly outer branches. The chair back was tied fast to the trunk and I intertwined branches in front of me to obscure any visible outlines. It was not an ideal place to shoot from but I thought the idea of sitting on a chair was better than trying to sit stiff legged and half paralyzed on a platform machan for hours on end.

The idea of building a machan utilizing the main trunk and branches, supported in the back by a couple of stout uprights was considered. I wasn't too hot on the idea because a year earlier I had sat up over a tiger kill on a similar rickety machan. I was only some ten feet off the ground which was low enough that any halfway athletic tiger could have joined me on the machan without much effort. Also I had hung my legs off the front of the platform since sitting cross legged, Buddha style, without moving, is an exercise in total torture. That night the tiger moved through the forest toward the bait without a single animal alerting me to its presence. I had been confident that a monkey or bird would signal me as it approached. Everyone was truly asleep at the switch that night and not a single alarm call was heard. Although I am not quite positive about what happened, I think the tiger approached directly under my machan without being aware of me only a few feet over his head. Either I moved or he caught my scent because the next instant there was a heart-stopping roar directly under me and then the machan swayed, leaves fell, and I was convinced I was being attacked by the tiger who was then, I thought, springing up into the tree. Whether in its startled anger the tiger had swatted the support posts upon first noticing me or if he had hit the supports as he swung his body to get out from under the machan, I'll never know. Then there was dead silence! With my heart beating like a gong I was sure the tiger was sitting directly below me waiting for me to make the first move. I couldn't move my rifle because I would have to unhook the battery cable to my light. During those few seconds fear did not really set in until later when the experience could be fully analyzed. With slow motion movements I drew up one foot and then the other till I could stand, expecting a full attack at any moment. When I could shine the light below me the arena was empty! My adversary had retreated into the night as quietly as he had come. Of course, his shock at finding me in the machan over his head, I am sure was as great as mine in discovering him below me. If he had hit the support posts a bit harder I would have fallen directly on top of him. I don't know who would have been more rattled, me or the tiger. I'm glad I didn't have to find out but I spoke in my sleep for many nights thereafter. With that experience behind me I convinced the village men that tying a chair to the trunk was the only way to go.

I had a shirt draped over the goat's head while I climbed up into my camouflaged chair. I had told the villagers to remove the shirt after I was fully seated so the goat would not be aware that I was in the tree. I was hopeful it wouldn't notice me after the men left and would become aware of its apparent abandonment and begin bleating to let someone know it had been left behind. Its protestations would be loud enough in the coming hours to alert the leopard. That was the plan, but plans have ways of going wrong!

The goat was fully grown and apparently was not terribly concerned about being left tied down in the woods. She called several times and then seemed contented and laid down to sleep. In my cramped position I envied her comfort. After some time I became very unhappy with my bait animal who refused to do what bait animals are supposed to do. I thought about the technique of clipping a paper staple through her ear to make her uncomfortable enough to make her call more often. But then I thought, possibly in the Buddhist way of thinking, that her fate was already determined and the staple would only be an unnecessary cruelty. Besides I didn't have a staple!

When morning came I climbed down and with my goat trailing along behind me on a string, I returned to the village to get some sleep. I instructed the men to tie out my other goats at several pre-selected places in hopes that the leopard might kill one and hopefully in a place where a sit-up would be possible.

I crawled into my mosquito net in a corner in the *Phuyai's* house and was quickly surrounded by some twenty children of all sizes and shapes. Each stared at what must have been to them the weirdest creature they had ever seen. It had hair on its arms, legs and chest like an ape. There was hair on its face, as a beard, that they had never seen before. Not only was the hair not black, like normal people possessed, but its eyes were blue like the sky and appeared to let daylight shine all the way through the skull. Surrounded by a whispering, gawking crowd, who meant no harm, but were overzealous with curiosity, muttering *"farang"* (stranger-foreigner) let me know how a caged creature in a zoo must feel. I turned my back and went to sleep while my every move and action continued as a never-ending fascination for the children.

The following morning a villager reported in that one goat was gone and he assumed the leopard had taken it. We looked at the kill site on a paddy dike and saw the pug marks of the leopard. The tether rope had snapped and the goat had been carried off. There was little blood on the hard ground which made it difficult to determine where the leopard had carried the kill. We made sweeping circles and soon discovered a splash of blood. Within a hundred yards we found what was left of the goat. The leopard had eaten a huge amount and there was little left to entice him to return for a second meal. The situation was complicated by the fact that there were only small stunted trees and bushes where he had dragged the kill. The nearest place to tie up my chair was well over fifty yards away and I doubted if my light would give a clear enough sight picture should the leopard return.

I climbed into my chair in the late afternoon and placed the camouflaging branches that I had tied in front of the seat. The forest was deathly still. In the distance I saw what I thought was movement in a tree. Turning my head as slowly as possible I stared at a black body in the upper branches. I knew the problem leopard had spots and I wondered if this was a black leopard or if the poor light and shadows made a spotted leopard appear black. It had a long tail, like a leopard, but moved on the branches in a slow deliberate way that didn't appear to be movements a leopard would make. As it cleared some foliage I realized I was looking at a Binturong, the so-called bear civet. The largest of its kind and almost totally arboreal. It is rarely seen and I regretted the quick ebbing of my light as darkness set in.

The long night again passed with no indication that the leopard had returned to examine his kill and at daylight I returned to the village. Everyone was disappointed, as I was, and the herd boys were anxious to take their goats back to better forage areas if only the leopard could be removed to make the area safe.

That day and night nothing was seen or heard of the leopard and my time to return to Songkhla was about to run out. I planned to stay two more days and then would have to leave the villagers to their own devices and hope for the best.

I decided on another sit-up with a live goat and had selected a large Banyan tree not very far from the village. This time I had the village men build a proper platform with a branch tied horizontally across the front upon which I could lay my rifle and the light. I had brought a battery-operated light this time with a strong beam. Lights attached directly to the barrel have various benefits but often also glare off the open sights blinding the shooter when a light is switched on when your pupils are fully dilated from sitting in the total darkness. Hunters, I have read and heard about, that claim to be able to see by starlight obviously possessed faculties beyond my own. Also those that claim to be able to distinguish between the rustle of leaves caused by a tiger or leopard and a rustle caused by a beetle, a slug or even a mouse leave many questions in my mind.

The goat tied up under my machan was a young billy with a good voice. As the men who had tied him left, he protested loudly and made it known that he didn't like being left alone one bit. He called constantly for over an hour and then just as the sun was starting to dip into the trees to my rear the goat suddenly became silent. It stood spraddle legged and stared hard at my tree but its eyes were focused at ground level and not on me. Whatever had caught its attention was behind me. The goat didn't move except to turn its gaze somewhat to my right. Whatever was being observed appeared to be circling my tree. I was afraid to make a movement and hoped sincerely it was my leopard. The light was still good enough to shoot and such an opportunity always seemed far better and safer than trying to make a shot by flashlight in the dark.

The goat tugged hard at the tether apparently deciding it no longer wanted to stay where it was. Then I saw movement in the grass directly next to my tree and in an almost fluid movement the leopard came into view. It was looking hard at the goat, like a customer examining a pork chop in the supermarket, but didn't seem to be in any hurry, as if confident the goat wasn't going anywhere. Noises from the village, children, chickens and an occasional dog could be heard quite clearly. The leopard seemed to pay them no mind. I fervently hoped he would hurry up and make his move to either attack the goat or come out into the open where I could get a shot at him. To try to move the rifle before he was fully engaged in making the kill was dangerous and in his elevated stage of alertness any move on my part would in all likelihood be quickly seen and in a flash he would be gone.

Then in a split second he made a spring, and with only a gurgle coming from the goat, he slammed it to the ground and fastened his teeth into the back of the neck. All movement of the goat ceased as his teeth crushed through the skull plate. Now was the time for me to make a move.

All such episodes tend to be anticlimactic and the leopard never guessed where the shot came from. I had a clear broadside at some twenty yards to aim at in a fairly good light. As the bullet slammed into his shoulder he lurched like a coiled spring but only with enough vigor to clear the goat and roll into the adjoining grass. I could see the body quite clearly but the light was fading fast and I wanted to be sure he was dead before leaving my machan.

My plans for a safe conclusion to the hunt were shattered when I could hear the sound of drums and gongs signalling the approach of people and dogs that sounded like a field maneuver of Cossack Cavalry coming my way. Having heard the sound of the rifle shot, they had naively assumed "The Tuan never misses and the leopard must be dead." It would have been nice to believe that their confidence was not misguided.

They charged up to the dead goat and by this time the village dogs also had discovered the dead leopard. Without giving a thought, as any prudent individual might, to determine if the leopard was truly dead or only wounded, they followed the dogs in to see the perpetrator of their miseries.

I climbed down in the semi-darkness and joined the crowd who were bowing to me with joined palms while the children stroked the hair on my arms, as one would to pet a dog, saying, "Well done Rover, well done."

TERROR
IN THE WATER

Crocodiles and Sharks

twenty

CROCODILE BITES OFF ZOO WORKER'S ARM

TAIPEI, TAIWAN—A ZOO worker had his forearm reattached Thursday after his colleagues recovered the severed limb from the mouth of a 440-pound Nile crocodile, an official said. The crocodile severed Chang Po-yu's forearm on Wednesday at the Shaoshan Zoo in the southern city of Kaohsiung when the veterinarian tried to retrieve a tranquilizer dart from the reptile's hide, zoo officials said.

The Liberty Times newspaper said Chang failed to notice the crocodile was not fully anesthetized when he stuck his arm through an iron rail to medicate it.

As Chang was rushed to the hospital on Wednesday, a zoo worker shot two bullets at the crocodile's neck to retrieve the forearm, said Chen Po-tsun, a zoo official.

"The crocodile was unharmed as we didn't find any bullet holes on its hide," Chen said. "It probably was shocked and opened its mouth to let go of the limb."

The 17-year-old reptile is one of a pair of Nile crocodiles kept by the Kaohsiung zoo. The crocodile is listed as an endangered species, and is rapidly disappearing from its native African habitat.

Chen said the zoo purchased the crocodile from a local resident who had kept it as a pet.

twenty-one

BEACH HAVEN: JULY 1, 1916

by Richard G. Fernicola

LESS THAN TWENTY MILES north of the gambling and saltwater taffy capital of Atlantic City lies a tranquil summer resort called Beach Haven. Eighty-five years ago (1916), located on the eighteen-mile stretch of Long Beach Island, Beach Haven was a place to where couples and families escaped for a true vacation, just as they do today. In the 1800s, the town's sole inhabitants were fishermen and whalers, but by the turn of the century, it was well known to outsiders for its appealing pristine waters, picturesque low-lying dunes, and a noncommercial boardwalk. According to John Bailey Lloyd, the noted historian of Long Beach Island, Beach Haven came into being in 1874 as the brainchild of Tuckerton railway founder Archelaus Ridgeway Pharo. Pharo's daughter actually wanted to name it Beach Heaven. It was, however, literally a haven from hay fever, as its paucity of mainland vegetation fostered a sneeze-free zone. The men who developed Beach Haven envisioned that their resort would be like no other. It was not on the edge of the bustling mainland, as were resorts like Cape May and Long Branch, but almost five miles at sea. As soon as the Tuckerton Railroad was completed in the 1870s, Pharo deeded 670 acres of his land at the southern end of Long Beach Island. The deeded land was divided into lots, and magnificent hotels like the Parry House, the Bay View House, and, later, the Engleside Hotel were constructed. Every weekend during the summer, steam trains arrived packed with beachgoers from southern New Jersey and Pennsylvania. The summer of 1916 was expected to be one of the most profitable and pleasant that Beach Haven had ever seen, and plans for a widened and lengthened boardwalk were to be implemented by summer's end. Two hundred shade trees adorned the town to welcome visitors, and the new express train from Philadelphia shortened the travel time to just under two hours. The Engleside Hotel and the other lavish island resort quarters opened on schedule by the third week of June. By the July Fourth weekend, the busiest of the year, hotels were fully booked. Since the Fourth fell on a Tuesday, vacationers were anticipating an extended fun-filled holiday.

On Saturday, July 1, 1916, the afternoon Number 8 train from West Philadelphia arrived at Long Beach Island. Among the travelers was twenty-five-year-old Charles Epting Vansant. Anyone who knows Philadelphia in the summer knows that its sweltering heat can be more than enough to send a young, tall, handsome, dark-haired, ambitious businessman racing for the invigorating Jersey surf. As one of the most promising graduates of the University of Pennsylvania's class of 1914, and with a bachelor's degree from the College of Arts and Sciences, Vansant had acquired a position with Philadelphia's Folwell Brothers brokerage firm, where his coworkers described him as a man "of unusual promise with an exceptionally winning personality and charm of a manner which brought to him many friends and admirers."* As a Philadelphia native, residing at 4038 Spruce Street, Vansant's college chums knew him as "Charlie" or "Van"; his popularity was further attested to by his role as glee club member, his position as business manager of the *Record* (the school paper), as well as his positions on the business staff of two other prominent school clubs. His athletic abilities landed him a slot on the varsity golf team and the junior varsity baseball team. Charles's spiritual side did not suffer because of his athleticism or popularity, for he was also an active congregant of the Walnut Street Presbyterian Church.

The Evening Bulletin, Philadelphia, July 3, 1916.

Vansant's scholastic achievements were supplemented by his privileged heritage and fortunate natural endowment. The Vansant family lineage distinguished it as one of the oldest family lines in the country. Charles was the only son of prominent Philadelphia nose and throat physician, Dr. Eugene L. Vansant, whose office was located at 1229 Chestnut Street. Dr. Vansant was a direct descendent of Stophel Garettson Vansant, an immigrant from Holland who ventured to New Amsterdam (New York) in 1647. Since 1700, the Vansant clan lived in Pennsylvania, and Charles and his dad were each entitled to membership in the Society for Founders and Patriots of America.

Besides their familiarity with Philadelphia, the Vansant family was also well acquainted with the pleasures of the southern Jersey Shore. In late June 1916, Dr. Vansant, somewhat preoccupied by the growing infantile paralysis epidemic in New York, suggested a family outing away from the city to take advantage of the long Independence Day weekend. On Saturday, July 1, Charles was joined on the train by his dad and two of his three sisters, Eugenia and Louise. Their ultimate destination was the plush Engleside Hotel, replete with seaside tennis courts and a magnificent spired tower.

The Beach Haven express left Camden at 3:35 P.M. and arrived in Beach Haven at a little after 5:00 P.M. Like an elite cruise liner, the large Beach Haven hotels had two dinner sittings that evening, 6:30 and 8:00 sharp. While the thermometer in Philadelphia was close to ninety, the Vansants were now grateful for the comfortable seventy-eight degree F. seaside temperature. After Charles and his family checked into the Engleside, he turned to his sister Louise and suggested a walk to the beach to take in the late-afternoon sun. Vansant also had another motive for the jaunt to the beach, taking the customary pre-dinner dip in the ocean.

While the Vansant family unpacked at the Engleside, Charles dashed off to the boardwalk bathhouses off Centre Street to change into his swim tights. The water temperature was an inviting sixty-eight degrees, just about average for a blistering day in early July. On his walk toward the surf, Vansant befriended a large Chesapeake Bay retriever and waved to his summer acquaintance, lifeguard Alexander Ott. Alex was just about to go off-duty after a long, hot day of guarding the beach, but he wasn't the type to shirk his late-afternoon duties. His eyes remained focused on every swimmer within his bathing area. Ott, athletic and in his mid-twenties, was not only well suited for his position but perhaps even overqualified. In 1910, Alex had been a prestigious member of the American Olympic swim team and had been guarding on the Jersey Shore for several summers.

By this time, Dr. Vansant and Louise arrived beyond the low dune and settled near the lifeguard stand, just as Charles waded into the surf. He frolicked for several minutes with the playful retriever and then he swam beyond the lifelines. Just beyond the breakers, in chest-deep water, Charles turned and began calling for the suddenly timid pooch. The dog was determined to make his exit from the surf, but Vansant continued calling to the dog in hopes that it would follow him.

Up on the beach, bathers ignored Vansant's shouts. At that same moment, however, a handful of people on the shoreline perceived a dark object just beyond the surf. A crowd gathered as the object came into view. What they saw looked like a black fin slicing across the water from the east toward Vansant. They began to shout heatedly to Vansant, who was unable to understand them and continued calling the dog. Suddenly, one shout from Vansant was louder and higher pitched than the rest, and he began struggling to the beach. (At this point, one can't help but visualize the scene from *Jaws* when the black labrador retriever disappeared in the surf during a game of fetch). At about fifty yards from shore, his shouts became shrieks, and he began frantically splashing. His splashes raised the crimson water airborne. Vansant saw his blood becoming one with the sea. He knew his life was departing with it. He made his way to about three and a half feet of water and got to within forty yards of the beach. Perched on his lifeguard stand, Alexander Ott knew immediately that Charles was in grave danger. He darted across the beach toward the pool of bright red blood encircling his friend. Without hesitation and without a thought for his own safety, Ott managed to get the flailing Vansant to waist-deep water. During the struggle to shore, the shark was never far away. Witnesses on the beach and boardwalk later swore they saw the shark affixed to Vansant's thigh during the entire rescue. W. K. Barklie of Broad Street in Philadelphia was on the beach at the time of the attack and later mentioned that the shark did not let Vansant free until its belly scraped the bottom of the sand. Ott finally received assistance amid the breaking waves from local residents John Everton and Sheridan Taylor. The men locked arms and grabbed Ott to create a human chain to hoist Vansant's quickly deadening weight onto the beach. As Charles lay basically motionless near the high-water mark, Louise Vansant stood frozen in horror, mesmerized by the wide stream of draining blood that flowed along the sand past her feet.

DURING THE EARLY YEARS of my 1916 attack investigation, my second move in research protocol, after perusing primary and secondary sources, was always to attempt to contact a witness or a relative of a witness. In reference to the Vansant attack of July 1, I drew blanks all the way around. I tried to find a Vansant family relation in Philadelphia and struck out. I attempted to find John Everton or Sheridan Taylor, but "no cigar," as they say. My most prolonged attempts were at finding anyone connected to Alexander Ott. Realizing that Ott would probably be in his mid-nineties in 1980, I knew that finding him would be a long shot. My calls to assorted Otts in South Jersey, and eventually to every Ott in the state, went completely unrewarded.

In February 1994, I decided to take a much-needed break from the rigors of my residency at NYU Medical Center to spend a nine-day respite in Kuai, Hawaii. A discovery made on the eight-hour airplane ride proved that an investigative historian should never lose hope. As I flipped through that year's *Sports Illustrated* swimsuit issue, I became intrigued by a feature story devoted to great American swimming pools and water shows. I glanced at the photos throughout the story, and I immediately zeroed in on an antique sepia-toned photo of a tall, handsome man in his early forties wearing vintage swimwear and holding an adorable blond kid with a Dutch-boy haircut. The caption beside the photo read, "In the '30s, crowds flocked to the prodigious pool at the Biltmore to see the aquatics of Jackie Ott the Aqua Tot and his father, Alexander." I almost dropped the magazine. I knew immediately that this could be no mere coincidence. This Alexander Ott was in the correct age range, and, of course, the swimming parallel was obvious. No wonder I could not find any trace of Alexander Ott in New Jersey. He had long ago traded in his summertime paradise of South Jersey for the perennial splendor of South Florida.

The *Sports Illustrated* article describes the Coral Gables Biltmore Hotel swimming pool, built in 1926, as the largest pool in Florida and, for many years, the largest hotel pool in the world. Motorboats could even tow water skiers through the L-shaped structure. Over a thirteen-year period, through the height of the Great Depression, Alexander Ott's Water Follies drew crowds of 3,000 people every Sunday. Legends like Harry Houdini, Olympic skater Sonja Henie, and the Flying Wallendas were headliners at the show. Long before Olympic great Johnny Weissmuller ever went to Hollywood to play Tarzan, he was a regular at Ott's Water Follies.

Ott's son, Jackie, the Aqua Tot, was touted as the most beautiful child in the world and was winner of six baby contests, including the prestigious baby parade contests of Asbury Park and Atlantic City.

Back in New Jersey, I searched the Miami information directory, only to find that there were no Alexander Otts listed. My next option, as well as my most realistic one, was to find Jackie Ott, the former Aqua Tot. Sure enough, a Jack Ott was listed, and I wasted no time in dialing.

"Mr. Ott?" I asked.

"Yes," he replied in a monotone.

"By any chance, would you be related to an Alexander Ott?" I gingerly asked.

"I guess so," he replied. "He's my father."

Jackpot. But in that instant I questioned myself and thought, "Who says that the attack on Vansant meant enough to Alex Ott for him to share it with his family?" Or, knowing the ultimate reliability of newspaper accounts, was it really Ott who was involved with the rescue? Nevertheless, I pushed on.

"When your dad used to be a lifeguard in New Jersey," I started, "I believe he helped a man who was involved in a shark attack. Did he ever tell you that story?"

"Sure he did," Jackie replied without hesitation. "I'll tell you the story if you want me to."

He continued enthusiastically. "My dad had been patrolling the beach one late afternoon when he saw a friend of his struggling just beyond the waves. When he got out to him, he saw a big shark still biting him. The sharked remained right next to them, and the man was swimming in a pool of blood. The shark followed them all the way to shore. When they got up on to the beach, my dad saw that the man's leg was badly injured, and blood was pumping onto the sand. He did the best he could with what he didn't have, and a woman was standing nearby [possibly Vansant's sister] and he grabbed the skirt of one of those old-fashioned bathing suits and ripped a piece of cloth to make a tourniquet. But the man died. . . ."

All the flesh along the back of Vansant's left thigh was stripped from the hip to the knee, leaving the bone exposed. There was also a huge gash on the right leg. Witnesses, many of whom said that they saw the shark still stubbornly affixed to Vansant's leg in about eighteen inches of water, described it as bluish gray or black, about nine feet long, weighing approximately five hundred pounds, and possessing a distinctly large triangular dorsal fin. One witness, a sea captain, described the shark as a Spanish shark (sandtiger shark) with a circumference of about forty inches. He had not seen a shark of this type on the New Jersey coast before this time. The sea captain stated that sharks are apparently attracted by the fishing grounds offshore, where fishermen routinely throw inedible fish remains overboard. He also pointed out that, a month prior, a fisherman reportedly captured a shark and found a man's leg in its stomach. Maritime literature of the day claimed that the Spanish shark was driven from tropical waters by Spanish-American War naval bombing. The newspaper quotation attributed to the sea captain may, therefore, be nothing more than a reporter utilizing a known myth to generate witness testimony.

Local newspapermen asked Vansant's sister Louise for her interpretation of the events. Louise responded in Beach Haven's *Courier*, saying, "My brother was a good swimmer and left the crowd near shore to swim out beyond the breakers. A few minutes before, he had been playing with a big dog. The crowd, believing that he was calling for the dog, paid no heed to his cries. Everybody was horrified to see my brother splashing about in the water as though struggling with a monster under the surface. He fought desperately and as we rushed toward him we could see great quantities of blood. When Charles was taken from the water, the terrible story was revealed. For his left leg had been virtually torn off."

Dr. Eugene Vansant, along with a medical student, rushed to Charles's aid on the beach. They quickly moved him to the manager's office at the Engleside and cleared the large wooden desk to create a bed. Dr. Herbert Willis of Beach Haven (who later became mayor in the 1920s) and Dr. Joseph Neff, former director of Public Health in Philadelphia, were summoned and swiftly attempted to assist in retarding the flow of blood from the pumping wound. Dr. Willis telephoned Dr. Buchanan at Community Hospital in Toms River (thirty miles to the northwest) in an effort to have the suffering Vansant transported urgently, but Willis soon made the decision that Vansant was too weak to make the bumpy journey. Vansant had already lapsed into unconsciousness near the beach and never regained enough strength to tell the story of the attack. Charles was pronounced dead by Dr. Willis at 6:45 P.M.

Besides making Vansant's the most legible of the 1916 shark-related death certificates, Dr. Willis also meticulously recorded Vansant's period of suffering to be "1 hour and 3/4." Dr. Willis reported the immediate cause of death to be "hemorrhage from femoral artery, left side" and recorded the contributory cause of death as "bitten by shark while bathing." Dr. Vansant had later stated that he felt the cause of death to be obvious massive blood loss (progressive-hemorrhagic shock), as the "shark virtually tore Charles' left leg from his body." The body was transported to Philadelphia for burial.

The southern portions of New Jersey and Philadelphia reacted to the Vansant tragedy with immediate horror. Surprisingly, however, even though it was the first recorded shark attack fatality of the East Coast of the United States, it received minimal coverage by the northern New Jersey and New York newspapers. The *New York Times* buried the account of the Vansant attack on page 18, referring to the culprit simply as a "fish" on three occasions in the short piece and reluctantly mentioned that it was "presumably a shark." Longtime Jersey Shore residents were astounded by what had transpired in Beach Haven, but since the shore's

economy relied on the daily trainloads of New York visitors, no great un-
rest was apparent.

James M. Meehan, the Fish Commissioner of Pennsylvania, and the
former director of Philadelphia's Aquarium in Fairmont, in an effort to
calm the beachgoers of Beach Haven, contributed to a *Philadelphia Public Ledger* article whose headline read: BATHERS NEED HAVE NO
FEAR OF SHARKS: FISH EXPERT DECLARES ONE THAT KILLED
SWIMMER MAY HAVE SOUGHT TO ATTACK DOG." In the *Public
Ledger* article, Meehan stated:

> Despite the death of Charles Vansant and the report that two sharks hav-
> ing been caught in that vicinity recently, I do not believe there is any rea-
> son why people should hesitate to go in swimming at the beaches for fear
> of man-eaters. The information in regard to the sharks is indefinite and I
> hardly believe that Vansant was attacked by a man-eater. Vansant was in
> the surf playing with a dog and it may be that a small shark had drifted in
> at high water, and was marooned by the tide. Being unable to move
> quickly and without food, he had come in to attack the dog and snapped
> at the man in passing.

Meehan conceded that the shark involved in the attack could have
been a genuine man-eater (great white) but thought it more likely to be a
blue shark. He also specified that if the shark of this length (approximately nine feet) were a true man-eater, it would certainly have taken
Vansant's leg completely off. Meehan also mentioned that if the shark
were a hammerhead, it would have easily been identified by the observers. In closing, he stressed that all sharks, dangerous or otherwise,
belong in deep water and rarely come in close to shore.

These theories were corroborated by those considered to be shark experts. Some spoke with firm skepticism about the prospect of a true unprovoked shark attack. Others, like the scholars at the American Museum,
thought the event so unique, bizarre, distant, and questionable, that "no
comment" was the best comment. Many experts believed that the question of analysis would disappear as the scientifically volatile event became
a blurry memory.

In preparation for the Independence Day crowds, Robert Engle, owner of the Engleside, announced that Beach Haven would protect its bathers by placing wire netting in the surf, three hundred feet distant from the shoreline and extending the entire length of the beach. Local cottage residents generated a fund to help install the nets and the local pound fishermen (pounds were immense netted containers situated four hundred yards offshore, in which fishermen would capture and store live catches) placed the pilings in and hung steel nets. The nets were similar to those used on naval torpedo destroyers. The hastily constructed nets would last until late August when the first fierce northeasterly storm blew in.

Back in West Philadelphia, preparations were made for Vansant's funeral, scheduled for Wednesday, July 5. The mass was to be conducted from Vansant's home on Spruce Street at 11:00 A.M. under the guidance of Charles's mother, Louisa, and his father. The funeral services were open only to friends, relatives, and members of the Class of 1914 of the University of Pennsylvania. The Reverend Archibald McCallum from Vansant's Walnut Presbyterian Church was to officiate. The interment took place at the picturesque South Laurel Hill Cemetery, just outside Philadelphia.

Charles Vansant was gone, as was the male legacy of the Stophel Garrettson Vansants of Holland. The untouchable mystique surrounding the Oelrichs reward was gone as well. Today, a visit to Vansant's grave reveals that he was laid to rest at a family plot. I'll never forget the phrase that the helpful cemetery caretaker used as he pointed to a map to show me Vansant's location: "You'll find your loved one right in this section." Vansant had predeceased other family members by several years.

twenty-two

ATTACK: CALIFORNIA

by Thomas B. Allen

ON AN AUGUST AFTERNOON in 1998, Jonathan Kathrein, a sixteen-year-old surfer, was about fifty yards off California's Stinson Beach, riding the waves on a small plastic boogie board, when he felt teeth sink into his right leg. A shark was pulling him, screaming, into the sea. As Kathrein went under, he somehow managed to grab one of the shark's gill slits and yank. The shark let him go, and Kathrein surfaced. He struggled back onto the board before friends and lifeguards pulled him ashore. A helicopter flew him to a nearby hospital. He survived, with a foot-long gash in his thigh. Teeth marks in his wetsuit identified the attacker as a great white about eight feet long. Police quickly posted shark warnings at Stinson, but within hours after the attack, surfers and swimmers were back in the water. Never before had a shark attack been recorded off Stinson. After all, Stinson was safe.

Sharks have so often bloodied the waters of a certain area off California waters that surfers call the region "the Red Triangle." From 1952 to 1999, there were seventy-nine attacks recorded off the U.S. West Coast, eight of them fatal. Forty-one of the attacks were in the Red Triangle—encompassed by the sea from Bodega Bay south to the Farallon Islands (about thirty miles offshore and twenty-eight miles due west of Golden

Gate Bridge); then back to the mainland near Santa Cruz, at the northern rim of Monterey Bay. Stinson Beach, although within the Red Triangle, was considered safe because shark-attracting seals were rarely seen off that popular surfing and swimming spot, and there had never been a great white attack recorded there. In fact the supervisor of lifeguards at Stinson said he had never even seen a dorsal fin in the twenty-three years he had been patrolling the beach.

There certainly were great whites some thirty miles away, because Peter Pyle, a shark researcher working in the Farallon Islands, later reported that on the day the great white attacked Kathrein, great whites attacked two surfboards placed in the Farallon waters in a study of shark behavior. But, after the Kathrein attack, most Stinson surfers decided that the attack was just a bit of aberrant conduct by one of "the men in the gray flannel suits"—bravado surfer-talk for great white sharks.

Then, on an August day almost exactly a year after the attack on Kathrein, a shark appeared about fifty yards off Stinson Beach. As the shark swam along, parallel to the shore, swimmers and surfers fled from the water, and lifeguards forbade them to go back in. "It's possible it's the same shark, because it's about the same size as last year's shark. But we can't say for sure," said John E. McCosker, a senior scientist of the California Academy of Sciences and a world authority on great whites. A seal was spotted in the surf, and McCosker surmised that "the seal was cruising the annual salmon run for a snack, which, in turn, draws the sharks, which want to dine on seal. A shark so close to shore isn't unusual, but typically sharks hunt underwater."

California divers and surfers know they share the sea with great white sharks, especially along certain parts of the coast. So, when Marco Flagg, an experienced, thirty-one-year-old diver, spotted a shark about twenty feet away, he quickly identified it as a great white and thought, *Gee, I got to see it without paying for a shark diving trip. It's just passing. It's not coming back or circling.*

Flagg was diving in June 1995 with two friends near Blue Fish Cove off Point Lobos, near Carmel and south of the Red Triangle. As he was preparing for his second dive of the day, a tourist asked him why he was diving. He told her that he was taking photos of great white sharks.

When she asked him if that was dangerous, he sardonically replied, "No. If a shark gets aggressive I just punch him on the nose."

Flagg was on a scooter and wearing a DiveTracker, an underwater location device. He cautiously turned the scooter and headed toward the diving boat. "I did not want to rush to the surface because I knew that was where most great white attacks occur. I remained calm," he later told *Dive* magazine.

"About thirty seconds after the sighting," he continued, "I sensed something on my left. I looked down and saw a huge, gaping circle of teeth coming straight at me out of the murk. The thought of being eaten alive by a shark sounds nightmarish, but the speed of the thing meant all I had time to think was *Oh sheeeet* before it had me sideways in its jaws, clamped down like a vice. I felt an incredibly severe and dull pressure on my body, but no cutting. I was locked in the shark's jaws, facing away from it. It happened so quickly that there was no time to escape or struggle.

"As quickly as it had grabbed me, it let me go and swam away. It was so quick that I did not really appreciate the horror of what was happening. I was conscious of a lot of pain in my legs, and my mind was racing, thinking the shark had bitten one of them off. I felt to see if they were both still there, and they were. The relief was overwhelming. You think your life is going to flash before you when something like this happens, but it does not. I did not think about my family or anything like that. Instead I concentrated on getting back to the boat."

He reached the boat, jettisoned the scooter, weight belt, tank, and gear, and painfully managed to get into the boat. He did not remove his wetsuit because, he thought, *This might be all that was preventing my guts from spilling out*. Then he leaned over the side to haul in his gear—and fell in. He got into his boat again and started off to pick up his friends, who were diving nearby. Ashore, he collapsed. In the ambulance, still unaware of the extent of his wounds, he wondered whether he was going to live or die.

"At the hospital," he recounted, "the doctors stripped off my wetsuit and found cuts and abrasions—and that was all. I had to have seventeen stitches for cuts on my left forearm, leg, and lower abdomen. For an attack by a great white shark, my injuries were amazingly light." (It is thirty inches from the three-inch gash in his arm to the V-shaped puncture on his leg—the span of a single bite.).

Flagg, who owned a company that produced the DiveTracker and other oceanographic equipment, had made more than 300 dives around the world. "I have seen plenty of sharks," he said. "My philosophy has always been this: If it's not bigger than me, then I have no reason to fear it. I reckon the shark took a test bite, tasted metal, and spat me out. If it had not been for the tanks and the navigation unit, I would probably be dead." Bite marks on the DiveTracker showed that it had almost certainly saved his life, acting as armor that had shielded his body.

As Flagg's description of the attack circulated among divers, some began to wonder what role his scooter had played. Did its sound or electromagnetic field attract the shark? Six months before, off San Miguel Island, Jim Robinson, an urchin diver, had been on a scooter when a great white zeroed in on him. The shark closed its jaws around him, killing him, just as he surfaced at his boat and passed the scooter up to a crewman.

Flagg doubted the connection. "My simple suspicion," he said, "is that it was hungry and I just happened to run across its path. Incidents such as mine are so rare that it's impossible to draw any meaningful conclusions. The shark did not attack the scooter, but my mid-section. From what I understand, the shark's final approach is guided by sensing electrical fields using sensors in its snout. And while it's true that a scooter emits a strong DC field, that field is uniform. I would suspect the animal is not attracted to field strength but to its variability, because many things in the water, such as dock and harbor structures, generate a DC field. This contrasts with a field generated by an animal, like one with a heartbeat."

A scooter's DC field is not necessarily steady, however. Most scooters have three speed settings, and during a dive a diver may frequently change speeds. Each setting produces a different DC field. More variances occur as the scooter's battery runs down.

McCosker contributed to the electrical-attraction debate by recalling that he once had had to release a healthy baby great white shark that had been repeatedly bumping into a certain spot on the wall of the Steinhart Aquarium's Roundabout tank. An electronics expert who examined the spot later detected there a very weak (about 0.125 millivolts) static electrical anomaly.

McCosker also remarked that while studying great whites along Australia's Great Barrier Reef he noted that they would "come up and mouth the shark cages in a funny way. Not attack them, but mouth them in a way suggesting it is part of a bioelectric stimulation. Have we demonstrated it? No. But let me put it this way: If a scuba diver forty feet down gets bitten, I would probably raise my eyebrows and ask, What gives? Because that's almost unheard of. But Flagg was forty feet down and holding onto a device pulsing an electrical DC field and making a noise, as it apparently did, that might incite a shark to mouth and bite, as it apparently did. That leads me to suspect that the scooter was probably contributory, but in ways we don't know. All the additional variables and attractive stimuli—sound, visual, electronic—complicate the issue. Sort of like *Murder on the Orient Express*. There are so many possible culprits." Whatever the scientific theories, many divers stopped using scooters, especially divers who, like Robinson, made a living harvesting sea urchins.

The attack on Flagg was not the first to occur in Monterey Peninsula waters. In 1981, Lou Boren was fatally attacked while surfing in Spanish Bay. Four years later, at Monastery Beach next to the Point Lobos Marine Reserve, Frank Gallo was about thirty feet underwater and about 150 yards offshore when a shark mauled him. He pushed the shark, which swam off as Gallo reached the surface. He called out a warning to his friends, who, ignoring their own safety, got him onto a diving mattress and towed him to shore, where they summoned help. Gallo, a paramedic and a competition scuba diver, was in superb shape and so survived a punctured right lung, and wounds—on his right shoulder, forearm, jaw, and neck—that required more than 600 stitches. In 1990, off the same beach, a shark gnawed a woman's leg, and then swam off. She also survived.

NATIVE AMERICAN COASTAL TRIBES encountered sharks close to the shores of what would become California. Members of the Pomo tribe said a prayer to guard themselves against sharks before they swam to outlying rocks on seal hunts.

Encounters remained unchronicled until the reporting of an attack in July 1926. A five-foot shark of unidentified species attacked a swimmer and his dog in San Francisco Bay, seriously injuring the swimmer. A boat launched from shore rescued him. The next reported attack came in 1950, this one off Imperial Beach in San Diego County. The victim was one of four swimmers treading water about twelve feet deep. The shark, probably a great white, came from behind, biting the swimmer on a leg and then attacking from the front, biting a leg as the victim kicked at it. The shark swam off. A lifeguard brought the man ashore. He recovered.

Coincidentally, in that same year the California Bureau of Marine Fisheries published a guide to local sharks that said the great white was "uncommon at best in our waters, and, since it rarely comes inshore, it is a negligible hazard to California swimmers." Two years after the guide was published, a shark killed another swimmer, and this time the attack was so thoroughly documented, there was no doubt that the killer was a great white.

Seventeen-year-old Barry Wilson was swimming off Pacific Grove on December 7, 1952, when something grabbed him. When he screamed, his cry was heard simultaneously by his friend, fifteen-year-old Brookner Brady, Jr. who was swimming nearby, and John C. Bassford, who was sitting on a rise directly above the beach. An instant before the scream, Bassford, an experienced diver, had noticed that the youth seemed to be frantically scanning the water around him. Then a large shark rose directly in front of him. As Bassford shouted a warning to Brady, the shark struck Wilson. Bassford saw Wilson's body thrust straight out of the water.

Wilson pushed both his hands against the shark, trying to free himself. But he fell sideways, still clutched by the shark, and was pulled under. Blood gushed upward and spread on the surface, forming a circle about six feet in diameter. Wilson suddenly bobbed to the surface in the middle of the circle, screamed again, and began beating the water with his hands.

Now the shark appeared again, part of its back showing above the surface. It swept past Wilson, returned, then disappeared. Brady, who had seen the attack, swam about fifty feet to reach Wilson and began towing him to shore. Meanwhile, four members of the Sea Otter Club, a divers group, swam out to Wilson and Brady, bringing with them a large inner tube. Three of the Sea Otters were trained investigators: Sergeant Earl Stanley of the 63rd Military Police Platoon stationed at nearby Fort Ord; Robert Shaw of the 313th Criminal Investigation Detachment at Fort Ord; and Frank M. Ambrosio of the California State Highway Patrol. The fourth Sea Otter was John L. Poskus, a mathematics and physics teacher at Monterey High School.

The four men managed to get the tube around Wilson's body and up under his limp arms. As they struggled in the water with the bulky tube, Wilson suddenly lunged forward. Startled, Shaw looked around to see that a shark had violently pushed Wilson and then turned away. Shaw and Ambrosio clung to opposite sides of the inner tube, pushing it, while Poskus pulled it with a nylon rope he had attached to it. Stanley kept to the back of the tube, supporting Wilson's head.

Through rough seas, the men headed for a small breakwater pier. During the twenty-minute swim to the pier, the shark constantly hovered close by the rescuers and the victim. Again and again—usually when the men stopped to prop Wilson's slipping body back into the tube—the shark appeared. Never did it strike.

Wilson was dead when a waiting physician examined him the moment his body was carried up to the pier. The lower part of his right buttock and nearly all of the back of his right leg, from the thigh almost to the knee, was ripped away. His left leg bore deep slashes.

Evidence showed that the killer had been a great white, twelve to thirteen feet long. Rolf L. Bolin, an ichthyologist from Hopkins Marine Station in Pacific Grove, said the teenager had been bitten at least four times. "The corroboratory evidence of the witnesses," Bolin reported, "indicates the sequence: first, on the lower left leg from behind, which strike wounded and startled him; second, on the medial surface of the right thigh, when the shark approached him from in front, and, passing partially between his legs, lifted him high out of the water; third, on the upper left leg from the back and side, when Wilson struck in desperation at the water, and, finally, on the back and side of the right thigh, while he was being placed in the tube and when he was undoubtedly already dead."

The rescuers and Bolin were able to provide one of the most detailed descriptions recorded up to that time at the attack site itself. All the information the investigators assembled would later be seen as important elements in analyzing attacks. *Weather:* partly cloudy. *Water depth:* about thirty feet. *Water temperature:* around 55°. *Water conditions:* murky because of dirt washed into the sea by rain the night before and a heavy concentration of plankton. Surf was running to heights of about eight feet. *Underwater visibility:* six to eight feet.

There were no more shark attacks recorded in California until February 1955, when a spear fisherman diving in Monterey Bay was grabbed about both ankles by a great white. It ripped off the ankle portions of the diver's wetsuit, tore off his right swim fin and a heavy wool sock, bit through his left swim fin, and swam off. Eight months later, a shark appeared near two divers swimming not far from shore off La Jolla, near the Scripps Institution of Oceanography. Hoping to positively identify the shark, a Scripps specialist in sharks, Arthur O. Flechsig, set out to catch it. The shark attacked his boat, leaving behind two teeth that gave a shaken Flechsig positive identification: a great white. Within two weeks, nine great whites were caught in the area. Now there could be no doubt that the 1950 state guide was wrong.

A scientist working in the 1950s and 1960s one day watched as a shark, undoubtedly a great white, seemingly pondered a possible attack on a scuba diver. His report is one of the earliest scientific accounts of shark attack-mode behavior: "The shark first appeared approximately 3 feet below the surface and moved directly toward the foot of the surface swimmer, who was wearing a black suit and green fins. The speed of the shark accelerated as it neared the flippers. When not more than 1½ feet away, it turned abruptly down, as the diver pulled his flipper up in a recovery swim stroke. The shark swam in a circle of about 15 feet, dropping to a depth of 6 to 10 feet. On the second approach, it turned away at a distance of 2 to 3 feet as the diver clung to the skiff. After the diver and his partner had entered the skiff, a shark (believed to be the same one) surfaced nearby, but avoided the pier of the nearby Scripps Institution of Oceanography.

There could be no doubt that great whites were appearing in California waters in increasing numbers. Tragic proof came again in April 1957.

Peter Savino and Daniel Hogan were swimming beyond the breakers of Morro Bay, near San Luis Obispo, when Savino became tired and Hogan started towing him toward shore. A shark appeared, nudged Savino, and drew blood when it rubbed him with its sandpaper hide. "I have blood on my arms!" Savino yelled to Hogan. "We'd better get out of here!" They began swimming separately. A moment later, Hogan turned to see whether Savino was all right. Savino had disappeared, without an outcry, and was never seen again.

Two years later came what Californians called the Year of the Shark. On May 7, 1959, Albert Kogler and Shirley O'Neill were treading water about fifty feet off Baker's Beach, San Francisco, when Kogler screamed: "It's a shark! Get out of here!" But Shirley O'Neill stayed. As she later recounted, "It was just blood all over—I knew I couldn't leave him—he just kept screaming and screaming. I could tell the fish was chewing him up. It was a horrible scream. He was shouting, 'Help me! Help me!' I grabbed for his hand, but when I pulled, I could see that his arm was just hanging on by a thread. So I grabbed him around his back. But it was all bloody and I could see the insides." She towed him to shore. He died that night.

Less than a month later, on June 14, Robert Pamperin, a husky, thirty-year-old aircraft engineer, was diving for abalone about fifty yards off La Jolla with another diver, Gerald Lehrer. Suddenly, Pamperin rose high out of the water. His faceplate had been torn off. He screamed once. "I was swimming about fifteen feet from Bob," Lehrer said later. "I heard him calling, 'Help me! Help me!' I swam over to him. He was thrashing in the water, and I could tell he was fighting something underneath . . ."

In the next instant, Pamperin went under. Lehrer peered underwater through his faceplate. The water, though bloodied, was remarkably clear, and he saw his friend's body in the jaws of a shark, estimated by Lehrer to be twenty feet long. "It had a white belly and I could see its jaws and jagged teeth," Lehrer said. "I wasn't able to do anything more." Lehrer, wanting to warn other swimmers, swam to shore, where several stunned bathers witnessed the attack. Pamperin's body was never found.

Eight days after the Pamperin attack, a twelve-foot shark was caught off Catalina Island, about sixty miles north of La Jolla. In its belly was a man's watch, too badly deteriorated to be identified. It could not have been Pamperin's, for he had not been wearing a watch. Had it come from a corpse or a victim? Now shark-conscious, the chief of San Diego lifeguards said that during the three months before the attack on Pamperin three people had disappeared in the area, and their bodies had never been found. Were they also victims of sharks?

Before 1959 ended, there were three more attacks in California. A hammerhead shark (*Sphyrna mokarran*) slashed a spear fisherman's left leg about 300 yards from where Pamperin had been devoured. Off Malibu, a shark raked a swimmer's left arm from wrist to elbow. And a great white bit a diver's swim fin, "shook me like a dog shakes a bone," and then released him, unharmed. Dr. H. David Baldridge, who had recently begun supervising what was then called the Shark Attack File, described 1959 as a "peak year," during which fifty-six attacks were reported throughout the world.

In California, public officials asked for some explanation for the shark boom. Oceanographers reported a rise in water temperatures off the coast of California in recent years. But no scientist could offer any answers to the officials' questions: Why had sharks suddenly appeared off California? Why had those specific people been attacked? And what about that lifeguard's remark: Was it possible that people who had disappeared were in fact victims of shark attacks?

To get the answers, scientists began a research effort that still goes on. From their observations in California have come not only ideas about the comings and goings of great whites but also unprecedented close-up observations of shark predation. By watching how sharks attacked their natural prey, scientists were able to produce scenarios that showed parallels to attacks on human beings. The epicenter of research is found in the Farallon Islands. In Native American legend the desolate, rocky isles were known as "the islands of the dead." Scientists have another name for the Farallons: "a white shark hotspot," a place so teeming with great whites that, after a series of non-fatal attacks there, sports divers have essentially abandoned the islands to the sharks, the pinnipeds, and the scientists.

Shark researcher Peter Klimley is one of those scientists. Klimley, a University of California professor, works out of the Bodega Marine Laboratory north of San Francisco. Klimley uses a Zodiac inflatable boat to ferry himself and other researchers to and from a research skiff tied to a buoy in a shark-watching bay. One day, while the skiff bobbed in large swells "like a large fishing jig" (in Klimley's words), a shark bolted toward the empty boat and attacked it. If anyone doubts whether sharks attack boats, just ask Klimley. But he believes that sharks do not actively seek human victims. And he believes that human beings entering California's waters should be aware of the sharks around them, particularly the great white, the shark that wounds and kills people more than any other species.

Klimley thinks that great whites sample unusual or unexpected prey, such as people, by first taking a bite. If that taste is satisfactory, they keep on eating; if not, they swim off. Klimley and two other scientists videotaped, above and below the water, 129 white-shark predatory attacks on northern elephant seals and California sea lions in the Farallons. In a typical attack—dubbed "feeding bout"—the sea explodes as a shark hits a seal underwater. Next, the seal appears in a widening blot of red as it bleeds to death. The shark then leaps out of the water and seizes the seal in its jaws. Neither the shark nor the seal is seen again.

Another researcher is Peter Pyle of Point Reyes Bird Observatory, who alternates annually between studying the birds of the Farallons and the sharks of the Farallons. The switchover comes in the fall when juvenile elephant seals haul out on the islands. Sharks prowl around the rocky ledges as the young seals struggle ashore. Sometimes the waves wash them back in the sea, and the sharks are waiting.

When a shark strikes, Pyle and Scot Anderson, a shark biologist, head for the kill site in a fourteen-foot boat. They lower underwater cameras and photograph the sharks eating their prey. From scars—probably inflicted during a food-fight misunderstanding—the scientists can identify the sharks. They have given the sharks names, such as Cut Dorsal and Notched Lobe, and have repeatedly watched them eat, sometimes consuming a seal (about 400 pounds of food) in about ten bites. Great whites seem to prefer elephant seals over sea lions, probably because the seals are loners that move slowly or, motionless on the surface, are literally sitting targets. The seals, which stay together and move swiftly, are more likely to spot a hunting shark and escape. African herd animals use the same many-eyes strategy against hunting lions.

As researchers analyze the great white's attack strategy for getting a seal, they see the act beginning as the shark launches a swift strike from below and takes a large bite, which usually causes death from loss of blood. Sometimes, however, the prey veers at the last moment—or the shark's aim is slightly off—and the seal escapes, either cleanly or raked by teeth. Researchers have seen many seals with scars testifying to such a near-death experience.

Most seals and sea lions suffered fatal wounds on their lower bodies. Sea lions usually survived the shark's first strike, unless that first strike decapitated the sea lion. The observers never saw a prey animal attacked on the surface.

Translating their observations from marine mammals to humans, the scientists compared a representative attack on a pinniped to an actual attack on a commercial abalone diver. A shark grabbed the diver as he paused about twenty feet below the surface to clear his ears. As the diver described the attack, "the shark swam up from underneath, seized me, carried me down for five to seven seconds, and suddenly let go and swam off." The diver, bleeding profusely, struck the shark with a club. Elephant seals are big enough to struggle successfully, surviving though scarred. And, like an elephant seal that fights as it is carried underwater by a shark, the diver had a similar experience—surviving with scars.

The observers also saw sharks sample an animal and then reject it, presumably as unappetizing. Unwanted meals included a brown pelican (*Pelicanus occidentalis*) struck from below. Hurled into the air, the bird bled and died from the strike. But the shark did not feed on it. Sharks also turned down rotting pinniped carcasses. Other observers had noticed that sharks bite but do not consume jackass penguins (*Spheniscus demersus*) and sea otters (*Enhydra lutris*), which are not eaten, though they sometimes are beheaded.

The scientific conclusion: "The birds, sea otter, and human are composed mainly of muscle tissue, whereas pinnipeds and cetaceans possess a great deal of superficial fat tissue. Sharks may prefer energy-rich marine mammals in favor of energy-poor prey." Sharks, probably for the same reason, selectively feed on whale blubber but not on muscle layers. "Fat," Klimley points out, "has twice the energy value that muscle does."

If that reasonably explains what sharks do as predators, why are the sharks there in the first place? Recent research by Klimley and his colleagues shows that white sharks are drawn, every summer and fall, to feasts offered by the seasonal arrival of seals and sea lions to waters off central California. In summer the sharks feed on seals and sea lions as far north as Oregon and occasionally the Gulf of Alaska; in fall, the sharks head south to prey upon pinnipeds living on offshore islands. Female white sharks migrate to southern California to give birth, an energy-draining event that presumably leaves them ravenous.

During the El Niño years of abnormally warm water, when both white sharks and their pinniped prey were found farther north, researchers noted a sharp increase in white shark predation. Great white shark populations seem to be increasing along the coasts of California and Oregon in concert with the booming populations of seals and sea lions, whose numbers have been growing since they gained federal-imposed sanctuary under the Marine Mammals Protection Act in 1972. The law made it illegal to hunt pinnipeds. Fifteen elephant seals were living within the Red Triangle in 1961. There were 5,000 by 1984, and the population began rising at the rate of 5 percent a year.

Another population is also increasing: divers, surfers, windsurfers, and ocean-going kayakers. And that means more encounters with sharks. Those California encounters, researchers discovered, resembled unprovoked attacks reported in Chilean, South African, Australian, Japanese, and Italian waters. Great white attacks, they observed, were "typically centered where pinnipeds are abundant, such as nearshore rocky outcrops and islands and often near the entrances of rivers." These are prime danger zones for human visitors.

Warnings of danger are not always heeded. California's recent attacks seem to follow a pattern: A shark bites or mauls a victim, who reaches shore and is saved by prompt and skilled medical attention. Divers and surfers may be venturing into sharky waters because, at least subconsciously, they know that expert emergency care is almost always available if the men in the gray flannel suits ruin a perfect day. Divers and surfers around Point Lobos knew there were seals in the area; Flagg saw some just before the shark grabbed him. And most of them knew that the seals attract hungry great whites. Recent victims like Flagg live to tell their shark tales because of modern rescue techniques and modern medical skills.

Recreation once meant refreshment of the spirits after toil—Isaac Walton's "calm, quiet, innocent recreation" of fishing, for example. But many who seek recreation in the sea today are looking for thrills. In the Red Triangle, the thrill involves statistics. Of the seventy-nine attacks recorded between 1952 and 2000, forty-one were in Red Triangle waters. The odds favor the human over the shark. As researcher Scot Anderson has observed, "California averages about two attacks per year, with a fatality once every five years. Statistically speaking, more people are killed by pigs in Iowa."

Abalone divers are not recreationists. They work the waters around the Farallon Islands, risking their lives for what could be a small fortune on a good day. They are not quite as foolhardy as they may appear. About 90 percent of all shark attacks happen at the surface, and most of the others take place between the surface and the sea floor. Once at the floor, a diver is relatively safe from attack.

"The first key to white shark safety is spotting him before he spots you, or at the same time he spots you," a diver told a Discovery Channel interviewer. "The minute he loses the element of surprise, we feel like that's a big factor, and the key thing again is to stay on the bottom, stay low to the rocks, climb into a hole if there's one nearby. Don't go anywhere. The guy who swims to the surface is going to get bit for sure." That diver carried a handgun modified to work underwater and, he hoped, capable of killing a shark within ten feet.

"We consider the springtime to be the relatively safe time of year," the diver said, "and we've always been somewhat lax. Up until this last month, I've never seen a shark at the Farallons in the springtime, not one. On this day, as I worked my way through a kind of flat, wide open bottom, and worked my way out into deeper water, like what would be thirty-five or forty feet for us, I saw a flash. I said, *That was a white shark.* Then I said, *No, that wasn't a white shark, whitey's not out here this time of year.* And then I looked down and picked an abalone, and I looked up and he was coming straight at me. This thing was huge. It was like laying on the street and having a station wagon drive over you.

"Normally, I would be getting the gun out at that point, and be ready to shoot it, if it got real close and got real aggressive with me. But it didn't come back, and I waited for about five minutes, and it didn't come back, and it didn't come back. I worked my way back to the boat, just hugging the bottom real close. I still didn't see it, still didn't see it . . . And when I got under the boat, I took my knee out from under the rock and made the fastest free ascent in the history of mankind. I happened to come up right at the ladder. And I pretty much walked on water the little distance I had to go, and then climbed up the ladder. I remember taking the regulator out of my mouth when I hit the deck. It was full of white foam, and I realized my mouth had gotten completely dry, and I kind of was just slobbering this white foam.

"I'm afraid of white sharks. I guess I'm not afraid enough to stop what I'm doing. I'm cautious. But I feel like we've achieved some kind of working relationship. We've achieved kind of a harmony where I can continue to work the areas that I'm working. The shark's looking for specific circumstances, and as long as I stay out of those situations, I'm going to be safe."

One abalone diver's luck ran out one day in September 1995, when he was surfacing after a dive in Shelter Cove, north of San Francisco. He was just putting an abalone in his diving bag when he felt a shark bite his left leg. "It pulled my leg and foot out of the water," he recounted. "I saw the shark's mouth with its ugly teeth. It was awful. I couldn't believe it." Abruptly, the shark swam off. The diver's partner and other divers got him ashore and to a hospital, where physicians took three great white teeth out of his leg and closed the wounds with fifty staples.

It happened again in August 1996 when another abalone diver found himself about ten feet above a great white, which was swimming in the same direction as the diver. Suddenly, the shark lunged upward, biting the thirty-five-year-old diver on the upper body. The shark took him to the surface—much as it would a seal that had been caught below—and inexplicably released him. The demonstration of prey-taking and prey rejection happened in the heart of shark territory: off Tomales Point, at the northern tip of the Point Reyes Peninsula. The diver, bleeding heavily, swam about twenty yards to his boat, from which his friends radioed for help. Ashore, he got medical help quickly and survived.

Ten months before, at Dillon Beach, not far from the abalone diver's attack site, a great white grabbed a surfer by a leg and flipped him and his surfboard over, then quickly released him, leaving him with a mauled leg. He was able to paddle to shore and get treatment for wounds not considered serious.

Kayakers are the newest members of California's shark-endangered population. And, like the surfers and the divers, kayakers have learned about the sharks of California.

A boat was sailing off Channel Islands Harbor, about forty miles north of Malibu, in January 1989 when a crew member saw the body of a young woman floating on the calm sea. A summoned Coast Guard craft retrieved the body and took it ashore, where a coroner examined it. The body, he said, bore "a classic shark bite"—a wound that had removed a piece of flesh nineteen inches wide from the front of the woman's left thigh. She had also suffered several other wounds, including a "defensive-type" bruise on the back of her right hand. That injury conjured up a woman trying to ward off a shark.

"The lungs did not show any of the classic findings of drowning," the coroner reported. "This was about as likely a fresh bite case as I've ever seen." She was bitten, he believed, before she died.

This "gorgeous young girl," as the coroner described her, was eighteen to twenty-six years old, had short brown hair, and was wearing a blue and black Spandex swimming suit with a blue and black zip-up jacket. The published description added that she had ear studs and wore a ring on her right hand. Not a swimmer or a surfer, the coroner deduced. He guessed that she had been a windsurfer.

He was wrong. Near the shore in the area where the body was found, searchers discovered a kayak paddle. At Ventura, just up the coast, the surfers kept surfing. "It's just one of those things you live with when you go surfing," one of the surfers told a Los Angeles Times reporter.

John McCosker, the shark researcher, said attacks were "entirely predictable" on anyone venturing far from shore. The kayaker—if that was what the unidentified woman was doing—was paddling through an area filled with sharks drawn to the Channel Islands, a breeding ground for sea lions and seals. "A shark looks up and sees a silhouette from something like a kayak, thinks he's got a big elephant seal, and swims up to take it."

Two fifteen-foot kayaks were found, lashed together, about five miles offshore, south of where the body was found. The underside of one of the kayaks bore abrasions and had been holed three times. Experts who examined it said a great white had probably attacked it.

When the body was identified as Tamara McAllister, a twenty-four-year-old UCLA graduate student, the mystery nearly ended. She and her boyfriend, fellow graduate student Roy Jeffrey Stoddard, twenty-four, had put their kayaks into the sea north of Malibu. They planned to paddle north about a mile and a half to Paradise Cove and return. Somewhere offshore they had tied the kayaks together, possibly to go for a swim, a common practice of kayakers. Whatever happened next will never be known.

There were not enough clues to determine whether a shark struck while the young man and woman were in the kayaks or in the water. The attack on Tamara McAllister was a characteristic great white hit-and-run. Stoddard's fate was not known because his body was not found.

The next kayak attack came in November 1992 when two paddlers chose to venture into what was undoubtedly the best place along the central California coast to confront great whites: Año Nuevo, a tiny island twenty-three miles north of Santa Cruz. Not only was Año Nuevo well within the Red Triangle; it was also an elephant seal rookery that one shark researcher compares to a supermarket for great whites: "It's stationary, it's open twenty-four hours a day, and it's full of things they like to eat." Like the Farallons to the north, Año Nuevo is a magnet for pinnipeds and their hungry predators. From December to March, about 8,000 northern elephant seals haul up on the bleak island, and massive males—called beachmasters—fight over female harems.

The two kayakers were Ken Kelton and Mike Chin. Although an experienced whitewater kayaker, Chin was paddling out to the open ocean for the first time. Kelton paddled a red kayak eleven and a half feet long; Chin's sixteen footer had a blue deck and a white hull. In the story Chin told on the Internet, the two circled the island, "gawking at the seals," then crossed the shallow channel between the island and the mainland, where seals also haul out. As they dawdled, looking for likely landing sites, Chin was about thirty or forty feet behind Kelton.

"I don't remember if it was sight or sound that first caught my attention," Chin wrote. "I vaguely recall hearing a thump & perhaps Ken saying 'What the . . . ???'" Chin saw something yanking and splashing at the stern of Ken's kayak. "Even though I couldn't yet see the shark in these first 1-2 seconds, I somehow knew exactly what was happening. I believe in this initial contact, the shark was mainly placing his jaws on the boat. In the next 3-4 seconds, the shark lunged horizontally out of the water with the boat clamped in his jaws, his belly skimming the water surface. I saw a dark dorsal fin, and the profile of the shark's immense bulk, dark on top turning to silver on the sides & fading to white on the belly. . . . It seemed that half the shark's length cleared the water, causing the stern to disappear, and it seemed that the shark had merged with the kayak/Ken. The shark seemed at once horrible, beautiful, powerful, terrifying & graceful.

"There was a rush of water like that of a breaking wave as the shark surged forward, up, & finally down. It seemed that the dorsal fin was towering over Ken's head as I finally lost sight of him amidst the spray. I was sure that I had just watched him die. After the shark submerged again, he abruptly let go and vanished; we never saw him again. Unbelievably, Ken was alive, unhurt, and still upright. Two thoughts were flashing through my head: white sharks rarely hit a victim more than once, and even more rarely do they attack rescuers.

"I paddled up nervously, scanning the water beneath my boat, slapping the water with my paddle, striving to not look like an injured seal. Ken yelled, 'What *was* that??!!' Somehow the humor of Ken not immediately realizing what had happened escaped me at that moment. I yelled back, 'Shark!'"

After a few moments of indecision—paddle seaward or shoreward?—Kelton landed his water-filled kayak on the mainland. There was a bite seventeen inches across a foot and a half behind the cockpit where Kelton had been sitting. At the waterline were several three- and four-inch gashes.

Not quite a year later after the Kelton attack, Rosemary Johnson went kayaking in another area known to be swarming with seals—and, of course, great whites. Johnson, in a blue kayak, paddled, with three other kayakers in separate boats, off the Sonoma coast, near the mouth of the Russian River. River mouths are a notorious rendezvous for sharks feeding on food items that float into the sea. Russian River has an added treat because seals haul out along the shore here. Johnson was on the ocean side of Arched Rock, a local landmark, when a white shark hit her kayak, lifting it out of the water and hurling Johnson out of the kayak. Confused, she thought she had hit a rock. The other kayaks sped to her side, got her into a kayak—hers had a large hole in it—and paddled to shore. She had not been injured. The shark was not seen again.

An analysis of seventy-four attacks along the U.S. West Coast showed that twenty-six attacks involved surfers (one in Washington, ten in Oregon, fifteen in central and northern California); and twenty-nine attacks involved divers from the same California areas. A close look at the fatalities shows that kayakers and swimmers died at a much higher rate than divers or surfers. Counting Stoddard as an attack casualty, of four kayakers who encountered sharks, two died. Of the five swimmers in the attack analysis, three died, compared to two of the twenty-nine divers and one of the twenty-six surfers. The probable reason is that swimmers tend to be solitary and often may not be able to get immediate help, as congregating surfers do.

There's something else. Surfers in southern California usually chose long, broad beaches, where there may be sharks but not pinnipeds. Along the coasts of northern California, Oregon, and Washington, surfers often chose places where there are pinnipeds and sharks. And on a board a surfer can look like a pinniped. Attacks again and again appear to be instances of mistaken identity, or perhaps it is a matter of territory—whose sea is this anyway?

twenty-three

ATTACK AT SEA

by Thomas B. Allen

IT IS ONE OF the grimmest reports in the battle-action archives of the U.S. Navy: "All bodies were in extremely bad condition and had been dead for an estimated 4 or 5 days. Some had life jackets and life belts, most had nothing. Most of the bodies were completely naked, and others had just drawers or dungaree trousers on—only three of the 28 bodies recovered had shirts on. Bodies were horribly bloated and decomposed—recognition of faces would have been impossible. About half the bodies were shark-bitten, some to such a degree that they more nearly resembled skeletons."

The report was written by the commanding officer of the U.S.S. *Helm,* a destroyer that sailed into bloodstained waters and snatched from the jaws of sharks the bodies and the survivors of the cruiser *Indianapolis*. Her legacy is not only what she did in World War II but what was done to her men by sharks.

On July 16, 1945, the *Indianapolis* departed San Francisco for a ten-day, 5,000-mile voyage. Traveling unescorted, she carried components for the first atomic bombs to the U.S. base at Tinian, the takeoff point for the dropping of the atomic bombs on Hiroshima and Nagasaki. After unloading her cargo, on July 28, again sailing alone, she made a brief call at

Guam and then headed westward for Leyte in the Philippines. At 12:15 A.M. on July 30, two torpedoes, fired by a Japanese submarine, struck her. She capsized and sank within minutes. There was no time to send an SOS. In those few moments, hundreds of survivors managed to plunge into the oil-slicked water.

Of the more than 1,190 men aboard, about 880—many of them badly burned, maimed, and wounded—made it alive into the sea in the early minutes of Monday, July 30. One of the men in the water, Woody James, a twenty-two-year-old sailor from Alabama, remembered that at first the sharks merely circled around, not striking anyone in his group. That was July 30, the first day, when the men in the water thought that help was inevitably on its way. Neither he nor any other survivors knew that U.S. Navy officials at Guam and Leyte did not realize that the *Indianapolis* was missing. The men—and the sharks—would be in the water for a long nightmare.

Another man in the water, Patrick Finneran, told what came with the dawn: "One by one sharks began to pick off the men on the outer perimeter of the clustered groups. Agonizing screams filled the air day and night. Blood mixed with the fuel oil. . . . It was a terror-filled ordeal—never knowing if you'd be the next victim." Survivors said they saw sharks by the hundreds, most of them swimming just below their feet, some of them rising to take a victim.

Both James and Finneran remember the third day, Wednesday, August 1, most of all. Numerous sharks—hundreds, by several estimates—swam amid the men, dorsal fins cutting through the blinding sun-glare of the oil. "By the third day," Finneran later wrote, "lack of water and food, combined with the unrelenting terror, began to take its effect on the mental stability of the men. Many began to hallucinate. Some, many who had taken in seawater, went slowly mad. Fights broke out. Hope faded."

"You'd hear guys scream, especially late in the afternoon," James remembered. "Seemed like the sharks were the worst late in the afternoon. . . . Then they fed at night too. Everything would be quiet and then you'd hear somebody scream and you knew a shark had got him."

By then, men around him were fighting and "going berserk." So he and a buddy tied their life jackets together and "kind of drifted off by ourselves."

On the fourth day, Thursday, August 2, the sharks were among them still. Many survivors clustered in groups, knowing now that the sharks picked off loners. The sharks also took the easiest prey, the corpses. Survivor manuals, if anyone could remember them in the delirium of blinding sun and desperate thirst, said it was safer to remain still. *But would that make you look like a corpse? Or did the manual say you should fight the sharks when they came close?* When they had the strength for it, men did kick and splash when a shark came into view. And, in a swift, sensible assessment of shark behavior, men kept together. Those who swam off were doomed to drown or be eaten.

At first, men took precious lifejackets off the corpses and pushed them off as lures for the sharks. As their strength waned, they were too weak to dispatch the corpses. And so the sharks kept coming among them, taking the living with the dead. Oil still covered everyone, but as the sea carried off patches of oil, men could look into the clear water and see the sharks swimming beneath their feet.

During the night, and now during the day, men were swimming off to die, sometimes in the jaws of a shark, sometimes because their minds and bodies had surrendered to the sea. At dawn one man noticed another floating down facefirst in his lifejacket. The sailor nudged him, thinking he was asleep. The head and torso flipped over. From the waist down there was nothing.

Later that morning, a Navy aircraft on routine patrol spotted some survivors. Thinking that a plane had gone down, the patrol craft radioed for a rescue craft to drop life rafts and set up a recovery operation. No one at the Navy's two Pacific headquarters yet officially knew that the *Indianapolis* had gone down and that there were hundreds of men in the sea. Responding to the rescue call late on the afternoon of August 2, Lt. Robert A. Marks, flying a Catalina PBY, spotted a long oil slick and many black, bobbing heads. He took the amphibious aircraft down to about 100 feet and began dropping life rafts. Then one of his crewmen saw sharks attacking the men in bloodstained water and shouted the news to Marks. He knew he had to save those men immediately.

PBYs were not rated to land in heavy seas. But he went into a power-on stall—tail low, nose high to keep the propellers from churning the waves—and put the plane down between swells, popping a couple of hull rivets. Sharks were attacking nearby men as Marks wove through the clusters, picking up the loners he judged to be most vulnerable. Men died swimming to the plane, but it slowly filled, and men were lashed to its wings. By nightfall, Marks's PBY had fifty-six survivors in it and on it.

Shortly after midnight, the destroyer *Doyle* arrived and took Marks' men on board. Other ships were arriving. The rescue of the *Indianapolis*' men had begun, on the fifth day of their ordeal. One of those ships was the destroyer *Helm*. At dawn, when the *Helm's* men began looking for survivors, they saw that the sharks were still there.

"From one to four sharks were in the immediate area of the ship at all times," the *Helm* report says. "At one time, two sharks were attacking a body not more than fifty yards from the ship, and continued to do so until driven off by rifle fire."

The *Helm* was recovering not just the occasional survivor but body after body. "For the most part," the report says, "it was impossible to get finger prints from the bodies as the skin had come off the hands or the hands lacerated by sharks. Skin was removed from the hands of bodies containing no identification, when possible, and the Medical Officer dehydrated the skin in an attempt to make legible prints. All personal effects removed from the bodies for purposes of identification, and the Medical Officer's Reports are forwarded herewith in lieu of the Bureau of Medicine and Surgery and the Personal Effects Distribution Center, Farragut, Idaho, on the assumption that such effects will be assembled from all ships recovering them. After examination, all bodies were sunk, using two inch line and a weight of three 5"/38 cal. projectiles. There were still more bodies in the area when darkness brought a close to the gruesome operations for the day. In all, twenty-eight bodies were examined and sunk."

The destroyer *French* made a similar report about the bodies: ". . . appeared to have been partially eaten by sharks . . . very badly mutilated by sharks . . . Body clad in dungaree trousers only. Badly mangled by sharks . . ." The search went on for six days. Of the 800 men who had gone into the water after the sinking, 318 had survived, and two of them would die soon after rescue.

THE "SHARK-INFESTED PACIFIC," AS war correspondents inevitably referred to that theater of war, was indeed well sharked, with at least 150 species, not including bottom-dwellers. The deep water where most survivors found themselves is the habitat of one of those species, the oceanic whitetip shark (*Carcharhinus longimanus*). Whitetips, large and aggressive, are the chief suspects when survivors disappear at sea. Whitetips live in deep water, prefer seas with temperatures around 70 degrees, and are rarely found near land (except for mid-ocean islands like Hawaii). There are probably more whitetips in the sea than any other species of large sharks. Blue sharks may outnumber them in places. No one knows the true population size of either species.

Whitetips are persistent predators, reluctant to leave a potential meal. Two eminent shark researchers cited their personal experience with the whitetip's stubborn attitude: "Once, while bailing bloody water from a dory, we time after time hit an attracted whitetip on the head with an oar. This backed it off a few feet, but it would soon again swim up to the dory and get another drubbing."

Reports of shark attacks came sometimes, but not always, after the sinking of a U.S. warship in the Pacific. Such reports followed a battle off the Savo Islands, for example. In that battle, Japanese warships sank three U.S. heavy cruisers and one Australian heavy cruiser in less than an hour on the night of August 8–9, 1942; a badly damaged U.S. destroyer went down after an air attack on August 9. More than 1,500 men were lost. Sharks killed countless survivors in the oil-covered water. After the Savo battle, lookouts aboard the destroyer *McCalla*, searching for survivors, noticed that bright aluminum powder cans, being used as lifebuoys, were luring sharks. Crewmen drove off the sharks with rifle fire.

After the torpedoed cruiser *Juneau* sunk off Guadalcanal on November 13, 1942, a shocked nation learned that the dead included five brothers. The five Sullivans, united in heroic death, became a symbol of patriotism at war bond rallies. But what happened to the *Juneau*'s men was not fully disclosed. Four of the Sullivans did go down with their ship, along with about 600 of the some 700 men aboard. The eldest brother, George, was one of about 100 men who went over the side and awaited rescue. But, like the men of the *Indianapolis*, the *Juneau* survivors faced a long ordeal. For eight days, sharks picked off man after man. No one knows who died of what, but George Sullivan almost certainly was taken, dead or alive, by a shark. When rescue ships arrived eight days after the sinking, they found ten survivors. The sharks were still there.

Reports of sharks did not follow the battle of Okinawa in April 1945, when Japanese kamikaze bombers sank dozens of ships and sent hundreds of men into the sea. Those waters, far to the north and west of battles earlier in the war, may not have been hospitable to whitetips. But sharks—among them tiger sharks and great whites—abound around Guadalcanal, Savo, and other islands of the Solomons. Native people long had worshiped sharks, made myths of their behavior, and often offered their dead to the sharks that lived in the islands. Presenting the dead to sharks was a chilling precedent for the taking of wartime dead.

Sharks still are a natural part of life in the Solomons. When the Solomon Islands became independent in 1978, the nation's new green and blue flag was emblazoned with frigate birds, a crocodile, and a shark.

Elsewhere in the seas of World War II, sharks frequently added their victims to the casualties of war. On November 28, 1942, a German U-boat torpedoed the troopship *Nova Scotia* in the Indian Ocean off South Africa. Most of the 1,000 men aboard safely abandoned ship. But they floated close to a shore notorious for shark attacks. Only 192 men survived, and many of the recovered bodies were legless. One of the survivors told David H. Davies, an authority on South African sharks, how one of the men died:

". . . he suddenly screamed and the upper part of his body rose out of the water. He fell back and I saw that the water had become red with blood and that his foot had been bitten off. At this moment, I saw the grey form of a shark swimming excitedly around and I paddled away as fast as I could."

In the South Pacific, after a Japanese submarine torpedoed the troop-ship *Cape San Juan* in the South Pacific on November 11, 1943, no one knows how many went over the side before the ship sank. Of the more than 1,400 men aboard, most should have been able to leap into the sea after the torpedoes hit. When the merchantman *Edwin T. Meridith* arrived, crewmen saw countless sharks attacking men on life-rafts. "Time after time," a *Meredith* crewman later said, "I heard soldiers scream as the sharks swept them off the rafts. Sometimes the sharks attacked survivors who were being hauled to the *Meredith* with life ropes." A soldier who survived recalled, "I was sitting on the edge of a raft talking to my buddy in the darkness. I looked away for a moment, and when I turned back, he wasn't there anymore. A shark got him." Rescuers picked up 448 survivors. No one will ever know how many the sharks got.

Leonard P. Schultz and Marilyn H. Malin, in their comprehensive worldwide list of shark attacks, devote a section to air and sea disasters, which lists the *Nova Scotia* and other ships lost in action and stalked by sharks. Among the sources for the Schultz-Malin list were the files of the U.S. Coast Guard's Search and Rescue Agency, which compiled eyewitness reports of shark encounters. One tells of a Navy pilot who ditched his aircraft in the central Pacific. Soon after the pilot and his radioman hit the water, sharks appeared. As they floated in their lifejackets, a shark seized the radioman's right foot. From the pilot's report in the files:

"I told him to get on my back and keep his right foot out of the water, but, before he could, the shark struck again, and we were both jerked under water for a second. I knew that we were in for it as there were more than five sharks around us and blood all around us.

"He showed me his leg and not only did he have bites all over his right leg but his left thigh was badly mauled. He wasn't in any particular pain except every time they struck I knew it and felt the jerk. I finally grabbed my binoculars and started swinging them at the passing sharks.

"It was a matter of seconds when they struck again. We both went under and this time I found myself separated [from the radioman]. . . . I was also the recipient of a wallop across the cheek bone by one of the flaying tails of a shark. From that moment on I watched [the radioman] bob about from attacks. His head was under water and his body jerked as the sharks struck it. As I drifted away . . . sharks continually swam about and every now and then I could feel one with my foot. At midnight I sighted a [U.S. patrol] boat and was rescued after calling for help."

U.S. soldiers, sailors, and airmen went to war in the Pacific with little knowledge of shark perils. An advisory to naval airmen told them that sharks "constitute a negligible danger to Navy personnel." In 1994, the Navy issued *Shark Sense,* a pamphlet that said, "There is very little danger from sharks." Fear of the shark, said the pamphlet, "has originated because of wild and unfounded tales"—a hearkening back to the beliefs prior to the New Jersey attacks of 1916. The advice was incredibly wrong:

"Remember that the shark strikes with his mouth opened wide, and his vision blocked. If you can avoid his mouth by moving a foot or so out of his path, it is a miss for the shark. . . . If you can attach yourself to him by grabbing a fin, when he turns for another attack, you aren't there; you are riding with him, behind his mouth and out of danger from his teeth. Hold tight and hang on as long as you can without drowning yourself. In the meantime, after missing his target, the shark may lose his viciousness and become his usual cowardly self."

George A. Llano, a U.S. Air Force research specialist who himself was a life-raft survivor, made a study of airmen who went down at sea during the war. Of 2,500 reports, only thirty-eight mentioned contacts with sharks. But, as Llano remarked, "When sharks are successful, they leave no evidence, and the number of missing airmen who may have succumbed to them cannot be estimated. . . . Men have spent hours in the water among sharks without being touched, and in view of the evidence some of the escapes seem little short of miraculous. The one feature all accounts illustrate is the fact that, though clothing cannot be depended on to prevent attack, sharks are more apt to bite a bare than a clothed body."

Fear of sharks, whether the Navy believed in it or not, forced Navy officials to seek a shark repellent, a search that still goes on. And servicemen still occasionally find themselves amid sharks. In 1995, for instance, a Marine fell from the aircraft carrier *America* and spent thirty-six hours amid sharks of the Arabian Sea. He said that sharks bit at his

fingers and toes but did not do any substantial damage. One wonders
what kind of sharks he had met.

AFTER WORLD WAR II, as surfing, diving, and boating became increasingly popular, sharks kept doing what they had always done: feeding on
prey. Now sharks were sensing—and sometimes coming into contact
with—more members of a relatively rare prey species, human beings. For
many human beings who were voluntarily in the water, as divers or surfers,
swimming with sharks became, if not routine, then at least a sporadic
thrill. Other human beings, safely in boats, did not expect such thrills.
But the unexpected happened, and shark researchers are trying to find
out why.

Shark attacks on boats have been going on for a long time. The 1963
Schultz-Malin list has a category on boat attacks, with entries going back
to 1804. Some are intriguingly cryptic: "Canoe pushed 100 yards" or
"6 sharks attacked" or "two boys; boat lifted a foot out of water" or "10-
foot boat: attacked 20 times" or "Sailboat capsized, 3 persons drowned."

One of the incidents was reported in 1953 by John MacLeod, a lobsterman, who said that a shark had smashed his white dory off the south-
eastern coast of Canada's Cape Breton Island. MacLeod had been found
clinging to the wreckage of the shattered dory. A fellow lobsterman, John
Burns, had drowned. MacLeod said a white shark that had been following the dory suddenly pounced, smashing an eight-inch hole in the bottom of the hull and throwing both men into the sea. The shark swam
on, leaving behind a tooth imbedded in a splintered board. William C.
Schroeder, of the Museum of Comparative Zoology and the Woods Hole
Oceanographic Institution, confirmed the story by identifying the tooth:
It came from a white shark about twelve feet long and weighing 1,100 to
1,200 pounds.

An amazingly similar attack was reported from Florida in 1959. A
boatman was sailing through water about eight to ten feet deep when a
shark started circling him. "It was a flat, calm day and he could look up
and see me clearly," the man reported. "Suddenly, he swam off about
twenty or thirty feet and turned extremely fast back to the boat. He hit

the boat right in the center and lifted the rear end clear out of the water. I have no doubt that he tried to knock me overboard." The boat owner said the rammer, which he identified as a tiger shark, ripped away a piece of fiberglass and wood about one foot in diameter.

During a 1998 fishing trip off the Adriatic coast of Senigallia, Stefano Catalani caught a sand shark and strapped it to the side of the boat, a thirty-foot cabin cruiser. Then, he later recounted, "All at once, I saw this large greyish fin." A great white first gobbled down a metal bait container attached to the boat. Next, it ate the sand shark and began circling the boat as if it was the next target. Catalani sped for shore. Next day—after Catalani's video of the encounter appeared on Italian television— authorities shut down beaches along thirty miles of the coast. It was the first time in memory that a great white had been seen in the Adriatic. A year later, an Italian fisherman reported a similar attack in the Adriatic. He said he had just caught a tuna when a great white shark appeared, ate the tuna, and began to attack the boat. "It looked like an elephant," he said. "In thirty years as a fisherman, I've never seen anything like it. I shot at it with a spear gun. But the dart just bounced off its skin." The shark ceased the attack and swam off.

In South Africa, sharks have leaped into boats, charged boats, and stopped at least one boat with a suicidal bite on the whirring propeller. In February 1974, while shark fisherman Danie Schoeman was looking for great whites in False Bay, sharks attacked his fifteen-foot boat five times. The first attacker jumped into the boat. Schoeman killed it with a lance. Two weeks later, a shark about the length of the boat charged and holed the boat above the waterline. Schoeman threw over a line baited with a small shark, and quickly hooked the big one. The infuriated shark dragged the boat for an hour and ten minutes, then turned and darted under the boat, rocking it violently in what turned out to be a death throe.

The third attack came in March 1974 when a shark banged the boat, putting another hole in it. In November 1976 a hooked sixteen footer dove, came up under the boat, and hit it so hard that the boat's stern rose nearly a foot above the sea. The shark chomped down on the transom, spitting out wood and fiberglass before Schoeman boated it. Schoeman also caught the fifth attacker, but only after it took another bite out of his scarred boat.

In March 1982 a shark stopped a ninety-foot boat operated by the National Oceanic and Atmospheric Administration. While the boat was off Jacksonville, Florida, the shark started chasing it and finally slammed into the rudder, killing itself by tasting the port propeller. Another killed itself off the Isle of Wight when it hurled itself into a twenty-three-foot fishing boat. "It turned towards the boat and dived," a man who was in the boat told the *Times* of London. "Everything was quiet for a moment, and we thought it had swum away. Then there was a great rushing noise and suddenly the shark came surging out of the water about five yards away. It landed across the boat, which is only nine feet wide, so its head and tail were sticking over each side. The impact nearly sank the boat and it killed the shark outright."

Attack records include many incidents involving divers, particularly people who dive off boats. Sharks have been known to follow or seemingly stalk boats, perhaps because of the refuse that is tossed overboard. A sudden splash attracts stalking sharks—a good reason to be extremely vigilant when swimming off a boat. A Florida father who was diving with his children in Tampa Bay in 1991 learned this lesson. Rick LeProvost and his three children were hanging onto a rope tied to the stern of a sailboat, playing a game he described as "jump off the boat and swim to Daddy." Suddenly, a shark grabbed his left thigh and tried to pull him under. His life vest probably kept him on the surface long enough to scream at his children to get into the boat and then get aboard himself.

"I got in the boat and lay on the deck. There was blood everywhere. I was lying there and I could just see over the side. I could see the shark just under the water, circling the boat," he told the *Petersburg Times*. He believed that the shark was waiting for the prey it had just tasted.

LeProvost and his sailing companion were both paramedics. So first aid was prompt and efficient. LeProvost only remembered two bites. But ashore, a surgeon found five bites—on his abdomen, left ankle, calf, and back thigh. He needed 120 stitches.

Researchers report numerous shark-boat encounters. From the field notes of S. D. Anderson and K. J. Goldman, shark researchers in the Farallon Islands:

> First one shark, then another. Bit boat engine twice within 5–10 seconds. Then boat was bumped on port side and tail slap shot water (two times) into boat (really across it). Got soaked good. Shortly thereafter (10–15 seconds) shark on starboard side bumped boat, bit engine and tail slapped multiple times. Got completely soaked. It was incredible. Then another shark appeared. These sharks were 'hot' so we headed off.

Great white attacks on boats are so numerous that some researchers believe a deep behavioral quirk is driving them. According to this theory, sharks, especially great whites, are attacking boats—and killing themselves on propellers—because they are investigating a strange entity in their ocean. The curiosity is perhaps comparable to the inquisitiveness that may trigger some of the "bump-and-bite" approaches to human beings. Because a 2,000- or 3,000-pound animal is doing the bumping, the impact can be disastrous to a boat or a person.

FOR CENTURIES SAILORS TOLD tales about sharks attacking survivors of shipwrecks. Most scientists scoffed at the stories, which always lacked dates and exact locations. And the human remains found in sharks could be explained away: They had drowned. But there often was a realistic, believable quality to those sea stories. Captain William Young recounted one that was told to him by a seafarer named Captain Ernie. Ernie had been working a ship out of Nassau, the *Una,* a small Bahamas steamer. She was bound for her homeport at Turks Island when she hit a coral reef.

"She had about seventy-five laborers aboard," Ernie recalled, "and when the little ship hit the reef, there wasn't much time for many of them to get into the lifeboats, or even on the life-rafts. Lots of them—God only knows how many—were dumped into the water and kept afloat by grabbing at whatever bobbed by. There wasn't much panic, though. That is, not until one of the passengers on a raft tumbled off and disappeared. Just one word was all he yelled: 'Shark!'

"All of a sudden, the sea was alive with those monsters from hell! They smashed into the rafts, overturning them and throwing screaming men into the sea. One of them even half-leaped out of the water and pulled a man right off a raft. Men tried to beat the sharks off with oars. The oars broke over their heads. Or a shark would grab an oar in his teeth and splinter it as if it was a toothpick. Some of the men went crazy and jumped right into the shark's jaws.

"How long the nightmare went on, Bill, I don't know. It ended as fast as it started. The sharks just disappeared. They didn't go away hungry, though. I'll vouch for that."

Since those days, shark researchers have documented many mass attacks on the dead and dying of air and sea disasters, tragedies that put human beings into the sea and sometimes add sharks to their torments. Each day in a world of desperate people, sharks stalk the makeshift craft that carry Cubans to Florida, Dominicans to Puerto Rico, illegal Asian immigrants to Australia. One such tragedy: A boat carrying about 160 Dominicans capsized on its way to Puerto Rico, a waystation on the voyage to a new life in America. Men, women, and children struggled in the sea. Forty or fifty sharks materialized. "It was an awful sight," a rescue worker said. The rescuers snatched about sixty people from the sharks.

A shrimp boat capsized in a storm off Australia's shark-prowled Queensland coast. Captain Ray Boundy, thirty-three years old, clung to the wreckage and watched sharks take his crew, Dennis Murphy, twenty-four, and Linda Horton, twenty-one.

The ferry *Doña Paz* collided with a tanker in the Philippines. More than 1,500 people died, said rescuers who, through the oily smoke and flames, saw sharks rising and eating. A ferry sinks in the Ganges-Brahmaputa delta, tipping 190 people into the water. Bull sharks take at least fifty of them. And those are only two of the crowded ferries that always seem to sink in the warm, turgid water that lures and hides the sharks.

When an airliner crashes into the sea, sharks may feast, but they do not kill. The tremendous impact may send out such a powerful vibration that the curious whitetips come from near and far. Those who have seen the autopsy photos say that airliner crash victims are already dead when the sharks arrive. But when a ship goes down, survivors live—to drown or to die in a shark's jaws.

Ships, little, unimportant ships, are always sinking in unimportant places. To name just one: A wooden cargo ship sailed from Aruba, off the coast of Venezuela, to deliver whiskey and frozen chickens to the Colombian port of Punta Gallinas, the northernmost point in South America. The ship had a captain and a crew of six. On May 29, 1998, somewhere in the Caribbean, a storm struck the little ship, breaking it up and hurling the crew and the chickens into the sea. And then the sharks came, drawn by the new, tantalizing scents. When the searchers found the wreck, there were three bodies ravaged by sharks. The others had mercifully drowned.

twenty-four

CROCODILE ATTACKS

by Peter Hathaway Capstick

WHAT'S WITH THE BIRDCAGE?" asked Paul Mason over his scrambled egg and impala liver breakfast. I glanced across the hard-packed earth of the safari camp to the slender figure of the young woman padding softly through the early light of the nearby lagoon.

"Fish trap, actually," I told him, ambushing a sausage from the platter Martin was passing. The woman disappeared into the bush, the cone-shaped cage of woven cane balanced lightly on her shaven head. "The women wade out into the lagoons along the river when they're low like this in the dry season and just slam the wide end of the trap into the bottom ahead of their feet. The bream and catfish are so thick when the water drops, they always get a few in the trap, then they just stick their hands through the open top and grab them."

Paul grunted, then spoke over his shoulder. "Martin! *Buisa maquanda futi!*" I was surprised that he even had the proper Q-click in the word for eggs. The old waiter, once the batman of a colonel of Kenya's crack regiment, the King's African Rifles, came to attention smartly, then trotted off to the kitchen for more scrambles. Mason grinned, proud of the Fanagalo he had picked up on his first two weeks of safari in the Luangwa.

Even if it wasn't the formal language of the country, Chenyanja, the Tongue of the Lakes, Fanagalo did the same job for central and southern Africa as KiSwahili served on the east coast. And, a hell of a two weeks it had been. Still in his thirties, Mason was fit and tough enough to hunt really hard, tracking twenty miles a day with nothing but an occasional breather, the kind of hunting that can produce the quality trophies he had taken. The third day out he'd busted a lunker lion from spitting distance with a better black mane than Victor Mature's and had built on that with a forty-eight-inch buffalo and a kudu that would necessitate an addition on his house if he planned to hang it on the wall. From the reports brought in by Silent, things looked pretty fair in the leopard department, too. The number three bait had been taken by a kitty that left a track like it was wearing snowshoes. Mason was one of the really good ones, a humble man who never thumped his chest, a fine shot and a better companion, a genuine pleasure to bwana for.

"What say we just screw around with some *Zinyoni* today, then hit the leopard blind about four?" I asked. "There's any amount of francolin and guinea fowl over by the Chifungwe Plains, and we could shoot the water hole on the way down for ducks and geese. Always the chance of picking up a decent elephant spoor in that area, too."

"You just purchased yourself a boy," he answered. "But, how's about we pot another impala? This liver's out of this world."

"Sure," I told him, "you've got two left on your license and the camp is getting kind of low on meat. That kudu filet's about finished and . . ."

The scream was low at first, more a cry of surprise than alarm, then crescendoed into a piercing shriek of pure animal terror echoing hollow through the *mukwa* hardwoods, up from the lagoon. Again it cut the cool morning air, even higher, a throbbing razor-edged wail that lifted my hackles and sent a shiver scampering up my spine like a small, furry animal. We both froze for an instant, Mason with a piece of toast halfway to his open mouth, his eyes wide in surprise. Reacting, I snatched the .375 H. & H. from where it leaned against the log rack on the low wall of the dining hut and loaded from the cartridge belt as I ran toward the lagoon. I heard Mason trip and curse behind me, then regain his feet and run, stuffing rounds into the magazine of his .404 Mauser action. My heart felt like a hot billiard ball in my throat as I bulled through the light bush along the 150 yards to the low banks of the lagoon, a reedy, dry-season lake that would join the Munyamadzi River 100 yards away at the first flooding rains. Bursting into the open, I could see a flurry of bloody foam fifty yards from shore, a slender, ebony arm flailing the surface at the end of a great, sleek form that cut the water with the ease of a cruiser. I raised the rifle. Should I shoot? What if I hit the woman? Like a mallet blow, I realized that even if I did hit her it would be a blessing, far better than being dragged inexorably, helplessly down by the huge crocodile. I lined up the sights and carefully squeezed off a 300-grain Silvertip, which threw a column of water just over the top of the croc's head, then whined off to rattle through the trees at the far side of the lagoon. A second later Paul fired, the big .404 slug meeting empty water where the croc had been an instant before, the giant saurian submerging like a U-boat blowing positive. Slow ripples rolled across the calm surface, waving the dark, green reeds until they lapped the low banks. Once again, the lagoon was silent. We stood helplessly, shocked into muteness, thinking of the woman. We could almost feel the tent-peg teeth deep in her midriff, the rough scaliness of the croc's horny head under her hands as she used the last of her strength to try to break loose before her lungs could stand no more and she would breathe dark death.

"Jesus Christ," said Paul in a hoarse whisper. It didn't sound like a curse. Silent, my gunbearer, Martin, and Stomach, a skinner, came running up. A glance at the floating fish trap and at the woman's sandals on the bank told them what had happened. Wading to his knees, Silent retrieved the cane trap and placed the other effects inside. He started a slow trot that would carry him to the woman's village, a miserable huddle of mud and dung huts called Kangani. Slowly we turned back to camp, the shock of witnessing the most horrible death in Africa leaving us numb. I took the rifles and unloaded them, placing a cartridge bullet-first into the muzzle of each to prevent mud wasps from starting nests in the bores, a bit of Africana that had cost hunters their sight and even lives when they forgot it. Martin came over to us and spoke quietly in Fanagalo. "There is nothing for it, Bwana," he intoned with the exaggerated fatalism of the bush African. "It has always been so. Always has *Ngwenya* been waiting; always will he wait."

Ngwenya, the crocodile, has been waiting a very long time. For 170 million years he has been lurking, patient and powerful, in the warmer fresh and salt waters of this planet. Virtually unchanged from his earliest fossil remains, he demonstrates with deadly efficiency the value of simplicity in design. The crocodile is the master assassin, the African Ice Man, combining the ideal qualities of cunning with ruthlessness and cold voracity matched with a reptilian intelligence far greater than his small brain would indicate. He is little more than teeth, jaws, and stomach propelled by the most powerful tail in nature. He will eat anything he can catch and digest almost anything he can eat. Someday, if you spend enough time around the watery haunts of *Ngwenya,* that may include you or—Lord forbid—me.

In these days of moon landings and lasers, it can be difficult to fathom the fact that crocodiles are still a very substantial threat to human life in Africa. Most Americans, were you to conduct a poll, would probably offer some vague impression that crocodiles are teetering on the brink of extinction in Africa today, hardly any threat to man. I've got some big news. By the most conservative estimates of professional researchers, something approximating ten human beings are dragged off to a death horrible beyond description *each day* in modern Africa. The figure may even be considerably higher since successful croc attacks, unless witnessed, normally leave no trace whatever of the victim, who may have died by any of the methods Africa has developed to make evolution a working proposition. The facts boil down to this: *Crocodylus niloticus* is the one man-killer who, if he's big enough and you're available enough, will eat you every time he gets a chance.

I was taught in Sunday School, I dimly remember, that it's not nice to hate anything. Nonetheless, I do hate crocs, an opinion shared rather vocally by such ne'er-do-wells as Winston Churchill and Theodore Roosevelt. I do not believe in their being driven to extinction, heavens no, because we find to our infinite wonder that everything in nature has its place. On the other hand, I have not an ounce of regret at having been in on the killing of about a hundred of them, all legally shot, I might add, and not for their hides. I have often wondered what stand the ultra-preservationists would take if we were to stock a few hundred crocs in New York's Central Park, where their philosophizing might become more than the armchair variety next time they walked their poodles. I'm sure it would lower the crime rate, if nothing else.

As with snakes there has been a great deal of exaggeration as to the length crocodiles may attain and at the same time a lack of appreciation of the weights they may reach. Adventure books are full of vivid reports of twenty-five- and even thirty-footers, but few realize how truly immense even a twelve-footer is. The Luangwa Valley of Zambia probably has the largest population of crocodiles in Africa, perhaps the world. Never having been hunted for their hides in this area, they have flourished in untold thousands. In a normal afternoon of hunting along the banks of the Luangwa and Munyamadzi Rivers, it is not unusual to see hundreds sunning themselves on the sand bars and banks, their mouths agape in sleep, oxpeckers and tickbirds hopping around their jaws with impunity. Yet of all the thousands I have seen, I must conclude that a twelve-footer is big and one of thirteen feet edging up to huge. The biggest croc I have ever seen, besides the one who killed the woman in the lagoon went about fifteen feet with three feet of tail missing, fairly common for some reason in very big crocs. That would make him roughly eighteen feet, which is one hell of a lot of crocodile. I've owned cars shorter than that! He crawled out to sun himself on a small island 150 yards from my camp one hot afternoon when I was between safari clients. I watched him for about a half-hour, out of film for my camera, of course, and God, but he was immense. He looked like a big, scaly subway car with teeth, that could have taken a buffalo and three warthogs with one gulp. To tell you the honest truth, I came very close to killing him. Crocs that big are very often man-eaters, learning the habits of native women until they try a couple and find they're a lot easier to handle than trying to pull a rhino in by his nose. But, I didn't have a license and knew that the locals would turn me in for the reward offered for violators, so I reluctantly let him go. At least they can't take away your white hunter's ticket for what you're thinking. When the next clients arrived two days later, he was never to be seen.

One famous hunter, shooting years ago in Kenya's Lake Rudolph, which has some Godzilla-league crocs in it, swatted over one hundred, of which only three beat fifteen feet, and those only by a whisker. The largest crocodile "officially" recorded was killed by the Uganda Game Department in the Semliki River along the Congo border in 1953. It was only three inches short of twenty feet. I have seen a mounted croc in a museum that tapes sixteen feet, and he stands higher than my waist, so you can imagine how colossal that nineteen-footer was. When crocs get over twelve feet or so, they gain tremendously in weight for each inch they grow. You could practically shoplift an eight-footer, but you had best have three strong friends along if you want to even roll over a twelve footer. I have never weighed a big croc, but I'll bet you a hangover that a fifteen-foot *Ngwenya* will outweigh a big buffalo, well over a ton. A croc this size will stand about four feet when walking and have a girth of about eight feet.

Crocodiles never stop growing their whole lives, so the age of an immense one must be very impressive. Consider that one Asian specimen, a saltwater crocodile, has been living in an American zoo for over thirty years and has grown only about four feet since his capture. Conceivably, a brute like the Semliki nineteen-footer may have seen two centuries turn over.

As much, if not more than, the lion, the history of African exploration is written around the crocodile. In fact, there is hardly an explorer or a missionary that doesn't mention a few squeaks with *Ngwenya*, *Mamba*, *Nkwena*, or whatever his local name may be, often with fatal results. By way of example, let's look at just one passage of the writings of Sir Samuel Baker on a military expedition in the great papyrus Sudd of southern Sudan:

"Among the accidents that occurred to my expedition, one man had his arm bitten off at the elbow, being seized while collecting aquatic vegetation from the bank. He was saved from utter loss by his comrades who held him while his arm was in the jaws of the crocodile. The man was brought to me in dreadful agony, and the stump was immediately amputated above the fracture. Another man was seized by the leg while assisting to push a vessel off a sand bank. He also was saved by a crowd of soldiers who were with him engaged in the same work; this man lost his leg. The captain of No. 10 tug was drowned [by a croc] in the dock vacated by the 108-ton steamer, which had been floated into the river by a small canal cut from the basin for that purpose. The channel was 30 yards in length and three feet deep. No person ever suspected that a crocodile would take possession of the dock, and it was considered the safest place for the troops to bathe. One evening the captain was absent and as it was known a short time previously that he had gone down to walk at the basin, he was searched for at the place. A pile of clothes and his red fez were upon the bank, but no person was visible. A number of men jumped into the water and felt the bottom in every portion of the dock, with the result that in a few minutes, his body was discovered; one leg was broken in several places, being severely mangled by the numerous teeth of the crocodile. There can be little doubt that the creature, having drowned its victim, had intended to return."

Several months later, sitting in the cool of the evening with Lady Baker and Commander Julian Baker, RN, Sir Samuel was accosted by one of his men, panicked almost into incoherency. To let Baker tell it:

"The man gasped out, 'Said, Said is gone! Taken away from my side by a crocodile, now, this minute!'

" 'Said! What Said?' I asked: 'There are many Saids!'

" 'Said of the No. 10 steamer, the man you liked, he is gone. We were wading together across the canal by the dock where Reis Mahomet was killed. The water is only waist deep, but a tremendous crocodile rushed like a steamer from the river, seized Said by the waist and disappeared. He's dragged into the river and I've run here to tell you the bad news.'

"We immediately hurried to the spot. The surface of the river was calm and unruffled in the stillness of a fine night. The canal was quiet and appeared as though it had never been disturbed. The man who had lost his companion sat down and sniffled aloud. Said, who was one of my best men, was indeed gone forever."

One can only hope that those of Baker's men working the No. 10 steamer got hazardous duty pay.

Arthur Neumann was the horrified witness to a classic croc attack on New Year's Day, 1896, on a river near Lake Rudolph in modern Kenya:

"Late in the afternoon, I went down for another bathe, with Shebane (my servant) as usual carrying my chair, towels, etc., and did the same thing again. It is a large river and deep, with a smooth surface and rather sluggish current; its water dark-coloured and opaque, though hardly to be called muddy, deepens rapidly, so that a step or two in is sufficient at this point to bring it up to one's middle, while the bottom is black, slimy mud.

"Having bathed and dried myself, I was sitting on my chair, after putting on my clothes, by the water's edge, lacing up my boots. The sun was just about to set behind the high bank across the river, its level rays shining full upon us, rendering us conspicuous from the river while preventing our seeing in that direction. Shebane had just gone a little way off (perhaps a dozen yards) along the brink and taken off his clothes to wash himself, a thing I had never known him to do before when with me; but my attention being taken up with what I was doing, I took no notice of him. I was still looking down when I heard a cry of alarm, and, raising my head, got a glimpse of the most ghastly sight I have ever witnessed. There was the head of a huge crocodile out of the water, just swinging over towards the deep with my poor Swahili boy in its awful jaws, held across the middle of the body like a fish in the beak of a heron. He had ceased to cry out, and with one horrible wriggle, a swirl and a splash all disappeared. One could do nothing. It was over; Shebane was gone . . . A melancholy New Year's Day indeed!"

Because there are far more blacks than whites in the range of the Nile Crocodile, it follows that the preponderance of victims are black. Most are women, the traditional duty of that sex being to draw water from the river bank where they are most vulnerable. However, crocs are equally partial to white meat, as the grisly case of William K. Olson, a Cornell graduate and Peace Corps volunteer attests. Olson was recovered in large chunks from the stomach of a thirteen-foot one-inch croc who killed and ate him while he was swimming—despite warnings—in the Baro River near Gambella, Ethiopia, on April 13, 1966. The croc was shot the next day by a Colonel Dow, a safari client of my friend, Karl Luthy, a Swiss white hunter operating in Sidamo Province. I have seen the photos taken by Luthy of removing the body from the croc's stomach, and if you are interested to see what Olson looked like after twenty hours in a croc's paunch, you may see one of them reproduced on page 200 of Alistair Graham's and Peter Beard's book, *Eyelids of Morning* (New York Graphic Society, 1973). I don't recommend it, however, unless you considered *The Exorcist* light comedy.

The inside of a croc's stomach is sort of an African junkyard. I have found everything from human jewelry to whole wart hogs to Fanta bottles and three-pound rocks inside them. One ten-footer I shot in Ethiopia even had a four-foot brother tucked in his belly. According to a reliable writer-hunter, one east African man-eater contained the following horribilia: several long porcupine quills, eleven heavy brass arm rings, three wire armlets, an assortment of wire anklets, one necklace, fourteen human arm and leg bones, three human spinal columns, a length of fiber used for tying firewood, and eighteen stones. I wasn't there, but that sounds just a touch exaggerated if only for the simple amount of the inventory. Stones are commonly found in the stomach of crocs, but whether they are picked up accidentally when the croc lunged for a fish or whether they are meant as an aid to the digestive process like the grit in a bird's crop is unknown. Maybe they're used for ballast.

The collections of indigestible items found in the stomachs of crocodiles points out their fantastic digestive powers. I have found good-size antelope leg bones that were almost dissolved; they would have to be since they were far too large to be passed through the normal process. The arm bracelets are worn by African women very tightly on the bicep, and the only way for them to be found free would be for the arm to have been digested.

The Nile crocodile holds the unquestioned title as the most accomplished of Africa's man-eaters. Some individual crocs have been credited with hundreds of human victims and since the species is more or less limited to water, there is only one factor that makes this possible—the incredible sense of fatality that the African holds toward the crocodile.

There are innumerable cases of scores of women being taken by crocs at the *same spot* every few days as they draw water for their families. Crocs easily learn where to wait and, apparently, the fate of the last person who filled her jug from a particular place has no effect whatever on the next one who may have even been present when the last victim was taken, I have lived with Africans in the bush for many years, but I have found it impossible to understand their total indifference to horrible death. I have seen this phenomenon from Ethiopia to South Africa, so it is not a matter of one particular tribe but a continent-wide indifference that defies explanation. Ask a woman why she takes her water from the same place where her sister was killed the week before and she will just shrug. It's weird.

I was once crossing a river in Mozambique by cable pontoon, which is a raft drawn across the stream by cables operated by government personnel. One man jumped off near shore to unfoul a line and was immediately taken by a croc in a swirl of bloody water and never seen again. Yet when I returned the following day, the surviving raft operators were happily splashing and washing not twenty yards from where their fellow worker was killed!

Crocodiles are considered "saurians" by science (as in dinosaur) and are available in a wide variety of flavors. Among these are their cousins, the alligators, gavials, and caimans. With the exception of the African or Nile crocodile (the same animal, even though found nowhere near the Nile) and the saltwater crocodile of the warm Asian islands, most of the clan is relatively inoffensive. Of course, the American alligator has caused some deaths and injuries, including a fully documented fatal attack that took place in Sarasota, Florida, in August 1973. A sixteen-year-old girl was taken by an eleven-foot gator and, despite efforts of onlookers to prevent it, partially eaten. Between 1948 and 1971 there were an additional seven unprovoked attacks, which produced various injuries but no fatalities. Although rare, there is an American crocodile reputedly as dangerous as the African breed.

The saltwater crocs of Asia are lumped under several types, including the marsh or mugger crocodile and estuarine types, all considered very dangerous. In fact, one of the greatest clashes between man and croc took place during World War II. At the time that Burma was being re-taken by the Allies, about 1,000 Japanese infantrymen became caught between the open seas and the island of Ramree, deep in mangrove swamps crawling with crocs, expecting to be evacuated by ships that never arrived. Trying to retreat, they found themselves cut off by the British Royal Navy in such a position that they could not regain the main-land. When night came, so did the crocodiles. Witnesses on the British ships have told of the horror of the mass attack on the men, of the terri-ble screaming that continued until dawn when only 20 men out of 1,000 were left alive. Certainly, some were killed by enemy fire and others by drowning, but all evidence points up that most were slaughtered by the big saltwater crocs.

Any animal as obviously dangerous as the crocodile is bound to have a thick layer of legend wrapped around its reputation. Of course, a lot of it is *marfi*, a polite term for droppings. Time and again tales are heard of people who have had an arm or leg removed, "snapped off in one bite," by crocs. Not so. One look at a croc's dentures point out that, because of their spacing and rounded design, they are intended for catching and holding rather than cutting. If you have ever tried to carve a London broil with a tent peg, you've got the idea. Anything a croc can get down his gullet at one try he will swallow whole, tilting his head back so the morsel falls to the back of his throat. Anything bigger, he must wait for decay to set in and soften the meat so that he can grip it and spin his body, ripping off a healthy chunk in the same way that a Frenchman tears off a piece of bread.

Another myth about the croc is his supposed ability to knock animals into his jaws by using his powerful tail, even from elevated river banks. No way. I have seen at least twenty animals taken by crocs, both on banks and in the water. All were caught with pure speed and surprise. No animal of the size and bulk of a croc cold possibly jump in such a way as to get his tail behind his meal and flip it toward him. Yet crocs have been reported as accomplishing this with animals on river banks six feet over them!

I had a good lesson in the speed a croc may generate late one after-noon when I was sitting in a leopard blind along the river. My client and I were watching a small troop of impala wander idly down a path to the water to drink, pausing thirty-one feet, by later measurement, from the river's edge. Instantly, a twelve-foot crocodile erupted from the water like a Polaris missile, crossing the ground to the nearest impala, a ewe, like a green blur. As she spun to escape, he was on her, grabbing her right rear haunch and effortlessly dragging her to the dark river. In less than a minute there wasn't even a ripple to mark where she had disappeared. Considering that the impala is one of the fastest of the African an-telopes, the speed a croc can crank out over a short rush must be well over thirty-five miles per hour. I can tell you I didn't walk as close to the river after the demonstration.

The awesome power of big croc has been demonstrated on large game many times. In a Tanzanian (Tanganyikan) game park in the late 1950s, a party of tourists were photographing a black rhino cow as she drank at a water hole. She was fair sized for a female, probably shading 4,000 pounds. As she stuck her odd, prehensile nose into the scummy water, the water exploded and a big croc clamped down on her muzzle. There followed an amazing test of strength between the two armored monsters, the croc trying to pull the rhino into the water and the rhino trying to pull the croc out of it. After an hour of straining, with neither gaining more than a foot, the rhino was actually inched toward the water. Thirty minutes later, her head was held under and, after a final flurry, she rolled over, drowned. The croc was estimated as about fourteen feet by the ranger driving the tour car.

The crocodile is a cold-blooded creature in more ways than one. Like most nonmammals, his ability to hang onto the last shreds of life would make a vampire wild with envy. So tough is the croc that there is an old hide hunters' maxim quite as valid today as it ever was: A croc ain't dead until the hide's salted, and even then don't count on it! Besides the fact that really large crocs—twelve feet and over—are sneaky as revenuers, the felony is compounded by their anatomy offering only the smallest of targets for a fatal shot. I have heard other professionals claim that a lung-shot *Ngwenya* will leave the water before he drowns, although I have never witnessed this. But then, to be fair, I have never shot a croc in the lungs. For my money the only way to anchor a crocodile where he lies and thus prevent his certain escape to the river where he will be lost or eaten by his pals is to separate him from his brain. Smaller than your fist, it's located just behind the eyes, an angle that can almost never be made from dead on or astern without at least 30 degrees of elevation above the croc. The brain is encased in some very impressive bone (I once broke a steel spearhead in two trying to drive it through the skull) and just can't be reached from a flat angle. The only reliable position for the brain shot is from the side, where your target will be about two inches high by three inches wide. Joe Joubert, a fine professional hunter who had a camp near mine in Zambia, was once shot in the face by a ricocheting .22 bullet when an excited client bounced it off the skull of a big croc in an attempted *coup de grace*.

Just how much pummeling a crocodile can absorb came to my definite attention during a safari in Botswana's Okavango Swamps, which had been pretty well picked over by professional hide hunters years before. Yet, after the market shooting was stopped, the crocs had come back strongly, if warily. I spotted one of a dozen feet sunning himself half out of the water on the base of an old termite heap. He was a good 400 yards out, and open water prevented stalking any closer. But, the croc was a good one for Okavango, and I knew my client to be an excellent shot with his "toy," a .257 Weatherby Magnum with a variable power telescopic sight, a flat-shooting iron too light for most game but perfect for a long shot like this.

We hunched along through the light *mswaki* scrub at the edge of a sand flat, the tsetse flies absolutely mobbing us. I have never seen them in greater numbers or more savage. Ignoring the saber-toothed mauling he was getting, my client rested the rifle across his hand on a broken wrist of branch, lined up with plenty of holdover, took his shooting breath, and sent one off Air Mail Special. I was amazed to see the little slug lash out and strike right on the money, a light mist of bone chips and brain matter erupting from the skull. Typical of a brain-shot croc, his prehistoric nervous system jammed in flank speed, his powerful tail whipping the water like a paddle wheeler gone aground.

As I watched through my binoculars, I could see the growing pink cloud in the water and the tail slowed to a stop. My gunbearers and skinners, who very wisely share a common sentiment of loathing anything to do with crocs, dead or alive, decided that they just weren't getting paid enough to help me drag that one back through open water. I stoked up the .470 with soft-points, removed my wallet, and, in the best Stewart Granger tradition, started wading. The water was only to my waist, and I wasn't nearly as worried about crocs as I was leery of the small herd of hippos who were eyeing me with some annoyance from seventy yards away. After a few minutes, however, the herd leader finally decided that I wasn't there to rape any of the ladies fair, and he ponderously ignored me. The big crocodile was lying mostly in the water, just his shattered head on the ant hill, so I was able to work him out into deeper water despite his bulk, which was largely negated by his buoyancy. With the end of his tail across my shoulder, I began to drag him back like a small ant with a dung beetle. I had made about forty yards when I noticed a tiny quiver through his body and began to reflect seriously on the prudence of my position. I didn't have much time to think about it because, with a tremendous wrench, he flattened me. The fist-sized crater in his head where his brain used to be had lulled me to the hasty conclusion that he was dead, a status he was clearly contesting.

I came up spitting muddy water, trying to get the double rifle free from where it was slung around my neck. He hit me again with his body, and I went back down, stumbling and thrashing to keep way from the jaws. I managed to break the rifle, pour the water out of the barrels and present the croc with 1,000 grains of high velocity tranquilizer right behind the smile. When the little pieces of the rest of his head stopped falling out of the sky, I grabbed him again and completed towing him back to shore. Polaroids appeared as if by witchcraft, and the client and I squatted down in the hero position and opened the jaws, the teeth gleaming like a nest of bloody *punji* sticks. Just as the camera clicked, there was a sound like an iron maiden being slammed, and people became very scarce. We jumped back as the croc began to thrash around, snapping his jaws and actually growling, a sound I have never heard one make before or since. My client belted him twice more with a .300 Magnum, his head looking like a jam jar somebody had stuck a grenade into. That calmed him down considerably. We finished the pictures and three of my men had to sit on the battered body to hold it down from nervous reaction as the belly skin was taken. Hunting back past the spot a few hours later, I was surprised to see the corpse surrounded by a ring of vultures, odd because normally they would have swarmed him and finished him up in short order. As we got closer, they flew off and I noticed something: a dead vulture was clamped tightly between the "dead" croc's jaws. That boy wasn't about to quit!

Paul Mason and I began to hunt the man-eater the same afternoon as the attack on the woman. I hadn't had much of a look at him beyond his obvious bulk, but that was so exceptional it would give him away if we ever saw him again. From the size of his head and the wake he was throwing, he had to be better than fifteen feet, and there just weren't many of that size anywhere. I decided to abandon the rule that the professional only shoots in case of a charge or imminent escape of dangerous game and split us into two groups on either side of the big lagoon, which was separated from the Munyamadzi by a sandy umbilical a hundred yards wide. We sat, rifles ready, through the long afternoon, watching the water until our temples throbbed for some sign of the huge croc, but not a ripple betrayed his presence. Crocodiles can hold their breath by only showing the tiniest tip of nostrils. As the last of the light disappeared, we pushed aching, cramped joints into action and returned to camp.

We ate early that night, not saying very much, and after a few belts of man's best friend went off to bed. It was still full dark when tea arrived and we shrugged off blankets in the chill morning air. Well before dawn, we were picking our way to the lagoon. Even in the growing half-light, I could see that we were too late. Across the sand spit lay a spoor like a half-track; a deep, wide belly mark flanked by huge tracks showed where the killer croc had crossed from the lagoon and entered the river. I said a bad word. We had a good chance of finding him in the limits of the lagoon, but now, in the expanse of river, where he could move at will, things looked much dimmer. Still, I thought, given enough time, hard work and a fifty-five-gallon drum of pure, Grade A, vitamin-enriched luck. . . .

Paul and I retraced our steps and wolfed down a fast breakfast of the remaining kudu steaks and plenty of sweet, black tea. Before heading for another long day on the river, I thought it best we check the "zero" of our rifles, having decided to switch from the heavier .375 and .404 to Paul's .25-06 Remington and my .275 Rigby Rimless, reasoning that any shot we might get would probably be a long one requiring the precision of the lighter rifles over the power of the heavier. My .275 didn't have the velocity of Paul's superhot Remington, but I had put so many rounds through it that holdover and windage were as indelibly ingrained in my subconscious as Raquel Welch's bustline. Satisfied that any misses could not be blamed on Messrs. Rigby or Remington, we headed back to the river.

In view of the fact that, considering the size of the area the croc could be in, our best approach would be a saturation campaign, I called all my staff together. There were twenty-six of them, a mixture of Sengas, Awizas, Baila, and even a couple of BaTonkas up from the Zambezi. There were cooks, waiters, skinners, trackers, gunbearers, water boys, laundry boys, *chimbuzi* boys, and firewood gatherers, all my bush family. Leaving only Martin to watch things around camp, I split them up into pairs with instructions to watch for the big croc at various vantage points on the river. If seen, one would stay while the other would come to fetch us. My strategy wasn't entirely hit or miss: it had been a cold night, and since crocodiles must regulate their body temperatures by alternate sunning and wetting, I was pretty sure that the man-eater would show somewhere within three miles in either direction of my camp. Therefore, I had somebody watching nearly every convenient sand bar.

The sun was an incandescent, white cueball on a blue felt sky when I saw the first smoke a half-mile downriver. Someone had seen the crocodile! I sent Silent to bring Paul, 300 yards upriver from me, and, when he arrived, breathless from running, we started off toward the tendril of smoke. On the way I met Chenjirani, partnered with Invisible, sent to fetch us if we did not notice the smoke. From a bend in the river, I climbed a small bluff and turned the binoculars on the shimmering water. Eight hundred yards away, the dark, water-wet form of a gigantic croc smothered the tip of a sand bar. It looked like we had him. I mentally marked a tree on the bank that was opposite the croc, deciding to use it as a firing point. I motioned to Paul that we should sweep in a large half-circle through the heavy brush so there would be no chance of the croc or his tickbird sentinels spotting us, and we came out at a point a few yards from the grass-skirted tree trunk.

It was a perfect stalk, the soft ground giving no warning that our tip-toe approach would set up vibrations that the animal could feel through the dense medium of water. The tree loomed nearer above the towering elephant grass until we were up to it. Ever so slowly, Mason moved up, slipping into firing position with the .25-06 clenched by the pistol grip ahead of him. We could see the edge of the upper part of the bar through the fringe of grass as I worked closer to Paul, ready for a backup shot if necessary. The croc should be only thirty yards away, sleeping in oblivion, a shot a blind man could make. I slid my hand forward to push the grass away from Paul's muzzle and we both popped up to find . . . *nothing. Nowhere. Empty.*

I was absolutely baffled. What in bloody hell could have spooked him? He must have just changed his mind about the sunbath during the ten minutes it had taken us to make the stalk. Or, maybe he had gotten to grow so big by realizing that to expose himself for any amount of time could mean the hot whiplash of a bullet. Whatever the reason, he simply was not there.

Two days later, our knees raw as minute steaks from crawling along the brushy banks looking for the croc, he still hadn't tipped his hand. I increasingly feared that, like many of his brethren who had achieved great age and size, he had figured out that safety lies in darkness.

"Paul," I said that night after dinner, pouring him something to dispel his mood, "we're gonna have to bait that croc to have any chance at him at all. I'm convinced he just isn't active during daylight or we would have seen him more than just once."

"Whatcha got in mind, Bwana?" he asked. "Want me to go fish trapping in the river?"

"Not 'til you pay your safari bill, I don't," I grinned back. "I think that big lizard has been hunted before. Shot at. Maybe he came all the way up from the Zambezi. After five months in this camp I've never seen him before or even cut tracks that big." I took a flaming splinter from the fire and lit the tip of a Rhodesian Matinee from the thirty-pack in my breast pocket. "Maybe he's not even in this section of river anymore, but I doubt that."

We ghosted the banks of the Munyamadzi the next morning until the sun was high in the cloudless, dry-season sky. September dust-devils swirled black grass ash thousands of feet up to rain back on us in a fine, grassy film until Silent joked that we were now dark enough that he might adopt us. Scores of crocs were basking on sand bars and small beaches, but nothing approaching the size of the man-eater. Then, as I swept the glasses across a stretch of calm water at the head of a pool, I caught two dark lumps that protruded oddly above the slick surface. As I stared, they disappeared without a ripple, as if they felt my stare. From the distance between the knobs, I knew they were the eyes of a monster crocodile, and I would take all bets that he was our boy. I crawled back from the bank and got Paul. We drove the hunting car quietly upriver a half-mile where a hippo herd lay in the tail of the current. Paul wedged himself into the sitting position and slammed a 400-grain .404 slug through the brain of a big, scarred bull, who collapsed without a twitch and disappeared into the black depths.

"How long, Silent?" I asked the spindle-shanked old gunbearer. He knelt down and felt the temperature of the water and glanced at the sun, calculating for a moment. A great poacher in his youth, Silent was never fifteen minutes off in predicting how long it would take a hippo's body to bloat and leave the bottom. Finally, he pointed to an empty piece of western sky where the sun would be when the hippo would rise to the surface. At five, we were back with the crew just in time to see the carcass balloon up and drift into a quiet eddy where we were able to rope it. After a long struggle we wrestled his tons into position where the Rover could winch him over in stages. When we were finished, he lay at the edge of a shallow bar beneath our ambush point, a low, riverine bluff thirty yards away and twenty feet high. Powerful ropes of his own hide held him to stakes driven deeply into the mud to prevent the crocs from pulling and tugging him into the current.

I showed Paul the big, wedge-shaped bits in the hide, tooth marks of crocs testing the degree of decomposition of the body. Usually, they would have to wait several days before the hide had rotted enough to be torn away, exposing the meat beneath, but this hippo would be table-ready. Already the skinners were busy struggling to slash away huge patches of the thick skin so the crocs could feed immediately. I suppose I should be able to tell you how crocodiles locate carrion, but I'm not really sure. I believe that they hunt living prey by both sight and sound of water disturbance, but I couldn't say how good their sense of smell is. Judging by the short time it takes a large number of crocs to find a decomposing carcass, though, they must have fairly decent noses, although whether they discern the odor from airborne scent or from tainted water evades me. Stomach brought over the corrugated ivory arcs of the fighting tusks and the smoother, amber rods of the interior teeth and presented them to Mason. Nearly dark, we drove back to camp and a couple of sun-downers followed by an excellent stroganoff of hippo filet. We were both dead to the world before ten o'clock.

"*Vuka,* Bwana, *tiye!*" I tried to drag myself back from deep sleep, the hissing glare of Martin's pressure lamp searing through my eyelids. I forced them open, taking the big tea mug and pouring the sweet, strong brew down in a few hot swallows. Martin laid out clean bush shorts and jacket for me, then refilled the mug.

"*Yini lo skati?*" I asked him, blearily squinting at my watch in the shadows.

"*Skati ka fo busuku,* Bwana," he answered. Jesus! Four A.M. I had better get moving if we were to be in position before first light. I shivered into the shorts and bush jacket and stepped into the sockless shoes, almost bumping into Mason on his way to the *chimbuzi.* He muttered something sleepily about idiots and disappeared into the toilet hut. I had finished my third tea and, while he swilled some coffee, I checked the rifles, deciding to go back to the big guns. If we got a shot this morning, it would be barndoor stuff and the .375 and .404, with their express sights, would be better over the dimly lit short range. If necessary, their big slugs would also penetrate water better.

Leaving the hunting car a full half-mile back on the track, I led the way toward the bluff in the velvety darkness, our bare legs and shoes soaked by the dew-wet grass before we had walked ten yards. A trio of waterbuck clattered off, caught in the slender beam of the electric torch, and an elephant could be heard ripping tender branches from a grove a hundred yards to our right. Somewhere in the night a hyena snickered and was taunted by the yapping of a black-backed jackal. Eyes sharp for the reflected sapphire of snakes' eyes, we sneaked closer until we were only fifty yards from the bluff. I kept the beam well covered even though I realized that the crocs on the carcass were deep in the hill's defilade and could not see it. After another twenty feet, I eased it off completely, slipping slowly forward in complete silence, the sugary river sand hissing beneath the soles of our shoes. Dully, from ahead, came the disgusting, watery sounds of crocs feeding on the hippo—the tearing rip of meat, the muffled clash of teeth, the hollow, retching, gagging sound of swallowing the big, bloody lumps of flesh. Ten feet from where I guessed the lip of the bluff was, Paul and I squatted and froze in the darkness awaiting enough light to slip up for a shot if the man-eater was there. If.

With maddening slowness, like a low fire heating the inside of a heavy steel barrel, the gun-metal sky began to blush. As we waited, cramped, listening to the crocs, the light swelled from mango to cherry to carmine tinged with thick veins of wavy gold and teal-wing blue. My outstretched hand began to take shape before my face. I nudged Paul to move with me to the edge of the overhang. The river was still black, but after a few seconds the darker blob of the hippo carcass loomed dimly, pale feathers of water visible as dozens of crocs swirled and fought over the meat. Behind a light screen of grass on the lip, I got Paul into a sitting position, his rifle eased up to his shoulder. Seconds oozed by like cold caramel as the dawn strengthened, the bulk of the hippo more discernible. I thanked our luck that we were on the west bank and would not be skylined by the growing light.

As I stared through the felt-gray shadows toward the water, smaller dark shapes began to take form and outline; then I saw one, partially behind the hippo, that was much larger than the others. I felt a thrill of triumph as I realized that our plan had worked. He was *there,* just thirty yards away, unaware that in a few seconds lightning was going to strike. A few more seconds and Paul could kill him. My stomach tightened as the giant length moved, then again. God, no! He was returning to the water with the dawn. The loglike outline moved again, two feet closer to deep water and safety, his head already in the river. Couldn't Paul see him? Didn't he understand that in a few seconds he'd be gone forever? Frustration coursed through me. I could not risk whispering. A tiny sound snicked through the half-blackness, and I realized it was the safety of the .404. Shoot, I willed him. Shoot now! He's still moving! He's going to . . . A yard of orange flame roared from Paul's muzzle, a brilliant stab of lightning that blinded me as the thunderclap of the shot washed over my arms and face. I was deafened, great, bright spots exploding wherever I focused.

"I think I got him," Paul yelled over the ringing of my ears. Twice more, the big bore rifle fired as Mason opened up on the spot where the croc had been. Slowly, my vision began to clear with growing dawn, the orange blossoms of light fading. I stared down at the dead hippo, my hope welling up as I saw the tremendous, dark shape beside it, half in the water. The great tail waved feebly as a shudder passed through the killer, then all was still. Paul knelt and put his last shot through the man-eater's skull. It was over.

Pounding each other's back in congratulations, we half-fell down the sandy bank and walked across the sand bar to the bodies, the odor of the dead hippo already sickly in our nostrils. Behind us came Silent and Stomach, their hands covering their open mouths in polite astonishment, muttering the usual, "Eeehhh, eeehhh," over and over. When two more men arrived, we were able to roll him onto dry land and examine him with mounting awe. Paul's first shot had been perfect, taking out the rear half of the brain as he faced away and below us. The rest hadn't mattered. One thing was for sure; he was the biggest croc I had ever seen up close, let alone killed. I put the tape on the two pegs we ran between snout and tail-tip, even though we couldn't get the tail all the way straightened out. The third unrolling of my six-foot measure totaled fifteen feet, two and one-half inches! We all guessed him at over a ton, perhaps quite a bit more. Crocs are very dense and heavy for their size.

After almost an hour had passed, the entire village of Kangani arrived to revile the dead reptile by spitting on him and kicking him in impotent frustration for the death of the woman. When Silent made two long incisions in the side and cut the stomach wall, we all gagged. From the slimy mass of hippo meat and crushed bones, slid the putrefacted arm of a woman, a copper bangle still tightly in place, gleaming dully from the croc's stomach acid.

Mason and I sat, smoking slowly in the warm sun, watching the men skin the man-eater and place what they could find of the woman in a plastic bag. Her head and one arm and shoulder were missing, as best I could tell. Somehow, the killing of the crocodile had felt anticlimactic, and I wondered if there wasn't something more to the episode than a woman being eaten and a croc being killed. No, I finally decided, it was exactly that simple. It had been going on for a million years and would continue as long as there were people, crocodiles, and water. But, at least, I thought on the walk back to camp, that's one *Ngwenya* who won't be waiting.

twenty-five

SCARFACE: DEATH IN DARK WATERS

by John H. Brandt

T HE RADIO OPERATOR AT Nakornsithamarat had received word
of the impending storm but, since typhoons are a rare occurrence on the Malayan Peninsula, he had not taken the weather
warning very seriously. He had shut down operations and gone home for
the night without notifying anyone.

Shortly, the small village of Lamthalupuk, which sits on a narrow
strip of land across the Ao Nakorn Bay from Nakornsithamarat, would be
totally destroyed. First the roar of wind had come from the Gulf of Siam
to the east and most of the houses and fishing boats had been swept
away. When the eye of the storm passed over the village everyone felt,
unfortunately incorrectly, that the calm indicated the storm was now
past. Shortly, the reverse winds which had forced water into the bay returned with a vengeance and waves eight to ten feet high washed across
the village to destroy what little was left. A few fortunate individuals had
tied themselves fast to trees and escaped the death by drowning to which
so many of their friends and neighbors had succumbed.

I had been sent to survey the damage to determine what assistance could be rendered. The storm had washed away any land approaches to the village and, accompanied by a number of Provincial officials, we proceeded by motorized sampan across the bay. The outward passage had been smooth but on our return a sharp wind had whipped up, churning the shallow water of Ao Nakorn into four- and five-foot waves. The sampan only rode a few inches above the water and bow waves soon started to spill over the freeboard. We all bailed frantically as the sun began to set, but by then the coastal mangrove was within sight. Soon, in complete darkness the boatman found the appropriate entry channel, which was totally invisible to me, and proceeded up a dark lagoon, overhung with creepers and vines, on the way back to a landing on the mainland. At that point one of my associates said, "At least we're lucky that we're not in Surathani because if our boat had tipped over we would only have drowned, but up there we would have ended up in the stomach of old Scarface." Since I was on my way to Surathani the following day, I called him aside and asked who and what old Scarface was. He had a most fascinating and horrifying tale to relate.

From where we were, the next province to the north on the peninsula was Surathani, which could only be reached by a train from Nakornsithamarat to Ban Doan Station, a distance of some 100 miles. There were no roads on the east coast at that time and the train was the primary means of transport other than walking. One common exception was that wherever small waterways existed people traveled by poled canoes or sampans propelled by a rat-tailed engine on a long, flexible shaft. For a period of several months, sampans around Surathani had regularly been attacked and turned over by a monster crocodile. Over a half-dozen people were known to have been dragged under and killed. A number of others were missing and were also presumed to be the victims of the crocodile. Some empty sampans had been found adrift with no one aboard and most likely the same horrible fate had befallen these occupants as well. No one knew exactly how many had died because the provinces had very poor reporting systems for such matters and many deaths went unrecorded. The villagers were terrified and many were afraid to go to the market. Canoe travel was the only way to get there and no one knew exactly where the crocodile lurked or where it would attack next.

Boats would often be totally unaware of the creature's presence until the entire craft was heaved into the air spilling the occupants into the water. In the fear of the moment, with everyone desperately splashing for shore, the dead were often not accounted for until a head count could be made. The croc would pull someone under so quickly that often there was no time to even scream for help. Not that any help would be available in any case!

The crocodile had been seen by survivors to have a large white mark on the forehead which had given it the name, "Scarface." Whether someone early in the croc's life had fired upon it at night while out hunting causing a large head wound that had healed, or whether the animal had been injured by the propeller of a motorboat was not known, but the prominent disfiguration made him distinctive from any other large crocodiles in the area.

The animal involved was the so-called saltwater or ocean-going crocodile which, in spite of its name, lives quite normally in fresh or brackish coastal waters. It is distributed extensively throughout southeast Asia and is the largest and most dangerous of the saurians in the area. Capable of ocean travel, it is found north as far as the Micronesian Island of Palau where I had had my first encounter with the dreaded creature some years earlier.

While living in Micronesia, I had been at Koror when an unfortunate villager had been brought to the hospital with both his buttocks torn off. Hemorrhaging extensively, he was at the point of death when the physicians began working on him. His tragic tale caused muffled laughter among the staff but wasn't funny to him at all. He had made a nighttime visit to the *benjo* which is an outhouse on stilts perched over the tidal flats. The tide was in and as he squatted, extended over the outhouse seat, a large croc had passed under him. Saltwater crocodiles consider man a part of their normal diet and this particular croc had surged out of the water and bitten the entire rear end off the screaming man who had desperately hung on to keep from being pulled into the water!

From Micronesia the animals extend into the Melanesian Islands, Indonesia and Australia. Among the largest of the crocodiles, there are recorded monsters of over twenty feet being killed in Borneo. In Singapore I observed a skull taken in the last century that, according to the measurements of the head alone, might have come from a crocodile over thirty feet in length! The enormity of a creature this size is frightening. Most full-grown males are in the eighteen to nineteen-foot class with only a few reaching twenty feet in length.

Saltwater crocs have been hunted extensively for their valuable skins, with those of lengths in the eight to nine-foot range being the most valuable. Consequently, they have been seriously depleted over much of their former range and, in the early 1970's, hunting of salt water crocs was fully restricted. With passage of such laws, all international trade in this animal was prohibited.

In 1987, a tourist from Colorado was pulled under and killed by a huge crocodile in Australia. Immediately prior to that in northern Australia, an enormous bull croc had taken on the terrifying habit of attacking the outboard motors on small fishing boats. A number had been attacked and swamped, with the panicked fishermen struggling to shore awaiting any moment to be pulled under by the monster. As this report came to the attention of the authorities, a number of attempts were made to destroy this animal. It became known by the name "Sweetheart." Although many fishermen aged rapidly as a result of their attacks, it was thought curious that Sweetheart only attacked the outboards and tore them savagely from their position on the stern. The men splashing in the water had never been directly attacked. This was only a small point in Sweetheart's favor but most of the victims had been virtually scared to death from their experience, even if they had no tooth marks to show for it.

When Sweetheart was finally killed it was thought that the huge nineteen-foot male may have mistakenly interpreted the purr of the outboard engine as the growling threat from another encroaching male crocodile. Lying on the bottom of the stream, the silhouette of a boat may have looked to him like a gliding croc on the surface. His attacks had been focused on the sound of the motor; his efforts to protect his home, although commendable, were experiences that would cause nightmares for years to come for the unfortunate victims. Sweetheart is now on display at the Darwin Museum and it is easy to envision the horror of a person subjected to an attack by such a creature. The few surviving victims of the croc at Surathani had similar gruesome experiences.

I proceeded the following morning by train to Ban Don Station, passing by the huge mountain called Khao Luang, the highest point on the peninsula with elevations over 6,000 feet. Upon arrival I immediately asked what the situation was concerning Scarface. All I had heard was quickly reaffirmed.

From Surathani north to the junction of Tha Chang no roads crossed the swampy delta of the Phum Duang River which emptied into the Gulf of Siam in Ao Ban Don Bay. Several tributaries, including the Yan River which connected from the north and the Tha Phi which flowed into the Phum Duang from the south, appeared to be the primary home areas of Scarface. Most of the attacks had taken place in the delta area and the adjoining mass of mangrove-lined lagoons.

Surathani Province is an area of vast mountainous jungle with no road connection at that time to the adjoining Province of Chumporn to the north or to any road across the entire Isthmus to Takua Pha in the west. The last settlement which had a track cut to it was the settlement of Kirirat Nikhom, almost in the middle of the vast central jungle. Just to the east of the settlement, the Yan River joined with the Phum Duang. It was here that I planned to start looking for the giant crocodile, proceeding eastward to the delta.

That night in Surathani I made arrangements for two canoes and purchased three new four-cell-battery flashlights. These, I felt, would throw an adequate beam to show up a croc's eyes at night. I had my .300 Mag along to hopefully use on the croc if we were fortunate enough to find him.

It took most of the next day to get to Kirirat Nikhom where we launched the canoes planning to drift downstream along the shore of the slow-moving stream until we reached the mouth of the Tha Phi.

The night was clear and stars were everywhere. We allowed the current to move us along as silently as possible. Occasionally we would strike a submerged log or rock and with every bump my heart would skip a beat and I would think, "Oh, my God, this is it! We're on top of Scarface and didn't see him!" But each time the smooth stream carried us along again without mishap. We periodically switched on the lights and on several occasions saw the red reflections of crocodile eyes along the bank or among the dense vegetation which grew into the water. But as quickly as they were spotted the eyes disappeared and it was impossible to even identify whether the croc was a big one or a small one. At day-break we made camp on the river bank and I slung a jungle hammock with mosquito netting on the sides and a nylon cover over the top to ward off the frequent rain showers. By afternoon, we were again ready to make preparations to continue on downstream.

The second night was as uneventful as the first one and several times when we passed small canoes the occupants always indicated that fur-ther downstream was the most likely place to find Scarface. We passed the mouth of the Tha Phi early the next morning and moved into the maze of channels that form the mouth of the Phum Duang near Tha Chang. Canoe traffic was getting heavier as we approached the more set-tled localities. We planned to spend the third night moving about in the delta area.

Late that afternoon we heard a large motor craft approaching up-stream on one of the channels. Upon seeing us, the craft veered our way and beached by our camp. Several government officials were on board and indicated they had been looking for us. Scarface had made an attack on a boat at midday not far from where we were camped.

On the launch was a very upset and grieving young soldier who, in the midst of his tears, regularly stood up and, vowing revenge, shouted tor-rents of violence into the watery wilderness. I asked one of the boatmen who he was and why he was so distressed. I was told that the latest vic-tim that Scarface had pulled under that day had been the soldier's younger brother, and he was vowing to kill the croc or give his life in the effort.

A crocodile, being unable to chew, grabs hold of its prey and pulls it under, never letting go of its grasp. Since it cannot bite off pieces to swal-low, it often pulls its victims to an underwater hideaway where the body can be secured among roots or vegetation until decomposition allows it to soften sufficiently for the crocodile to eat. In eating, the croc grabs a secure hold and then twists its body in the water until the mouthful comes free. In this way, arms and legs are easily wrenched from the dead body.

We were asked to accompany the group to a nearby backwater where the attack had occurred. The plan was to use long poles to prod the edges of the huge pool to see if the body could be dislodged—if it could be found. At least the soldier intended to give his younger brother a decent funeral ceremony.

Several hours went by and the sun was rapidly setting behind the trees. My boat was poling along an embankment about 100 yards from the launch. Everything was silent as death as the grim search continued. Suddenly, we heard loud shouts from the launch indicating that the body had been found. Decomposing gases had forced it to the surface once the prodding poles had jostled it loose. We turned to join the launch when suddenly a massive explosion rocked our boat. In the semi-darkness my first thought was that the launch had exploded, but I could see no fire. We hung onto our canoe to keep it from tipping over when the air was rent by another muffled explosion. This time we were close enough to see the huge geyser of water.

The young soldier had pulled the pin of two fragmentation grenades and had tossed them, at the moment of detonation, into the vegetation near where his brother's body had surfaced hoping that the croc was lurking nearby. This was a most unexpected event and I wondered then, as I have wondered since, why shrapnel didn't penetrate the boat bottoms. The water must have slowed the fragments down, but the concussion was of stunning magnitude.

Quickly, flashlights played on the surface of the water and loud shouts came from the launch that the crocodile had surfaced. Keeping our lights on the floating croc we proceeded to within fifteen yards not knowing for sure what the animal would do. It was still very much alive. We found out later that the grenades had apparently broken some ribs and had severely crippled the beast. Since crocodiles are known to be able to sustain massive injuries and still survive, I, together with two armed men on the launch, fired a series of nine shots. The shooting was difficult in the bobbing boats since every time we aimed, someone would move the flashlight off to some other point of interest until someone shouted a command of, "Dammit, hold still!" and with the proper lighting some good shots were finally made.

A rope was thrown over Scarface and he was taken in tow to the village. In his stomach was found a large collection of beads, a bracelet and a set of keys. Surprisingly, he was not as large as we had anticipated, measuring slightly over eleven feet in length. Although not a giant among crocodile, Scarface was as big as any I had ever seen, and his opened jaws looked large enough to drive a VW inside without crowding!

I returned home fully satisfied with our killing of Scarface and felt assured that now canoe travel would again be safe in this area. The event was not forgotten, but I was to meet Scarface again.

Many months had elapsed and in the northeastern town of Korat, hundreds of miles away, where I happened to be visiting, a small fair was being held. My servants came to tell me that the famous man-eater, "Scarface," was going to be on display. Surely, he was dead, and I couldn't imagine what advertisements my servants had seen.

I drove into Korat and pushed through the crowd gathered around a sign that proclaimed, "Scarface, killer of hundreds of people." Allowing for such exaggeration at carnivals, I hurried to see the animal. Apparently, some Chinese entrepreneurs had purchased the crocodile and quickly saw that they could make some money with the animal. Since no taxidermists existed in that part of the world, they had concocted a trough large enough to hold Scarface and had submerged him in a mixture of formaldehyde and alcohol. Poor Scarface had shrunk horribly and his mouth was grotesquely propped open. The white scar on his forehead was still prominently visible. For a small fee, viewers were permitted to stick their hands into the gaping maw of Scarface's mouth to get the imagined feel of being swallowed by a true man-eater. I couldn't help but feel a bit sorry for him in that his days were ended in so undignified a display.

No one who has ever had a boat turned over by a crocodile, or who has seen red eyes glide over the waters at night, or has even seen a formaldehyde-soaked rendition of a salt water crocodile is ever likely to soon forget the experience. It would quickly establish a firm conviction that if God would grant a choice in manner of dying, death by a man-eating croc would not be the one to choose.

twenty-six

RETURN OF THE MAN-EATERS

by Peter Hathaway Capstick

THE LAST DAWN OF Sweetness Vilakazi's short life edged the sere, brown horizon of KwaZulu with typical and terrible heat. As the shimmering globe of sun flooded over the drought-tortured crops and into her beehive-shaped grass *kaia*, Sweetness rolled from her simple bed, balanced on stacked bricks to raise it above the reach of the dreaded *tokoloshe*—the Zulu equivalent of a free-lance leprechaun—and checked to be certain none of the hairy water spirits lurked beneath, ready to render her unworthy of a husband. Satisfied that she was alone, she shrugged into a faded calico shift and stepped outside.

Already, many of the married women had left for the fields, hoes on shoulders, before the first threat of the January summer day began to hammer down, and were now sweating in the parched, khaki-colored mealie patches that should have been as green as the wing of the *isithathabantwana*, the praying mantis—the-green-one-who-takes-children. It would be a very bad year, Sweetness thought, scuffing the powdery dirt with coated toes. This should be the time of the rains, yet her KwaZulu homeland was still burned and naked. What, then, would happen when the dry winter came in April? Ah, well, decided Sweetness Vilakazi, thoughts were for men. . . .

As she had done since the time her mother had trained her to balance a tiny vegetable tin on her head as a child, she swung up the envied plastic jerry can and started on the worn path to the Hluhluwe River, which muttered the muffled speech of dark water beneath high banks, some 200 yards away. "*Sakubona*, Sweetnessi," called a woman as she passed, and Sweetness smiled easily on her way to death, which lay, unseen, only twenty long, barefoot paces ahead, waiting and hungry a few feet from the well-worn notch in the red clay bank where women drew murky water for their families. "Hua!" thought Sweetness Vilakazi, "but that hussy Beauty Mkunzi was foolish to let that crocodile take her water can." And, she remembered, just the next day Bongiwe Mkwandi had been caught by the hand by a big *iNgwenya* but had pulled free, although the crocodile had badly hurt her. She was still in the *hospitali* at Empangeni, Sweetness recalled, and cast her eyes quickly about in hopes of seeing Bongiwe's strapping husband, who might well be getting lonely by now. What foolish women, decided Sweetness, to let themselves nearly be caught by *iNgwenya*. Humming a snatch of "The Wedding Song," she felt the cool caress of the river water sluice over her toes as the slow, brown liquid flowed into the neck of the jerry can.

Of course, she never saw it, the camouflaged log just beneath the torpid surface. An explosion of muddy water and ivory teeth erupted before her, savage fangs and irresistible power crushing the bone of her arm that gripped the water vessel and clamping her flesh as solidly as a lion trap. Her scream of protest and agonized surprise had just welled in her constricted throat when, with a wrench and a twist, she was under the surface, the panic of her filling lungs unfelt because of the agony of her splintered arm. In seconds, the calm, brown waters of the Hluhluwe had closed, only the flirt of swirling, slow current marking the place where Sweetness Vilakazi had ceased to exist.

Sweetness Vilakazi was never seen after that day in early January 1983. Nor have the corpses of nine other human crocodile victims killed in the Nkundizi area of Hlabisa been recovered in the roughly four months since they began to die.

Why were they not more careful, knowing the danger only too well? I doubt that it could ever be explained to a non-African; perhaps it is just the way of things with the hunter and the hunted.

I can never seem to stop a small shake of my head every time I pick up a newspaper or magazine and see the Nile crocodile enshrined with the Cudjoe Key beach mouse, the California condor, the Hawaiian monk seal, or the rusty numbat under the enveloping wings of the word *endangered*. It may seem a touch strange, but I would suggest, as have some enlightened wildlife experts, that in some very extensive areas of Africa, the odds of getting eaten by a crocodile are about as good—or bad—right now as you read this as they were a hundred or more years ago.

I suppose that, these days, when the lightning development of mind-boggling technology is so astounding as to numb us, it's hard to keep in mind that some things *never* change. For sure, one of them is the croc. The other, as typified by the killing and eating of Sweetness Vilakazi, is the fact that man is a quite natural prey for old *iNgwenya*, which has been snacking on lithe, dusky maidens for as long as they have been hanging around the banks of lakes and rivers. This is, of course, much less than the 170 million years that the crocodile has been open for business, but it seems that it has filled in its idle moments admirably since humans came on the scene.

It's worth an instructive look at the particular situation in which Sweetness Vilakazi had all her life memberships canceled, because the circumstances are, at least in my experience, classic croc fare that still seem beyond belief to the average American.

The Nkundizi area of Hlabisa, a section of the Zulu homeland of KwaZulu, sounds exotic enough, but in fact lies only about two hundred miles from the ultrasophistication of Johannesburg, the City of Gold. Call it a round trip between New York and Philly. Well, the Hluhluwe (Shlush-shloo-weh) River has plenty of crocs, make no mistake, but it's not especially noted for its saurian population. The interesting thing is that of the nine humans recently eaten in company with 114 cattle, nine goats, and three dogs, not a single one of the late tribesmen was reported to the authority responsible, the KwaZulu Nature Conservation Department.

The *indunas*, or headmen, had for generations taken the croc danger as just a normal ingredient of bush living or, as they put it, a "natural disaster." Actually, they were informed only in the 1950s that they would be prosecuted for such unenlightened, anticonservationist activities as trying to kill the crocodiles that were regularly eating their people. Although it could have been little consolation to widow Pauline Dlamini, whose fifteen-year-old son and breadwinner was eaten by a croc in January of 1983 while gathering aquatic wild plants, protests against the wave of human slaughter were finally lodged with the local magistrate. No, no, and no again ruled the various parks boards and conservation departments. They would try to remove a *particular* man-eater, but, as was the case with the Hluhluwe crocs, there was no way to determine which crocs were guilty. A general thinning of the crocs was declared liable to "disturb the ecology." The Zulus would just have to take more care or find someplace else to get their water.

I suppose one could make a point that the Zulus living along the Hluhluwe have it pretty easy compared with the Zambian natives resident in the Kapinda region of Zambia's border with Zaire on Lake Mweru Wantipa. According to the Zambia *Daily Mail* (which, one presumes, would hardly go out of its way to advertise such a primeval state of affairs in a country as enlightened as Zambia), an average of thirty people a *month* are killed and eaten by crocs. That's one a day, as of July 15, 1982! The Kapinda villagers report that a shortage of fish, the mainstay of the local diet for both people and crocodiles, has led to the crocs becoming so fierce and aggressive that they are hunting humans as far as 550 yards from the water's edge. At an average of thirty per month, it would seem that the tactic works pretty well!

Certainly, it shouldn't be presumed that Zambian crocs have some sort of racist preference; it's just that the obvious population proportions in rural Africa dictate that blacks are thousands of times more likely to turn up on the menu than whites. A terrifying exception to the rule was Andrew Theunissen, a senior police official who came about as close to being crocodile fodder as you can get while he was swimming in the massive Lake Kariba, part of the border between Zambia and Zimbabwe (formerly Rhodesia).

According to the report in the *National Enquirer,* which Theunissen wrote in June of 1982, he was in the croc-infested water in the first place because of his own pet theory, which proclaimed that crocs won't attack a man where fish are plentiful. Well, Andy, back to the old drawing board. . . .

Theunissen, who was checking out the equipment on a police boat near the town of Binga, was suffering from a headache and decided that a dip would be just the ticket. It was nothing compared with the headache he was about to get. Floating quietly about two hundred feet from where he had dived off a dock, he was paralyzed with terror when an eight-foot crocodile grabbed him by the head, an armory of teeth shearing his scalp and grating on Andrew's skull with "an unbelievable crunching, grinding noise." He reached up and tried to grip the jaws with his hands, noticing how dark it was inside the croc's mouth, all air shut off from his bursting lungs. Theunissen struggled for all he was worth, feeling the savage teeth peg deeply into his hands and fingers. Suddenly, he was free!

In a growing cloud of watery blood, the policeman tried to fend off the reptile with his hands and feet, barely avoiding the terrible slashing of fangs as the croc snapped repeatedly at him. Upright in the water and belly-to-belly with the animal, Theunissen fought until he was able to kick and push himself off. He thrashed out in desperation and finally felt the greasy mud of the bank under his fingers, pulling himself clear in a last burst of terrified energy. Fortunately, his fellow officers saw him and got him to a hospital. Despite a major collection of stitches, Theunissen was really very lucky that the extent of his injuries was a severed nerve in his lacerated scalp, which left one side of his face permanently numb, and several severed finger tendons.

Just as in the case of Sweetness Vilakazi, though, and probably thousands of others, the pattern was completed the next day; another policeman in a different part of the lake was attacked by a crocodile. He didn't have Theunissen's luck, however. The "endangered" croc killed and ate him.

It seems to me that those folks who don't tend to think of croc hunting as among the more diverting of Africa's hunting pleasures haven't tried it. A big croc, accompanied as it normally is when sunning by tick birds and plover sentinels, is tougher to get within range of than a paranoid bull turkey, and is certainly one of the greater stalking challenges in the world of hunting. Add to that a fatal target zone of only a few square inches that can only be hit from side angles or above, and you have a classic game animal for the precision rifleman. Still, the real problem and challenge of croc hunting is *after* the shot, trying to retrieve the carcass. The perfect placement of a brain shot normally causes a few seconds of tremendous tail flurry, which often carries the body into the water to be lost to the jaws of its pals. If you're lucky and the croc was pointed the right way when you shot it, though, you now have the interesting project of dragging it back to land.

This was the proposition facing a pal of mine in southeast Africa whose safari client had shot a big croc on a river sandbar a few seasons back. For count-on-it sure, his African safari staff weren't *about* to go get it and drag the water-supported carcass back. The client allowed that he hadn't paid his bill yet, and that left my friend, John. Walking down to the bank, he fired a few rounds from his .458 into the water to spook off any close acquaintances of the deceased dragon and started wading up to the base of his chest, the rifle held above. About twenty yards short of the dead croc, he felt something grab his left leg with terrifying power, and the next instant he was flipped off his feet, the water closing over his head. Breaking the surface, in the sloshing billows of dirty liquid now rapidly staining with big red blossoms, he saw that a big croc had the calf and shin of his leg meshed tightly between its teeth and was spinning to tear off the living meat and bone. He got a lungful of water as he was knocked down again, trying to contain his panic but gagging and screaming in terror. Somehow, he realized that he still had his .458, a Brno bolt-action stoked with 500-grain solid bullets. Despite the fact that the rifle was full of water, he reckoned he was as good as dead anyway, and fought to flip off the safety catch. Feeling it under his thumb, he jerked the trigger while the gun was still beneath the surface. There was a violent *whump!,* the exploding barrel badly lacerating his hand as the action was blown apart. As he dropped the gun, he felt the croc release him. Floundering toward land, half dead with shock and pain, he was relieved to see the client run in to help him ashore. That the French hunter happened to be a physician probably saved John's life, since the man was able to stop the bleeding long enough to make the six-hour drive to a clinic.

Africa doesn't have a monopoly on crocodile attacks (a man who wounded an American crocodile in Biscayne Bay in Florida in the 1800s was killed by it when he tried to—of all things—kick it), and a recent report by United Press International from Kuala Lumpur, Malaysia, is certainly interesting. Although not the Nile crocodile of Africa, the equally deadly "mugger" or marsh crocodile (or possibly a saltwater croc, a species that killed most of a Japanese force of one thousand men stranded between Ramree Island and the Burma mainland in World War II), was reported at twenty-six feet and having a track record of at least eleven successful human kills as well as having bitten several more people who weren't inclined to stay to dinner. Over a three-year period, according to the UPI report, this particular beastie had terrorized long stretches of the Lupar River in Sarawak, formerly a prime prospecting ground for commercial hide hunters.

As of October 31, 1982, the super saurian was still giving the Lupar constabulary the slip, although the brute had been reported seen at noon several times; alas, no sharpshooter had been able to perforate its skull with a bullet. There is hope, however. Six veteran Malay witch doctors and two scientists of indeterminate qualification have joined the dragnet. It's not clear what the witch doctors are doing, but the scientists have been wandering the riverbank with their Sonys or Hitachis, playing the recorded chirpings of newly hatched crocodiles in hopes of either stirring maternal instinct in the (almost surely) female man-eater or tempting her to infanticidal cannibalism, which would be far more likely. So far, no go. Wonder what the score is up to by now?

Before leaving the different species of crocodiles to their continued depredations, bear in mind that we have only discussed *two* African locations. Even the relatively urban Zulus don't think much of reporting chopped damsels to the authorities, so you can guess what may actually go on in the *real* boondocks. Just a bit of finger counting can only leave one with the conclusion that the thousands of people killed in such remote areas as Mozambique, Angola, Ethiopia, or Congo-Brazzaville—all crocodile strongholds—must aggregate huge numbers.

For our sins, we in the southern United States are gifted with the alligator. And, for my money, the 'gator is the classic case of "preservation" gone stark, raving bananas.

When I was a kid, alligators spent most of their time seemingly queued up at the back door of Johnson, Smith and Co., the world's biggest novelty house, which sold bushels of the babies by mail order along with exploding cigars, chameleons, and highly realistic fake dog droppings. Placed on the federal endangered species list in 1967, the alligator had a record of attacking man outside of Gary Cooper Everglades movies that was pretty unimpressive. Ah, but that was before they got federally subsidized.

Today, conservative official estimates figure 'gator populations in just three Gulf counties at about ninety thousand! A fifteen-footer got itself arrested casually wandering down a street of $200,000 houses in Missouri City, Texas, just last June. Charming. Zany. Colorful, right? Not if you are one of the growing number of people who have been or will be mutilated or killed by alligators.

It wasn't funny to Sharon Elaine Holmes, who never got past the tender age of sixteen. You see, she was the first documented case of fatal alligator attack in the United States. She was dragged to her death—with her father trying to pull her out of the 'gator's jaws by her hair—drowned, and partially eaten in a state park near Sarasota, Florida, in 1973, back when 'gators were still considered endangered. That was seven years after the species became strictly protected, and four years before it was downgraded to "threatened" status. At the time, game biologists and state officials declared the terrible tragedy a "freak incident." Turns out it wasn't. In fact, it was just a preview. . . .

Since the death and dismemberment of Sharon Holmes, alligator attacks have been increasing with spooky frequency, from zero between the time of the first Spanish settlers through Sharon's death in 1973. Just last August, two University of Florida students were fortunate to rescue an even-more-fortunate classmate from the jaws of a ten-footer near Gainesville. Chris Palumbo, a twenty-year-old engineering student, was spotted in a local lake disputing possession of his left arm with a 'gator, which was trying with some success to eat it. The alligator took off when the two rescuers got close with a boat, but Chris's arm was reported severed in two places.

Mr. Dennis David, who is coordinator of the Nuisance Alligator Program for the Florida Game and Freshwater Fish Commission, advised UPI in June of 1982 that alligator bites are rare, averaging about three per year, with the last official death by 'gator in 1979. Presumably he is speaking of the Florida population only, which is composed of 500,000 to one million 'gators, depending upon whom you choose to believe. (That still seems like one heck of a lot of 'gators to be called "threatened," at least by me!) My notes show some thirteen 'gator attacks that featured major bites around the United States in 1981 alone. And these are just the ones that made the newspapers. In less than five months of 1982, for example, there had been 2,336 officially lodged complaints against nuisance, problem, or dangerous alligators (or all three) in thirteen Florida counties alone! Consider that the statistics included the cold months of January and February, when 'gators tend to be sluggish, and there is some indication of how big the problem is getting.

There is little doubt that the alligator is suffering from the same "familiarity syndrome" that affects such otherwise people-wary species as African lions and grizzly bears. That familiarity breeds contempt through close association and loss of predator respect of man in artificial circumstances, such as those of parks and reserves, is easily borne out by the alarming increase of attack rates by alligators. Those animals, once naturally frightened of man, may have now grown blasé by over-protection and increased association to the point that they are now deadly dangerous. I doubt that it will be the case, but perhaps a clipping I found in August of last year is a foreboding indicator of the future:

ALLIGATOR FOUND IN NEW YORK RESERVOIR

New York (SAPA-AP): After years of debunking stories of alligators living in New York sewer systems, municipal officials were astounded to find a small alligator in the reservoir.

"I couldn't believe it," said Mr. Andrew McCarthy of the Department of Environmental Protection.

Officials began hunting last week when residents near the reservoir began calling to say that they had seen an alligator.

On Monday two department employees spotted the alligator on a rock. It jumped into the water and swam away before they could get to it.

Later that night, accompanied by an expert from the zoo and a Mrs. Myra Watanabe, a university professor who has captured alligators in China, among other places, they succeeded in bagging it.

The alligator was taken to the Bronx Zoo, where experts examined it, pronounced it healthy, and placed it in a cage.

I suppose it won't be long before it's "Hey! Canada! Look out behind you!"

twenty-seven

AUSTRALIA: SALTIES RULE SUPREME

Michael Garlock

RUSSELL AUGUST BUTEL, fifty-five, owned a successful aquarium supply business near Vashon Head, north of Darwin. He was influential and well-liked within the industry. He was also an accomplished scuba diver who liked to combine his vocation with an avocation. In October 2005, that merger resulted in almost instant death.

Butel was collecting fish, coral, and sea cucumbers for his business, diving in Trepang Bay about 15 nautical miles east of Cape Don off the Cobourg Peninsula in the Northern Territory. It was later speculated that he'd probably been splashing around in the water—not a wise thing to do when curious crocs are in the area. They usually bring the kind of attention people can live without (or die with). Local residents are aware that crocodiles inhabit the bay and are understandably very reluctant to go into the water.

The 13-foot-long saltie lined Butel up, instantly went through the vectoring process that included estimating the distance to the target, and submerged. The croc tucked its legs close to its body to reduce drag and water resistance, and with a few powerful swings of its tail, began his silent, unseen attack, which encompassed a distance of between 328 and 656 feet (100 to 200 meters).

At the last second, when escape was impossible, the croc surfaced next to Butel, opened its jaws wide, and guillotined his victim's head off. In one horrible instant just before he died, the victim no doubt saw the gaping, tooth-filled mouth and the elongated, triangular-shaped tongue, right before the powerful jaws snapped close, exerting thousands of pounds of force per inch on Butel's neck.

The victim's headless body was found floating around a mile from the attack site at about 4:30 P.M. The assault was witnessed by the victim's horrified diving partner, a forty-one-year-old New Zealand man who immediately scrambled safely into a nearby dinghy. He marked the exact location of the attack with an emergency beacon and used a satellite phone to notify authorities. Divers said the victim was working in an area where there was a high risk of attack. Police said they would not shoot the croc.

THE KAKADU NATIONAL PARK guide who escaped a freshwater crocodile attack was fortunate. A twenty-three-year-old German tourist was not so lucky.

Isabel von Jordan was killed by a 13-foot croc while swimming at night in a natural pool. Nine people had gone into Sandy Billabong at 11:30 P.M. as part of a four-day tour. It was hot, the moon was nearly full, and the water looked inviting. The victim's sister Valerie, twenty-one, later told the German diplomatic representative in Darwin that a tour guide had assured the group it was safe to swim in the billabong because it held only innocuous freshwater crocodiles who rarely if ever attacked humans.

It's a wonder they didn't notice the many conspicuously posted signs that warn of the eight adult salties that live in the billabong. It's their residence, and their buffet table.

Isabel and Valerie had come to Australia from Bali to call on friends who had been evacuated to a Darwin hospital after being wounded in the terrorist attack at the Sari Club, a popular Bali nightclub. Valerie said they left the club only an hour before the deadly explosion. On that occasion Isabel was very fortunate indeed.

A scant ten days later, however, her luck came to a screeching halt.

James Rothwell, twenty-four, a resident of Sussex, England, said he felt a croc brush against his leg. A few seconds later he heard the victim scream and disappear under the water. Then it was all over. It had taken less than a minute. Rothwell said he shone a flashlight on the water and saw two red croc eyes swimming away from the spot where Isabel had disappeared, and then, the blurred outline of a crocodile highlighted against the night sky.

Search parties worked through the night and finally discovered the German tourist's lifeless body about a mile upriver from where the attack had occurred. Park rangers had to harpoon the killer croc the following morning in order to convince it to release the victim's body.

GROOTE EYLANDT, A REMOTE Northern Territory island in the Gulf of Carpentaria off Arnhem Land, was the last place British-national Russell Harris saw on earth. The thirty-seven-year-old mines superintendent's lifeless body was found in September 2005 at the mouth of Eight Mile Creek.

He had been snorkeling with another man off rocks approximately 330 feet north of Picnic Beach. They became separated, and Harris was last seen about 65 feet from shore. Local police said a saltwater crocodile had been previously observed at the mouth of the creek where his body was discovered. The place of discovery was about a mile from where Harris was last seen alive. The croc apparently grabbed the victim from underneath and pulled him under the water, where he drowned.

Fifteen years earlier, forty-three-year-old Albert Juzelionas, a Telecom worker from Jabiru, had met a similar fate when he was killed by an 8-foot croc while swimming on Groote Eylandt. And less than a week after Russell Harris met his maker, a fifty-five-year-old man was killed by a croc while scuba diving with a friend on the Cobourg Peninsula (not far from Groote Eylandt) in the Northern Territory.

SIXTY-YEAR-OLD BARRY JEFFERIES LIKED to fish. In August 2005 he found himself in the extremely unenviable position of being the catch of the day for an 882-pound saltwater crocodile.

Midway Waterhole on the Normanby River in Lakefield National Park, northwest of Cooktown in northern Queensland, is a popular place with locals and tourists. Famous for its scenic beauty, the area is familiar to tour operators. Lakefield is Queensland's second-largest park. It comprises 19,395 square miles (50,000 square kilometers) of savannah and riverine flats drained by large rivers, and contains magnificent wetlands that are home to water birds, barramundi, and both saltwater and freshwater crocodiles. In the dry season, rivers are transformed into a series of water holes; in the wet season the park is an inaccessible wetland.

There are twenty-one campsites that provide few amenities. Campers must be relatively self-sufficient and, it is presumed, fairly knowledgeable not only about the terrain, but also about the different types of animals that make Lakefield their home.

Jefferies and his wife Glenda were fishing at dusk from a canoe, enjoying life and being on the water, when the croc silently attacked him, grabbed one of his arms, effortlessly dragged him out of his flimsy craft, and killed him. His body was never found.

People familiar with the area said the croc, which was later killed by park rangers, was an old animal that had lived near this water hole (and others) for many years. Had the croc become habituated to people? Was it too old to hunt for its normal prey? Had it turned to humans instead, developing a taste for people? No one ventured an opinion.

Jefferies's wife Glenda later told authorities she saw the crocodile approach them before it submerged. It cleverly followed a baited fishing line up to the side of the canoe and then propelled itself up and out of the water. It lunged and expertly caught her husband, who tried in vain to fight the huge reptile off with a paddle.

During the process of dragging the ill-fated victim into the water, the croc capsized the canoe, which vanished into the water hole. Glenda Jefferies surfaced as the saltie was biting her husband to death. Knowing she could not save him and fearing the croc might turn on her after finishing its grisly task, she frantically swam to shore as fast as she could. It took her twenty minutes to drive to the ranger station where she raised the alarm.

Helicopters and boats were used in the ineffectual search for Barry. Torn clothing was found several hundred yards from their campsite, but no physical evidence of Barry was ever discovered. A large croc was shot and killed the following afternoon, but no human remains were found in its stomach. Was it the croc that had killed Barry? No one knows. (However, after about a week in a crocodile's stomach, human bone takes on the consistency of very rubbery gristle, so it's doubtful that the rangers shot the right croc.)

Tour operator Tom Rosser expressed surprise that the couple had taken a canoe into known crocodile habitat. Many conspicuously posted warning signs advise against doing such a foolish thing. He said that people have fished in the river quite often, but typically they're in at least a 14-foot or larger dinghy, which is wider, more stable in the water, and more imposing-looking to the crocodiles. A larger craft reduces the chance of attack considerably. Canoes are notoriously unstable even in calm waters. When they are assaulted by an animal weighing a ton or more, they are almost certain to capsize.

In defense of their territory, saltwater crocodiles will attack just about anything, and it doesn't necessarily have to be edible. Being in a larger watercraft does not guarantee immunity from an unprovoked and violent assault, but it does give the occupants a better chance of survival.

KEL LUSCOMBE AND STEVE "Chilli" Pye were fishing 1.24 miles (two kilometers) offshore in Princess Charlotte Bay in October 2002 when their 14-foot-long aluminum boat was attacked by a 16.5-foot-long monster croc. The saltie used its head as a battering ram, and knocked the boat sideways for a distance of at least three feet, according to Pye. His partner, who has been fishing in the area for thirty years, added that the croc was probably larger than 16 feet.

"We spotted him 3,040 meters [1.89 miles] away, near a sand quay, and he kept pace with us for a while, then moved closer and closer before he reared out of the water and went for us. The noise when he hit was like a car crash and he nearly threw me out of the boat." The boat didn't tip over and the three men were none the worse for the experience.

* * *

A KAYAK IS AN even worse choice when venturing out into croc-infested waters. Pom Jason Lewis, thirty-seven, was traveling around the world in 2005. He made it as far as Cape York Peninsula when his luck nearly ran out. When paddling from the appropriately named Lizard Island to the mainland, Pom suddenly found himself being intensely scrutinized by two large crocodiles.

The attack came late in the afternoon as he neared the sandbank, where he intended to pitch his tent and spend the night before continuing his journey the following morning. The two salties silently slithered off the bank and into the water as he got closer.

Pom saw the crocs and didn't think much about it. He had seen crocs before, except this time one of them started following him. That had never happened to him, and it frightened him. Pom paddled as fast as he could in an attempt to reach the beach and the safety he assumed it provided, but the croc kept on closing the distance between them.

He finally made it safely to the beach, but the curious croc refused to go away. When Pom foolishly tried to drive the beast off with his paddle, his only means of propelling his kayak through the water was destroyed. He survived the night in spite of the watchful eyes of the patrolling croc. The next morning he used his satellite phone to call a seaplane, which subsequently rescued him. It could have been a lot worse.

ALMOST EXACTLY A YEAR earlier, eleven-year-old Hannah Thompson decided to take a cooling dip in Margaret Bay near the top of Cape York Peninsula, when she was attacked by an 11-foot-long saltie who figured it had just caught a very easy and tender meal.

Hannah's life was saved by Ray Turner, a famous croc hunter who providentially happened to witness the assault from his nearby boat. When he saw the croc grab the diminutive Hannah by her arm and start to drag her under the water, the fifty-seven-year-old Turner took immediate action. He launched himself out of his boat like a human bullet and landed on the reptile's back.

With complete disregard for his own safety (and life), he assaulted the attacking reptile. After Turner gouged the croc's left eye; the reptile lost his appetite for little Hannah and broke off the attack, although it continued to circle the boat that was now occupied by Turner and his intended victim.

The celebrated croc hunter took Hannah and the rest of her group to Haggerstone Island, where she was medivaced to Thursday Island Hospital. Although she suffered deep puncture wounds to her lower arm, Hannah made a full recovery.

LAKEFIELD NATIONAL PARK IS accessible only by four-wheel-drive vehicles, and is renowned for viewing freshwater and saltwater crocodiles in the wild. The vast majority of people who camp and enjoy other recreational activities do so without incident, although officials do urge visitors to exercise common sense when in croc country.

Saltwater crocodiles may appear slow and lumbering when on land, but that does not mean they won't venture out from their natural habitat—water—in search of a meal. Like their Nile counterparts in Africa, salties know an opportunity when they see one.

Just ask thirty-four-year-old Andrew Kerr.

Bathurst Bay is a popular fishing spot 155 miles north of Cooktown in the remote Cape York Peninsula, in Far North Queensland. The Kerrs and a group of friends from Brisbane were taking an annual holiday, camping at the same spot they had visited for the past five years. They were familiar with the area and all the different animals that lived there. What could possibly go wrong?

Andrew, his wife Diane, and their three-month-old son Kelly were peacefully sleeping in their tent on a beach in October 2005 when their pleasant dreams suddenly turned into a horror show. A 14-foot-long (4.2-meter) saltie that weighed 661 pounds (300 kilograms) snuck up on them and lunged through the tent at the ungodly hour of 4:00 A.M.

Diane later told the *Brisbane Courier-Mail* that after she heard a thud, she got up and looked through the netting on the tent door and saw an immense crocodile staring back at her. She woke her husband in a panic, and when he sat up, the croc charged him.

The marauding monster grabbed one of Kerr's legs in a viselike grip and attempted to drag him back to the water. Kerr's wife Diane held onto the bassinet that contained their son with one hand and her husband with her other hand and started screaming for help as loud as she could. The croc dug his heels into the sand and effortlessly pulled all three of them (including the bassinet) out of the tent.

Diane's shrieks woke the Sorohan family camping nearby. Mr. Sorohan later said they'd heard screams, so they jumped up and raced out of their tent. Andrew would not have had the chance to yell or do much of anything, as the croc had him in his mouth.

Alicia Sorohan, a sixty-one-year-old grandmother who tips the scales at a feathery 121 pounds (55 kilograms), probably thought the croc had gone after the baby. Without giving it a second thought, she jumped on the reptile's back. The croc immediately released its grip on Andrew Kerr, turned around, and smashed her face with its head, breaking her nose. Then it clamped its jaws on one of her arms, almost tearing it from its socket, and started to haul her toward the water. Her husband ran back to their tent to fetch an ax.

While he was doing that, the croc was still trying to lug Alicia to her certain death. Their son Jason, thirty-three, positioned the barrel of a high-powered handgun against the back of the croc's head and pulled the trigger, instantaneously killing the animal.

By the time Alicia Sorohan had reached Andrew Kerr and jumped on the croc's back, Kerr was already badly mangled. One of his legs was shattered, and his entire body was hideously perforated and slashed. Bits of flesh were hanging off of him. The tent floor was covered in slowly congealing blood. Andrew Kerr was as limp as a rag doll.

Other campers on the beach activated a Cospas-Sarsat beacon (an emergency position radio), whose signal was detected by two quarantine officers who were eradicating wild pigs in the area. The signal also alerted the Rescue Coordination Center in Canberra, which immediately dispatched a Queensland Park Wildlife Service (QPWS) helicopter with a medic on board to the scene.

After a ninety-minute flight, the QPWS chopper touched down and evacuated the badly wounded Andrew Kerr and Alicia Sorohan, taking them to the ranger station. On the way the pilot alerted the Royal

Flying Doctor Service (RFDS). Another helicopter dispatched from Cairns was also en route to the park after stopping at Cooktown to pick up a doctor.

Kerr and Sorohan were given emergency treatment at the ranger station by the RFDS before being medivaced to the Cairns Base Hospital. A flyby of the area confirmed that the killer croc was dead.

The attack was subsequently investigated by the QPWS, which believed the croc may have been tempted to the area by fish and food morsels carelessly and inconsiderately discarded by fishermen.

Kerr underwent several operations and months of recovery time, but he survived the ordeal. His wife and baby son were unscathed. Needless to say Kerr and his wife were extremely grateful. Alicia's actions had saved their lives.

Alicia Sorohan spent two weeks in the hospital and endured months of physiotherapy. She lost the full use of the arm the croc chewed on, now badly disfigured, and her hand no longer rotates properly. In spite of her ordeal, Alicia continues to return to the same camping spot. She told reporters that she liked crocs before the unfortunate incident, and she continues to like them.

"They are fascinating creatures," she added.

THE FINNISS RIVER IS 50 miles southwest of Darwin in the Northern Territory. Although certain channels are only about 4 feet deep, they and most of the river can safely be navigated by large boats that are 14 feet wide. At its widest point the river is 329 feet across, and it's slightly less than 6 miles long. The river is prime saltwater croc habitat.

It is also possible to ride all terrain vehicles (ATVs) on broad, lush, verdant paths that run parallel to the river and follow its course as it meanders in a series of gentle arcs and curves in a north by northwesterly direction. ATV riding is a popular recreational activity in the area.

In late December 2003, tropical cyclone Debbie tracked south by southwest and dumped between 6 and 12 inches of rain over a large area, causing significant rises in water levels and local flooding as it skirted the Northwest Territory. The combination of Debbie, the Finniss

River, and resident crocs created an unforeseen set of rarely combined circumstances that forced two young men to witness a friend being eaten alive.

Shaun Blowers and Ashley McGough, both nineteen, and Brett Mann, twenty-two, had been riding their ATVs parallel to the Finniss River for most of the day. The track, although muddy and full of potholes, was nevertheless navigable. All three of the young men were experienced, safety-conscious riders who knew how to have fun without taking unnecessary risks.

Their scheduled, day-long Sunday ride began uneventfully, and by afternoon they had parked their ATVs above the riverbank and were ready to go down to the river to wash the mud and sand off themselves and their clothes. Brett Mann left the safety of the sandy bank and ventured out a little farther.

It was a fatal mistake.

The recent rains had swollen the river and increased the speed of the current. Taken unawares, Mann lost his footing on the moss-slippery rocks and pebbles and was swept away. Blowers and McGough immediately jumped in and swam to his rescue. After they reached him, they positioned themselves in front of him, shielding him from the current. They were in the process of leading him back to shore when Blowers walked past a lurking, 13-foot-long croc. He didn't see the reptile, but McGough did, and yelled a warning. McGough and Blowers swam to the nearest tree and scrambled up the trunk. Mann was nowhere to be seen. There had been no splashing, no scream *in extremis*—no sound whatsoever.

A few minutes later the huge reptile surfaced with the lifeless body of Brett Mann firmly clamped between its jaws. It swam toward the treed pair as if showing them a trophy. Then it swam away, only to reappear approximately five minutes later. Brett Mann was no longer between its jaws. Apparently the croc had wedged the victim's lifeless body against submerged rocks or logs, where the corpse would no doubt remain for several days, curing.

In the meantime, the saltie was hoping to nab another victim. It cruised close to the tree, looking up, hoping one of the lads would fall down where he would be an easy catch. The persistent, patient croc hung around all night as Blowers and McGough clung to each other, shivering in the cold darkness. They were afraid to go to sleep while the still-hungry croc lurked below them. They knew the river was rising. Would the water level climb high enough to enable the croc to jump up and grab one of them? The saltie finally gave up and left the following morning. They had been in the tree for twenty-two hours.

When they failed to return as expected Sunday night, concerned family and friends called police, who immediately launched a search mission. They were finally discovered by a helicopter at 3:30 P.M. that afternoon and winched to safety.

Blowers and McGough were treated for exposure and shock at Royal Darwin Hospital before being released. Authorities used a helicopter, ATVs, and several dinghies when they searched for the remains of Brett Mann. Deteriorating weather later forced police to call off the search. Neither the croc nor Mr. Mann was ever found.

THE RIVER WAS ALSO the haunt of a crocodile that became a legend in its own time, and after its untimely death, achieved iconic status in the Northern Territory. Nicknamed "Sweetheart," because it dominated Sweet's billabong (about 34 miles southwest of Darwin), this saltie weighed 1,720 pounds and reached a length of 17 feet. During the 1970s, the croc terrorized thousands of boaters for many years by ramming them and biting their propellers.

Because it was very territorial, the croc regarded any incursion into its domain as a threat, and it reacted accordingly, no matter how big or small the craft was. Scars lined its back and several teeth were chipped, evidence of several violent confrontations with propellers.

Wildlife officials used a tranquilizer dart to finally subdue the animal in 1981. Unfortunately, the drugged reptile sank to the bottom of the river, where it became snagged on a submerged log and drowned. Divers recovered its body and moved it to the Northern Territory Museum and Art Gallery in Darwin, where the remains are viewed by thousands of people a day.

* * *

ABOUT A WEEK AFTER Russell Harris and Barry Jefferies wound up as dinner for hungry saltwater crocodiles, another attack occurred. Ric Burnup and his children, ten-year-old Chantal and older brother Simon, were vacationing at Doubtful Bay off the Kimberly Coast, 218 miles northeast of Broome in northern Australia. Mrs. Burnup remained at home in Busselton.

They had rented a boat in the first week of October 2005. The family traveled by dinghy up an estuary to a water hole near the mouth of the Safe River. They were swimming and snorkeling for about twenty minutes when Ric saw his daughter suddenly disappear. What Chantal suddenly saw through her mask were the jaws of an 8-foot-long saltie, opening wide and closing around her.

Ric grabbed his daughter by one arm while Simon punched the croc in the head. The saltie, probably distracted by this unexpected retaliation, released its grip, enabling Ric to haul a very frightened Chantal to a nearby rock, where they saw that the croc was still watching them.

Miraculously, the cuts on one of her arms and a leg were not life-threatening. The girl was airlifted by helicopter to a farm at Mount Hart, about 150 miles northeast of Derby, where a doctor was to meet her. Later she was taken to Derby Hospital where she was treated for her injuries and released.

ANOTHER VERY LUCKY ESCAPEE is nineteen-year-old Manuel Pascoe. In November 2003 he was returning home along a creek near the Blyth River, about 250 miles east of Darwin, capital of the Northern Territory. Tired from hunting geese all day (and from the effort of lugging their carcasses home), Pascoe evidently forgot that crocs are very attracted to the smell of blood.

The 10-footer that lunged up from the bottom of the creek Pascoe was imprudently walking in probably thought he was in for a good meal—Pascoe *and* his dead, still-bleeding geese. What the croc could not have anticipated was getting punched in the snout by Pascoe's aunt,

Margaret Rinbuma, who was hunting with Pascoe when he got attacked. Diverted and confused, the croc let go of Pascoe's leg and retreated. The victim suffered muscle damage to his left leg, but was found to be in otherwise stable condition when he got to the local hospital.

A YEAR LATER, LACHLAN MCGREGOR, seventeen, was hunting magpie geese at Dhipiri, a remote water hole near the Glyde River in the Arnhem Land region of the Northern Territory. He made the near-fatal mistake of stepping on the head of a submerged crocodile.

He later told reporters that he and his group were walking back at a leisurely pace. When he stood on the croc's head, it latched onto his leg and pulled him back into the water, but released him after three or four seconds. After that he ran as fast and as far as he could. Witnesses said they thought the 8.5-foot-long croc was a mother protecting her hatchlings. If that was indeed the case, in all likelihood it saved McGregor's life.

SHORTLY AFTER RUSSELL HARRIS and Barry Jefferies were killed and Chantal Burnup was attacked, Northern Territory authorities sent a proposal to the federal government that would have allowed twenty-five trophy crocodiles (longer than 13 feet) to be killed on safari hunts each year. Australia rejected the plan. The environment minister said that permitting visitors to blast away at Australia's wildlife would convey an inaccurate idea about the country's pledge to preserve its indigenous fauna. He added that safari hunting, in his opinion, was not consistent with a modern-day approach to animal welfare and responsible management. Moreover, it was highly unlikely that amateur hunters would be able to kill a crocodile from 50 yards away in a humane manner with the first shot.

The government will continue to permit 600 crocs a year to be shot and trapped by experts, to be used for farming, to harvest their hides and meat, or because they pose a real threat to humans.

* * *

ANOTHER HUNTER WAS SAVED from almost certain death on November 22, 2003, when a forty-year-old woman from the Pirlangimpi Aboriginal district became detached from a group that had been searching for mud mussels on Melville Island in Arnhem Land in the Northern Territory. The woman foolishly tried to traverse a creek at night during a high tide.

She never saw the saltie that sprung up and bit her on the back. She successfully defended herself by whacking the reptile with her bag of mussels. Like Blowers and McGough, she climbed a tree where she remained overnight. The following morning the croc left the area, and its intended victim went on her way, basically none the worse for wear except for a minor wound that was treated at a local hospital.

Trees are often the only way to escape from an attacking saltwater crocodile. Once high enough, a person can usually wait until the croc gives up and goes away. The main issues for someone in a tree are falling asleep, and the risk that rising waters will put the croc within leaping reach.

A CERTAIN MS. PLUMWOOD, an academic from Sydney, decided to go canoeing alone on the ominously named East Alligator River in Kakadu National Park in 1985. Her story of escape and survival ranks among the most miraculous and improbable in the annals of northern Australia croc attacks.

Plumwood ran into what she thought was a floating log. The log was in fact a very large saltie that instantly went after her frail craft, bumping the canoe repeatedly with its bone-hard nose and threatening to tip it over and hurl its occupant into the water. Knowing that if she were to wind up in the river she would face almost certain death, Plumwood sensibly decided to make a dash for the riverbank.

She made it without incident to the bank and managed to climb a tree that easily supported her weight. No doubt she believed she was safe—for a fleeting second. However, that illusion was brutally shattered when the reptile lunged up and out of the water and managed to get ahold of her legs in a grip as strong as a bear trap. Unable to hold on, Plumwood, suffering from deep puncture wounds, was snatched out of the tree in a heartbeat. Once the croc landed back in the water, it did two death rolls. Normally this would have been enough to either render unconscious or outright kill most victims, but Plumwood was no ordinary item of prey.

When the croc released her in order to get a better and final grip, the plucky Plumwood made a second sprint for the same tree she had just been snatched from moments ago. Not to be denied its dinner, the croc lunged again and was able to chomp down and secure its intended victim in its jaws for a second time.

Holding her firmly by her thighs, the croc plunged back into the water, dragging the helpless Plumwood with it. Amazingly, the reptile released her once again in order to get a better grip and administer the fatal coup de grace. Seizing yet another improbable opportunity to escape with her life, Plumwood wisely eschewed the tree and instead hauled her painfully bleeding body up the bank and as far away from the water as possible.

Park rangers found her sometime later in a swamp, bleeding profusely from her injuries. A large part of one of her thighs had been bitten off by the croc and was hanging on by tendons. But Plumwood survived to tell the tale.

THREE YEARS LATER IN Kakadu, an attack had an entirely different and infinitely more gruesome outcome. A local man went fishing at the Oenpelli border crossing at the junction of Arnhem Land and Kakadu. It was (and still is) common for native peoples to catch their dinner on the end of a well-baited line. Thinking the fishing was better elsewhere, he was able to wade to the far side of the crossing. There he contentedly cast his lure for several uneventful hours.

He was not alone. Watching him with intense interest was a large saltwater crocodile. In and of itself, this was nothing to get concerned about. Salties are found in great numbers throughout the area, and the sight of one did not necessarily precipitate a horrendous event. Indigenous people get used to crocs. They learn to live with the reptiles and in general, they exercise sound judgment in their presence.

However, the penalty for complacency can be catastrophic.

When he had finished fishing, the man waded back along a causeway in the direction of his parked car. But by this time the water had risen and he inexplicably fell or slipped into deeper, faster-moving water. He started to float downstream. A group of American tourists were sitting and relaxing on the riverbank, watching and wondering if they should intervene and help the man.

Gathering himself up, he regained his footing and scrambled to the riverbank. The Americans were glad they didn't intercede. It was obvious the man was safe. But it was slippery and muddy. The man was encumbered by a fishing net, and, according to witnesses, a beer which he held in his other hand. Everything conspired to slow him down just long enough to enable the submerged croc to explode out of the water.

The croc had already completed his attack run, and he executed the final phase to perfection. Every variable had been considered and factored into the final equation. The croc had maneuvered himself extremely close to the fisherman. Jaws agape, the reptile seized the already doomed man's head with his long, pointy teeth and clamped down as hard as he could.

The fisherman was instantly decapitated. The croc submerged with the head in his jaws and the corpse, spewing blood from a ghastly stump between the shoulders, floated lazily down the river past the Americans. No remains of the fisherman were ever found. It is entirely possible that alcohol impaired the man's judgment and was a contributing factor in his death.

LOOKING DIRECTLY INTO THE gullet of a saltwater crocodile is a terrifying experience. A man's head can easily fit into a saltie's mouth. Not many people have been in that predicament and lived to tell the tale.

In Cairns, North Queensland, in December 2004, eighteen-year-old Drew Ramsden was having a few drinks with a group of friends when he went to the lip of the Barron River at a basin named Lake Placid at approximately 10:30 P.M. to wash his face. He knelt down, leaned over, and plunged his head into the water. Unfortunately he was unable to hear his mates as they frantically shouted at him, trying to warn him of the 8-foot-long croc that was stealthily approaching. They threw rocks and beer cans at the reptile, but were unable to deter it from getting closer and closer.

Drew lifted his head out of the water just in time to hear his friends' hysterical warnings; then, he felt the reptile's teeth scraping his skull. When Drew raised his head, it more than likely saved his life. The croc was unable to get a firm grip on him, allowing the extremely lucky beer drinker to escape with only a few minor puncture wounds and teeth marks on his head and chin.

ANOTHER RIVER WAS THE scene of a fatal attack in 1985, when Beryl Wruck, forty, attended a party on the banks of the Daintree River, north of Cairns, Queensland. Everyone in the group was from the area, well aware of the crocodiles that lived in the river and the dangers they posed. Perhaps they did not know that the safety net erected to protect the site where they were partying had been removed for repairs, and had not yet been repositioned.

In any case, it was a hot December night, and several members of the group decided to wade into the river to cool off after hours of dancing and drinking. The water was very shallow, only 18 inches deep. Surely there was no danger. A witness who was standing next to Beryl said he was rudely shoved aside as the croc rushed toward its victim. When the saltie took hold of Beryl, it threw her upwards, somersaulting her into the air. There were no screams, only a loud splash as she landed back in the water and the saltie dragged her to certain death.

An ensuing search party looked for a week, but nothing was ever found—no Beryl . . . no croc.

EVEN LARGE, LAND-BASED MOTOR vehicles are not exempt from salt-water crocodile attacks. In late January 2006, a croc catapulted itself at a passing four-wheel-drive truck on the Kakadu Highway near Jabiru. The 6.5-foot-long croc had abruptly materialized from a culvert drain and hurtled itself into the path of the truck, which was driven by a local scientist.

The animal died on impact and was given to local Aborigines, who cooked and ate it. It happened so suddenly, the driver hadn't had any time to react and try to avoid the airborne reptile. Croc experts said the animals often move into culvert fishing sites and stay there for the entire wet season because they're attracted to the fish.

Garry Lindner, a crocodile management officer at Kakadu National Park, said the croc was probably startled by the passing vehicle and just leapt in the wrong direction when it heard the vehicle coming.

A POLICE BLUNDER IN March 2005 nearly resulted in tragedy. Officers in Kununurra in the far north of Western State responded to an emergency call from a shocked woman who returned home earlier than expected from a holiday and discovered a 6-foot saltwater crocodile in the laundry room of her home.

The saltie had been caught by a friend of her son's, who was a licensed croc catcher. He had intended to take it to a nearby sanctuary the next day and release it. In the meantime, he'd stashed the croc for safekeeping in the mother's home.

Believing the animal to be a relatively harmless freshwater croc, the police took it to Lily Creek Lagoon, a popular swimming hole, and set it free. When they learned of the mistake, alarmed wildlife officials immediately warned all residents, especially children (and including dogs) to avoid the area.

After a massive search that lasted several weeks, the croc was found 28 miles upstream from where it had been released. Attempts to trap and remove the saltie from the lagoon were unsuccessful, leaving officials no choice but to shoot the animal.

THE RETURNING VACATIONER WASN'T the only one who got a nasty surprise. Ian White, an employee of the Northern Land Council in Jabiru, was sitting at his desk at home one Sunday in February 2006 when he happened to look out the window at his garden. The sun bounced off something black and gold. Ian thought it was a goanna (a large lizard), but then realized it was a croc. Rangers removed the 6.5-foot-long reptile from Ian's carport and later released it at the South Alligator River boat ramp.

A 3-FOOT SALTIE TOOK advantage of one of Darwin's many amenities when it went for a swim in a public swimming pool in Palmerston, south of Darwin, in January 2005. Swimmers were quite alarmed when they realized they were sharing the Olympic-sized pool at the Palmerston Leisure Center with the 3-foot-long male reptile.

Police and Parks and Wildlife personnel had no difficulty in getting people to evacuate the pool while they easily captured the animal. The croc was very calm and seemed to be in poor health.

twenty-eight

TERROR ON THE ZAMBEZI

by Hannes Wessels

IT WAS A MAGNIFICENT Easter Sunday morning when canoe guide Phil Longden led his party of German tourists into a channel skirting the great Zambezi River, which separates Zambia and Zimbabwe in southern Africa. Their trip had been a happy one and the spectacles they had come in search of had filled their cameras. The vista ahead promised more of the same. Waterbuck and impala grazed quietly on the green riverine grasses while brilliant white egrets danced at the feet of Cape buffalo as their hooves unearthed a well-stocked larder of insects. Unmistakable brown blobs rippled the calm water downriver as hippos grunted and chortled. On the sand banks crocodiles basked in the sun, languid but alert.

Longden was tall, with an Olympian physique. No newcomer to these waters, he had coursed the big river in his fiberglass shell many times. The Zambezi practically ran in his veins. He loved the sweaty smell of the "Dagga Boys," the old buffalo that glared back at him when he paddled by their retirement homes on the islands. And he loved the scenic magnificence of the floodplain that lay at the feet of the rugged mountains that formed the Zambezi escarpment.

That morning Longden had called the little flotilla together to relax and savor the beauty. He organized a "leg-over," where the occupants place their feet in the adjoining canoe to hold the canoes parallel. The group rested their paddles and sat back to relax and let the current take them slowly down. The tranquil scene was shattered when an unseen hippo burst out of the reed-bank adjacent to them and crashed into the water. The guide reacted immediately and shouted for the paddlers to disengage.

"Watch out!" he screamed as he kicked a canoe away. But as he drew his foot back, a pair of gaping jaws with massive white incisors surged out of the water below and clamped onto his leg. With awesome brute strength and four tons of muscle and bone, the attacking hippo shook Longden like a rag doll, tearing into his flesh and bone.

The guide struck out at the attacker with his paddle but was pulled into the river and dragged down. Terrified, the entourage screamed and lashed out at the water with their paddles. Miraculously, Longden surfaced. He was immediately pulled aboard another canoe and hauled to shore. His lower leg was a bloody mess of lacerations, still connected to the top half, though tenuously. Part of his leg was numb, but Longden felt a searing pain above the knee. The guide looked at his mangled leg and knew that a few disastrous seconds had changed his life forever. Then the scene was quiet again. Amid the chaos, Longden noticed his blue paddle drifting slowly away. He was sad to see it go; it had been with him all the time he'd been on the river and he felt like he was seeing the last of an old and trusted friend. He looked up at the big blue African sky and felt sadness overwhelm him.

On this same Easter Sunday, a party of five people were on their way from the Zambian capital of Lusaka to a camp about a hundred miles downriver from where Phil Longden lay stricken. They were on their way to relax and fish and had no idea of what had just transpired.

The group consisted of Alistair Gellatly, Arthur and Fay Taylor and Fay's parents, Clive and Brenda Kelly, who were visiting from England. Both Gellatly and Taylor were professional hunters who were taking time off to relax for a few days and fish the Zambezi. They were both hard men who had spent years in the bush.

MAYDAY, MAYDAY!

On Tuesday morning they were aboard their powerboat, just up from the Mupata Gorge, in the middle of the river drifting for Tiger fish. It was another perfect day; the sun shone brilliantly and not a soul was in sight. Elephants frolicked on the north bank, and to top it all off the fish were biting. Life could hardly have felt better. That was about to change.

Suddenly there was a thunder-clap and the boat's prow exploded out of the water, sending the party sprawling into the stern. The boat was at a precarious angle, and another thud capsized them. In seconds they were in the water, swimming for their lives. For some strange reason a lone hippo had decided the boat was unwelcome and had attacked it. They saw their assailant only briefly as he snorted contemptuously, submerged and disappeared. All of them knew instinctively that they were smack in the middle of the river, at a point where the crocodiles ruled. Worse still, Clive and Brenda Kelly could not swim.

Taylor was a strong man and an excellent swimmer. He and his wife grabbed Brenda and swam for the nearest sand bar. Gellatly and Clive managed to grab a rope trailing from the boat, which had settled in the water with its hull inverted. They climbed on top and found a semblance of sanctuary. Meanwhile, Taylor and his wife battled the current to reach the sandbar as Brenda hung on for dear life. Fear drove them on. Exhausted, they made it to the shallows and staggered to the center of the little island.

Once he had recovered his breath, Arthur launched himself back into the river and swam back to the boat. With Gellatly's help he then managed to get Clive back to the sandbar. It was midday and the sun was beating down. Their situation was desperate. They could wait and hope for another boat to pass by, but on this remote stretch of river there were no guarantees.

Gellatly and Taylor also knew that the river level was dictated by the floodgates at the Kariba dam 200 miles upstream. If those gates were opened, the river would rise and their island sanctuary would disappear, leaving the party no choice but to swim for it.

Gellatly decided that the best way to get help was for him to swim to the bank and run to a nearby fishing camp, about five kilometers away. He was well aware that his swim might cost him his life, but he was the only single man in the party; his great friend Arthur had a wife and family. He dove into the river and swam for the riverbank.

Two hundred meters of water flowed between life and potential death.

INTO THE RIVER

A smoker and a lover of beer, Gellatly was not exactly a fitness fanatic, but he pounded the water for all he was worth as he struggled to narrow the gap. Breathless, and after what seemed a lifetime, he finally touched the bank.

He frantically tried to extricate himself. He clawed at the soil and tried to clamber up, but to no avail. The side was too sheer. Out of breath, his strength sapped, he looked upriver and saw an inlet. He swam toward the opening and entered the calm water, observing with relief that the land joined the river at a gentler grade here, which would allow him to exit the water more easily. He swam briskly through the mirrorlike calm. It was deadly quiet around him. Looking up, he realized why. Directly in front of him the armor-plated head of a crocodile lay motionless on the water.

Then a gentle ripple formed a small bow-wave around the croc's snout as the huge reptile began to come alive. Gellatly waited motionless, knowing the croc would take him down into the dark depths and tear his body apart. With nowhere to go, Gellatly dove. In a second the crocodile attacked; Gellatly was winded by the body blows that hammered into him. The big man kicked and punched in a furious panic in the dark. Somehow he kept the teeth at bay but the crocodile stayed close and circled him eagerly, looking for a limb to grab hold of. Then suddenly the croc was gone. Gellatly surfaced, gasping for air. For a brief moment there was quiet. Then all hell broke loose as Gellatly felt the full length of the crocodile's body thrust against his as it powered out of the water and fastened onto his right arm at the elbow. Down he went again. This time he knew what was coming and made the only move he could. The old hunter knew the croc would launch itself into a tail-driven spin and wrench his arm from its socket, tearing him literally limb from limb. Before the animal did so, Gellatly clasped his legs around the reptile's torso, so as the croc spun he went with him. As long as he could hang on, the crocodile would not have the leverage to wrench his arm off. Gellatly remembered someone once told him that jamming a finger in a croc's eye will make it break its grip. He plunged his left thumb into the beast's eye socket and gouged with all the strength he could muster.

"I thought I had broken my bloody thumb off and left it in his head," Gellatly recalls. "The pain was incredible. It had absolutely no effect on him."

Seconds away from death, Gellatly made one last effort to save himself. He jammed his free hand down through the gap in the crocodile's jaws and clawed at the back of its throat where he felt soft flesh. He ripped at it in a frantic final effort to gain release.

Incredibly, he had reached the epiglottis and breached the flap of the skin at the rear of the croc's throat that acts as a valve. This intrusion allowed water to pour into the crocodile's lungs, effectively drowning it. The croc spat Gellatly out, surfaced briefly and then disappeared in a dive. Gellatly lunged for the bank, staggered ashore and collapsed.

His right arm was severely mutilated; the elbow was dislocated and bones were shattered. Blood poured from the wounds and he knew he had to stanch the flow or die. He also knew his wounds contained deadly parasites, courtesy of the crocodile's mouth and teeth. Without swift medical attention, severe infection and the loss of his arm would be inevitable. Gellatly moved to a shallow part of the river, where he tried to wash his wounds as best he could and then ripped a strip off his shirt and secured a tourniquet to stem the bleeding. Too weak to walk, he looked for somewhere to lie down and rest. He looked up at the same blue sky that Phil Longden had peered into two days earlier and felt the same sad loneliness as he pondered his destiny.

A STRANGE VISITOR

Back on the sandbar the rest of Gellatly's party were deeply despondent, since they hadn't seen or heard from their companion. They were now trapped and their worst fears were being realized. The river was rising fast. From covering their ankles, it was now at their knees. A nearly full moon loomed in the east and Taylor well realized that come nightfall they would be fully exposed to the crocodiles.

With no means of defense apart from his bare hands, he knew a horrible death was almost inevitable. He watched as the sun slunk away over the mountains in the west and prepared for the worst. Then, as if it were sent from heaven, he spotted something blue drifting downriver toward him. Astonished, he tried to make sense of what it was. Then, to his utter joy, he realized it was a paddle. Taylor raced into the water with reckless abandon and secured it. Miraculously, Phil Longden's paddle had made it all the way down a hundred miles of channels and sand banks and had arrived in his hands at a moment of most dire need. Taylor's spirits soared. Now he had a weapon to stave off the attacks that would surely come. The marooned party had a fighting chance.

Meanwhile, on the shore, Gellatly made a bed of leaves among a pile of rocks and gathered together a bunch of stones with which to protect himself from prowling predators. It was a feeble defense but it was all he had.

Lions, leopards and hyenas were all around and the sunset would bring them from their daytime hideouts to follow the hunting trail.

"I was scared witless," Gellatly recalls. "I knew how many hyenas there were in the area and I had left a serious blood trail behind. They weren't going to have a problem finding me."

With the light fading fast he made himself as comfortable as he could. A breeze blew off the river and the chill, combined with the aftershock of his encounter, made his body shake. He flinched as he heard the crack of twigs nearby—something was approaching. From the heavy footfalls, he suspected it was something large: An elephant? A hippo? Scanning the thick riverine brush he saw the head and then the horns . . . Cape buffalo!

He drew breath and his heart pounded as he watched the bull head toward him. Had it seen him or was it a mere coincidence that it was on his trail? And if suddenly startled, would it give chase?

He steeled himself as his worst fears were realized—the buffalo broke into a run, heading straight at him. "There was nothing I could do," Gellatly recalls. "I just waited for it to come onto me and nail me."

Resigned, he waited for the end. Then something miraculous occurred. The buffalo broke his charge a few feet away, came to a complete halt, looked the human in the eye, put his nose in the air and shook his huge head high.

"I couldn't believe my eyes. He stopped just short of me and looked at me as if he knew I was in trouble and had just come to see what the score was," says Gellatly. "Then he turned and followed the blood spoor slowly back to the water, in effect following my tracks. He went to the water and stood motionless for a while, then ambled back and lay down nearby. I couldn't believe what was going on. The old bull was trying to protect me!"

For a man who made a living out of hunting big game, it made no sense. One of the most formidable animals on the continent was now taking it upon himself to show a softer and gentler side. The aggressor had become the protector.

As night fell Gellatly heard the first whoops of approaching hyenas. The sound sent nervous shivers through his broken body, but he took heart in the sight of the great beast casually chewing his cud just a few steps away, contemptuous of all those out there who might threaten. Through the night the hyenas called but kept their distance.

"I just don't know what would have happened if that buffalo had not stayed there, but his presence gave me strength."

THE RIVER RISES

Meanwhile the foursome in the river was living a nightmare. While they could still stand, they could do so only with great difficulty as the current bore down on them. In the moonlight they could see eyes sparkling in the water, each pair representing an animal that was determined to kill and eat them. The silhouette of the lonely quartet was stark for all to see. As nightfall arrived Taylor commenced beating the water with the paddle to frighten the circling crocs off. His efforts were effective but tiring, and periodically he had to take a break. His rests were short, however. As soon as he stopped lashing the water, the assailants would renew their assault.

"I just beat the water like a madman, and when they came too close we all yelled like crazy and caused a commotion to scare them off."

Fortunately his powerful build, driven by fear, was up to the task. On at least two occasions he used the paddle to beat attacking crocodiles over the head but they maintained their deadly vigil through the night. A few hundred meters away Gellatly lay curled up in a ball trying desperately to keep his senses. He knew he had to carefully regulate the tourniquet. If he cut off the blood supply entirely his lower arm would perish. But he could not allow it to flow unrestricted or he might bleed to death. Roughly every 30 minutes he loosened the knot for a few seconds and then waited. Finally exhaustion overtook him and he lost consciousness.

This might have spelled disaster for him, but fate intervened once again. Red ants, attracted to the blood, attacked him by the thousands, covering his body and invading his wounds. Gellatly awoke to the agony of a thousand bites and lashed out at the insects as best he could. He couldn't rid himself of all of them, but this rude awakening kept him conscious and he went back to work on his tourniquet. This painful providence almost certainly saved his arm and probably his life.

The sound of birds in the early morning cheered him. Soon it would be light and he would have a chance to find help. No sooner was the first blush of a sun-streaked dawn upon them than the old buffalo brought himself slowly to his feet, stretched his legs, gave his stricken acquaintance a quick backward glance and sauntered off. Gellatly looked on, incredulous. If he survived, no one was going to believe what he'd tell them.

Summoning his remaining strength, Gellatly staggered off in search of help. He could see someone across the river and his hopes rose. But the man was far off and Gellatly did not have the strength to shout. He tried to indicate his distress by raising his blood-soaked arm, but the man in the distance failed to understand. Later it turned out he thought Gellatly was a falconer and the makeshift bandages armlets for birds. Utterly frustrated and totally exhausted, Gellatly eventually collapsed. All he could do was wait and hope.

A WILD RESCUE

That afternoon, Arthur Taylor and his family found relief with the blessed arrival of canoeists, who recovered the desperate party—almost 24 hours after they had capsized.

Gellatly's salvation came in the form of fishermen on the southern side of the river, who spotted his hand waving feebly in the distance. They came immediately, carried him to their boat and took him to a bush airfield in Zimbabwe where there was a radio. A plane was radioed to evacuate him to a hospital in Harare. He remembers the sweet sound of the aircraft engine. "The best sound I ever heard," he says.

"It had been more than twenty-four hours since the croc had ripped me up. I knew gangrene was a growing possibility and time was short."

Phil Longden made it back to his base camp later Easter night. By good fortune there were two visiting doctors in attendance. Sadly their best efforts were not enough to stave off the gangrene that resulted from the hippo's bite. In the morning he was flown to Harare, where his leg was removed above the knee. Gellatly made a remarkable recovery. Apart from severe scarring and an impairment of the dexterity of his right arm, he was ready to go hunting again nine months later.

THE WORST
OF THE REST

Monkeys, Wolves,
Pigs, Deer, Hippos, and
Other Animal Attacks

twenty-nine

TWO NIGHTS
IN SOUTHERN MEXICO

by Anonymous

A CAPITAL PLACE THIS for our bivouac!" cried I, swinging myself off my mule, and stretching my arms and legs, which were stiffened by a long ride.

It was a fairish place, to all appearances—a snug ravine, well shaded by mahogany-trees, the ground covered with the luxuriant vegetation of that tropical region, a little stream bubbling and leaping and dashing down one of the high rocks that flanked the hollow, and rippling away through the tall fern towards the rear of the spot where we had halted, at the distance of a hundred yards from which the ground was low and shelving.

"A capital place this for our bivouac!"

My companion nodded. As to our Mexican arrieros and servants, they said nothing, but began making arrangements for passing the night. Curse the fellows! If they had seen us preparing to lie down in a swamp, cheek by jowl with an alligator, I believe they would not have offered a word of remonstrance. They are themselves so little pervious to the dangers and evils of their soil and climate, that they never seem to remember that Yankee flesh and blood may be rather more susceptible; that *niguas* and *musquittoes,* and *vomito prieto,* as they call their infernal fever, are no trifles to encounter; without mentioning the snakes, and scorpions, and alligators, and other creatures of the kind, which infest their strange, wild, unnatural, and yet beautiful country.

I had come to Mexico in company with Jonathan Rowley, a youth of Virginian raising, six and twenty years of age, six feet two in his stockings, with the limbs of a Hercules and shoulders like the side of a house. It was towards the close of 1824; and the recent emancipation of Mexico from the Spanish yoke, and its self-formation into a republic, had given it a new and strong interest to us Americans. We had been told much, too, of the beauty of the country—but in this we were at first rather disappointed; and we reached the capital without having seen any thing, except some parts of the province of Vera Cruz, that could justify the extravagant encomiums we had heard bestowed in the States upon the splendid scenery of Mexico. We had not, however, to go far southward from the chief city, before the character of the country altered, and became such as to satisfy our most sanguine expectations. Forests of palms, of oranges, citrons, and bananas, filled the valleys: the marshes and low grounds were crowded with mahogany-trees, and with immense fern plants, in height equal to trees. All nature was on a gigantic scale—the mountains of an enormous height, the face of the country seamed and split by barrancas or ravines, hundreds, ay, thousands of feet deep, and filled with the most abundant and varied vegetation. The sky, too, was of the deep glowing blue of the tropics, the sort of blue which seems varnished or clouded with gold. But this ardent climate and teeming soil are not without their disadvantages. Vermin and reptiles of all kinds, and the deadly fever of these latitudes, render the low lands uninhabitable for eight months out of the twelve. At the same time there are large districts which are comparatively free from these plagues—perfect gardens of Eden, of such extreme beauty that the mere act of living and breathing amongst their enchanting scenes, becomes a positive and real enjoyment. The heart seems to leap with delight, and the soul to be elevated, by the contemplation of those regions of fairy-like magnificence.

The most celebrated among these favoured provinces is the valley of

Oaxaca, in which two mountainous districts, the Mistecca and Tzapoteca, bear off the palm of beauty. It was through this immense valley, nearly three hundred leagues in length, and surrounded by the highest mountains in Mexico, that we were now journeying. The kind attention of our chargé-d'affaires at the Mexican capital, had procured us every possible facility in travelling through a country, of which the soil was at that time rarely trodden by any but native feet. We had numerous letters to the *alcaldes* and authorities of the towns and villages which are sparingly sprinkled over the southern provinces of Mexico; we were to have escorts when necessary; every assistance, protection, and facility, were to be afforded us. But as neither the authorities nor his excellency, Uncle Sam's envoy, could make inns and houses where none existed, it followed that we were often obliged to sleep *à la belle étoile*, with the sky for a covering. And a right splendid roof it was to our bedchamber, that tropical sky, with its constellations, all new to us northerners and every star magnified by the effect of the atmosphere to an incredible size. Mars and Saturn, Venus and Jupiter, had all disappeared; the great and little Bear were still to be seen; in the far distance the ship Argo and the glowing Centaur; and, beautiful above all, the glorious sign of Christianity, the colossal Southern Cross, in all its brightness and sublimity, glittering in silvery magnificence out of its setting of dark blue crystal.

We were travelling with a state and a degree of luxury that would have excited the contempt of our backwoodsmen; but in a strange country we thought it best to do as the natives did; and accordingly, instead of mounting our horses and setting forth alone, with our rifles slung over our shoulders, and a few handfuls of parched corn and dried flesh in our hunting pouches, we journeyed Mexican fashion, with a whole string of mules, a topith or guide, a couple of *arrieros* or muleteers, a cook, and one or two other attendants. While the latter were slinging our hammocks to the lowermost branches of a tree—for in that part of Mexico it is not very safe to sleep upon the ground, on account of the snakes and vermin—our *cocinero* lit a fire against the rock, and in a very few minutes an iguana which we had shot that day was spitted and roasting before it. It looked strange to see this hideous creature, in shape between a lizard and a dragon, twisting and turning in the light of the fire; and its disgusting appearance might have taken away some people's appetites; but we knew by experience that there is no better eating than a roasted iguana. We made a hearty meal off this one, concluding it with a pull at the rum flask, and then clambered into our hammocks; the Mexicans stretched themselves on the ground with their heads upon the saddles of the mules, and both masters and men were soon asleep.

It was somewhere about midnight when I was awakened by an indescribable sensation of oppression from the surrounding atmosphere. The air seemed to be no longer air, but some poisonous exhalation that had suddenly arisen and enveloped us. From the rear of the ravine in which we lay, billows of dark mephitic mist were rolling forward, surrounding us with their baleful influence. It was the *vomito prieto,* the fever itself, embodied in the shape of a fog. At the same moment, and while I was gasping for breath, a sort of cloud seemed to settle upon me, and a thousand stings, like redhot needles, were run into my hands, face, neck—into every part of my limbs and body that was not triply guarded by clothing. I instinctively stretched forth my hands and closed them, clutching by the action hundreds of enormous *musquittoes,* whose droning, singing noise now almost deafened me. The air was literally filled by a dense swarm of these insects; and the agony caused by their repeated and venomous stings was indescribable. It was a perfect plague of Egypt.

Rowley, whose hammock was slung some ten yards from mine, soon gave tongue: I heard him kicking and plunging, spluttering and swearing, with a vigour and energy that would have been ludicrous under any other circumstances; but matters were just then too serious for a laugh. With the torture, for such it was, of the *musquitto* bites, and the effect of the insidious and poisonous vapours that were each moment thickening around me, I was already in a high state of fever, alternately glowing with heat and shivering with cold, my tongue parched, my eyelids throbbing, my brain seemingly on fire.

There was a heavy thump upon the ground. It was Rowley jumping out of his hammock. "Damnation" roared he, "Where are we? On the earth, or under the earth?—We must be—we are—in their Mexican purgatory. We are, or there's no snakes in Virginny. Hallo, *arrieros!* Pablo! Matteo!"

At that moment a scream—but a scream of such terror and anguish as I never heard before or since—a scream as of women in their hour of agony and extreme peril, sounded within a few paces of us. I sprang out of my hammock; and as I did so, two white and graceful female figures darted or rather flew by me, shrieking—and oh! in what heart-rending tones—for "*Socorro! Socorro! Por Dios!* Help! Help!" Close upon the heels of the fugitives, bounding and leaping along with enormous strides and springs, came three or four dark objects which resembled nothing earthly. The human form they certainly possessed; but so hideous and horrible, so unnatural and spectre-like was their aspect, that their sudden encounter in that gloomy ravine, and in the almost darkness that surrounded us, might well have shaken the strongest nerves. We stood for a second, Rowley and myself, paralysed with astonishment at these strange appearances; but another piercing scream restored to us our presence of mind. One of the women had either tripped or fallen from fatigue, and she lay a white heap, upon the ground. The drapery of the other was in the clutch of one of the spectres, or devils, or whatever they were, when Rowley, with a cry of horror, rushed forward and struck a furious blow at the monster with his *machetto*. At the same time, and almost without knowing how, I found myself engaged with another of the creatures. But the contest was no equal one. In vain did we stab and strike with our *machettos*; our antagonists were covered and defended with a hard bristly hide, which our knives, although keen and pointed, had great difficulty in penetrating; and on the other hand we found ourselves clutched in long sinewy arms, terminating in hands and fingers, of which the nails were as sharp and strong as an eagle's talons. I felt these horrible claws strike into my shoulders as the creature seized me, and, drawing me towards him, pressed me as in the hug of a bear; while his hideous half-man half-brute visage was grinning and snarling at me, and his long keen white teeth were snapping and gnashing within six inches of my face.

"God of heaven! This is horrible! Rowley! Help me!"

But Rowley, in spite of his gigantic strength, was powerless as an infant in the grasp of these terrible opponents. He was within a few paces of me, struggling with two of them, and making superhuman efforts to regain possession of his knife, which had dropped or been wrenched from his hand. And all this time, where were our *arrieros*? Were they attacked likewise? Why didn't they come and help us? All this time!—pshaw! it was no time: it all passed in the space of a few seconds, in the circumference of a few yards, and in the feeble glimmering light of the stars, and of the smouldering embers of our fire, which was at some distance from us.

"Ha! That has told!" A stab, dealt with all the energy of despair, had entered my antagonist's side. But I was like to pay dearly for it. Uttering a deafening yell of pain and fury, the monster clasped me closer to his foul and loathsome body; his sharp claws, dug deeper into my back, seemed to tear up my flesh: the agony was insupportable—my eyes began to swim, and my senses to leave me. Just then—crack! crack! Two— four—a dozen musket and pistol shots, followed by such a chorus of yellings and howlings and unearthly laughter! The creature that held me seemed startled—relaxed his grasp slightly. At that moment a dark arm was passed before my face, there was a blinding flash, a yell, and I fell to the ground released from the clutch of my opponent. I remember nothing more. Overcome by pain, fatigue, terror, and the noxious vapors of that vile ravine, my senses abandoned me, and I swooned away.

When consciousness returned, I found myself lying upon some blankets, under a sort of arbour of foliage and flowers. It was broad day; the sun shone brightly, the blossoms smelled sweet, the gay-plumaged hummingbirds were darting and shooting about in the sunbeams like so many animated fragments of a prism. A Mexican Indian, standing beside my couch, and whose face was unknown to me, held out a cocoa-nutshell containing some liquid, which I eagerly seized, and drank off the contents. The draught (it was a mixture of *citron* juice and water) revived me greatly; and raising myself on my elbow, although with much pain and difficulty, I looked around, and beheld a scene of bustle and life which to me was quite unintelligible. Upon the shelving hillside on which I was lying, a sort of encampment was established. A number of mules and horses were wandering about at liberty, or fastened to trees and bushes, and eating the forage that had been collected and laid before them. Some were provided with handsome and commodious saddles, while others had pack-saddles, intended apparently for the conveyance of numerous sacks, cases, and wallets, that were scattered about on the ground. Several muskets and rifles were leaning here and there against the trees;

and a dozen or fifteen men were occupied in various ways—some filling up saddle-bags or fastening luggage on the mules, others lying on the ground smoking, one party surrounding a fire at which cooking was going on. At a short distance from my bed was another similarly composed couch, occupied by a man muffled up in blankets, and having his back turned towards me, so that I was unable to obtain a view of his features.

"What is all this? Where am I? Where is Rowley—our guide—where are they all?"

"*Non entiendo*," answered my brown-visaged Ganymede, shaking his head, and with a good-humoured smile.

"*Adonde estamos?*"

"*In el valle de Chihuatan, in el gran valle de Oaxaca y Guatimala; diez leguas de Tarifa*. In the valley of Chihuatan; ten leagues from Tarifa."

The figure lying on the bed near me now made a movement, and turned round. What could it be? Its face was like a lump of raw flesh streaked and stained with blood. No features were distinguishable.

"Who are you? What are you?" cried I.

"Rowley," it answered: "Rowley I was, at least, if those devils haven't changed me."

"Then changed you they have," cried I, with a wild laugh. "Good God! have they scalped him alive, or what? That is not Rowley."

The Mexican, who had gone to give some drink to the creature claiming to be Rowley, now opened a valise that lay on the ground a short distance off, and took out a small looking-glass, which he brought and held before my face. It was then only that I began to call to mind all that had occurred, and understood how it was that the mask of human flesh lying near me might indeed be Rowley. He was, if anything, less altered than myself. My eyes were almost closed; my lips, nose, and whole face swollen to an immense size, and perfectly unrecognisable. I involuntarily recoiled in dismay and disgust at my own appearance. The horrible night passed in the ravine, the foul and suffocating vapours, the furious attack of the *musquittoes*—the bites of which, and the consequent fever and inflammation, had thus disfigured us—all recurred to our memory. But the women, the fight with the monsters—beasts—Indians—whatever they were, that was still incomprehensible. It was no dream: my back and shoulders were still smarting from the wounds that had been inflicted on them by the claws of those creatures, and I now felt that various parts of my limbs and body were swathed in wet bandages. I was mustering my Spanish to ask the Mexican who still stood by me for an explanation of all this, when I suddenly became aware of a great bustle in the encampment, and saw every body crowding to meet a number of persons who just then emerged from the high fern, and amongst whom I recognized our arrieros and servants. The new-comers were grouped around something which they seemed to be dragging along the ground; several women—for the most part young and graceful creatures, their slender supple forms muffled in the flowing picturesque *reboxos* and *frazadas*—preceded the party, looking back occasionally with an expression of mingled horror and triumph; all with rosaries in their hands, the beads of which ran rapidly through their fingers, while they occasionally kissed the cross, or made the sign on their breasts or in the air.

"*Un Zambo muerto! Un Zambo Muerto!*" shouted they as they drew near.

"*Han matado un Zambo!* They have killed a Zambo!" repeated my attendant in a tone of exultation.

The party came close up to where Rowley and I were lying; the women stood aside, jumping and laughing, and crossing themselves, and crying out "*Un Zambo! Un Zambo Muerto!*" the group opened, and we saw, lying dead upon the ground, one of our horrible antagonists of the preceding night.

"Good God, what is that?" cried Rowley and I, with one breath. "*Un demonio!* A devil!"

"*Perdonen vos, Senores—Un Zambo mono—muy terribles los Zambos.* Terrible monkeys these *Zambos.*"

"Monkeys!" cried I.

"Monkeys!" repeated poor Rowley, raising himself up into a sitting posture by the help of his hands. "Monkeys—apes—by Jove! We've been fighting with monkeys, and it's they who have mauled us in this way. Well, Jonathan Rowley, think of your coming from old Virginny to Mexico to be whipped by a monkey. It's gone goose with your character. You can never show your face in the States again. Whipped by an ape!—an ape, with a tail and a hairy—O Lord! Whipped by a monkey!"

And the ludicrousness of the notion overcoming his mortification, and the pain of his wounds and bites, he sank back upon the bed of blankets and banana leaves, laughing as well as his swollen face and sausage-looking lips would allow him.

It was as much as I could do to persuade myself, that the carcass lying before me had never been inhabited by a human soul. It was humiliating to behold the close affinity between this huge ape and our own species. Had it not been for the tail, I could have fancied I saw the dead body of some prairie hunter dressed in skins. It was exactly like a powerful, well-grown man; and even the expression of the face had more of bad human passions than of animal instinct. The feet and thighs were those of a muscular man: the legs rather too curved and calfless, though I have seen Negroes who had scarcely better ones; the tendons of the hands stood out like whipcords; the nails were as long as a tiger's claws. No wonder that we had been overmatched in our struggle with the brutes. No man could have withstood them. The arms of this one were like packets of cordage, all muscle, nerve, and sinew; and the hands were clasped together with such force, that the efforts of eight or ten Mexicans and Indians were insufficient to disunite them.

Whatever remained to be cleared up in our night's adventures was now soon explained. Our guide, through ignorance or thoughtlessness, had allowed us to take up our bivouac within a very unsafe distance of one of the most pestiferous swamps in the whole province. Shortly after we had fallen asleep, a party of Mexican travellers had arrived, and established themselves within a few hundred yards of us, but on a rising ground, where they avoided the mephitic vapours and the *musquittoes* which had so tortured Rowley and myself. In the night two of the women, having ventured a short distance from the encampment, were surprised by the *zambos*, or huge man-apes, common in some parts of Southern Mexico; and finding themselves cut off from their friends, had fled they knew not whither, fortunately for them taking the direction of our bivouac. Their screams, our shouts, and the yellings and diabolical laughter of the *zambos*, had brought the Mexicans to our assistance. The monkeys showed no fight after the first volley; several of then must have been wounded, but only the one now lying before us had remained upon the field.

The Mexicans we had fallen amongst were on the Tzapoteca, principally cochineal gatherers, and kinder-hearted people there could not well be. They seemed to think they never could do enough for us; the women especially, and more particularly the two whom we had endeavoured to rescue from the power of the apes. These latter certainly had cause to be grateful. It made us shudder to think of their fate had they not met with us. It was the delay caused by our attacking the brutes that had given the Mexicans time to come up.

Every attention was shown to us. We were fanned with palm leaves, refreshed with cooling drinks, our wounds carefully dressed and bandaged, our heated, irritated, *musquitto*-bitten limbs and faces washed with balsam and the juice of herbs: more tender and careful nurses it would be impossible to find. We soon began to feel better, and were able to sit up and look about us; carefully avoiding, however, to look at each other, for we could not get reconciled to the horrible appearance of our swollen, bloody, and disgusting features. From our position on the rising ground, we had a full view over the frightful swamp at the entrance of which all our misfortunes had happened. There it lay, steaming like a great kettle; endless mists rising from it, out of which appeared here and there the crown of some mighty tree towering above the banks of vapour. To the left, cliffs and crags were to be seen which had the appearance of being baseless, and of swimming on the top of the mist. The vultures and carrion-birds circled screaming above the huge caldron, or perched on the tops of the tall palms, which looked like enormous umbrellas, or like the roofs of Chinese summer-houses. Out of the swamp itself proceeded the yellings, snarlings, and growlings of the alligators, bull-frogs, and myriads of unclean beasts that it harboured.

thirty

THE KILLER BABOONS
OF VLAKFONTEIN

Peter Hathaway Capstick

TH E IMAGE OF THE old baboon was surprisingly clear through the Bushnell 2.5X-8X scope. Even the brown of his sharp, hard eyes gleaming through the slight waver of heat haze was distinct as I steadied the crosshairs about twenty inches over his savage face.

As softly as possible, I raised the bolt handle and lowered it, cocking the action on a 270-grain Kynoch .375 H&H Magnum round in the old Model 70. With the scope at full power and the Pachmayr Lo-Swing snug, the 450 yards between the baboon and me seemed like a few feet in the laser-like sunshine of the Rhodesian [Zimbabwe] afternoon. Sweat sheeting down my dirty face after the long stalk, I paused to get my shooting breath, watching him through the scope.

He surveyed the area, alert and cautious, an aloof but lonely figure among his clan, which he disdainfully ignored. The silver edges of his hair ruffled in a light swirl of wind, and I removed my finger from the trigger to see how the gust would flow. The Winchester was zeroed at two hundred yards, and I knew the holdover at four hundred would be about twenty-seven inches. So, at an estimated 450 yards, I had better allow a good thirty inches to drop that big, soft-point surprise smack into the boiler room.

I watched the grass stalks and dull mopane leaves, deciding on a three-quarter breeze of about five miles per hour, and shifted my hold a whisker left. The rifle was propped against the edge of an old termite hill—solid as a benchrest—with my crushed beret for insulation. Revenge would now be mine.

I started my squeeze and was startled when the big rifle roared. After what seemed a very long time, I saw the big baboon slam backward from his perch atop a rock. A glimpse of his face showed the purest astonishment. He rolled over once and lay on his side in the short grass.

Bedlam rocked the hillside with the arrival of the bullet's sonic crack. I quickly worked the bolt and lined up on another huge male that had paused in flight, confused by the echoes of the muzzle blast. As he looked over his shoulder, I sent him an Air Mail Special COD that passed through his back and continued on to throw a cloud of topsoil from beyond him. He threw up his arms and rolled down the hill like a bad guy in a grade-B Western movie. The crosshairs swung past a female with a baby clutched to her chest, and pulled ahead of another male. The hurried shot landed just short, showering him with high-velocity dirt and gravel. He gave a shriek that was piercingly loud even at my distance as he jumped an easy ten feet into the air and cleared the ridge before I could jack another round up the spout.

I kept perfectly still, scanning the hill for movement, but nothing showed after a full five minutes. I opened the action and clicked in fresh rounds. With the rifle at the ready position, I cautiously started across the low valley and up the little hill, which was snaggled with boulders and tangles of grassy cover.

The old baboon lay where he had fallen, the exit hole of the bullet through his spine. His terrible madman eyes were still open and staring unglazed at my feet. Lordy, but he was huge—at least ninety pounds of iron muscle and tent-peg fangs that could disembowel a tom leopard as easily as a man opens a Ziploc bag.

"Tag, you're it," I muttered softly, rolling him over with my foot, an odd feeling of ancestral murder running through the dark back of my brain.

A chorus of outrage erupted from the trees, well out of range. I went to inspect the other big male farther up the slope. He lay in a huddled lump. I prayed he was dead; finishing off wounded *mabobojan* was spooky. They are just too bloody human—nasty as the creatures are.

As I walked toward him, I had to pass a large jumble of boulders about six feet high that formed a shadowy cave of solid rock. When I was fifteen yards away and just even with it off my right elbow, I chanced to glance into the dark corner. I got the absolute fright of my misspent life.

In a blur of hairy motion, the shade exploded with an earsplitting series of screams and assorted intensely unpleasant sounds as a gigantic male baboon launched himself at me. He was a terrifying, nightmare creature, bounding with amazing speed straight at my sweet young body. His lips were pulled back from the black mask of his Doberman muzzle, displaying his awful fighting fangs. Nearly two inches of switchblade ivory displayed in that manner is not likely to go unnoticed. I'd be lying if I said I wasn't downright spooked. But I'll promise you one thing, brother, I wasn't having any of *him!*

If I'd passed five yards closer, it would have likely been the ball game— no hits, no runs, one major error. I reflex-shot him from the hip at about ten feet. The big slug lucked into his left eye and took out everything west of his teeth. The impetus of his final leap brought his corpse almost to my feet, in spite of the impact of the .357 Mag's bullet. I jumped aside and swatted him again, no matter how unnecessarily. When they try to bite you, you can't make them *too* dead.

I lit a cigarette and got my heart restarted on the third try. I promise you faithfully that I approached the other male on the slope with one eye on the rest of the rocks. The bullet had taken him dead-on, and he was dead-off when I turned back down the hill. Watching the vultures vol-plane lower, I wondered what bright day they would be stopping off to visit what might be left of me. Africa has a very effective way of stifling any ideas one may entertain of immortality.

Well, I thought, trudging back toward my temporary camp, I'd finally won a skirmish with the Vlakfontein baboons. But the war was still very much in question. At the rate I was going, I'd be tripping over my beard before I could induce the huge troop to pack up and change territories.

In 1975, when things got a bit sticky for palefaces in Zambia, and extremes of weather and overhunting had made Botswana less than it used to be, I had entered into a deal to conduct client safaris in Rhodesia. The area I was to work in was the Matetsi Wildlife Area Safari Unit No. 4, about fifty miles south of Victoria Falls and the Zambezi River. I had chosen as headquarters an abandoned house originally built in 1902 by a chap who had actually driven an ox wagon all the way from Capetown. (The feat was, in those days, the same as flying a single-engine aircraft to the moon and back would be today.) I preferred canvas or grass huts for most safari work, but the solid, plaster-covered adobe walls of Vlakfontein (Flackfohn-tain, from the Afrikaans term meaning "Fountain on a Plain") offered excellent cover from surprise machine-gun fire and mortar bomb fragments. They were the rage in that area of the world during the bush war.

The land surrounding Vlakfontein is like a coral reef in the open sea or an oasis in the Sahara. Deep, cool springs, alive with delicious tilapia bream, were bearded with ancient groves of fig, acacia, and fruit trees planted when the place was a going concern. The trees were now in poor shape, but still offered a gigantic smorgasbord for a baboon troop. Lions roared, rattling the remnants of windows from what I brazenly called "the lawn," a grassy *vlei* with the tall grass crushed flat by buffalo herds in the dry season. Leopards lurked in the rocky hills, singing their love and territorial songs anytime they felt like it. Herds of sable and zebra ghosted the edge of the bush off the veranda, and bull kudu drank daily at the nearest springs, with the brassy early light accentuating their ivorytipped corkscrew horns.

Heavily enlaced by deteriorating barbed wire was an enclosure fifty yards from the back door, containing the grave of the last owner of Vlakfontein. The man had killed more than 150 lions here in a single year to protect his cattle herds, and still failed. Vlakfontein, you see, borders the Wankie National Park, which supplied beef-hungry lions a lot faster than he and his men could kill them.

One day, when he was prepared to call it quits anyway, he walked out into the backyard, smack into a bull buffalo that didn't like the way he parted his hair. They buried what was left when the hyenas had tired of him.

But, if Vlakfontein was a miniature paradise for other game, it was pure, undiluted heaven for the yellow baboon. The creatures had procreated until I estimated the local troop had more than one hundred members. They foraged in close company that discouraged all but the most occasional attack by marauding leopards, which normally keep their numbers down more than any other animal. The bloody baboons were everywhere, and to make matters worse, they had chosen a magnificent grove of *mfuti* of Prince of Wales feather trees as their sleeping place. They had been living about half a mile from the ramshackle house for most of the years the place had been uninhabited.

The first notification I had of the location of their dormitory was an odoriferous waft of wind that would haunt the dreams of a sewer cleaner. Their accumulated dung beneath the trees was inches thick, the smell hitting you like a wet blanket. Their night-long screeching and whooping insomnia, as well as their constant raiding of the papaya trees next to the house, soon made it clear that somebody was going to have to find new digs. It wasn't going to be me.

On numerous instances previously, I had had nuisance problems with baboon troops becoming overbold, but killing a couple usually solved the problem, at least for a span of time. Unfortunately, and fatally for one of my staff, I was to find the Vlakfontein troop very different indeed.

From the outset, I can tell you that, despite my general revulsion of them as some sort of human parody, I greatly dislike killing baboons. The problem lies in the fact that the baboon, if unchecked, can be one of the worst scourges of agriculture, game, and young livestock on earth. They are the epitome of savage, calculating, cruel, and extraordinarily intelligent varmints. I have twice been in leopard blinds and witnessed baboons catch doves that came to drink at nearby waterholes, only to completely pluck them for the sheer fun of it, leaving the bird alive. Through a career never noted for great doses of boredom, I have been in on the demise of some of my own species with, strangely, less regret than I felt at having to kill a baboon. After all, they're only trying to make a living as best they can, although often at the expense and risk of man.

Perhaps it will make little sense to you, but baboons, especially frightened or wounded ones, can sometimes seem even more human than man himself. They can sometimes offer heartrending gestures of supplication I'd as soon not get into here. The idea of arbitrarily shooting even a big, murderous "dog" baboon gives me a case of the ancestral creeps.

It may be that there's a very good reason for the creepy regret I feel when I have to destroy a baboon: Man and old *bobojan,* as he's called locally, go back a long way together in Africa. We probably share some misty common ancestor, the baboon taking one evolutionary road while we took another. If you doubt this, feel the size of the sockets of your eyeteeth or canines. Notice how immense they are in comparison to your bicuspids; we once had fangs like the baboon. But according to some of the best conjecture of our time, we lost them through evolution as we transferred our fighting weapons from dental to hand-held sticks and rocks. In short, the size of our fighting teeth has diminished because we didn't need them.

Well over a million years ago, a very nasty, though efficient, little chap dubbed *Australopithecus africanus* or "southern ape-man" did his thing, among other places, around three cave sites in South Africa. In one of his caves he left forty-two baboon skulls—just the heads, no bodies. Most clearly show that the animals were killed by right-handed blows from the hand-held leg bone of an antelope. All forty-two skulls had had the brains extracted and, with macabre certainty, eaten. Nice family we share, cousin!

At least one baboon partially squared the score in the first half of this century in what is now Tanzania, East Africa. According to the highly reliable hunter, soldier, and traveler Major P. J. Pretorius, a tremendous, man-eating baboon operated from a six-mile-wide mangrove swamp on the Ruvuma River. The swamp was threaded by a footpath used by the natives to cross the swamp to higher ground. In his classic book *Jungle Man,* Pretorius wrote:

> Here this ferocious baboon had taken up its quarters, and when an isolated native came past it would attack and tear open the stomach of its victim. It would then *break the skull, tear out the brains, which it devoured, and leave the rest of the body* [my emphasis]. The natives were unable to catch it and were so terrified of the brute that eventually they left their village.

Pretorius does not record the number of victims of the Ruvuma Man-eater. However, for a lone, homicidal baboon to drive an entire village of armed Africans to leave their home, he must have had a pretty respectable score.

The quickest of glances will convince you that baboons are nothing to fool around with, despite the impish charm of the juveniles. Their primate intelligence and attack behavior, coupled with their strength, agility, fangs, and powerful hands, make them among the most dangerous close-quarters animals in Africa's formidable collection of bad news for the stupid, over-brave, or unlucky. I'd have to have a couple of long ones and a half-pack of smokes before deciding between the unpleasant choice of tangling hand-to-hand with a baboon or a leopard.

All things considered, I just might choose the leopard, despite the claws. That's because of the baboon's terrible biting technique. He anchors his great fangs in your meat and, keeping his jaws locked, uses his steel-strong arms and legs to push himself away. This maneuver rips out a chunk of meat that would just about fit into a one-pound dog-food tin. A big male's muzzle may be eight inches long, and, pound for pound, he's three times as strong as a human wrestler. I know of no wrestlers who ever had teeth that big, either!

The relationship between the leopard and the baboon as predator and prey depends upon the terrain, the baboons, leopard populations, and other factors. No leopard that had not been overdoing the catnip would dream of trying to take a member of a troop that was not incapacitated or on the very fringes of the group. Even trying for an isolated or vulnerable small or female baboon can be the equivalent of Russian roulette for a leopard.

Three times I have found the bodies of baboon-killed leopards, caught by the sentinel males. In one case, the deed had been done to a full-grown tom by two old males, both of which had taken something of a lacing themselves. I didn't witness the actual fight, but I sure heard it!

Many humans are mauled in African parks, often severely, by baboons that have become overly familiar with man. At Khwai Lodge in Botswana, which I once ran between safaris, I had to snipe about ten members of a troop that were becoming cheeky enough to charge right into the open dining area to beg or steal food. They were a real threat to the guests. I used a .22 long rifle in this case, taking only head shots from chalet windows before they caught on and kept their distance.

In 1963, a large baboon of the *chacma* subspecies, very similar to the yellow baboons of Rhodesia, was killed by South African police. It had harassed natives for two years by throwing rocks at them! It was later discovered that this was the same old male that had forced two African girls, aged five and thirteen, over a hundred-foot cliff to their deaths in 1961.

Three years later, a farm laborer was terribly mauled by a baboon while looking for strayed sheep in the Cape Province. He survived, but not by much, oddly reporting that the rest of the troop had just sat around and watched while he was attacked. Lucky for him, as baboons often mass-attack in a screeching gang of flashing fangs. Only two months later, also on the Cape, a pair of baboons terrified a mother and her two children by trying to break into their home. The baboons banged on the doors and windows, until police, who arrived just in time, shot them in the garden.

Although baboons can be quite cheeky and downright bold when they know a person to be unarmed (they have reliably stolen many children throughout Africa), unprovoked, flat-out attacks are rare. The male that tried to take me apart on the hillside near Vlakfontein clearly was cornered. He had ducked into the rock grotto while I was firing. Probably because he could still see the troop leader, the first dead male, he had remained confused until I surprised him.

Just as man has evolved socially, the baboon is doing the same thing at an accelerated pace right now, and in a very spooky way. Since the turn of the century, he has greatly expanded his predatory carnivore instincts, shifting faster and faster from a voracious herbivore to an accomplished killer and meat-eater. Looking through my collection of antique African books, I cannot find a single reference to baboons killing smaller antelope, sheep, goats, or other livestock as they so commonly do today.

In the tsetse fly-free regions of southern and central Africa, where livestock may be kept, baboons commonly rank near the hyena and leopard as stock killers. Considering the relative helplessness of women and children in the African bush, it doesn't seem unreasonable to me that one troop or another may finally get the same idea as that one-baboon horror show of Pretorius's on the Ruvuma Swamp. Then Africa is going to have a problem that will make the "killer bees" seem like gnats.

MY FIRST REAL BRUSH with the enemy at Vlakfontein took place near dusk the second day I was camped there. Like most of the jams I get into, this one was my own damn-fool fault. I broke a rule learned over years the hard way: don't wander around the bush unarmed, no matter how safe the real estate appears.

On an impulse, I grabbed a small hand-line and a few scraps of eland meat, intent on catching a bream or two before dark. With only my hunting knife, I wandered down the *vlei* toward the water, two hundred yards from the ruined house. A narrow trail led through the higher grass to the water's edge.

Still fifty yards from the springs, I looked up smack into the face of a huge male baboon, the leader of a string of a great many. To say that we were both startled would be tantamount to observing that Cheryl Tiegs ain't bad looking for a girl. His surprised *"Waughh"* of warning mingled with my own strangled shout. Two more males leaped up to join him as he reared on his hind legs, ten feet away. As he gave an unforgettable display of his dental work, the grass around us went crazy with sound and motion as the rest of the troop fled the unseen threat. I yelled back at them as one bounced forward in a feint, barking so loud my ears hurt. Remembering the Randall skinner at my belt, I dropped the fishing line and whipped it out in the best Alan Ladd tradition.

I knew we were too close to count on the baboon's natural fear of man to scare them off, and with the rest of the troop to protect, any one of them might try something heroic. I stood perfectly still, my attention on the biggest, as he demonstrated, snapping jaws and tearing up grass. My eyes were locked with his in the weirdest feeling of communication. Remembering the old adage about the best defense being a good offense, I brandished the knife and took a very reluctant and slow step toward them. I shouldn't have done that.

For a second I was sure they would call my bluff, all three going insane, snapping and roaring. Still facing them, I took a step backward with equal care and that seemed to calm them down a touch. Another step to the rear, and, to my immense relief, they turned and were gone.

I had been hunting the troop of apes with rising irritation and frustration. I carefully stalked them, only to have one of their binocular-eyed sentinels catch a glimpse of motion or be tipped off by birds like the gray lourie whose warning cry of *"Go-Waaaaay"* would cause a scampering exodus of the feeding troop. By sheer persistence, I had killed eight of the gang of marauders, including the three males on the hillside. Yet, if on one hand they had become more cautious of me, on the other they had become even bolder around the house and native huts. When they saw me leave in the vintage Land Rover, they brazenly raided the fruit trees and even entered the camp itself, much to the distress of my personnel. Then, six days ago, it had happened while I was off at Matetsi for supplies.

A small garden had been planted in a plot of rough earth fifty yards from the huts thrown up by my temporary laborers. It was being weeded that morning by the wife of one of my bricklayers, a bright MaShona woman of twenty-six named Wedu. On her back, as is the custom, she supported a four-month-old infant boy in a length of cloth. She was completely unarmed, not even carrying a digging stick.

She was pulling weeds by hand, when she had the strange feeling of being watched. As she paused in her work to look around, she was startled to see four big male baboons stalk out of the nearby bush. They began to advance on her, demonstrating very aggressive behavior, grunting and bouncing stiffly on knuckles and feet. With remarkable presence of mind, she threatened them back and threw a stone. This, instead of having the normal effect of sending them packing, seemed to infuriate them more. They drew closer to the now thoroughly frightened woman, surrounding her as she began to scream for help.

As she tried to wrestle the baby from the hammock on her back to protect it with her arms, one of the baboons raced in from behind and, with a ferocious tug, pulled the child free. He immediately gripped it with his jaws. The woman, panicked to madness by the sight, charged the baboon, only to have one of his mates snap viciously at her leg. The male who had the child shook the pathetic bundle and dropped it, turning on the mother.

It happened at that moment that Amos and Rota, respectively my gunbearer and tracker, were returning from the spring when they heard the woman's cries. They came upon the scene at a sprint. Both were armed with spears, and they immediately attacked the baboons, shouting at the top of their lungs. Seeing the determined, armed men bearing down on them, the baboons broke off their harassment of the poor woman and began to stalk reluctantly back toward the bush.

Their retreat was sufficiently grudging that Rota, who was younger and faster, got within range and was able to plant a thrown *assegai* through the thigh of one of the males. While he bit and fought the steel blade, Amos was able to spear him to death as the other three turned tail and left.

The woman was hysterical and had several nasty lacerations. When I treated these, I concluded that the baboons' fangs had cut across her skinny shin bones. There was no hope for the child. A set of massive fang holes had punctured him through the chest, and, although he lived a few minutes, he was dead by the time he could be carried to the huts. We buried him deeply that night, as custom dictates—on his right side, knees drawn up, facing the rising sun he would never see again.

That was enough. It had not taken ten minutes for the entire labor camp to agree that these baboons were, in reality, vengeful witches and warlocks. This is a common belief among bush Africans about any man-eaters or marauders.

Was the *Inkosi* a blind man, they asked themselves in whispers, that he could not see the *mabobojan* wanted revenge for their dead and would strike any time they had an opportunity? Disgusted, I paid off those who wanted to leave and called a conference with my hunting staff for that evening. They, no matter how personally spooked by the strange attacks of the baboons, never would have dreamed of inviting the stigma of cowardice by quitting. They were *madoda*, warriors, not *mafazi* to run from danger, skirts flapping.

In the manner of any formal discussion with African natives, there is a great deal of bush-beating before getting down to the meat of the matter.

But I knew custom well enough never to interrupt, so I listened to them speak for hours. I would occasionally interject polite questions as speakers gave their ideas starting with their lowest-ranked and ending with my most senior man, Gladstone. He is a *madalla* or elder of the Amandebele Zulu, who was referred to by the honored title of *Baba* (Father) by all my staff. He finally distilled the best of the arguments. After a somewhat windy appraisal in Fanagalo/Sindebele, a local form of the common language of southern Africa, he observed that the baboons did not relate my sniping them to their residence in the area. Also, since the baboons were no longer a nuisance but a full-blown menace, we would have to concentrate them for a quick and decisive slaughter. He recommended the classic buffalo assault formation of his grandfather's regiments. Finally, he said, piercing me with a bloodshot eye, if we were not able to do this, the baboons surely would kill me.

I sat alone long into the night in the canvas camp chair, watching the sparks streak upward like tracers at each addition of a fresh mopane log. Gladstone was undoubtedly correct on his first two points. I had used the wrong tactic in picking them off piecemeal because they did not relate the harassment to their presence in my area. To them I was just some big, white ape killing them for the hell of it. Further, he was right that the troop had to be maneuvered into some position where I could get their attention with some real firepower. What bothered me was his last observation.

After well over a decade in the bush, I was sufficiently Africanized to feel my hackles getting a bit of involuntary exercise when I considered this revenge motive. What if they really *were* trying to get even? They could easily have enough intelligence; that I knew from observation. Where would they be likely to strike next? And at whom? I kept getting flashes of the end of the film *Sands of the Kalahari* and what happened to Stuart Whitman when he ran out of ammo for his Weatherby, after severely picking on a troop of yellow baboons.

Slowly, as the ember of a new cigarette began to glow deeply with a drag, an idea began to form and kindle brighter. I reached over for the web-belt holster of the MAC-10 submachine gun I always kept near me in camp in case of uninvited two-legged unpleasantries. I unrolled the lumpy, home-stitched, buffalo-hide bandolier carrying ten double-stick magazines of 9-mm ammo, carefully taped together for quick reloading. I had purchased the little gun with gold sovereigns, (very handy coins to someone in a hurry and faced with currency restrictions) from a farmer who had decided to pack it in. I had also been able to pick up his suppressor attachment or silencer, 1,800 rounds of hard-nosed military ammo, and twenty extra thirty-six-round stick clips. With its wire stock retracted, it was not much larger than a good-sized pistol, and it had a rate of fire of about seven hundred rounds per minute. I preferred it vastly to the standard FN assault rifle in 7.62 mm that most people carried in their bush cars. I thoughtfully examined the little brute and extracted the overlapped magazines. As the firelight licked silently at its dull finish, my idea formed more solidly with each throb of my thoughts.

I slept rather late the following morning, until the sun was high and I was sure the entire baboon troop was off foraging. After a leisurely breakfast, I whistled up the eight men on my hunting staff, leaving two spearmen to guard the work area, and went with the rest to reconnoiter the feather tree grove where the troop roosted.

The impossible stink of the place soon permeated our very clothes and skins. We determined which of the trees were most heavily used, deciding on four or five about in the center of the grove. Their bark was worn as smooth as Venetian crystal from the repeated touch of thousands of paws, and the dung was thick at their bases. It was not my intention to annihilate the whole troop. That would have been impossible on a practical basis without high explosives. But I did want to give them a severe enough mauling for them to be forced into changing their range entirely. They must be made to understand that they could no longer use this roost, and after the terrible affair of the dead baby and the potentially dead mother, I had absolutely no regrets about showing them the hard way. With my battle plan firmly in mind, I walked back to camp to make preparations for my personal version of the Entebbe Raid.

Being a professional small boy at heart, my camp was never short of wondrous and fascinating paraphernalia, which included six magnesium aerial flares and a dozen or so nifty little monsters called "thunderflashes." These are really super firecrackers made to simulate grenades for training exercises. But they're no joke and easily could blow most of your throwing arm from here to the Carpathian Alps if you didn't get rid of one in time.

The sun looked like a giant red balloon as it finally began to slip down behind the trees, leaving the sky with thick varicose veins of gold and orange. Through my binoculars, I watched the first of the troop file into the grove and disappear into the murk of shadow, their hoots and barks threatening as they vocally sneered at us. I decided to go ahead and dine, waiting for full darkness. That should give the baboons time to settle down and doze off.

We took our positions about fifty yards from the trees. Amos stood to my right with the heavy bandolier of double magazines for the MAC-10. I had removed the submachine gun's silencer for more noise confusion. With several clips in position to hand to me, Amos was ready for the attack. On my left was Rota, holding the cocked flare launcher, another cartridge ready in his hand. Flanking us were my six other men. Three on the right carried spears, and three on the left, who blew casually on embers of campfire wood, carried the slingshots so common among Rhodesian tribesmen for knocking off doves or francolin. These slingshots were loaded with thunderflashes ready for lighting and launching.

"*Lungile manje,*" I whispered up and down the line—"All set!"

Amos gave the low hoot of an owl. I caught the small flash of a match flaring at the far side of the thickness of the grove. The tiny spark roared and grew, racing in a two-hundred-yard semicircle around the far side of the grove, where we had scratched a shallow trench. We had soaked the trench with a mixture of more than one hundred gallons of gasoline, kerosene, and old crank case oil. The fire cut off the escape of the troop effectively. No baboon, even with courage born of desperation, would try to pass through that five-foot wall of hell. I watched the flitting form of the boy Amos had sent to light the trench fire dashing closer, until he was panting beside us. It was time to go to work.

At that moment, Rota fired the first flare on my command. It arched like a giant firefly over the trees. I signaled the slingshot men and watched the sparkle of three thunderflash fuses in a high trajectory.

A second later, they exploded in a ragged procession of perfect airbursts on a far side of the grove.

Rota's flare then burst under its parachute, lighting the area brighter than midday. For an instant there was silence, then the baboons went berserk. I've never been in a riot in a madhouse, but this couldn't have been much different. Instantly, dark forms began to drop and scamper from the trees, most racing in terrified panic straight for us, their eyes half-blinded by the flare. Some very icy second thoughts scampered up my spine as they poured down on us. Could I stop them with the little gun, or had we bitten off a bit too much?

I fired three quick squirts into a group of ten headed right at us. It may have been the best of dumb luck that I had removed the muzzle-flash-hiding suppressor as the two baboons not caught in the sleet of slugs veered off to the left. I let them go because one was young, and the other was a female.

The sight of Wedu's mutilated baby flashed through my mind as I ripped a long burst into a scrambling group of seven, sweeping the gun in a long arc that chopped all but the last as my magazine ran dry. Certainly, one thing was obvious: there were a lot more than a hundred baboons in that grove. More than that had already run the gamut of my selective automatic fire. About a third of their number was killed as I punched out short, accurate bursts at no more than twenty-five yards.

Again the magazine was empty, and my eyes were down, changing the clip when I heard Amos shout, *"Basopa, madoda!"*

I glanced up just in time to see two males skewered in midair by the spearmen on my right flank as the baboons bore down on us in a desperate charge. There was no need to finish either of them as my men decapitated each with a single slice of their *pangas*.

Finally, the screeching and grunting died down and the movement lessened. The tabloid of death was pinned like some great diorama in the sterile light of a new flare. Another twenty or so baboons remained alive in the grove, scampering and dodging as they sought to break our deadly ring of flame and lead. I killed two more big males, but let another six or eight go, spurred on by a couple of bursts behind them. To have left the troop completely shattered, without any of the leadership and protection that are the duty of the adult males, probably would have meant their complete extinction.

Exhausted, back at my temporary camp, I poured a nightcap while cleaning the MAC-10. I sat beside Amos, who was reloading the emptied magazines, each with thirty-six staggered rounds.

Frankly, I was having a lousy bout of depression over the slaughter, wishing it had not been necessary. Amos, quietly clicking in the gleaming rounds, seemed to catch my mood.

"*Haya kataza, Inkosi,*" he said, pausing to roll a cigarette of newspaper and black shag tobacco. "Don't worry about it. They would have killed you if they could. It is just the way of things that a man must fight his enemies to hold his kraal and his women."

I thought about what he had said for a long time, and realized his wisdom. The troop simply had to be moved, and, after killing the baby, there was no choice left to me as to means. They would settle again, perhaps twenty miles away, maybe along the Bemba. They would build their tribe again, until they had reached a natural balance with the leopards and disease. Africa would go on again as it had for the baboon since the days of the South African caveman.

thirty-one

WOLVES AND HYENAS

Peter Hathaway Capstick

IF YOU HAVE NOT already suspected such to be the case, there is no animal's supposed man-eating habits which encompass such a great degree of controversy and hard feelings between people of different emotional persuasion as those of the wolf, *Canis lupus.* The only indisputably true thing that can be said is that the wolf, at this moment, is at the very edge of a grinding, cutting, violent conservational tectonic plate, which increasingly shakes even the most emotional aspects of the study of animal behaviorism.

Perhaps you've noticed how many more books there have been published recently on wolves, particularly the rearing and keeping of them in captivity or semiconfinement, sometimes in a *Born Free* motif of returning the animal to the wild. In fact, although I draw no special conclusion because of its insertion beyond subliminal, one of the pictures in Caras's chapter on wolves is captioned: "The submissive posture of a female wolf in a highly socialized pack. The woman is Joy Adamson, author of *Born Free,* founder of the 'Elsa Wild Animal Appeal.'" This seems to imply that Ms. Adamson, who is petting or touching the wolf, approves of wolves, particularly because she is smiling broadly. I'm not sure what the message of the picture is supposed to be, but it would take a flamingly vivid imagination to believe that cringing and submissive lady wolf is any tougher than a ten-year-old mink coat.

I'll give you one piece of good advice: if you happen to take a stance other than that of the New Wolfmen, you might be well advised to stay off talk shows with them. They're not exactly the most logical of reasoners and can get very excited about what a bad guy man has been to the wolf over the years. Further, they would be mostly completely correct.

Since there is so much controversy around the "goodness" or "savagery" of the wolf, I can't see any approach to this subject of man-eating other than purely statistical and base any conclusions we do reach purely upon the most reliable records we can dig up. As in most matters controversial, my guess is that the truth will be found, cringing like a wounded rabbit, somewhere pretty close to dead center between views.

To give you a practical idea of what we're up against, the first thing that James Clarke tells us about wolves is that, although it's mighty strange, the wolf has never been known to eat a man in North America. Yet, John Pollard, who wrote *Wolves and Were-Wolves* (John Hale, London, 1966), a pretty definitive book about European wolves, sees the beast as sufficiently "cruel" to justify the old and quaint custom of sewing up the lips of captured specimens and then having them skinned alive! Good Lord, but is *anybody* being remotely objective?

Although I promised to keep this subject as free of personal conjecture as possible, one facet of the human-wolf relationship is undeniable: it is ancient, going back as far as we do. We have always been impressed by the efficiency of the wolf as a predator, which is understandable as that's what we're in business for ourselves. Since the development of firearms and a much more active competition for prey animals, man has beaten up on the wolf undeniably, basing his relatively arbitrary policy of emnity upon a variety of both valid and invalid excuses. There's no black and white with wolves *or* people. Sure as shootin' wolves kill stock. One, the legendary Custer wolf, who was killed in 1920, had a bounty of $500 on his head and was, interestingly, accompanied by two coyotes during most of his ten years of devastation in South Dakota and Wyoming. Some estimates reckon he killed $25,000 worth of stock. Twenty-five grand bought a lot of lamb chops in 1920, too.

Probably because the wolf is good at what he does and kills as a group, man got an early impression that, if he was of such a mind, the wolf, because of his obvious intelligence, would not only be a potential problem but clearly represented the forces of evil. I'm sure howling at night while early man sat around a dying fire, trying to protect his newly domesticated stock didn't help the wolf's popularity either. Thus, just as the Africans have their traditional bad actors such as leopard-men and werehyenas and werelions, we have the werewolf, the transmutation of the most crafty and intelligent predator we recognized. The idea was so popular that it hangs on today as Little Red Riding Hood, the sexual "wolf," the "wolf whistle," to "wolf down" food, "the big bad wolf " etc. Wolves have a bad image among the average Joe, deserved or not.

In Medieval Europe, there may be pretty good documentation that the reputation of the wolf as a man-eater was justified, too. When Paris was still a walled city, in 1447, 45 years before Columbus got lucky, there was an infamous bobtailed wolf called Courtaud, who led a pack of about a dozen other wolves and terrorized the suburbs all summer and fall. That winter, Courtaud and his gang are reported, reliably or not, to have gotten through the wall and eaten 40-odd people before being baited to the square in front of Notre Dame Cathedral where they were speared and stoned to death. True? Probably at least to some degree.

There was sure no question about the "Beast of Gevaudan," which Pollard records as a single animal. Barry Holstun Lopez, quoting a C. H. D. Clarke, a Canadian naturalist (whose original material I cannot find in Lopez's bibliography of *Of Wolves and Men*; Charles Scribner's Sons, New York, 1978) maintains that clearly there were two animals involved, ergo, Clarke is credited with bringing the "Beasts of Gevaudan" to an English-speaking audience.

Fortunately, there's a good cross-reference to this version in *The World of the Wolf* by Russell J. Rutter and Douglas H. Pimlott (J.B. Lippincott Company, Philadelphia and New York, 1968) which reveals Clarke to be a Doctorate holder with the Ontario government. The manuscript Clarke wrote was never published and is undated. Because of physical details of both wolves as recorded by an original research source, Abbe Francois Fabre, in 1901, from old parish records and such

I'll buy it that there were two wolves instead of Pollard's version of only one man-eater of Gevaudan.

The story begins in June of 1764 on the central plateau of France, which Pollard figures had more wolf casualties than any country in the world. A single wolf rushed a woman herding her cattle but she was un-injured as the animals drove the wolf away. But, then, on July 3rd, a teenage girl was dismembered and eaten, best guesses indicated by two wolves. By the time October rolled around, ten children were eaten and six more before New Year's day. The fact that three people were eaten over the holiday and three more on the 6th and 7th of January seems pretty conclusive that more than one wolf was doing the eating or he would have developed heart problems from being so overweight. By the end of 1765, despite tremendous hunting pressure and huge drives, the death toll had risen to 50 persons.

The single animal version of the Beast has him killed on June 19, 1766 by a 60-year-old farmer named Jean Chastel, one of more than 300 hunters in the La Tenaziere forest, the wolf having totalled 60 kills. In the two-wolf version, the first animal was killed in September of 1765 and the second in June of 1767. By any standard, they were very large, one recorded at 130 pounds and the other at 109. Because of a comment one writer makes, at least the skull of one of the Beasts must survive as it has been measured. Dr. Clarke is reported to have wondered in his "phanton" manuscript if, through description, they were not wolves at all but hybrids with dogs. Whatever they were, they killed at least 64 people and attacked about 100 overall.

The European and North American wolves are the same animal, which makes for an interesting question as to why the European variety seem to have such a record of human depredation whereas it is very dif-ficult to pin down a genuine case of man-eating in North America, let alone a determined attack. Of course there are dozens of races of *Canis lupus*, but they are all variations on the same theme, with one exception, that of the Red wolf group, which are members of the *Canis* family but not of the *lupus* group, being of the *niger* classification. So far as we're concerned, this discussion only extends to *lupus*, no matter what the race.

Some views have been expressed that the European wolf has the history of attacking because of the much longer association with man through the relatively late discovery and colonization of America. This doesn't seem to hold water, under scrutiny. Nowhere can I find a strong tradition of man-eating by wolves among the American Indian, although the joint must have been crawling with wolves when the bison was in his heyday. There are plenty of reports of wolf attack by settlers, but these traditionally are fanciful and almost none will withstand investigation. Another to ponder is that European wolves, even in very recent times since World War II, and probably even today are still eating people in Europe and Asia!

World War II was manna from Heaven for the wolf population of Europe. All the hunters were off fighting each other and the glut of abandoned corpses in the wilder places (imagine how many bodies the combined Germans and Russians left unburied during the Russian Campaign?) insured that the weakest of cubs would survive. After the war, particularly in the north, where there was less habitat disruption, a lot of problems developed when the war ended and all that easy food disappeared. On the border between Poland and Rumania in 1946, a pack of more than 50 wolves ate two soldiers before they were chased off with automatic fire and grenades. Finland was having such a problem by 1949 that it had a whole campaign mounted against wolves which had been eating both stock and people. Despite the use of aircraft, machine-guns and even mines, only a few wolves were killed, the rest coming back out of the deep forest as soon as the pressure was off. Eleven children were eaten by wolves in Portugal (Portugal!) in 1945. In ten years, reported only up to 1955, there were just short of 7,000 wolves killed in southern Yugoslavia. Although the wolf is probably no longer found in its old stronghold of France, a schoolteacher was eaten in her own classroom in 1900 and the last reported death in that country was in Dordogne, in 1914, where so long ago poor Neanderthal probably was cooked and eaten by Cro-Magnon. She was an eight-year-old girl eaten near her house.

Spain has always been rife with wolves and still is in the wilder areas. Italy also has very viable wolf packs, including recent man-killers.

A postman was killed and eaten about two hours drive from Rome in 1956; you read right, not 1856! Six years earlier a soldier was torn apart after defending himself with his bayonet, killing one wolf before the rest got him.

The vastness of the Russian steppes and taiga have always been ideal wolf habitat, and man-eating has never been rare. The village of Pilovo, according to James Clarke, was damned near wiped out during a food shortage by a concerted wolf attack in 1927, the survivors under siege conditions until rescued by the army. The cheery Pollard tells the apparently true story of a caravan being completely wiped out by man-eating wolves in the Ural Mountains about 1914. The Russians reported 30,000 wolves shot in a single year in the 1960's and more than 70,000 assorted barnyard animals killed by them, plus 11 people eaten out of 168 reported attacks on man.

One of the most bloodcurdling aspects of wolf attack (not man-eating) and certainly one of the most common causes, is that of rabies. In fact, it is almost unquestionably the single greatest factor. Wolves being social animals, rabies can spread quickly through a pack. An entire section would be devoted to this aspect of sheerly horrible behavior, but we had better stick on the tracks which lead from man-eating to man-eating, at least for the sake of space.

Having clearly determined that the European wolf has a definite, certified history of man-eating, it would seem time to take another look west and see what the records show for North America. Was James Clarke right that there has never been a confirmed case in North America? Of actual man-eating—even if some attacks might have logically resulted in the losing man being consumed—there exists no evidence I can consider "hard" and I've turned over one hell of a lot of reference rocks. Of course, some of this becomes a matter of judgment. Elmer Keith, that great *Maestro* of the six-gun and other related matters, wrote to Roger Caras of knowledge of a man's skeleton being found on a island off southeast Alaska along with a weathered Smith and Wesson .357 Magnum revolver (which dates the incident to no earlier than 1935, when that caliber was developed) and the associated skeletons of three wolves can only be considered circumstantial. There is no proof that the man didn't attack the wolves, have a heart attack himself and get eaten after death by the crows. Perhaps he was simply killed by a wounded wolf or wolves. *Maybe* it was a genuine case of unprovoked man-eating, the trouble is that there are too many other possibilities, no matter what one prefers to read into the imagined "probabilities" of the evidence, it is just not conclusive.

Certainly, there have been reputable recorded instances of attack in Canada and the United States by wolves. A beauty was reported, complete with witnesses in a scientific journal of the Royal Ontario Museum, which includes the sworn testimony of one Mike Dusiak, the victim, the train crew that battled and finally killed the wolf and the wildlife official who investigated the incident. Although it reads classically like a report of rabid behavior, nowhere in Dr. Randolph L. Peterson's paper, *A Record of a Timber Wolf Attacking a Man* (*Journal of Mammology*, 1947) is there any mention of rabies. However, as Rutter and Pimlott are quick to point out in their reproduction of the paper, rabies tests were not normally carried out at that time and, through extreme good fortune, Dusiak was either not bitten or did not contract the disease, the only basis for serious consideration that the attack was preliminary to possible consumption. Here's what happened, paraphrased from Peterson's rendition of Dusiak's testimony:

Mike Dusiak, a railway section foreman, was driving his "speeder" (I presume a slang term for a hand car or similar vehicle) slowly west of Chapleau, Ontario, expecting to meet a scheduled train. Suddenly "something" smashed into him and grabbed him by the left arm, hitting him hard enough to knock both him and the speeder off the tracks. (If it grabbed his arm that hard wouldn't the skin have been broken?) It was such a powerful blow he thought he'd been hit by a locomotive. Getting to his feet, he saw a wolf about 50 feet away, which immediately charged him. He grabbed a pair of axes, one in each hand, and laid open the wolf's belly with a stroke and lost one axe. The wolf then started a circling attack, so close that Dusiak was able to smack him in the skull with the second axe a couple of times, but seemingly with no effect. All the time, he was growling and gnashing his teeth and after what Dusiak thought was 15 minutes, he had been able to brain the wolf five times, each time he broke the circle and jumped at the man. Another ten minutes went by as

Mike was able to keep the animal off, crossing the tracks and fighting until the train came along, stopped and the foreman got help from the engineer, fireman and brakeman, who together killed the persistent wolf with picks and shovels! The wolf was thought to be in excellent health, but was not tested.

Earlier, in 1926, there was a huge flap when what most authorities reckon was a rabid wolf walked into a small town of Churchill, Manitoba. As James Clarke reports, the army was called in to get the wolf, which was now missing, and within a short time most of the town's huskies and at least one local Indian had been shot. A tourist later ran over the wolf with his car, presumably an accident.

Those are the hard and rather remote facts about the wolf as a man-eater. In Europe, guilty as charged; elsewhere, no. I have looked long and hard for any other conclusion, but it doesn't seem warranted.

Why? Nobody knows, let alone agrees, but I have at least one idea. There's an interesting parallel between the wolf and the African hunting dog, *Lycaon pictus,* the incredibly efficient, highly socially-organized predator of the plains and savannahs of Africa. As rich in what would only be considered elaborate abstract ceremony and behavioral ritual, exactly as is the wolf, this truly fearsome killer, from which all game less than the elephant flee, is also one of the only predators of this continent capable of eating man who has never been reliably reported as doing so.

Now, that's more than just curious.

In my opinion, the reason the wolf is reticent as a man-eater when healthy and well-fed, even in Europe, is that he is a methodical hunter. He's not like a consistent man-eater such as the more solitary cats, who make quick decisions and attack targets of opportunity. The wolf hunt, from first howl to last bloody scrap is a masterpiece of organization. As such, I believe that the wolf recognizes us not only as a danger, but as another predator, not a prey animal. If you've ever seen the efficiency with which wolves kill, you'll join me in hoping that it stays that way!

IF THERE IS AN animal as universally loathed, ridiculed and secretly feared through all the lands of those who know him, it is the hyena. As what may possibly be the most accomplished processor of human meat of all, both as a scavenger and newly recognized super-predator, old *Fisi* as most of the old East African types call him, has a very annoying habit that tends to rankle humans of every color: he always has the last laugh.

Hyenas are fascinating bloody animals. Despite the presumption that they are some sort of dog designed by a committee with their grinning, quite expressive faces and tremendous jaws, seemingly crippled, slanting downward hindquarters and one-man-band repertoire of the goddamnd-est collection of noises one ever did hear, they give a most erroneous im-pression of being some sort of animal fugitive from all that good fun on *The Gong Show*. Spend a little time in the bush with *Fisi*, pal, and it won't be long, if you pay attention, that you'll respect him more than the lion.

It's interesting, considering all the big, fat grants that have been fi-nancing African animal research for the past 60 years, that it's only quite recently that we have started to get away from the traditional concept of the spotted hyena, (*Crocuta crocuta*), as some olfactory offense to mankind, some "fringe" species of little value to anybody except for the processing of animal garbage and the entertainment of insomniac tourists. That, as an individual and small hunting band, the hyena may be the most successful predator of them all, in some places turning the tables so severely that the lions follow the hyenas and eat *their* scraps, as we've discovered is quite common, was not well known until just a few years ago, after the work of men like Dr. Hans Kruuk, and Hugo and Jane van Lawick-Goodall.

But, let us trip lightly back onto the path of man-eating and the hyena. For purposes of space, let's consider just the most populous of the group, the spotted, and leave the fringe of the family out of it although the striped hyena does eat people in Asia.

The biggest problem with the hyena is the fact that he has a rude ten-dency to eat and run. If you spend some time in Africa, you will see some people around with faces that would cause you to gag up last Easter's jelly beans. As the late Robert Ruark, who I suspect strongly of having had a fondness like mine for hyenas, despite the way he reviled them in print, learned, there is quite often a relationship between those people with profiles that end abruptly below the eyeballs because of hyena bite and a fondness for the American equivalent of Old Stumpblower. Africans who drink themselves into the death-like stupor produced by some of this homemade liquid form of Roto-Rooter, sooner or later may be noticed as they are passed out near a dying fire. *Fisi,* albeit a bit prematurely, decides to sample what he's going to get anyway a few years down the road and SNAP! Look, Ma, no face! Depending upon individual circumstances, it may be no arm, foot, fingers or—let your imagination roam. Oh, yes. That happens, too.

Hyenas in general are brighter than some people I have worked for. At better than 150 pounds for a biggie, living around a clan is sort of like sharing an apartment with "The Munsters." I am convinced that, except for the primates, the hyena is the only animal I have seen who seems to have a sense of humor. It takes a while, but when you've spent years in Africa as I have, without TV and even sufficient light to read by on many nights—as if you would have had the strength—the hyena can become a frequent source of entertainment. I have recorded hyenas imitating lions in most convincing fashion, unless one happens to know the voices of all the resident lions well enough to differentiate. Really, I am positive the hyena will imitate lion roars, and I can't think of any reason other than for the hell of it.

I wish I could use the space to tell again my experiences in Botswana with my hyena "retrievers" when sand grouse shooting, but you can find it in *Death in the Long Grass* (St. Martin's Press, New York, 1977). It'll point up the fact that free enterprise is not fading among the *crocuta!*

Unfortunately, my misplaced affection for the species is somewhat watered down upon realizing that, as a man-eater, he's probably a "natural" such as the crocodile. African custom has dictated abandonment of dead and dying people, leaving them for the hyenas so that the eating of people, dead or alive, has become ingrained.

A white by the name of Balestra killed two big man-eating hyenas who had ingested the village idiot of the Mlanje District of Malawi back in 1955. The killer hyena ate everything but the man's clothes, which I'm surprised were left behind as hyenas commonly eat even the blood-stained handles off knives, as they did to my faithful Randall skinner.

A little after this, an old woman was taken bodily—and I do mean bodily—from her hut, but although a tribesman drove off the hyenas, her arm had been completely bitten off and carried away by the attackers. She died the next day of shock and additional bites around her throat. The next victim of the Mlanje hyenas was a six-year-old child, who had been killed with the ever popular technique of biting the child's face off. The hyenas had been joined by others, now, and ate the entire body but for the skull, half of which was left.

Between 36 and 60 people were eaten by this hyena group until 1961, all taken during the warm months when they were sleeping outside. Not too bright, guys! At last things died down, no pun intended. Balestra was never sure if there was *mbojo* or lycanthropic witchcraft mixed up in the matter as George Rushby found the case in Tanganyika.

I see little point to a long, drawn-out history of man-eating by hyenas, because it's not very entertaining except in a few cases I have already written about elsewhere. Suffice it to say that the hyena is a casual killer who will take whatever flesh he can get whenever an opportunity presents itself. The problem is, that includes you and me; although I promise you, everything else equal, it's a lot more likely to be you than me. You see, I've been there, Charlie!

thirty-two

ONE TOUGH TRAPPER

by Larry Kaniut

TEN YEARS AGO WADE Nolan and I returned to Anchorage from an ice-fishing trip. The day before we had sadly watched Andy Runyan's cabin burn to the ground near Lake Louise, Alaska. Wade spun a tale about a trapper whose innovation spoke volumes about his courage and desperation. I could never find the trapper and asked Wade to recount the story from memory.

IN THE EARLY WINTER of 1979 or 1980 I completed six months' work in Nome. I boarded a flight out of Nome back to Anchorage, probably a two-hour flight. As I sat in my seat, this big guy, a grizzled, bearded old trapper, sat down next to me.

We both looked at magazines before and after takeoff.

After a while I looked over and noticed his hand was all scarred up. It looked like he'd stuck his hand into a bag full of razor blades. The scars were healed but they were relatively new, not ten years old. Later on I glanced over at his face. It, too, was heavily scarred as was his other hand.

As time went on, we started talking. I think his name was Jack, but I'm not positive. I'm going to call him Jack for the sake of the story.

He was a lone trapper with a line up in the Kigluaik Mountains, north and east of Nome. They are their own little mountain range, right in the middle of nowhere. They're so remote it takes forever to get to any place from there.

Jack's trapline was similar to others' in that he had a base cabin with a number of small trapline cabins. These small, often crude cabins provide overnight shelter—a place to get in out of the weather, to skin animals, to sleep. His line was circular and took several days to cover. He worked out of his home cabin and snowshoed the line checking traps and stopping at several-mile intervals at his line cabins.

One winter Jack made the rounds of his traps, clad in his parka, his backpack slung on his back, and his webs rhythmically slicing along the trail. He resembled many an old-time trapper. It was late in the afternoon when he neared the end of his line, between the last line cabin and his main cabin. Each of the many traps he'd just checked held remnants of eaten carcasses of pine marten or mink. He had recently noticed wolverine tracks and knew that pirate of the north had beaten him to his traps.

Wolverines are secretive and rarely seen by the foot traveler in the wilderness. They are sly and hold a reputation for gluttony and ferocity.

Jack reset the traps and tossed aside the animal remains. He traveled on, thinking little of the glutton but more of his main cabin and warmth and food. That's when he noticed some ptarmigan. He shouldered his .22 rifle and shot three of the pigeon-sized fowl, which would make fine table fare that evening.

Walking along with the birds in his mittened hands, Jack paid no heed to the blood occasionally dropping from the birds onto the trail. He noticed a weather front closing in on him as it started snowing. The storm built so fast he knew he couldn't reach the cabin before it reached its zenith. He decided to hole up until the storm blew over.

Knowing the country well, he hurried to a nearby hill studded with rock outcroppings. He reckoned an outcropping would provide safety away from the wind where he could back in under a ledge for protection and sit out the storm.

He left the main trail and found an appropriate ledge. Jack took off his pack and laid it down beneath the ledge. He crouched down and backed underneath the ledge—there was just enough room to sit with his knees up under his chin. He laid the ptarmigan in front of him at the mouth of the ledge.

What he didn't know was that the trap-raiding wolverine had been following him. The carcajou, knowing the rewards to be found along a trapper's trail, had keyed on the blood from the ptarmigan. It walked right up to the top of the ledge, just above the trapper's head. Spotting the ptarmigan below, the wolverine pounced down on the birds where they lay just a few feet in front of the trapper.

Startled by the blur of an object dropping in front of his face, Jack jerked back in surprise, automatically raising his hands. Instead of bounding away like most any other animal would have done, the wolverine instantly jumped onto the trapper.

Jack pushed against the wolverine with his mittened hand. The wolverine was a windmill of razor-blade paws. Even though this big, brawny trapper was doing his best to hold the wolverine away from him, the animal's claws whirled and slashed around his face. Jack repeatedly pushed the animal away, and the wolverine kept pouncing back at his face.

Moments into the attack Jack's mittens were ripped off. He pushed with his exposed hands. In short order the animal shredded Jack's hands.

Compounding Jack's efforts to free himself of the furious attack, the beast caught a claw in the hole on his parka zipper. Somewhat trapped, the wolverine went crazy. Old Jack said it felt as if the fight hadn't begun until then because the wolverine went into high gear, fighting for its life. Jack saw only whirling claws and teeth.

In spite of his cramped quarters and the animal's attachment, finally Jack shoved the wolverine back far enough to break its hold. The wolverine landed on the snow two to three feet away. The animal glanced at Jack momentarily, grabbed the ptarmigan in its mouth, and trotted off, leaving the badly bleeding trapper.

Jack had so much blood in his eyes he could hardly see. Wounds on his face, hands, and wrists were bone-deep. Jack knew his very survival dictated reaching his home cabin, even though the storm was now raging.

Picking up his pack, Jack crawled from beneath the ledge. Trailing blood, he struggled off along his trapline in the diminishing light.

Before darkness closed in on him Jack reached his cabin. His clothes were matted with blood. He shuffled through the door knowing it would be nearly as cold inside as outside. Jack's survival necessitated getting a fire going in his woodstove. Coupled with his weakened condition from the loss of blood and his injuries, finding a lantern and starting the fire was an ordeal.

His next step was to evaluate and care for his injuries. In the glow from the lantern the mirror reflected a mask of death. His only help would have to come from his own efforts. Jack found his sewing kit. He propped up the mirror in front of him next to the lantern on the table.

He fumbled for a needle and thread. Sitting there in the gathering warmth of his fire and the glowing lantern light, Jack slowly and painfully inserted the needle into his skin, pulled the thread through and tucked the wound together, one stitch at a time.

As he sewed, he blacked out. Later he came to and continued sewing. He doesn't know how many times he blacked out; but all night and into the wee hours of the morning Jack alternately stitched his wounds and passed out. Finally, exhausted, he'd closed the major wounds on his face and his hands.

He climbed into his bunk. Without a radio or any way to contact help, he had no other choice. He didn't know what he was waiting for . . . he was just trusting that something would happen. He could only wait.

As the Lord would have it, He saw fit a couple of days later to send a bush pilot. Passing low over Jack's cabin, the pilot noticed no smoke was coming from the chimney, so he landed. He entered Jack's cabin and found him in serious condition in his bunk. The pilot loaded Jack into his bush plane and flew him back to Nome, where after weeks in a hospital Jack survived.

thirty-three

TEXAS BOAR FEEDING FRENZY

by Don Zaidle

WHAT HAS BAD BREATH, big teeth, a shaggy coat of coarse hair, a leg at each corner, weighs up to 600 pounds, and likes to eat people? Before you waste a lot of time trying to figure out if it's your mother-in-law, consider the following:

In October 1993, seventy-nine-year-old Willie Heinen was working outdoors around his home when he noticed his dogs had been strangely absent all day. He whistled for them and heard a commotion of feet running toward him from behind the house, but it sure wasn't his dogs. A sounder of twelve wild hogs came boiling around the corner of the house, running straight for him in a flat-out charge.

Being an old southern-Texas bush hand, Heinen was well familiar with hogs and knew he was in trouble. Unarmed and effectively cut off from the house by the rapidly closing gang of killers, he looked around for a refuge and spotted his pickup truck parked some twenty-five yards away. "Relief" is too mild a word to describe Heinen's emotions when his hand closed on the pickup's door handle. Relief melted into terror, however, when he tried the latch—locked! The hogs were almost on him, leaving no time for other options. Resigning himself to the inevitable, he raised his heavy mesquite walking stick and turned to face the rushing conglomerate of hooves, tusks, and death.

The first hog rushed in and was met with Heinen's cane crashing over its head. Three-inch tusks crunched around the stick, snapping it in half and ripping it from Heinen's grasp with a violent jerk. Electric fingers of pain gripped him as a second hog ripped at his thigh while a third savaged his ankle, yanking him down flat on his back on the ground. The rest of the pack swarmed him, powerful jaws splintering bones and shredding flesh in his right hand, a 200-pound boar hooking at his left leg and tearing away flesh with a soggy *thwop*. Willie Heinen literally was being eaten alive.

Deciding to go down swinging. Heinen threw a fist at the nearest hog. He wasn't certain where the punch landed, but for sure it was the right place. The hog screamed in surprise and pain and ran off toward the brush, the others following with cannibalistic intentions. Heinen struggled through the pain to his feet, then hurriedly hobbled inside before the hogs came back. He somehow managed to telephone a neighbor before passing out.

Six months later, he was still recovering from wounds painfully infected by the pathogens in the rotting meat on the hogs' tusks. If it hadn't been for that lucky punch, Willie Heinen would today be fertilizing the grasses of some *sendero* as hog droppings.

Man-eating hog stories have been circulating for years, reflected in such macabrely humorous colloquialisms as "So-and-so went to the outhouse and the hogs ate him" and "I haven't had this much fun since the hogs ate my little brother." Hogs feeding on human corpses is a confirmed fact, but no verifiable case of man-killing has ever been documented. There's probably a good reason for that: When hogs kill you unwitnessed in the woods and eat you, they eat *all* of you, bones and all. With no witnesses and no body, what is there to document? I once found a boot, a tattered, chewed-on hunting boot, bearing vestiges of what *might* have been bloodstains. Nearby lay the broken half of a broadhead-tipped aluminum hunting arrow. Contemplating the possibilities of how the two objects came to be found together in a dense thicket crawling with wild hogs is an exercise I try to avoid, especially when I am bowhunting.

It may comfort you to know that wild hogs (*Sus scrofa*) do not inhabit all of the U.S., just most of it, in numbers estimated at two million strong.

thirty-four

PIGSTICKING MADE PERSONAL

by Peter Hathaway Capstick

THE PALE STREAKS OF the winter dawn were showing through the feathery *alamo* trees when Chiche Bilo reined his horse up short. He swung from the gaucho saddle and with the rolling gait of the professional horseman approached the mutilated sheep. Inserting the toe of his *alpargata* under the edge of the stiffening carcass, he flipped the carcass, exposing the massive damage to the animal's underside. Bilo's brown Basque eyes stared hard at the long, irregular wounds in the sheep's chest and at the big tear across the paunch where the internal organs had been dragged out and eaten. I saw his gaze flicker to the churned desert earth as it followed the series of deep, split grooves that led into the heavy chaparral. His jaw muscle was twitching as he spoke.

"*Jabalí*," he said quietly. "Wild boar, and a hell of a big one."

I held in my horse as it skittered at the blood scent. "You mean it was a wild boar that killed this ram?" I asked incredulously. "What the hell, I've never heard of pigs killing animals to eat." The carcass looked like the remains of an ax murder. "I thought boars lived on acorns or truffles and that sort of stuff."

"Not in Argentina, they don't," answered Chiche as he remounted in one smooth movement. "We had one boar operating about twenty miles from here that killed over eight hundred sheep and heifers over a three-year period until I finally was called in to take care of it. This kill isn't more than three hours old," he continued, rubbing a clot of blood between his fingers. "Let's head back to the *estancia* and pick up the *Dogos*."

I slid the shotgun back into its scabbard, all thought of hunting the sporty desert partridge called *copetonas* now far from my mind. Chiche's *estancia*, I knew, was a working ranch and nothing came before the protection of his stock—including my *Saga* assignment to investigate the rumors of fantastic bird shooting to be found here in the Patagonian region of western Argentina. Anyway, I was glad of an opportunity to see his famed *Dogos Argentinos* at work.

We rode back through the dry sage and maquis of Chiche's fifteen thousand hectares at an easy canter. Angel, a giant gaucho in balloon pants with a heavy, silver-handled knife stuck through the back of his waist sash, rode heavily behind me, a grin as wide as a watermelon slice on his weathered face. Chickens and puppies scattered as Chiche led us through the apple orchard into the dusty courtyard where the big, white boar dogs strained against their staked-down leads. They seemed to sense a hunt in our pounding hoofs, and whined with excitement as we reined up.

Chiche called for maté, the traditional herb tea of the pampas which was brought in silver-trimmed gourds by his slender, blue-eyed wife. She handed me a gourd and spooned sugar over the dry mixture, adding enough hot water for one noisy sip through the silver straw. I inhaled mine down in approved gaucho fashion while Chiche untied three of the biggest dogs. Released, they stood silently listening to his whispers in Araucano, the ancient tongue of the fierce Patagonian Indians, the only language he would use with his fighting animals. He explained to me that in the confusion of a boar fight, men shout in Spanish. Since the dogs might misunderstand a shout between hunters, Araucano was his only language of command.

The night before, over a grilled *parrillada mixta*, the wonderful Argentinian national dish of assorted meats, Bilo had told me about his

Dogos Argentinos. Originally developed by Dr. Nores Martines, the *Dogos* are probably the most effective breed of boar-hunting animals ever developed.

When the European wild boar, *Sus scrofa,* was imported into Argentina in the middle of the last century to provide sport on the estates of the wealthy, it was soon found that conditions in Argentina were just about perfect for wild pigs. The result was that *jabalí,* as boar are called locally, grow bigger and tougher here than anywhere else in the world. Bilo has killed several better than six hundred pounds, and there are records of boar better than seven hundred. It didn't take long to find that imported European dogs were no match for these huge pigs, particularly in the heavy bush of the western areas.

A further complication arose when it was found that boar were beginning to kill stock, an almost unheard-of thing elsewhere in their vast range. Bilo said that nobody knew if they were killing stock because the breed had gotten so big, or whether they had gotten so big by killing and eating sheep. At any rate, by 1900 they had become a major menace for ranchers throughout most of Argentina.

It took until the 1930s before Dr. Martines, a dedicated hunter and dog breeder, had developed the bloodline into what is today the standard *Dogo Argentino.* He used Spanish pointer, mastiff, pit bull, bloodhound, and a half-dozen other strains to develop the qualities necessary for a real fighting dog: tenacity, ferocity, and fearlessness. After Dr. Martines's death, the development of the *Dogo Argentino,* now a national pride, was unofficially adopted by Chiche Bilo. At his ranch on the banks of the Rio Negro near the town of Allen (pronounced locally Azzhen), Bilo has about fifty of the best *Dogos* in the world.

A full-grown *Dogo* weighs about ninety to one hundred pounds of white-sheathed muscle. Their teeth and jaws are tremendous, as they must be to grab and hold boar, but they are strangely gentle, making excellent house pets, although I doubt they'll ever replace the poodle.

Although *Dogos* have a natural instinct for boar fighting, Bilo won't let his dogs hunt without having actually fought boar in his arena, an enclosure specially constructed for young dogs to learn tactics the hard way, in the hope that experience here may save their lives later. Moderate-sized captive boar are used in these fights, but despite this, many *Dogos* are killed or disabled before they ever take up a wild scent.

The tactics of the *Dogos,* Chiche explained to me, are to follow the boar's spoor silently, and to jump the big pig as a team. One dog will grab an ear while the others take legs or flank. Since *Dogos* almost never bark when hunting, curs follow them and sound off when the fight starts, indicating the location of the struggle to the hunters.

"Then," said Bilo casually, "I kill the *jabalí* with the knife."

"You *what?*" I asked.

"The *arbolito*—the gaucho knife. I kill the boar with it."

"Now, let me get this straight. You walk up to a five-hundred-pound wild boar and stab him to death? Isn't that just a little bit tricky?"

"Oh, yes, *Pedro,* many men are killed trying it. But really, it is all in knowing when to make your attack, when to—how do you say—stab."

"Where the hell did you get this idea?" I asked him, lighting a *cigarro negro.*

"We gauchos have always considered it a man's way to hunt," he answered simply. "The object of hunting *jabalí* is not to make it as easy as possible, but as hard as possible. If I just wanted a dead pig, I would buy one."

God, I thought, these crazy cowboys . . .

Followed by the three boar hounds and a pair of scruffy-looking mutts, we rode back to the grove of *alamos* and the dead sheep. A desert eagle flapped off heavily as we reined in. Chiche dismounted and whistled the *Dogos* over to the spoor. They snuffed the pungent boar scent with low nasal snorts, milled about for a moment, then forged ahead with Bilo's lead bitch, Day, in the lead. The mongrels whined and followed at a trot.

We cantered after the pack for about a mile through the thorny scrub without a hint of sound to guide us until we came to a broad plain hemmed with gray brush. Bilo stopped, and, like an acrobat, he steadied himself and rose standing on the saddle, his eyes shaded across the desert. There was no sound but the low moan of the dry wind and the whisper of the *alamos.* Dropping back into the saddle, he told me he felt the boar would probably make for the thick stuff along the river and possibly cross the

jungled islands near the north bank. We rode in the direction Chiche indicated, straining to hear the bark of the curs. Finally, like the faraway ring
of a small bell, it came.

Whack! went the flat rawhide whip against the rump of Chiche's
mount as he spurred off at a flat run, with Angel and me behind, eating
his dust. Sharp branches slashed at us as we crashed through the scrub
toward the green of the river a mile ahead. Twice I swerved my horse just
in time to avoid deadly *viscacha* holes, knowing it would mean a broken
leg for my animal and a possible broken neck for me if he stepped into
one of the rodent's burrows at full speed. Coveys of *perdices*—tailless
Argentine quail—burst from under our hammering hoofs like brown
grenade fragments, and one smashed into my face like a thrown rock,
blinding me for a moment. I hung on to the pommel with white knuckles, head down against the lashing branches, until my vision cleared.

As we flashed across the pampas, a high, quivering cry cut the air like
a sword. It was the ancient Basque war cry that Chiche used to encour-
age his dogs to fight on until he got there. Ahead, I caught a glimpse of
one of the curs running toward us, his tail tucked between his legs.
Chiche thundered on into the cover, and I saw the icy flicker of steel as
he drew his long knife. Hauling his horse back into a skidding cascade of
flying dirt, he hit the ground running and disappeared from view. I pulled
the scattergun, loaded with slugs, from the scabbard and followed him
on foot. When I caught up after fifty yards, he was standing in a clearing,
completely still, staring at something on the ground. It was Day, the
leader, and she was dying.

Chiche knelt by her and inspected her wounds. A froth of bloody pink
bubbles oozed from her chest where a razor-sharp tusk had penetrated
her lung. A bulge of snaky intestine protruded from a straight incision in
her paunch. She whined and struggled to rise. Chiche's eyes misted over
as he realized she wanted to go on with the hunt.

Angel wiped her face with a grimy fist and lifted the dying dog in his
arms, placing her gently over his saddle. She feebly licked his hand.
Chiche rode off and returned fifteen minutes later with the remaining two
hounds, both filthy with dirt-smeared blood, but not really wounded. Taking a curved needle and gut from his wallet, Chiche began to sew them up.

They never even whimpered as he sterilized their wounds with brandy. I could see the muscle in Chiche's jaw twitching again as he swung onto his horse and began the ride home. I knew better than to say anything.

The pale sun had just set when Angel patted the last spadeful of red earth into place. Chiche took the shovel and drove the head marker deeply into the dirt: *Day de Trevelin—364 Jabalíes.* Drawing his fighting knife, he sank it hilt-deep to the right of the marker and Angel stabbed his to the left. I knew they did it for the same reason an Englishman breaks his champagne glass, so that never may a lesser toast be drunk from it.

AMADEO "CHICHE" BILO IS one of the few great hunters who has become a legend in his own time, not only in his native Argentina, but anywhere strong men hoist a glass and speak of great hunting deeds. He is among the last of the most ancient line of noble sportsmen who fight the most dangerous prey on foot with hand weapons.

The entire way of life of the early warrior-nobles of northern Europe and England during medieval times was based on combat and the development of skill at arms. When there wasn't a stack of Saracens handy for an afternoon's sport, or some other target available for some good rough-and-tumble, the man of action got a few buddies together and went out boar hunting.

The oldest surviving book on hunting dates from the 1360s and is entitled *Livre de la Chasse.* Written by Gaston Phoebus, by whose name the book is more familiarly called, it provides the first and best records of hunts and killing techniques, and is guaranteed to frost the sideburns of the toughest modern Tarzan. Concerning the spearing of boar on foot with a lance fitted with a crosspiece (so the boar wouldn't come up the shaft at you), old Gaston told it like it really was:

"As soon as the point has entered the boar's body, take the heft under your armpit and press and push as hard as you can and never let go the haft, and if the boar be stronger than you then you must turn from side to side as best you can without letting go the haft until God comes to your aid or some other assistance."

Bear in mind, now, that Gaston considered spearing to be the *easy* way. By his reckoning, the killing of a charging boar from horseback with a sword was really doing it right, "a finer thing and more noble" than the methods employed by the pantywaists with the pigstickers. In a technical discussion, Phoebus mentioned that the major problem in filleting your pig from the saddle was the chance of cutting off your own arms and legs while chopping away at the boar, who was himself occupied with the vivisection of your horse. The author laments the many mounts that were killed under him by boar.

It must have been a tough and short life, being in the employ of Master Phoebus. We can only hope his staff received combat pay, as Gaston recites in an antiseptic manner that he had lost many good squires and servants at the tusks of boar that would "slit a man from the knee to the breast and slay him all stark dead at one stroke so that he never spoke thereafter."

Presumably, Phoebus must have figured the odds on coming home after a tête-à-tête with a boar while on foot and armed only with a knife were too short to even call it sport, and has not mentioned it in his book. He would have been very impressed with Chiche Bilo. Perhaps the difference was in the skill of the hounds, but that would be hard to believe. There are surviving tapestries and drawings showing boar dogs that would make the Hound of the Baskervilles look like a Chihuahua. A skilled boar dog has always been highly prized, and with good reason. An experienced hound was one that had lived long enough to develop a style in his tangles with boar without getting permanently ventilated. Other members of the pack would learn from him, thus decreasing the mortality rate of the entire pack. German paintings from the eighteenth century often show pack leaders wearing expensive chain-mail coats to protect them against the deadly tusks.

It is interesting to note that the quality of silence among boar dogs was as popular eight hundred years ago in England as it is today in Argentina. A letter survives at the Tower of London, written by King John in 1213 to Roger de Neville, mentioning that the king was sending, among other breeds, "fifteen varlets . . . and forty-four *de mota* (mute) dogs to hunt boars in the park at Bricstok. . . ." One speculates whether they were mute naturally or perhaps had been operated on in some way.

A boar hunt in Europe, by the 1500s, had become sort of a combination between the opening day of rabbit season in New Jersey and the Super Bowl. Huge beats took place for the pleasure of hundreds of sportsmen, driving great numbers of boar and other game before the huntsmen. As there were considerable pauses between the furious action, one Frenchman, Jacques de Fouilloux, suggested that between the more active phases of the hunt, a gentleman should have a young girl of the village at hand to take care of his more idle moments. You can see that hunting isn't what it used to be.

One of the only men of the modern era to hunt boar on foot with a knife for the sheer hell of it was Sir Samuel White Baker, an early explorer of the tributaries of the Nile River. In one of Baker's first books, *The Rifle and the Hound in Ceylon,* he describes chasing down Ceylonese boar on foot and killing them in the identical manner of Bilo. Baker, twenty-two years old at the time, favored a cut-down Highland Claymore, a double-edged piece of steel that was sharp as a razor, with an eighteen-inch blade. Weighing about three pounds, it was really a short sword. Describing the scene he would meet after a long run through jungle and ravine following his hounds and finally bringing the boar to bay in the thickest part of the forest, Baker said:

The huntsman approaches the scene of the combat, breaking his way with difficulty through the tangled jungle until within about twenty yards of the bay. He now cheers the hounds on to attack, and if they are worthy of their name, they instantly rush into the boar regardless of wounds. The huntsman . . . immediately rushes to the assistance of the pack, knife in hand.

A scene of real warfare meets his view—gaping wounds upon his best hounds, the boar rushing through the jungle covered with dogs, and he himself becomes the immediate object of his fury when observed.

No time is to be lost. Keeping behind the boar if possible, he rushes to the bloody conflict, and drives the hunting knife between the shoulders in the endeavor to divide the spine. Should he happily affect this, the boar falls stone dead; but if not, he repeats the thrust, keeping a good lookout for the animal's tusks.

If the dogs were not of sufficient courage to rush in and seize the boar when *halload* [sic] on, no man could approach him in a thick jungle with only a hunting knife, as he would in all probability have his inside ripped out on the first charge. They are wonderfully active and ferocious, and of immense power, constantly weighing four cwt [400 pounds]. The end of every good seizor is being killed by a boar. The better the dog the more likely he is to be killed, as he will be the first to lead the attack, and in the thick jungle he has no chance of escaping from a wound.

Chiche confirmed to me what Baker had said. Without big, fearless dogs to hold the boar for him, a man wouldn't have a chance. A boar charges as straight as a spear, with his head low and shrieking like a banshee with a stubbed toe. He'll flatten a horse and unzip him with his razor tusks quicker than it takes to tell. Contrary to popular opinion, boar don't gore or slash with their tusks; they bite like a pair of shears. The lower tusks loop up and whet against the uppers, keeping them sharper than a carving set. When a boar is warming up to subdivide your carcass, the whetting sound is much like that made by your butcher just before he carves you a good steak.

A boar will almost always charge a man when fighting with dogs. If the dogs are weak from loss of blood or don't have a good grip on the boar, the pig may shuck them off like so many sparrows. Boar dogs are like dominoes—if one loses a grip, the others may be thrown off balance. Then, big shot, there's nothing between you and a quarter-ton of uncooked pork but a foot-and-a-half blade and your two shaking feet. I know, it happened to me.

THERE WERE NEEDLES OF ice around the rim of the horse trough as we sucked up the last of our *maté* and mounted for the hunt. Two more *Dogos,* trotting behind the horses in their grim silence, joined the survivors of yesterday's fight. Chiche led us toward the river, about a mile downwind of the thicket where Day had been killed. Chiche and Angel had both whetted new knives and presented me with one as a gift. My sense of honor forced me to leave the shotgun in the corner behind the ranch house door. I later regretted it.

Puffs of cold dust were thrown from our horses' hoofs as we walked the mounts in line-abreast formation through the chaparral. In the distance, a pair of guanaco, desert cousins of the llama, stared and bolted away. To my left, a giant Patagonian hare hunched beneath a bush, frozen into hiding, then burst with a blur of speed into the surrounding thorny scrub.

A low whistle brought our eyes from the packed ground. It was Angel. "*Se fue por aquí, Patrón,*" he said, addressing Chiche and pointing to the set of tracks leading across our path. We dismounted as Bilo inspected the spoor and followed it, leading his horse. After fifty yards, a fresh pile of droppings lay on the trail. It was full of matted wool. Bilo gave me an odd smile, as if to say, "same one as yesterday."

Angel brought up the dogs on a multiple tether. Shaking with excitement, they were released and disappeared like silent wraiths on the spoor, with the little curs running behind. The lead dog was Tahpei, a big male given his Araucano name for bravery. He didn't look like the sort of dog you'd want to try to take a bone from.

Spurring forward, we followed at a canter, Chiche ahead and the big gaucho trailing me. I shifted the knife in my belt where the hilt dug into my ribs.

We covered three miles following the dogs, never hearing a sound from the curs. Four times the trail of the *Dogos* went off at a tangent with the pig's spoor until Angel shouted to stop for a moment. He jumped from his horse and stared at the ground. Grimacing, he pointed to the trail. Even I could see that the big boar had been joined by two others that were a little smaller and probably sows.

"*Pedro,* we've really got to ride now," Chiche said with a frown. "If those *Dogos* tangle with three pigs at once, we'll lose the whole pack. It's happened before. They're bred for fearlessness and won't hesitate to go for a dozen boar." As if to answer him, a distant barking came to us from the river edge.

We covered the last mile as if possessed, and pulled up in the heavy cover near the riverbank. Fierce grunts and squeals mixed with the hysteria of the curs sounded like a steam calliope gone wild. Following Chiche and Angel with drawn knife, I bulled through the snags and thorns, wishing like hell I was going the other way.

I felt the wind whistling through my burning lungs as I ran with Bilo's wild Basque yell ringing in my ears. Suddenly, ahead I could see the movement of white dogs flicker through the small gaps in the bush. At twenty yards, a long slice on the side of Tahpei glistened a wet red as I saw him rush in like a mamba snake to grab the ear of a big sow. She shrieked and snapped her head, lifting the big dog off the ground with a lightning wrench, breaking his grip and tearing his powerful teeth through her ear skin. He landed on his back and regained his feet just before the pig hit him, her frothing, open mouth snapping shut like a bear trap just past his leg. A few yards to the right, the other three *Dogos* were trying to hold on to an enormous female, one dog on each ear and the third with his fangs sunk into the fat of her rump. She dragged them along the ground like a pro fullback in a Little League game, but none would break his vise-like grip.

There was a blur of Chiche coming in like a falcon from the sow's side, his left arm extended and the knife held low in his right. I saw him grip deeply into the pig's bristles, and drive the steel behind her shoulder, working the blade in the wound. The sow gave a terrible scream and began to thrash around with redoubled fury, lifting the heavy hounds holding her ears like two marshmallows. Chiche withdrew the knife and struck again, this time between the shoulder blades, sawing to find the spinal cord, holding on with one hand as the sow bounced him like a doll in her frenzy. Then, as if axed, she dropped without a quiver and lay still. He had found a joint between the vertebrae.

A hoarse shout ripped through the clearing. It was Angel yelling, "*Cuidado, Patrón! A la izquierda!*" Bilo leaped from the dead pig in time to see the other female bearing down on him, Tahpei being dragged behind with his teeth fastened deep in her flank. Three white streaks tore straight at her as Bilo shouted in Araucano, "*Kiah!*" Kill!

The *Dogos* rushed as one at the charging female. The center dog feinted at the animal's head, and, as she snapped at him, the other two leaped to her flank and grabbed her by the side of the throat. Slowed momentarily, she turned to slash at them and the middle *Dogo* joined Tahpei on the opposite flank. Bilo motioned Angel back and measured his charge. The split-second opening came and he was on her like a madman, stabbing and ripping. Her screeches turned to deep gurgling as thick blood gushed from her snout and open mouth, staining her clashing tusks crimson. With a last grunt she fell heavily on her side, kicking feebly in the grip of the dogs. A shudder ran up her spine and she was dead.

Blood-smeared and panting, Chiche got to his feet and called off the dogs mauling the carcass. They backed off and shook themselves, licking at wounds.

"*A Dios gracias*," puffed Chiche, "*que se fue el macho.*" I looked at him questioningly. "I say, thank God that son-of-a-bitch male took off," he repeated in English. "He's a smart old bastard and left the sows to cover for him while he got away."

"Where do you think he went?" I asked.

Without answering, Chiche walked to the other side of the clearing and showed me the trail of the boar where it led down the riverbank and into the water. He pointed to a large island covered with thick undergrowth. "That's where he'll be, *Pedro*, and it'll be a rough place to worm him out."

Angel tied the horses to a bush while Bilo flipped off his *alpargatas* and I also removed my boots. Bilo said that even though it would be cold, we had better wade rather than bring the horses over. Cold? What a masterpiece of understatement. I felt like an icicle from the chest down as we struggled ashore with the dogs. Angel had to carry the curs, since there was no way they could be coaxed to enter the icy current, demonstrating considerably more sense than we did.

Walking slowly along the border of reeds where the shore met the river, Bilo found where the boar had come ashore and pushed his way through the heavy riverine growth. His path looked as though somebody had rolled an oil drum through the foliage. Even Angel's eyebrows went up. "Beeg wahn, no, *Pedro*?" Hell, yes, he was a "beeg wahn." My pig-sticker began to look more like a paring knife. I was about to excuse myself to go back for my cigarettes when Bilo let the dogs loose. Bilo slapped my back and said, "*Pedro,* give me a hand with this one, eh? He'll be a real trophy." I was about to tell him that I wasn't really all that fond of fresh bacon when he turned and started after the *Dogos.*

The island wasn't as big as I thought it was, because within two minutes the little mutts began to sound off again. We heard the sound move about fifty yards, then steady and swell with the murderous grunts of the boar as he took on the dogs. Running full speed through the brush, I could hardly see Chiche and Angel until I burst into a clearing ringed by a heavy wall of nearly impenetrable brush. At several points in this wall, there were small tunnels bulled out by generations of wild boar. From one of them, surrounded by lunging *Dogos,* stuck the head of the biggest, meanest-looking, crook-nosed pig I have ever seen. His head was the size of a barrel, set with flaming red eyes above hooked tusks. The immensity of him made the 350-pound sows look like something out of "The Three Little Pigs."

Except for an occasional snort, the strange fight was silent. The boar had backed into the opening and knew his back and flanks were protected. Brave as they were, the *Dogos* also knew that it was suicide to attack head-on. He was huge, and he was smart, refusing to lose his advantage by attacking from his hole, no matter how the dogs baited him.

When he saw me, he changed his mind.

It was a dream where you couldn't run. As tall as my waist, hairier than a bear, and looking for murder, he burst from the tunnel straight for me. As he cleared the hole, the four *Dogos* were all over him, slashing for a hold in his flanks and backside. He paid absolutely no attention to them. I was fifteen yards away when he began his rush, but with the flood of adrenaline pumping into my brain, I had thought of and rejected three different ways to meet the charge before he covered half the distance. Not knowing what else to do, I ran straight at him, hoping my unexpected tactic might throw him off stride. As he was almost on me, I sidestepped to the right and he tore by, snapping his tusks.

Screaming with frustration, he wheeled around and lunged again, but two *Dogos* had grabbed his ears and fouled up his timing, leaving me somehow behind him. I made a leap for his tail and hung on to it with one hand, the other clutching for a grip in his hair. I hung on for all I was worth as he spun like a dog chasing his tail, banging one of the *Dogos* into my head each time he tried to reach me with his tusks. His snapping jaws were so close to my face they sounded like a bank vault closing.

Amid the tangle of dogs, pig, and me, I saw Chiche advancing. He screamed for me to hang on and lunged with his knife against the boar's unprotected shoulder as the pig swung to snap at me again. As if in slow motion, I saw the boar's left hind foot leave the ground and loop lazily to land perfectly in the center of my forehead. I saw stars for a moment, and then everything went black.

I don't know how long it was before I shook the cobwebs from my scrambled brain, probably only a few seconds. I was still holding the boar's tail with one hand as Chiche gently slapped my cheeks. Warm blood coursed down my face where the pig's hoof had split the skin of my forehead, dripping into the darkened earth already sodden with pig and dog blood.

I let go and rolled free, promptly falling on my head again. Chiche helped me up and steadied me. Angel lay on the ground, writhing as if in agony, tears welling from his eyes. I imagined him to be disemboweled. Finally I figured out that he was laughing too hard to stand up. Between peals of smothered mirth, he said something to me in Spanish. I asked Chiche what he wanted.

"He says you would make a very good *Dogo Argentino,* even though you were not supposed to catch the boar, but kill it." I began to realize I had never even drawn my knife!

Regaining as much composure as possible under the circumstances, I asked Chiche to advise the big, still giggling lummox that any damn fool could get a boar with a knife—we *norteamericanos* always used our bare hands. I was just a little rusty, that's all.

It took a couple of hours to load the three dead pigs onto the horses and walk them the five miles back to the *estancia*. On the granary scale in Chiche's barn, the big one tipped the balance at 596 pounds. I call him six hundred, because he must have left at least four pounds of blood in my clothes. That night, an *asado,* the traditional gaucho fiesta, was held in honor of the barehanded *gringo* boar-catcher. The whole town of Choelechoel turned out—all ten residents.

Chiche told the story of my prowess in fits and starts between the peals of laughter until it was time to carve the roasting boar. Before the first cut was made, the mayor called for attention. In Spanish, he explained that he had a token from his people in appreciation for demonstrating my new way of boar hunting, a trophy I had earned.

I carefully unwrapped the small box he presented to me. There, by the flickering firelight, I saw the ultimate trophy of my Argentine boar hunt—the freshly severed tail of my prey.

The next day we went back to the bird shooting I had traveled ten thousand miles to sample. It was great, but somehow anticlimactic. After all, how do you follow a pig act?

thirty-five

TERROR IN THE WILD

by Krista Hanson Holbrook

HUNTING THE REFUGE ALWAYS held the promise of surprise. In addition to the deer and wild hogs we typically pursued, we could encounter anything from alligators to eagles, bobcats to rattlesnakes. But when we set out that morning, I had no idea we would encounter a situation far more frightening than anything I could have imagined.

My husband, Sterling, and I had been bowhunting in this 4,000-acre wilderness in southern Alabama for eight years. We shoot traditional archery tackle; Sterling even makes his own bows and arrows. When I first started hunting, the most difficult thing for me to master was remaining calm under pressure.

Instinctive shooting requires intense concentration on the exact spot you want to hit. In the early years I tended to get excited and shoot at the whole animal rather than pick a spot and concentrate. How else could I miss a 200-pound deer at 10 yards?

The fourth year I finally harvested a nice four-point buck. In the traditional Native American fashion, I used the animal's brain to tan its hide and made myself a hunting quiver. I guess that was a real turning point for me, as I made the connection with nature and became an active participant in the food chain.

On this day we had brought along a canoe to access a new area, and our excitement grew as we made the 20-minute boat ride up the Tombigbee River. We pulled the canoe out of the Boston Whaler and began to paddle across the lake. The view was spectacular. Managed primarily for waterfowl, the ponds, lakes and tributaries of the refuge are wintering grounds for tremendous numbers of ducks. Hundreds of coots, wood ducks and mallards took flight as we glided in among them. Putting our backs to it, we quickly covered the few miles to shore on the far side of the lake and then continued up the twisting creeks farther into the swamp.

After about an hour in the canoe, we arrived at a large bluff falling off rapidly to the swamp where we intended to scout.

A few steps from the canoe, we intersected a heavy game trail with tracks on top of tracks. As we traveled along, other trails paralleled and then joined it until we reached a well-worn crossing. Sterling promptly claimed the area and went to retrieve his tree stand from the canoe. I had a brief longing for the old days when Sterling had coddled me. We would have spent hours finding the perfect tree for me, but now I had to fend for myself. Leaving him, I paddled across the creek to explore a large finger of land surrounded by swamp and marsh.

Sterling, on the other hand, was quickly into the hunt. Laying his handmade Osage orange flat bow and western larch arrows close by, he prepared to put up a tree stand. Still squatted at the base of his tree, he heard a grunt. Scarcely had he grabbed his bow when a hog emerged from the thicket onto his trail. Up came the bow arm and away flew the arrow in a graceful arc. The boar saw him just as he released and whirled to run as the arrow made impact. It appeared that the arrow had hit too far back and too low for a lethal shot. Sterling had made perfect shots on the other three hogs he had harvested this year and was sorely disappointed with this one. We had spent countless hours conducting necropsies while field-dressing game, discussing arrow lethality and proper shot placement.

Experience had shown us that it was best to delay tracking an animal when poor arrow placement was suspected, so he climbed the tree and spent several hours worrying over his shot. When he finally took up the trail, his fears were confirmed by the lack of a blood trail and the sign on his recovered arrow. Easing down the trail, he could follow the large fresh tracks of the big hog, and after slowly covering about a hundred yards while making low grunting sounds, he heard the hog in thick saw grass. There wasn't much opportunity for a shot, but it was likely to be the best chance he would get. Creeping within ten yards, he slowly drew an arrow and made another shot. He could see his bright yellow fletch as it deflected off the thick grass, barely creasing the top of the hog's neck before sailing across the swamp.

The hog bolted toward him and Sterling grabbed a handy limb and swung himself up as the big boar charged past. Thinking the hog was mortally wounded from the first shot, Sterling dropped to the ground and was off in rapid pursuit. Occasionally hogs will stop, whirl around and stand their ground, offering a finishing shot, or go through a clearing large enough that another shot can be taken as they move.

At a dead run, Sterling managed to stay in sight of the big boar until it ran out a very narrow finger that was thick with scrubby trees. He could see that the finger opened into a knoll or peninsula surrounded by swamp, and as darkness was setting in he chose not to disturb the hog further.

I paddled across to pick him up just before dark and he related his hunting experience. We commented on the fact that the hog had run up the very trail where Sterling had been standing while making its escape. You hear stories of wild hogs charging a hunter, but we always believed that they were trying to flee and simply found the trail blocked.

We had supper but didn't talk much. Sterling was anxious about the hog. He wondered whether he had made a lethal shot or whether the animal was scarcely hurt and would recover. Early the following morning, we prepared for the day's hunt as we waited for daylight to depart down the river. I was about to lace on my soft deerskin moccasins when Sterling suggested I wear snake boots. I like the moccasins for stalk-hunting, but I followed his example and pulled on my knee-high, snake-proof boots.

Fog lay like a blanket over the water and it was a cold ride. Having mapped a quicker canoe route the previous day, we quietly made our way out the finger to where Sterling had last seen the hog. As I waded a deep muddy spot, one of many too wide to jump, I was glad I had worn the high-top boots.

Near the end where the finger widened out, there were several downed trees in a brier thicket with more open woods beyond and to the right. Sterling indicated that he would take a stand while I stalked around the edge of the swamp. He figured that if I jumped an animal it would likely run up this trail and offer a clear shot. It took me ten minutes to stalk around the edge. When I was back to within about 50 yards, Sterling called to me asking if there was any place beyond me where the hog might have bedded. I said I didn't think there was, as none of the trails that I had seen leading into the thick grass looked fresh.

Walking a few yards toward me, Sterling stepped up onto one of the downed trees in the brier thicket separating us. He then broke through into a small opening perhaps ten yards across. Glancing up he spied the hog hiding in the thick cover of a downed tree. Its beady eyes were open and focused directly on him and it made a low grunting noise. "Stop!" he called to me. "Stay where you are; I see the hog." I froze in place about 40 yards away and caught the odor of feral swine. It was obvious the hog had seen and smelled both of us and had stood its ground. Less than a second passed when I heard a startled yell followed by, "Help, he got me! Help, quick!"

I tore through the thicket toward Sterling, hanging up on briers and vines as I went. My heart was pounding hard in my chest. Hearing another frantic cry, I redoubled my efforts to reach him. I felt as though I were caught in a nightmare. The briers and vines clung and tore at my skin and clothing as I tried desperately to reach him.

When I finally arrived within sight, I could scarcely believe my eyes! Sterling lay on his back kicking at the attacking beast. He was dwarfed by the massive hog, which outweighed him by more than 65 pounds. Yelling and kicking, he was fighting for his very life! The hog slung its huge head, bloody tusks glistening in the morning sun, knocking chunks of leather from the soles of Sterling's heavy boots. I could see the hog was in full attack, trying to break through his guard and rush into Sterling's vulnerable rib cage. With a powerful thrust of his head, the hog suddenly knocked Sterling's leg aside and charged right up his middle, trying to hit him in the lower abdomen. Sterling instinctively lunged up and grabbed an ear with each hand. Amazingly, the hog froze in place.

Jerking my bow loose from a clinging vine, I was finally clear enough for a shot and I reached for an arrow with trembling hands. I took a deep breath, nocked the arrow on the string and bore in on the very hair I wanted to hit. The autopsy classes were about to pay off, as I took a quick step to the right, affording myself a better angling forward shot. Noting that I would be hitting mere inches from Sterling's knee, I focused intense concentration on the exact spot I wanted to hit as I drew my bow to anchor.

The heavy, 670-grain larch-wood shaft and Zwicky Eskimo broadhead hit with a satisfying thump, and still neither animal moved. We were in a seemingly frozen tableau, Sterling on his back, a death grip on the big black ears, the hog, poised just inches from his groin, still standing between Sterling's bent knees, my yellow fletch protruding just behind its shoulder. From the ground, Sterling could not see my arrow and said, "What happened? Quick, shoot again!"

But I couldn't shoot again. In my desperate struggle to reach him, my quiver had hung in thick vines and I had lost all but the one arrow I had just shot. As I realized my predicament, the hog pulled away from Sterling and turned toward me. It took two steps in my direction and then fell over dead. I had severed its aorta.

Suddenly my knees felt as if they might give way, but there was no time for that. I noted blood on the hog's tusk and on Sterling's leg. During the first charge, the hog had buried its tusk deep in Sterling's calf. The only thing that had prevented a long, deadly, ripping cut had been the heavy snakeproof boot.

I was anxious to depart for the hospital. Sterling, however, was loath to leave the big boar and wanted me to field-dress it and see if we could drag it to the creek. As I tied a bandage on his leg, I promised to return and complete the harvest only if he would leave for the hospital immediately.

We reached hunt camp in just under an hour, and as good fortune would have it, many of our friends were back already. One promptly volunteered to transport Sterling to the hospital, while another offered to help me to recover the hog. An autopsy revealed my fatal heart shot and the fact that Sterling's shot had indeed hit low and was not fatal at all. Until the attack the hog was not even seriously injured, just very mad.

Sterling went first to a family emergency center in a small town located close by. There the resident neurosurgeon administered strong antibiotics and shipped him off to the closest major hospital. The news had preceded his arrival, and although extremely professional, the staff was intently curious regarding the hog attack. Dr. Cady pronounced Sterling incredibly lucky regarding the damage. Another quarter-inch in either direction and there would have been major nerve or artery damage. The cut would require a drain, along with numerous stitches and antibiotics, and would likely result in a bad scar. Fortunately, there would not be serious permanent damage. Although months later his lower leg is still numb and tender, things certainly could have been much worse if he hadn't worn snake boots.

Dr. Cady told of a hunter he had treated who had been gored by a deer antler and eventually died of the injuries. We were fortunate our story had ended so much better. I had learned a respect for the wildness of our prey and would be more cautious and wary when hunting in the future. I would also carry a big knife.

thirty-six

SNAKE ATTACKS

by Don Zaidle

IF THERE IS AN animal more universally loathed and feared on a worldwide basis than snakes in general, I don't know what it is. Of the hundreds of snake species indigenous to North America, only four basic types are considered dangerous: rattlesnakes, water moccasins, copperheads, and coral snakes.

Note that there is no emphatic proclamation that these are the only *poisonous* snakes, for we are continually dismayed to find that many snakes once considered nonvenomous actually do possess poison glands and fangs. They remain in the "not considered dangerous" category because their poison-delivery mechanisms are located sufficiently far back in the mouth to make human envenomation *almost* impossible. Species in this category include the lyre, Texas cat-eyed, black-banded, and Mexican vine snakes, plus—get this—the ubiquitous garter snake! Yep, the ones you played with as a kid.

In November 1975, an eleven-year-old California boy was bitten on the hand by a garter snake he found on the playground at his school. A short time later, his arm began to swell, his shoulder turning black. He and the snake were flown to the Los Angeles County/University of Southern California Medical Center, where Dr. Findlay E. Russell, a leading authority on the treatment of venomous bites, verified that the boy had indeed been poisoned by the snake. Within days, Russell received nine additional reports of venomous gartersnake bites from doctors around the country.

As far as my research indicates, no human deaths have been attributed to the bite of a "harmless" snake, but the same cannot be said of the genuine article. In this country, ten to fifteen people are annually killed and hundreds more are less-definitively bitten by rattlesnakes alone, mostly the Eastern and Western diamondback varieties. A discussion of the normal circumstances under which most bites occur seems unnecessary, but here are a few nontypical episodes you might find interesting:

In 1996 a jury awarded a San Antonio, Texas, man $6,000 for medical expenses after he was bitten by a rattlesnake while shopping in the automotive department at Wal-Mart. The man was reaching for an air filter when a twenty-four-inch rattler struck him on the right hand from the shelf. This was the store's second rattlesnake incident; an employee narrowly avoided being bitten when another snake struck her plastic name tag—and you know where they are worn.

That it is unwise to make fun of a rattlesnake was illustrated by the 1995 experience of an Arizona man. While showing off with his "pet" rattlesnake, the man in mockery stuck out his tongue, which the snake promptly bit. Within minutes his throat swelled nearly shut, and only prompt medical attention saved his life.

Anyone skeptical of stories about people bitten by "dead" snakes needs to talk to thirty-six-year-old Texas resident Paul Russo, who in October 1995 was bitten on the arm by the decapitated head of a diamondback rattler. On the way to the hospital, ambulance attendants twice had to resuscitate Russo when he stopped breathing. He remained on life support for several days but eventually recovered.

There is at least one case on record of a rattler putting a man in the hospital without laying a fang on him. Five minutes after killing one huge rattlesnake, a Thomasville, Alabama, turkey hunter nearly stepped on a second one he hadn't seen. It didn't bite him, but it frightened him so badly that he swallowed the rubber diaphragm turkey call he had in his mouth, and was hospitalized for two weeks after it was extracted. If they can't get you one way. . . .

Space prohibits a detailed discussion of the effects rattlesnake venom have on the body. The viscous, amber juice is composed of a variety of toxins, including neurotoxins, but is mostly hemotoxic, which simply means that it digests your tissues from the inside out, a less than pleasant sensation.

Although I have never had a rattler catch up with my rapidly retreating backside, a few years ago I did have a close encounter with a copperhead, whose venom is similar to a rattler's but not as virulent. The snake latched onto my left hand when I picked up the log it was coiled under. The initial sensation was exactly like the sting of a yellow jacket, which is what I thought it was until I saw the orange and coppery-brown reptile dangling from my index finger, one fang embedded to the hilt between the second and third knuckle.

Rather than bore you with all the gory details, let it suffice to say that I had a rather interesting time of it for a couple of weeks, without benefit of medical treatment. (Antivenin costs $200 a vial, and my body size would have required at least twelve vials. I knew death or serious complications were unlikely, so I opted to tough it out and save a few bucks.) One aspect of the experience bears telling, a curious phenomenon I have never seen alluded to elsewhere: People who spend a lot of time in copperhead country are familiar with the serpent's "musty" smell, and can frequently detect a snake's presence by scent alone without seeing it. When the swelling in my arm began to go down, I started smelling copperhead.

At first I thought it was all in my head, but the phenomenon was confirmed as real when I got within nose-range of an acquaintance who recognized the scent. "Damn! You stink like a copperhead," I believe were his exact words. Anyway, the more the swelling subsided, the stronger the smell became, oozing out with my sweat and permeating my clothes with the acrid odor. Toward the last, my wife (who has also been bitten, as has her nephew) made me undress outside each day so I wouldn't stink up the house. It was nearly three weeks before all the poison processed out of my system and I once again smelled more or less human.

That more people are not killed by cottonmouths probably owes to the watery inaccessibility of their preferred habitat, otherwise cemetery-plot futures would be on the S&P Top 10 list. Besides being big and possessing a most virulent hemotoxic poison, the cottonmouth is of a decidedly nasty disposition. Given half a chance, rattlers and copperheads will avoid you. Not a cottonmouth. Bestir his ire, and he'll come for you. His ire is easily bestirred.

When I was a kid, the other ranch urchins and I used to amuse ourselves by catching cottonmouths alive, then releasing them out by the barn to watch the dogs fight them. We accomplished this feat by arming ourselves with sticks and burlap feed sacks (we always called them "tow sacks") and wading down the creek until a big moccasin was spotted sunning on an overhanging limb. When prodded with a stick, nine out of ten would launch themselves into the water and swim faster than most people can believe straight at us, the lining of their open mouths bright white against the mottled-brown to dirty-black background of the undulating body. At the last second, we'd scoop it up in one of the tow sacks, then go looking for another one. Why none of us got bitten remains one of the great mysteries of our times.

About the only way to get bitten by a coral snake is to pick it up and fool with it, and even then you'll probably have to stick your finger in its mouth which is purely delightful news, considering that its venom is a paralyzing neurotoxin quite similar to a cobra's.

Back in the 1980s, one of the members of a hunting party I was part of came close to finding out what it is like to die of coral-snake bite. We had arrived late the evening before opening day and immediately started setting up camp. Several of us scoured the forest by flashlight for firewood to prepare the evening meal. The next morning, I was stoking up the breakfast fire when I spotted the unburned half of a coral snake sticking out of the ashes. Somebody had accidentally picked it up and carried it into camp with an armload of wood. We never did figure out who, but knowing my luck. . . .

Though it is beyond the geographic purview of this work, there are a couple of things you might like to know about giant snakes—you know, man-eating pythons and such. As you probably already suspect, I am not about to waste any pulp rehashing other writers' strenuous attempts to debunk such beliefs; I'd rather prove them as fact. According to a September 1995 Associated Press report, a twenty-three-foot python in Malaysia killed and was in the process of eating twenty-nine-year-old rubber-plantation worker E. Heng Chuan when its meal got rudely interrupted by some other workers. The snake had already swallowed the man's head and crushed some of his bones when discovered. Another AP story, dated 30 April 1969, recounts the death and subsequent consumption of an eight-year-old Pakistani boy by a python of unspecified size. I rest my case.

thirty-seven

WHEN BIG BUCKS TURN BAD

by Don Zaidle

SO MEWHERE IN THE BACK of our minds, in what Jung called man's "collective unconscious," we carry ancestral, saber-toothed memories of things that want to kill us. Niggling thoughts of great carnivores make us wonder what might be watching and waiting in the shadows as we huddle around our dying campfires. On the other hand, not everything that comes for you intends to eat you, nor does it always come at night.

On a dry, dusty day in late October, Ron Smith and his nephew Aric Alvarez trudged along the Trinity River upriver from Vance's Camp, a well-known gathering place for North Texas fishermen. The walk was tiring, but finally the pair reached their destination, a brush-shrouded bend about two miles downriver from Eagle Mountain Reservoir. It was the kind of crappie hole that was worth a long hike. Smith baited up and sat back in the grass, more interested in solitude than fishing. Alvarez went upstream to cast for bass.

A half-hour later, Smith was on the brink of a serious nap when he was roused by the sound of something moving in the brush. Thinking Alvarez had returned, he sat up and was surprised to see a nine-point buck eyeing him from the far side of the river, scarcely 20 yards away. Smith and the whitetail watched each other for several seconds; then the deer stepped into the river and began to swim toward the fisherman. Smith had never seen such a buck so near in the wild and hoped that the animal would swim closer and give him an even better look. Smith didn't realize just how close a look he was about to get.

The deer crossed the river and clambered out, shaking itself like a dog. Just ten yards away now, the whitetail turned and looked straight at Smith as if seeing him for the first time. It stretched its nose toward him and sniffed the air. Suddenly, its demeanor changed from one of simple curiosity to one of pure malevolence. The deer's ears, previously cupped forward, swiveled back flat along the animal's neck. As Smith watched, every hair on the whitetail's body seemed to bristle. The buck's head dropped slightly and cocked to one side as the deer stared balefully at Smith through slitted eyelids. The angler sensed he was in danger and for some reason remembered the date: October 31, Halloween. Trick or treat.

The buck pawed the ground once, dropped its head low and charged Smith with astonishing speed. Smith tried to get up from the ground to run and was halfway to his feet when the crazed animal smashed into him. He fell backward into the river, reflexively grabbing the antlers and pulling the whitetail in after him. Momentum carried man and deer deep beneath the water. Smith clawed to the surface, sputtering muddy water as the buck bobbed up scant feet away. Smith gained the shore first and clambered out. He figured the impromptu dunking might have made the buck remember that it was a deer, and not a Cape buffalo, but no such luck. The whitetail climbed out seconds behind the shivering man and was on him again in a flash.

The impact of the second charge slammed Smith to the ground and onto his back, knocking the wind out of him. The buck pressed the charge, stabbing at the man's face with the brush-honed spikes on its head. Smith grabbed a double fistful of antler and hung on. He didn't realize until too late that he had seized an antler tip. The buck's next lunge drove the point of the right main beam through the palm of his left hand and into the ground. Smith tore his hand off of the spike and scooted from under the buck. Struggling to his feet, he shifted his grip on the antlers and somehow managed to bulldog the nine-pointer to the ground.

A NEAR THING

Alvarez was out of sight around the bend when he heard his uncle's cries and the subsequent splashing. Figuring Smith had accidentally fallen into the river, he dropped his pole and ran to help. A whirlwind of flying dust and flailing arms and legs greeted Alvarez when he crashed out of the brush and onto the scene. He sized up the situation and ran in to deliver the hardest kick he could muster to the buck's ribs. The deer didn't flinch. Alvarez looked around for a weapon and found a large tree limb. Smith looked up just as Alvarez was about to swing the club down on the buck's head, which was within inches of his own. "For heaven's sake, don't kill me!" he screamed.

Realizing that he might further injure his bleeding uncle, the teenager cast the limb aside. Frantic with concern that his uncle was about to be gored, Alvarez tried unsuccessfully to pry off the buck. He was about to give the club another try when he recalled that Smith wore a fillet knife on his belt. Careful to avoid the buck's slashing hooves and antlers, Alvarez reached beneath the embattled man for the knife. Smith held on while Alvarez cut the buck's throat and didn't let go until he was sure the animal was dead.

Finally, Smith rolled away from the buck and rested on the trampled grass while he regained his breath. Although Smith didn't know how badly he was injured, he was covered in blood—his and the buck's—and experienced severe pain in his hand, ribs and abdomen. Just as the first waves of shock set in, Smith instructed Alvarez to go back to Vance's for help, then lapsed into semi-consciousness.

Other than considerable blood loss, Smith's most serious injuries were the hole in his left hand and a few bruised ribs.

An isolated case of an animal bypassing its genetic code and going berserk? Hardly. Such run-ins with whitetail bucks, though aberrations, are more common than you might think. On average, several people are attacked each year by bucks. And an aroused, mature buck weighing 150 pounds or so is a savage force.

CRAZY IN LOVE

Most biologists attribute attacks by bucks to rut behavior. Rutting bucks routinely destroy everything from saplings to concrete lawn ornaments as they vent hormone-heated steam. A case that took place two years ago in Illinois serves as a classic example. Paul Cheatham, 61, was scouting for deer on his farm near Herrin one November day when he came upon a six-point buck that was wooing a doe. The deer didn't seem to be particularly alarmed by the man's presence and continued to gambol about in front of him. Watching the animals interact, Cheatham was amazed when the buck left the doe and started moving toward him, sniffing his trail as it came. When the buck got to within six feet, Cheatham's curiosity was transformed into concern. He was one step into backing away when the buck snorted, dropped its head and charged.

Like most living members of the "Bashed-by-Bambi Club," Cheatham grabbed antlers and held on. The buck tossed him around for quite a while before the man remembered his pocketknife. Holding onto an antler with one hand, the man reached into his pocket with his free hand and got the knife, opened it with his teeth, then repeatedly stabbed the buck's neck and chest until it lay still.

While the Cheatham case involved a wild deer in a rural setting, whitetails whose habitat overlaps that of suburban homeowners are more frequently the offenders. Last November, for example, a buck attacked a 61-year-old woman while she was hanging laundry in her backyard in Durham, N.C. A neighbor, John Hughes, who ran to investigate her screams, said he saw the buck toss the woman in the air and repeatedly gore her legs. He finally drove the deer away and summoned an ambulance.

Sometimes deer take the initiative in what some might call preemptive strikes. A few years ago, Raymond Rebels was hunting near Garrison,

Tex., when a buck boiled out of the brush and nailed him in a sneak attack from behind. Rebels, his rifle jarred from his grasp, wrestled with the deer for some time and finally climbed a tree to get away. While self-preservation by flight is the whitetail's normal course of action unless cornered, the onset of the rut apparently can make at least some bucks feel ten feet tall.

Testosterone run amok is a handy, catchall rationale to explain why some whitetails go after humans. Yet bucks don't follow form in all instances.

In June 1994 (a long time from rutting season), a velvet-antlered buck nearly killed a Texas woman in her driveway. A passerby saw the unconscious woman within minutes of the attack and called authorities. He couldn't render immediate aid to the victim, because the buck stood guard over her. A Brazos River Authority ranger, Mike Cox, had to kill the buck before paramedics could tend to the injured woman. She survived with multiple lacerations, bruises, a concussion and several broken bones.

Unprovoked whitetail attacks unrelated to the rut are not regional phenomena. Incidents of varying severity have occurred in most U.S. states and Canadian provinces with whitetail populations. Last March, 21-year-old Brian Keister engaged a seven-point whitetail in hand-to-antler combat after it charged him during a coyote hunt near Beavertown, Penn. The hunter had laid his .22 rifle aside prior to the attack. Keister told investigators he heard something coming through the brush and saw the deer, which immediately charged and "threw me all over the place."

Keister grabbed the buck's headgear to avoid puncture wounds. After a prolonged shoving match, Keister finally managed to break away and scramble the ten yards to his rifle. He was able to get off one hurried shot that inflicted a minor flesh wound, but the deer stopped long enough to give Keister the opportunity to escape. Wildlife conservation officer Harold Malehorn later encountered the bizarre-acting buck and killed it not 40 yards from the attack scene. It took six hours of surgery to patch Keister's injuries.

IT GETS WEIRDER

Rare as fatal buck assaults are, more exceptional are those incidents that involve bucks staying on the scene long after their victims are dead. It is not unheard of for non-carnivores to guard their "kills." Last year, an Asian elephant that had killed a forest ranger in India carried around the body for two weeks before relinquishing it. The few dozen wildlife biologists and ethologists I quizzed regarding such behavior answered with a collective shrug.

In the fall of 1990, central Texas sheriff's deputies investigated a van that, according to a citizen's report, had been parked beside the road for two days with its driver-side door open. On exiting the patrol car, the law officers noticed a large buck in the brush about ten yards from the van, thrashing a sapling with its antlers. As the deputies approached the vehicle, the buck charged them.

The deputies backed off and the buck did likewise, but it would not allow them to get near the van. Reconnoitering from a safe distance, the lawmen discovered the buck wasn't "guarding" the van, but rather a body lying in the ditch near the vehicle's open door.

The lawmen finally killed the buck after it fought off all of their attempts to reach the body of 61-year-old Buddy Coleman. The official cause of death was a crushed skull, but Coleman probably would have bled to death anyway from the more than 100 puncture wounds in his back, stomach and face from the buck's hooves and antlers. Coleman died in the unprovoked attack within sight of his home while picking up aluminum cans along the road. The buck, a "monster" by Texas standards at 160 pounds, tested negative for any disease that would account for its behavior.

Bucks raised by humans from infancy tend to stay put after they have attacked one or more "parents," if only because they are conditioned to remain in familiar surroundings. One gruesome case, which occurred in September 2000, involved an eight-year-old pet deer that gored its 75-year-old owner to death in Mapleton, Kan. The woman's husband found her body after she did not return from cooping her chickens for the night.

Police killed the six-point, 200-pound buck, which the husband had locked in its pen. In October last year, a captive buck killed a 54-year-old York, Ontario, man on his farm. Police speculated the animal viewed its keeper as a rival for the 18 does kept in the same enclosure.

A former U.S. Fish & Wildlife Service agent quoted in published reports of the Ontario assault said: "Deer attacks in the wild don't happen, but there are four or five cases of attacks by domestic bucks that are kept in captivity. You've got a much better chance of winning the lottery or being hit by lightning, though, than of being attacked by a buck deer—domestic or otherwise."

The former agent's contention that there are only "four or five" such cases on record, involving both domesticated and wild whitetails, is an understatement. As for the "lightning" analogy, in the same sense that people who stand under tall trees during thunderstorms are at greater risk, the odds of becoming hors de combat are greater for people who share their environment with whitetails.

Nowadays, that's apt to be just about anywhere in North America except major cities. Anyone who walks in the woods or trims crabgrass from the lawn stands a chance, albeit remote, of being confronted by a deer that has forgone its docile nature and is ready to fight.

thirty-eight

DEATH CHARGE

by Hannes Wessels

DAWN SPREAD OVER THE mopane trees like a wave of gold. Another glorious African day was upon me. I had been hunting professionally for 15 years and my work had taken me all over south-central and eastern Africa, but I considered every day I spent on those rolling plains in Maasailand in northern Tanzania a great privilege. I was one of a fortunate few capable of making a living amid this wild magnificence.

With Kilimanjaro towering omnipresent in the background and the untamed unknown stretching out before me, there was always the smell of excitement in the cool breeze that drifted over the savannah. Slicing through the territory like angry old scars were the mostly dry riverbeds lined by the combretum thickets that provided daytime shelter for the area's many Cape buffalo. I had hunted in these tangled growths for buffalo many times before, and each time I had felt the adrenaline charge that comes from encountering this grand adversary up close.

My client, Paul Hicks, was a young cattle trader from Dallas. He was an American classic, with dark good looks that introduced a thoroughly decent man—exuberant, energetic and steadfast. Thanks to him I live, and sit here today to write this story.

WOUNDED AT DUSK

It was around 4 P.M., and the big bull on the edge of the thicket looked straight at us as we looked at him. He held his head high as his nose worked the wind. Paul took a careful bead on the brisket and I watched the rifle jerk under his sweat-soaked cheekbone as he fired, but the moment I heard the thud and saw the reaction of the bull I knew we had a problem. The look on Paul's face told me he was not happy with his shot.

I looked over at my tracker, Miragi, and noted his frown with concern. He had been with me since my arrival in the country five years earlier, had helped me find my feet and had shown commendable patience as my Swahili tutor. A slight whip of a man with a sparkling smile, boundless energy and a most pleasant disposition, he excelled at not listening to me when it suited him. He could irritate the hell out of me, but he was a loyal and willing trooper and we had formed a strong alliance.

I was fearful as I watched the big bull disappear. The next stage was almost certainly going to be unpleasant. The vegetation lining the riverbeds was a snarl of dense thorn, and the rocky ground would make tracking difficult and dangerous. The thick cover offered little visibility, ensuring that our next encounter would be at close quarters.

The specks of blood we discovered brought more bad news. An aerated, pink hue would have been a heartening sign of a lethal lung shot, but the dark red blood we saw indicated the likelihood of a muscle wound.

We entered the thicket and moved quickly and perhaps a bit recklessly, but as night was falling, I was in a hurry to close in and kill the bull. I could see Miragi was wary yet I cut him no slack. In the last moments of daylight I spotted a solid, indistinguishable black lump up ahead. I crept closer and realized it was a buffalo, though I couldn't be sure it was the wounded one. I considered opening fire but restrained myself and moved closer still. Regrettably, the animal sprang into action and bolted away. My stomach sank as I noted the pool of blood where he had been lying. I had missed my chance to bring the proceedings to an end. Heavy of heart, we made our way back to camp.

At 5 A.M. the next day, I switched on my shortwave radio to the BBC

News and was delighted to hear that my boyhood friend Nick Price had won the British Open. I couldn't help but smile at the tapestry that is life as I considered our wildly disparate situations.

As dawn arrived, we positioned ourselves back on the tracks. Initially, we made good progress, but then the blood spoor petered out. I knew there was a chance that the animal was only lightly wounded. But there was also the possibility that the shot had raked down the body, missing the vitals and puncturing the stomach. This would inflict terrific pain and ensure a slow, agonizing death. I wanted to avoid this.

The temperature rose and the sweat from the sun, frustration and fear poured forth. Impatient, I pushed Miragi harder, to little avail. I decided to move ahead of Miragi and Paul and try to flush the wounded bull. I caught sight of a dark shape and tried to crawl closer, but he crashed away. Furious, I gave chase and raced after him, determined to start shooting as soon as he gave me a chance. He broke out into the open, however, and outpaced me before veering back into the thicket. My eyes blurred with sweat as I ran full tilt after him into the brush. I tried to close in for the kill but the thorns ripped me to a standstill.

AMBUSHED

As if in a bad dream, I found I could not make any headway. Exasperated, I flung myself down and snaked forward on my belly. I arrived in a small clearing and halted while straining my senses for any sign of the bull. The silence was overwhelming. I knew he was close, but with ghostly skill he had disappeared. Now he was hunting me.

The bull was smart, he was upwind and he knew where I was. I inched forward, searching for any sign of him. My rifle shook in my hands. I knew one shot from my Winchester .375 H&H would be all I'd get. I heard a crash and he was upon me. As I turned to face him his hulking mass smashed into my hip and I was airborne, my weapon lost to me. It is a testament to the skill and cunning of these great brutes that I failed to dispense a shot.

I hit the ground winded and helpless. I saw the bull lower his great head and power into me again. It was all dust and sickening pain as I felt one blow after another, and then suddenly I was in the air again, impaled on his right horn, which had entered my groin and thrust deep inside. Airborne, I hung motionless briefly, and then with awesome ease he tossed me onto his back.

It's quite bizarre what goes through one's mind in times such as this, but I remember thinking to myself what a bloody fool I must look—and thanked the good Lord that the audience was a small one. I tried to grasp the bull's tail in a vain attempt to maintain my position on his back, but he bucked and spun around, sending me hurtling back to the ground. His beady black eyes bore into me as he came at my head. I lifted my arm to ward him off and noticed that my left bicep had been separated from the bone with one slash. I watched the bull, transfixed, waiting for the deathblow. Almost in slow motion, he swung his huge black head away just prior to plunging his horns back into me when a rifle shot roared. The bull's mighty head jerked upward, taking with it the horns that had almost succeeded in killing me.

Paul had stormed to my rescue and his shot had saved my life. It slammed into the animal's shoulder, pummeling him back. I looked on in helpless bewilderment as another round from Paul's .375 cracked overhead. His next shot brained the beast and the great animal crumpled like a boxer bludgeoned to the canvas. Unfortunately, the bull fell astride my prostrate body, smothering me as his great weight crushed my broken torso.

WAITING TO DIE

I struggled to comprehend my plight. The abdominal pain was exquisite and I felt warmth running down my legs. I could feel my innards sloshing around inside and I knew there was an unholy mess in there. My mouth was dry and full of dirt. Gathering my senses, I forced my hand under the buffalo's rib cage and worked it into the hole in my inner thigh, feeling the bone that was my left femur. Certain that my femoral artery had been severed, I concluded I had hunted my last hunt.

With a calmness that surprised me, I explained my situation to Paul and asked him to perform some tasks after my departure. I felt for the poor man—he was shaken and emotional. I tried to prevail upon him to feel no remorse on my behalf. For reasons still not entirely clear to me, I found myself very much at peace and unafraid of death. I did take some solace from the thought that I was dying with some honor, and I was determined also to depart with some dignity. I was at ease knowing that an animal I had always admired and respected had accounted for me in a conflict of my choosing.

Confronting death, I searched my conscience as I think most people would in a similar situation. Throughout my hunting career I had grappled with the righteousness of what I was doing. Like many in my game, I had always felt a sincere attachment to the animals I hunted and often killed. To the outsider this sounds paradoxical, but it is true, and the realization that I was to pay with my life for some of what I had taken was a relief. I felt no animosity toward the animal that had savaged me—only affection, some sadness and enormous respect.

My mind flashed to the people most dear to me, in particular my family. Blessed as I had been with devoted parents and wonderful siblings, I gave Paul details about how to make contact with them and express my thanks and say farewell. Then, I thought, I was ready to die.

Paul asked to say a prayer.

Although of no serious religious persuasion, I happily agreed and closed my eyes and tried to follow the words. I prepared myself for the unknown. Everything went terribly quiet. . . .

Well, I must say that there is something very embarrassing about going to considerable lengths to die stoically and then not doing so because one fails to expire, yet that was the ridiculous predicament in which I found myself! After about five minutes, I realized I could not have suffered the injuries I imagined. A punctured femoral artery would certainly have rendered me unconscious and I was very much alert. My self-diagnosis had been wrong.

Sheepishly, I opened my eyes to register the same situation I thought I was departing. I looked into the eyes of a puzzled Paul. Feeling a little guilty about being alive and realizing that maybe all was not lost, I asked him to summon the others and remove the buffalo from its present location. They were reluctant to do so. Africans are deeply suspicious of being close to death, so it was with some timidity that they approached. On seeing that I was alive, however, they rolled the animal off me. I could then see my legs and see that the bleeding, although severe, was not life threatening. I removed my gun belt and used it as a tourniquet. I then instructed Miragi and the scout to disappear at speed and collect my vehicle.

Four hours later I found myself on the floor of a light aircraft headed for Nairobi. I have never wanted to kiss another man, but the doctor who stood at the door of the plane after we landed and pumped in the morphine that ended my agony was, for a brief moment, an object of genuine desire.

I am happy to say that after extensive surgery at St. George's Hospital in Nairobi I made a full recovery. To those good people who cared for me I am eternally grateful.